Presented
to

Judy Geib

by
First Methodist Church
April 11, 1965

THE
BOOK
OF
WORSHIP
for
Church and Home

THE
BOOK
OF
WORSHIP

for
Church and Home

With orders of worship, services for the
administration of Sacraments, and aids
to worship according to the usages of

THE METHODIST CHURCH

The Methodist Publishing House
NASHVILLE, TENNESSEE

Scripture quotations unless otherwise noted are from the Revised Standard Version of the Bible, copyrighted 1946 and 1952 by the Division of Christian Education, National Council of Churches, and are used by permission.

Acknowledgment is made to the following who have granted permission for the use of copyrighted material as listed below:

Abingdon Press for prayer from *A Book of Pastoral Prayers* by Ernest Fremont Tittle; copyright © 1939 by Pierce & Washabaugh (Abingdon Press). Prayer from *Let Us Break Bread Together* by Fred D. Gealy; copyright © 1960 by Abingdon Press. Prayers from *Lift Up Your Hearts*, Enlarged Edition, by Walter Russell Bowie; copyright © 1939 by Pierce & Washabaugh (Abingdon Press). Communion table dismissals, pp. 202-4, from *Communion Table Dismissals* by John Keith Benton, by permission of Abingdon Press.

Basil Blackwell & Mott, Ltd., for prayers from *A Book of Prayers* by A. Campbell Fraser.

The Board of Publication of the Lutheran Church in America for prayer from *Helps on the Road* by C. M. Jacobs.

The Board of Publication of the United Church of Canada for prayer from *The Book of Common Order* of the United Church of Canada.

Cassell and Company, Ltd., for prayers from *A Book of Prayers*, edited by Richard Tatlock.

The Central Conference of American Rabbis for prayer from *The Union Prayerbook for Jewish Worship*.

The Church Pension Fund for prayers from *The Book of Offices*.

The Commission on Liturgy and Hymnal of the Lutheran Church in America and the American Lutheran Church for prayers from *The Occasional Services for the Use of the Lutheran Churches Cooperating in the Commission on the Liturgy and Hymnal*.

The Committee on Public Worship and Aids to Devotion of the General Assembly of the Church of Scotland for prayers from *Prayers for the Christian Year* and *The Book of Common Order*.

The Diocese of Massachusetts of the Protestant Episcopal Church for prayer from *Prayers for the Church Service League*, copyright 1937.

E. P. Dutton & Co. for prayers from *The Book of Common Worship* by W. P. Thirkield and Oliver Huckel and *A Free Church Book of Common Prayer*.

Epworth Press for prayers and litanies from *Divine Worship*.

Harper & Row for prayers from *Prayers of the Spirit* by John Wallace Suter, *A Book of Public Prayers* by Harry Emerson Fosdick, and *Prayers for Private Devotions in War Time* by Dean W. L. Sperry.

Bishop L. S. Hunter for prayers and litanies from *Devotional Services for Public Worship* by John Hunter.

Industrial Christian Fellowship for prayer from *The Prayer Manual* by F. B. Macnutt.

John Knox Press for litany of intercession from *An Experimental Liturgy* by J. G. Davies, G. F. Cope, and D. A. Tytler.

Longmans, Green & Co. Ltd. for prayers from *Family Prayers* by A. F. Thornhill and *The Cambridge Bede Book* by Eric Milner-White.

The Lutheran Church in America for prayers from the *Common Service Book of the Lutheran Church.*

Lutterworth Press for prayer from *The Book of Jeremiah* by Elvet Lewis.

Morehouse Barlow Co. for prayer from *A Book of Prayers* by John Heuss, copyright 1957 by Morehouse Barlow.

A. R. Mowbray & Co. for prayer from *The Prayer Manual* by F. B. Macnutt.

Oxford University Press for prayers from *Prayers of the Christian Life* by John Underwood Stephens; copyright 1952 by Oxford University Press, Inc.; reprinted by permission. Prayers from *The Pastor's Prayerbook* by Robert N. Rodenmayer; copyright © 1960 by Oxford University Press, Inc.; reprinted by permission. Prayers and litanies from *The Kingdom, the Power, and the Glory*, copyright 1933 by Oxford University Press, Inc., renewed 1961 by Bradford Young; used by permission. Prayers from *The Order of Divine Service for Public Worship* by W. E. Orchard; used by permission. Prayer from *Prayers for Parish Worship*, compiled by C. F. Miller; used by permission.

The Pilgrim Press for prayers from *Church Worship Book* by Charles W. Merriam, *A Book of Church Services,* and *Prayers of the Social Awakening* by Walter Rauschenbusch.

Rivingtons, Ltd., for prayers from *The Sanctuary* by Percy Dearmer.

Caspar L. Roberts, Executor, Estate of Jennie M. Newton, for prayers from *Altar Stairs* by Joseph Fort Newton.

SCM Press for prayers from *A Book of Prayers for Schools,* edited by Hugh Martin, and *A Book of Prayers for Students.*

S.P.C.K., London, for prayer from *Acts of Devotion,* compiled by F. W. Dwelly.

Charles Scribner's Sons for prayer adapted with the permission of Charles Scribner's Sons from *A Diary of Private Prayer,* p. 89, by John Baillie. Copyright 1949 Charles Scribner's Sons.

John W. Suter for prayer from *Prayers for a New World,* compiled by John W. Suter, Charles Scribner's Sons, 1964.

The Synod of the Church of South India for prayers from *The Book of Common Worship of the Church of South India.*

J. M. Todd for prayers from *Prayers and Services for Christian Festivals.*

United Church Board for Homeland Ministries for prayer from *A Book of Worship for Free Churches.*

Westminster Press for prayers by Henry van Dyke from *The Book of Common Worship;* Revised; copyright 1932, The Board of Christian Education of the Presbyterian Church, U.S.A.; copyright renewed 1960; used by permission. Prayers from *The Book of Common Worship,* copyright 1946 by the Board of Christian Education of the Presbyterian Church, U.S.A.; used by permission.

Acknowledgment is also made to the following individuals for permission to reprint their prayers: Bishop F. R. Barry; Dr. Paul Burt; Bishop D. H. Crick; Dr. Fred D. Gealy; Bishop Nolan B. Harmon; The Rev. Donald R. Jessup; Dean Sherman E. Johnson; Dr. Reinhold Niebuhr; Mrs. Ursula Niebuhr; Dr. Gregory Vlastos; Mr. Edwin B. Womack.

Preface

The Book of Worship for Church and Home, prepared by an earlier Commission on Worship under the able leadership of Bishop Ivan Lee Holt and adopted by the General Conference of 1944 for "optional and voluntary use," won such wide acceptance by The Methodist Church that the General Conference of 1956 ordered a revision to help further meet an awakened and growing need.

This present volume, adopted by the General Conference of 1964, is the consequence of this action and the labors of subsequent Commissions on Worship during the intervening eight years. An interim report, known as the "Green Book," was accepted by the General Conference of 1960 "for trial use and study." Through this study, carried on by countless individuals and groups who relayed their thoughts and experience to the commission, the entire Church has been involved in the process that brought this book into being. The members of the commission dare to hope that, through this widespread participation, the usefulness of the revised *Book of Worship* to all Methodist congregations and individuals will be enhanced, and that the all but unanimous acceptance of the book by the General Conference will be reflected in the favor with which it is accepted throughout the Church.

In Sections I and IV, *The Book of Worship* contains orders and offices for the official rites of the Church. Section II presents an anthology of Scripture, prayers, and other liturgical material as Aids for the Ordering of Worship, in accordance with the Order of Worship which introduces Section I. Some of these aids are arranged according to the Christian Year and others according to the sequence in the Order of Worship. They are available equally for the ordering of special services and for family and private devotions. The Order of Worship provides for a larger use of Scripture in our services, whether in lessons, sentences, or acts of praise. To this end a new Lectionary of readings has been created, for which the members of the commission acknowledge their indebtedness to William F. Dunkle, Jr. For the most part Scripture quotations are given in the Revised Standard Version and are identified by references.

Section III, entitled Acts of Praise, consists of a Psalter and a collection of other Acts of Praise. Section V contains services and material recalling our Methodist tradition.

The Book of Worship is designed to provide significant structure for the worship of the Church. It is not intended in any way to fetter the spontaneity or reject the reliance upon the Holy Spirit which have characterized Methodist worship throughout its history. Rather *The Book of Worship* seeks to claim for the Church and its people the total Methodist heritage in worship. John Wesley himself, by his devotion to the Book of Common Prayer and his ordering of the "Sunday Service of the Methodists in America," has made us heirs of the deeply meaningful historic forms of devotion of the universal Church. As we make these our own we shall find that the Holy Spirit will move among us with mighty power.

THE COMMISSION ON WORSHIP

Emory Stevens Bucke	Will Hildebrand
Warren A. Bugbee	James R. Houghton
Paul Burt	J. deKoven Killingsworth
William R. Cannon	Austin C. Lovelace
Virgil Y. C. Eady	Joseph D. Quillian, Jr.
J. Robert Hammond	Daniel L. Ridout
Earl E. Harper	Mrs. Floyd W. Rigg
Nolan B. Harmon	Amos A. Thornburg
Charles S. Hempstead	Edwin E. Voigt

Editorial Consultant: Fred D. Gealy

Contents

CONTENTS

CONTENTS

CONTENTS

CONTENTS

III. ACTS OF PRAISE

IV. OCCASIONAL OFFICES OF THE CHURCH

CONTENTS

V. SERVICES IN THE METHODIST TRADITION

I.

The General Services of the Church

The Order of Worship

† *Let the people be in silent meditation and prayer upon entering the sanctuary. Let the service of worship begin at the time appointed.*

† *At the end of all prayers the people shall say Amen.*

PRELUDE

SCRIPTURE SENTENCES, OR CALL TO WORSHIP † *To be said or sung.*

HYMN † *The people standing.*

PRAYERS † *Here the minister may use an invocation or collect and prayers of confession and the Lord's Prayer.*

PSALTER OR OTHER ACT OF PRAISE † *To be read responsively or in unison, the people standing; then shall be said or sung the* Gloria Patri.

ANTHEM

THE SCRIPTURE LESSONS

AFFIRMATION OF FAITH † *The people standing; then may be sung a doxology.*

PASTORAL PRAYER

OFFERTORY

† *Here parish notices may be given.*

† *The minister may read Scripture sentences before the offering is received. An anthem may be sung during the receiving of the offering. Following the presentation of the offering a prayer of dedication may be said or sung.*

† *At the discretion of the minister, the offertory and prayers may follow the sermon.*

HYMN † *The people standing.*

THE SERMON

INVITATION TO CHRISTIAN DISCIPLESHIP

HYMN † *The people standing.*

BENEDICTION † *The people may be seated for silent prayer.*

POSTLUDE

The Order of Worship

† *Let the people be in silent meditation and prayer upon entering the sanctuary. Let the service of worship begin at the time appointed.*

† *Scripture sentences, alternate prayers, affirmations of faith, and benedictions may be found in* The Book of Worship *and* The Methodist Hymnal.

† *At the end of all prayers the people shall say Amen.*

PRELUDE

SCRIPTURE SENTENCES, OR CALL TO WORSHIP   † *To be said or sung.*

HYMN   † *The people standing.*

† *If a processional, the hymn may precede the Scripture sentences.*

INVOCATION   † *By the minister, the people standing.*

Almighty God, from whom every good prayer cometh, and who pourest out on all who desire it, the spirit of grace and supplication: Deliver us, when we draw nigh to thee, from coldness of heart and wanderings of mind, that with steadfast thoughts and kindled affections, we may worship thee in spirit and in truth; through Jesus Christ our Lord. **Amen.**

CALL TO CONFESSION   † *By the minister, the people standing.*

Dearly beloved, the Scriptures move us to acknowledge and confess our sins before almighty God, our heavenly Father, with a humble, lowly, penitent, and obedient heart, to the end that we may obtain forgiveness by his infinite goodness and mercy. Wherefore I pray and beseech you, as many as are here present, to accompany me with a pure heart and humble voice, unto the throne of heavenly grace.

† *Or the minister may say,*

Let us confess our sins to almighty God.

GENERAL CONFESSION   † *To be said by all, the people seated and bowed, or kneeling.*

Almighty and most merciful Father, we have erred and strayed from thy ways like lost sheep. We have followed too much the devices

4

and desires of our own hearts. We have offended against thy holy laws. We have left undone those things which we ought to have done, and we have done those things which we ought not to have done. But thou, O Lord, have mercy upon us. Spare thou those, O God, who confess their faults. Restore thou those who are penitent, according to thy promises declared unto mankind in Christ Jesus our Lord. And grant, O most merciful Father, for his sake, that we may hereafter live a godly, righteous, and sober life, to the glory of thy holy name. Amen.

PRAYER FOR PARDON OR WORDS OF ASSURANCE † *By the minister.*

O Lord, we beseech thee, absolve thy people from their offenses, that through thy bountiful goodness, we may be delivered from the bonds of those sins which by our frailty we have committed. Grant this, O heavenly Father, for the sake of Jesus Christ, our blessed Lord and Savior. Amen.

THE LORD'S PRAYER † *To be said by all.*

Our Father, who art in heaven, hallowed be thy name. Thy kingdom come, thy will be done on earth as it is in heaven. Give us this day our daily bread. And forgive us our trespasses, as we forgive those who trespass against us. And lead us not into temptation, but deliver us from evil. For thine is the kingdom, and the power, and the glory, forever. Amen.

Minister: O Lord, open thou our lips.

People: And our mouth shall show forth thy praise.

Minister: Praise ye the Lord.

People: The Lord's name be praised.

PSALTER OR OTHER ACT OF PRAISE † *To be read responsively or in unison, the people standing; then shall be said or sung,*

Glory be to the Father, and to the Son, and to the Holy Ghost; as it was in the beginning, is now and ever shall be, world without end. Amen.

ANTHEM

THE SCRIPTURE LESSONS † *Here shall be read two lessons, one from the Old Testament, and one from the Epistles or Gospels.*

5

AFFIRMATION OF FAITH † *The people standing; then may be sung a doxology.*

Minister: The Lord be with you.

People: **And with thy spirit.**

Minister: Let us pray.

COLLECT † *By the minister, or the minister and people, the people seated and bowed, or kneeling.*

O Lord, our heavenly Father, almighty and everlasting God, who hast safely brought us to the beginning of this day: Defend us in the same with thy mighty power; and grant that this day we fall into no sin, neither run into any kind of danger, but that all our doings may be ordered by thy governance, to do always that which is righteous in thy sight; through Jesus Christ our Lord. **Amen.**

PASTORAL PRAYER

OFFERTORY

† *Here parish notices may be given.*

† *The minister may read Scripture sentences before the offering is received. An anthem may be sung during the receiving of the offering. Following the presentation of the offering a prayer of dedication may be said or sung.*

† *At the discretion of the minister the offertory and prayers may follow the sermon.*

HYMN † *The people standing.*

THE SERMON

INVITATION TO CHRISTIAN DISCIPLESHIP

HYMN † *The people standing. This may be a recessional hymn.*

BENEDICTION † *The people may be seated for silent prayer.*

POSTLUDE

The Order for the Administration of the Sacrament of Baptism

† *Our ministers are enjoined diligently to teach the people committed to their pastoral care the meaning and purpose of the Baptism of children and to urge them to present their children for Baptism at an early age.*

† *When youth and adults present themselves for Baptism, the minister shall take due care that they have been instructed in the meaning of Christian Baptism.*

† *This Sacrament should be administered in the church in the presence of the people in a stated hour of worship. But at the minister's discretion this Sacrament may be administered at another time and place.*

† *This Sacrament may be administered by sprinkling, pouring, or immersion.*

† *The minister shall see that the names of all baptized children are properly recorded as preparatory members on the permanent records of the church, and in each instance he shall deliver to the parents or sponsors a certificate of Baptism.*

† *Children baptized in infancy shall be reported annually in the number of preparatory members until they shall have been received into full membership in the church or shall have attained their adulthood.*

CHILDREN

† *Parents or sponsors presenting a child for Baptism should be members of Christ's holy Church.*

† *The parents or sponsors, with the child to be baptized, shall stand before the minister, who, addressing the people, shall say,*

Dearly beloved, Baptism is an outward and visible sign of the grace of the Lord Jesus Christ, through which grace we become partakers of his righteousness and heirs of life eternal. Those receiving the Sacrament are thereby marked as Christian disciples, and initiated into the fellowship of Christ's holy Church. Our Lord has expressly given to little children a place among the people of God, which holy privilege must not be

7

denied them. Remember the words of the Lord Jesus Christ, how he said, "Let the children come to me, do not hinder them; for to such belongs the kingdom of God."

† *Then the minister shall address the parents or sponsors, saying,*

Beloved, do you in presenting *this child* for holy Baptism confess your faith in our Lord and Savior Jesus Christ?

We do.

Do you therefore accept as your bounden duty and privilege to live before *this child* a life that becomes the Gospel; to exercise all godly care that *he* be brought up in the Christian faith, that *he* be taught the Holy Scriptures, and that *he* learn to give reverent attendance upon the private and public worship of God?

We do.

Will you endeavor to keep *this child* under the ministry and guidance of the Church until *he* by the power of God shall accept for *himself* the gift of salvation, and be confirmed as a full and responsible member of Christ's holy Church?

We will.

† *Then the minister shall take the child in his arms, and shall say to the parents or sponsors,*

What name is given this child?

† *And then, repeating the name, though not including the surname, the minister shall baptize the child, saying,*

N., I baptize you in the name of the Father, and of the Son, and of the Holy Spirit. **Amen.**

† *Then the minister may have the people stand, and, addressing them, may say,*

Brethren of the household of faith, I commend to your love and care *this child,* whom we this day recognize as *a member* of the family of God. Will you endeavor so to live that *he* may grow in the knowledge and love of God the Father, through our Savior Jesus Christ?

† *Then the people shall say,*

With God's help we will so order our lives after the example of Christ, that *this child,* surrounded by steadfast love, may be established in the faith, and confirmed and strengthened in the way that leads to life eternal.

† *Then the minister shall say,*

Let us pray.

O God, our heavenly Father, grant that *this child,* as *he grows* in years, may also grow in grace and in the knowledge of the Lord Jesus Christ, and that by the restraining and renewing influence of the Holy Spirit *he* may ever be *a* true *child* of thine, serving thee faithfully all *his* days.

So guide and uphold the *parents (or sponsors)* of *this child* that, by loving care, wise counsel, and holy example, they may lead *him* into that life of faith whose strength is righteousness and whose fruit is everlasting joy and peace; through Jesus Christ our Lord. **Amen.**

† *Then the minister may give this or another blessing:*

God the Father, God the Son, and God the Holy Spirit bless, preserve, and keep you, now and forevermore. **Amen.**

YOUTH AND ADULTS

† *The person or persons to be baptized shall stand before the minister, who, addressing the people, shall say,*

Dearly beloved, forasmuch as all men have sinned and fallen short of the glory of God, and our Savior Christ said, "Unless one is born of water and the Spirit, he cannot enter the kingdom of God," I beseech you to call upon God the Father, through our Lord Jesus Christ, that of his bounteous goodness he will grant that *this person* may receive the forgiveness of sins, be baptized with water and the Holy Spirit, and may be received into Christ's holy Church, and be made a living *member* of the same.

Let us pray.

Almighty and everlasting God, the aid of all who need, the helper of all who call upon thee for comfort, the life of all who believe, and the resurrection of the dead: We call upon thee for *this* thy *servant,* that *he,* coming to thy holy Baptism, may receive remission of *his* sins and be filled with the Holy Spirit. Receive *him,* O Lord, as thou hast promised by thy well-beloved Son, and grant that *he* may be faithful to thee all the days of *his life,* and finally come to the eternal kingdom which thou hast promised; through Jesus Christ our Lord. **Amen.**

† *Then, addressing the person or persons to be baptized, the minister shall say,*

9

Well beloved, you are come here desiring to receive holy Baptism. We have prayed that God, through our Lord Jesus Christ, would grant to receive you, release you from sin, sanctify you with the Holy Spirit, and give you the kingdom of heaven, and everlasting life.

Do you truly and earnestly repent of your sins and accept Jesus Christ as your Savior?

I do.

Do you believe in God, the Father Almighty, maker of heaven and earth; and in Jesus Christ his only Son our Lord; and in the Holy Spirit, the Lord, the giver of life?

I do.

Do you desire to be baptized in this faith?

I do.

Will you then obediently keep God's holy will and commandments and walk in the same all the days of your life?

I will, by God's help.

† *Then the minister shall say,*

Let us pray.

O merciful God, grant that all sinful affections may die in *this* thy *servant,* and that all things belonging to thy Spirit may live and grow in *him.* Grant that *he* may have the power and strength to triumph over evil, may receive the fulness of thy grace, and ever remain in the number of thy faithful and beloved children; through Jesus Christ our Lord. **Amen.**

† *The minister, asking the name of each person to be baptized, and then repeating the same, though not including the surname, shall baptize him, saying,*

N., I baptize you in the name of the Father, and of the Son, and of the Holy Spirit. **Amen.**

† *Then the minister may have the people stand, and addressing them, may say,*

Brethren of the household of faith, I commend to your love and care *this person,* whom we this day recognize as *a member* of the family of God. Will you endeavor so to live that *he* may grow in the knowledge and love of God the Father through our Savior Jesus Christ?

† *Then the people shall say,*

With God's help we will so order our lives after the example of Christ that, surrounded by steadfast love, you may be established in the faith, and confirmed and strengthened in the way that leads to life eternal.

† *Then the minister may give this or another blessing:*

God the Father, God the Son, and God the Holy Spirit bless, preserve, and keep you, now and for evermore. **Amen.**

The Order for Confirmation and Reception into the Church

† *This service shall be conducted in the church in the presence of the people at such a time in a stated hour of worship as the minister may determine.*

† *All who are to be confirmed as members of Christ's holy Church shall have been baptized, and instructed in the doctrines and duties of the Christian faith.*

† *Those to be confirmed shall stand before the minister, who, addressing the people, shall say,*

Dearly beloved, the Church is of God, and will be preserved to the end of time, for the conduct of worship and the due administration of his Word and Sacraments, the maintenance of Christian fellowship and discipline, the edification of believers, and the conversion of the world. All, of every age and station, stand in need of the means of grace which it alone supplies.

These persons who *are* to be confirmed *have* received the Sacrament of Baptism, *have* also been instructed in the teachings of the Church, and *are* now ready to profess publicly the faith into which *they were* baptized.

† *Then the minister, addressing those who are to be confirmed, shall say,*

Do you here, in the presence of God, and of this congregation, renew the solemn promise and vow that you made, or that was made in your name, at your Baptism?

I do.

Do you confess Jesus Christ as your Lord and Savior and pledge your allegiance to his kingdom?

I do.

Do you receive and profess the Christian faith as contained in the Scriptures of the Old and New Testaments?

I do.

Do you promise according to the grace given you to live a Christian life and always remain a faithful member of Christ's holy Church?

I do.

† *Then the candidates shall kneel, and the minister, laying his hands upon the head of each severally, shall say,*

N., the Lord defend you with his heavenly grace and by his Spirit confirm you in the faith and fellowship of all true disciples of Jesus Christ. **Amen.**

† *Those confirmed shall rise, and the minister, addressing the people, may say,*

Let those persons who are members of other communions in Christ's holy Church, and who now desire to enter into the fellowship of this congregation, present themselves to be received into the membership of The Methodist Church.

† *Then those confirmed and those to be received from other communions shall stand before the minister; and he, addressing them, shall say,*

Will you be loyal to The Methodist Church, and uphold it by your prayers, your presence, your gifts, and your service?

I will.

† *Then the minister may say,*

Let those who are members of other congregations of The Methodist Church, and who now desire to enter into the fellowship of this congregation, present themselves to be welcomed.

† *Here a lay member, selected by the Official Board, may join with the minister in offering the right hand of fellowship to all those received.*

† *Then the minister may have those received face the congregation, and, causing the people to stand, he shall address them, saying,*

Brethren, I commend to your love and care *these persons* whom we this day receive into the membership of this congregation. Do all in your power to increase *their* faith, confirm *their* hope, and perfect *them* in love.

† *Whereupon the people shall say,*

We rejoice to recognize you as *members* of Christ's holy Church, and bid you welcome to this congregation of The Methodist Church. With you we renew our vows to uphold it by our prayers, our presence, our gifts, and our service.

† *Then the minister may say,*

Go forth in peace, and be of good courage; hold fast that which is good, rejoicing in the power of the Holy Spirit. And the blessing of God, Father, Son, and Holy Spirit, be with you and remain with you forever. **Amen.**

† *On any day when persons are to be received by transfer only, the minister will use only that part of the service which applies to them.*

14

The Order for the Administration
of the Sacrament of
the Lord's Supper or Holy Communion

† *It shall be the duty of the pastor to administer the Sacrament of the Lord's Supper at regularly appointed times to the people committed to his care, remembering the charge laid upon him at the time of his ordination: "Be thou a faithful dispenser of the Word of God, and of his holy Sacraments."*

† *The order for the administration of this Sacrament to the sick, to those confined to their homes, or to others in circumstances where the full service is impracticable, should include the Invitation, the General Confession, the Prayer for Pardon, the Comfortable Words, the Prayer of Consecration, the Prayer of Humble Access, the Words of Distribution, the Prayer of Thanksgiving, and the Benediction.*

† *At the time of Holy Communion, the Lord's Table shall have upon it a fair white linen cloth. The elements of bread and wine shall be placed thereon. The pure, unfermented juice of the grape shall be used.*

† *It is our custom to deliver the elements into the hands of the people while they kneel before the Lord's Table. But at the discretion of the minister, the elements may be served to any or to all of the people while standing, or while seated in the pews.*

† *Upon entering the church, the people shall bow in prayer and shall remain until the entire service is concluded.*

† *All people who intend to lead a Christian life are invited to receive this holy Sacrament.*

† *The service may begin with a prelude.*

† *A hymn may be sung, the people standing.*

† *Or the minister may begin the service with one or more of the following or other suitable sentences from the Scriptures:*

Behold, I stand at the door and knock; if any one hears my voice and opens the door, I will come in to him and eat with him, and he with me.

Revelation 3:20

I am the living bread which came down from heaven; if any one eats of this bread, he will live forever; and the bread which I shall give for the life of the world is my flesh. *John 6:51*

The cup of blessing which we bless, is it not a participation in the blood of Christ? The bread which we break, is it not a participation in the body of Christ? Because there is one loaf, we who are many are one body, for we all partake of the same loaf. *I Corinthians 10:16-17*

Beloved, let us love one another; for love is of God, and he who loves is born of God and knows God. In this the love of God was made manifest among us, that God sent his only Son into the world, so that we might live through him. *I John 4:7, 9*

Christ our Paschal Lamb is offered up for us, once for all, when he bore our sins on his body upon the cross; for he is the very Lamb of God that taketh away the sins of the world: Wherefore let us keep a joyful and holy feast with the Lord.

From I Corinthians 5:7-8; I Peter 2:24; John 1:29

What no eye has seen, nor ear heard, nor the heart of man conceived, what God has prepared for those who love him, God has revealed to us through the Spirit. For the Spirit searches everything, even the depths of God. *I Corinthians 2:9-10*

† *Here the minister, facing the people, shall say,*

> The Lord be with you.

People: **And with thy spirit.**

Minister: Let us pray.

† *Then, kneeling or bowed, the minister and people together shall say,*

Almighty God, unto whom all hearts are open, all desires known, and from whom no secrets are hid: Cleanse the thoughts of our hearts by the inspiration of thy Holy Spirit, that we may perfectly love thee, and worthily magnify thy holy name; through Christ our Lord. Amen.

Our Father, who art in heaven, hallowed be thy name. Thy kingdom come, thy will be done on earth as it is in heaven. Give us this day our daily bread. And forgive us our trespasses, as we forgive those who trespass against us. And lead us not into temptation, but deliver us from evil. For thine is the kingdom, and the power, and the glory, forever. Amen.

† *Then, standing, all shall sing or say,*

16

Glory be to God on high, and on earth peace, good will toward men. We praise thee, we bless thee, we worship thee, we glorify thee, we give thanks to thee for thy great glory: O Lord God, heavenly King, God the Father Almighty.

O Lord, the only begotten Son, Jesus Christ: O Lord God, Lamb of God, Son of the Father: that takest away the sins of the world, have mercy upon us. Thou that takest away the sins of the world, receive our prayer. Thou that sittest at the right hand of God the Father, have mercy upon us.

For thou only art holy; thou only art the Lord; thou only, O Christ, with the Holy Ghost, art most high in the glory of God the Father. Amen.

† *The minister, facing the people while they remain standing, shall say,*
Ye that do truly and earnestly repent of your sins, and are in love and charity with your neighbors, and intend to lead a new life, following the commandments of God, and walking from henceforth in his holy ways: Draw near with faith, and take this holy Sacrament to your comfort, and make your humble confession to almighty God.

† *Then the minister, kneeling and facing the Lord's Table, and all the people, kneeling or bowed, shall make together this general confession:*
Almighty God, Father of our Lord Jesus Christ, maker of all things, judge of all men: We acknowledge and bewail our manifold sins and wickedness, which we from time to time most grievously have committed, by thought, word, and deed, against thy divine majesty. We do earnestly repent, and are heartily sorry for these our misdoings; the remembrance of them is grievous unto us. Have mercy upon us, have mercy upon us, most merciful Father. For thy Son our Lord Jesus Christ's sake, forgive us all that is past; and grant that we may ever hereafter serve and please thee in newness of life, to the honor and glory of thy name; through Jesus Christ our Lord. Amen.

† *Then the minister shall pray, saying,*
Almighty God, our heavenly Father, who of thy great mercy hast promised forgiveness of sins to all them that with hearty repentance and true faith turn to thee: Have mercy upon us; pardon and deliver us from all our sins; confirm and strengthen us in all goodness; and bring us to everlasting life; through Jesus Christ our Lord. Amen.

† *The minister, standing and facing the people, shall say,*

Hear what comfortable words the Scriptures say to all that truly turn to the Lord:

† *Then the minister shall say one or more of the following sentences:*

Come to me, all who labor and are heavy-laden, and I will give you rest.
Matthew 11:28

God so loved the world that he gave his only Son, that whoever believes in him should not perish but have eternal life. *John 3:16*

The saying is sure and worthy of full acceptance, that Christ Jesus came into the world to save sinners. *I Timothy 1:15*

If we confess our sins, he is faithful and just, and will forgive our sins and cleanse us from all unrighteousness. *I John 1:9*

If any one sins, we have an advocate with the Father, Jesus Christ the righteous; and he is the expiation for our sins, and not for ours only but also for the sins of the whole world. *From I John 2:1-2*

† *Here the minister may offer a pastoral prayer, or he may say,*

Let us pray for the whole state of Christ's Church.

† *Then may follow this prayer, the minister beginning, the people responding:*

Most merciful Father, we humbly beseech thee to receive these our prayers for the universal Church, that thou wilt confirm it in the truth of thy holy faith, inspire it with unity and concord, and extend and prosper it throughout the world.

We beseech thee also, so to guide and strengthen the witness of the Church to those in authority in all nations, that they may maintain the justice and welfare of all mankind.

Hear us, we beseech thee, O Lord.

Give grace, O heavenly Father, to all ministers of thy Church, that both by their life and doctrine they may set forth thy true and lively Word, and faithfully administer thy holy Sacraments.

And to all thy people give thy heavenly grace, that with willing heart and due reverence, they may hear and receive thy holy Word, truly serving thee in holiness and righteousness all the days of their lives.

Hear us, we beseech thee, O Lord.

And we most humbly beseech thee, of thy goodness, O Lord, to support and strengthen all those who, in this transitory life, are in trouble, sorrow, need, sickness, or any other adversity.

Hear us, we beseech thee, O Lord.
We remember with thanksgiving those who have loved and served thee in thy Church on earth, who now rest from their labors (especially those most dear to us, whom we name in our hearts before thee). Keep us in fellowship with all thy saints, and bring us at length to the joy of thy heavenly kingdom.

Grant this, O Father, for the sake of Jesus Christ, our only mediator and advocate. Amen.

† *Then shall be read the lesson(s) from the Holy Scriptures. If two lessons are read, let one be the Epistle and the other the Gospel. An anthem or a hymn may be sung after the first lesson.*

† *Here the minister and people may say the Apostles' Creed or another of the Christian affirmations of faith, the people standing.*

† *Then shall follow the sermon.*

† *Here parish notices may be given.*

† *A hymn may be sung. The minister shall uncover the elements, and shall proceed to receive the offering from the people. When the offering is presented, the people shall stand, and a prayer of dedication shall be said or sung.*

† *Where custom prevails, an offering may be left by the people at the chancel when they come forward to receive the elements.*

† *The people shall remain standing, and the minister, facing the people, shall say,*

> Lift up your hearts.

People: **We lift them up unto the Lord.**

Minister: Let us give thanks unto the Lord.

People: **It is meet and right so to do.**

† *Then the minister, facing the Lord's Table, shall say,*

It is very meet, right, and our bounden duty that we should at all times and in all places give thanks unto thee, O Lord, holy Father, almighty, everlasting God.

† *Here may follow the proper preface,[1] or else the minister immediately shall say,*

Therefore with angels and archangels, and with all the company of

[1] See p. 23.

19

heaven, we laud and magnify thy glorious name, evermore praising thee, and saying:

† *Then shall all sing or say,*

Holy, holy, holy, Lord God of hosts: Heaven and earth are full of thy glory! Glory be to thee, O Lord most high! Amen.

† *The people shall kneel or bow; the minister, facing the Lord's Table, shall offer the Prayer of Consecration:*

Almighty God, our heavenly Father, who of thy tender mercy didst give thine only Son Jesus Christ to suffer death upon the cross for our redemption; who made there, by the one offering of himself, a full, perfect, and sufficient sacrifice for the sins of the whole world; and did institute, and in his holy Gospel command us to continue, a perpetual memory of his precious death until his coming again:

Hear us, O merciful Father, we most humbly beseech thee, and grant that we, receiving these thy creatures of bread and wine, according to thy Son our Savior Jesus Christ's holy institution, in remembrance of his passion, death, and resurrection, may be partakers of the divine nature through him:

Who in the same night that he was betrayed, took bread [*here the minister may take the bread in his hands*], and when he had given thanks, he broke it, and gave it to his disciples, saying, Take, eat; this is my body which is given for you; do this in remembrance of me. Likewise after supper he took the cup [*here the minister may take the cup in his hands*]; and when he had given thanks, he gave it to them, saying, Drink ye all of this; for this is my blood of the New Covenant, which is shed for you and for many, for the forgiveness of sins; do this, as oft as ye shall drink it, in remembrance of me. **Amen.**

† *The minister shall kneel before the Lord's Table. After a brief silence, the minister and people together shall pray, saying,*

We do not presume to come to this thy table, O merciful Lord, trusting in our own righteousness, but in thy manifold and great mercies. We are not worthy so much as to gather up the crumbs under thy table. But thou art the same Lord, whose property is always to have mercy. Grant us therefore, gracious Lord, so to partake of this Sacrament of thy Son Jesus Christ, that we may walk in newness of life, may grow into his likeness, and may evermore dwell in him, and he in us. Amen.

† *Here may be sung or said:*

O Lamb of God, that takest away the sins of the world, have mercy upon us.

O Lamb of God, that takest away the sins of the world, have mercy upon us.

O Lamb of God, that takest away the sins of the world, grant us thy peace.

† *The minister shall first receive the Holy Communion in both kinds, and then shall deliver the same to any who are assisting him. Then the minister or those assisting him shall deliver the elements in both kinds to the people.*[2]

† *During the distribution of the elements, appropriate hymns may be sung or played.*[3]

† *When the bread is given, one or both of the following sentences shall be said:*

The body of our Lord Jesus Christ, which was given for thee, preserve thy soul and body unto everlasting life.

Take and eat this in remembrance that Christ died for thee, and feed on him in thy heart by faith with thanksgiving.

† *When the cup is given, one or both of the following sentences shall be said:*

The blood of our Lord Jesus Christ, which was shed for thee, preserve thy soul and body unto everlasting life.

Drink this in remembrance that Christ's blood was shed for thee, and be thankful.

† *When all have communed, the minister shall place upon the Lord's Table all that remains of the elements, covering the same.*

† *Then the minister, standing and facing the people, shall say,*

> The peace of the Lord be with you.

People: **And with thy Spirit.**

Minister: Let us give thanks unto the Lord.

† *Then the minister, kneeling before the Lord's Table, and the people, kneeling or bowed, shall pray, saying,*

---

[2] See pp. 202-4 for table dismissals, if desired.
[3] See topical index in *The Methodist Hymnal.*

O Lord, our heavenly Father, we, thy humble servants, desire thy fatherly goodness mercifully to accept this our sacrifice of praise and thanksgiving; most humbly beseeching thee to grant, that, by the merits and death of thy Son Jesus Christ, and through faith in his blood, we and thy whole Church may obtain forgiveness of our sins, and all other benefits of his passion.

And here we offer and present unto thee, O Lord, ourselves, our souls and bodies, to be a reasonable, holy, and lively sacrifice unto thee; humbly beseeching thee that all we who are partakers of this Holy Communion may be filled with thy grace and heavenly benediction. And although we be unworthy, through our manifold sins, to offer unto thee any sacrifice, yet we beseech thee to accept this our bounden duty and service, not weighing our merits, but pardoning our offenses;

Through Jesus Christ our Lord, by whom, and with whom, in the unity of the Holy Spirit, all honor and glory be unto thee, O Father Almighty, world without end. Amen.

† *Then a hymn may be sung.*

† *Then the minister shall let the people depart with this blessing:*

The peace of God, which passeth all understanding, keep your hearts and minds in the knowledge and love of God, and of his Son Jesus Christ our Lord; and the blessing of God Almighty, the Father, the Son, and the Holy Spirit, be among you, and remain with you always. **Amen.**

† *A postlude may follow.*

Proper Prefaces for Certain Days, to Precede the Sanctus in the Order for Holy Communion

Christmas

Because thou didst give Jesus Christ, thine only Son, to be born as at this time for us; who, by the operation of the Holy Ghost, was made very man, and that without spot of sin, to make us clean from all sin.

Therefore with angels, *etc.*

Epiphany

Through Jesus Christ our Lord; who, in substance of our mortal flesh, manifested forth his glory, that he might bring us out of darkness into his own glorious light.

Therefore with angels, *etc.*

Easter

But chiefly are we bound to praise thee for the glorious resurrection of thy Son Jesus Christ our Lord, who by his death hath destroyed death, and by his rising to life again hath restored to us everlasting life.

Therefore with angels, *etc.*

Pentecost

Through Jesus Christ our Lord; according to whose most true promise, the Holy Spirit came down as at this time from heaven, lighting upon the disciples, to teach them, and to lead them into all truth, whereby we have been brought out of darkness into the clear light and true knowledge of thee, and of thy Son Jesus Christ.

Therefore with angels, *etc.*

A Brief Form of the Order for the Administration of the Sacrament of the Lord's Supper or Holy Communion

† *This form for the administration of Holy Communion may be included in an order of worship, following the sermon.*

† *The minister shall uncover the elements, and shall proceed to receive the offering from the people. When the offering is presented, the people shall stand, and a prayer of dedication shall be said or sung.*

† *Where custom prevails, an offering may be left by the people at the chancel when they come forward to receive the elements.*

† *The people standing, the minister, facing the people, shall say,*

Ye that do truly and earnestly repent of your sins, and are in love and charity with your neighbors, and intend to lead a new life, following the commandments of God, and walking from henceforth in his holy ways: Draw near with faith, and take this holy Sacrament to your comfort, and make your humble confession to almighty God.

† *Then the minister, kneeling and facing the Lord's Table, and all the people, kneeling or bowed, shall make together this general confession,*

Almighty God, Father of our Lord Jesus Christ, maker of all things, judge of all men: We acknowledge and bewail our manifold sins and wickedness, which we from time to time most grievously have committed, by thought, word, and deed, against thy divine majesty. We do earnestly repent, and are heartily sorry for these our misdoings; the remembrance of them is grievous unto us. Have mercy upon us, have mercy upon us, most merciful Father. For thy Son our Lord Jesus Christ's sake, forgive us all that is past; and grant that we may ever hereafter serve and please thee in newness of life, to the honor and glory of thy name; through Jesus Christ our Lord. Amen.

† *Then the minister shall pray, saying,*

Almighty God, our heavenly Father, who of thy great mercy hast promised forgiveness of sins to all them that with hearty repentance and true faith turn to thee: Have mercy upon us; pardon and deliver us from all our sins; confirm and strengthen us in all goodness; and bring us to everlasting life; through Jesus Christ our Lord. **Amen.**

24

THE SACRAMENT OF THE LORD'S SUPPER OR HOLY COMMUNION

† *The minister, standing and facing the people, shall say,*

Hear what comfortable words the Scriptures say to all that truly turn to the Lord:

† *Then the minister shall say one or more of the following sentences:*

Come to me, all who labor and are heavy-laden, and I will give you rest.
Matthew 11:28

God so loved the world that he gave his only Son, that whoever believes in him should not perish but have eternal life. *John 3:16*

The saying is sure and worthy of full acceptance, that Christ Jesus came into the world to save sinners. *I Timothy 1:15*

If we confess our sins, he is faithful and just, and will forgive our sins and cleanse us from all unrighteousness. *I John 1:9*

If any one sins, we have an advocate with the Father, Jesus Christ the righteous; and he is the expiation for our sins, and not for ours only but also for the sins of the whole world. *From I John 2:1-2*

† *The people shall kneel or bow; the minister, facing the Lord's Table, shall offer the Prayer of Consecration:*

Almighty God, our heavenly Father, who of thy tender mercy didst give thine only Son Jesus Christ to suffer death upon the cross for our redemption; who made there, by the one offering of himself, a full, perfect, and sufficient sacrifice for the sins of the whole world; and did institute, and in his holy Gospel command us to continue, a perpetual memory of his precious death until his coming again:

Hear us, O merciful Father, we most humbly beseech thee, and grant that we, receiving these thy creatures of bread and wine, according to thy Son our Savior Jesus Christ's holy institution, in remembrance of his passion, death, and resurrection, may be partakers of the divine nature through him:

Who in the same night that he was betrayed, took bread [*here the minister may take the bread in his hands*], and when he had given thanks, he broke it, and gave it to his disciples, saying, Take, eat; this is my body which is given for you; do this in remembrance of me. Likewise after supper he took the cup [*here the minister may take the cup in his hands*]; and when he had given thanks, he gave it to them, saying, Drink ye all of this; for this is my blood of the New Covenant which is shed for you and for many for the forgiveness of sins; do this, as oft as ye shall drink it, in remembrance of me. **Amen.**

† *The minister shall kneel before the Lord's Table. After a brief silence, the minister and people shall offer the following prayer:*

We do not presume to come to this thy table, O merciful Lord, trusting in our own righteousness, but in thy manifold and great mercies. We are not worthy so much as to gather up the crumbs under thy table. But thou art the same Lord, whose property is always to have mercy. Grant us therefore, gracious Lord, so to partake of this Sacrament of thy Son Jesus Christ, that we may walk in newness of life, may grow into his likeness, and may evermore dwell in him, and he in us. Amen.

† *The minister shall first receive the Holy Communion in both kinds, and then shall deliver the same to any who are assisting him. Then the minister or those assisting him shall deliver the elements in both kinds to the people.*[1]

† *During the distribution of the elements, appropriate hymns may be sung or played.*[2]

† *When the bread is given, one or both of the following sentences shall be said:*

The body of our Lord Jesus Christ, which was given for thee, preserve thy soul and body unto everlasting life.

Take and eat this in remembrance that Christ died for thee, and feed on him in thy heart by faith with thanksgiving.

† *When the cup is given, one or both of the following sentences shall be said:*

The blood of our Lord Jesus Christ, which was shed for thee, preserve thy soul and body unto everlasting life.

Drink this in remembrance that Christ's blood was shed for thee, and be thankful.

† *When all have communed, the minister shall place upon the Lord's Table all that remains of the elements, covering the same.*

† *Then the minister, kneeling before the Lord's Table, and the people, kneeling or bowed, shall pray, saying,*

[1] See pp. 202-4 for table dismissals, if desired.
[2] See topical index in *The Methodist Hymnal.*

O Lord, our heavenly Father, we, thy humble servants, desire thy fatherly goodness mercifully to accept this our sacrifice of praise and thanksgiving; most humbly beseeching thee to grant, that, by the merits and death of thy Son Jesus Christ, and through faith in his blood, we and thy whole Church may obtain forgiveness of our sins, and all other benefits of his passion.

And here we offer and present unto thee, O Lord, ourselves, our souls and bodies, to be a reasonable, holy, and lively sacrifice unto thee; humbly beseeching thee that all we who are partakers of this Holy Communion may be filled with thy grace and heavenly benediction. And although we be unworthy, through our manifold sins, to offer unto thee any sacrifice, yet we beseech thee to accept this our bounden duty and service, not weighing our merits, but pardoning our offenses;

Through Jesus Christ our Lord, by whom and with whom, in the unity of the Holy Spirit, all honor and glory be unto thee, O Father Almighty, world without end. Amen.

† *Then a hymn may be sung.*

† *Then the minister shall let the people depart with this blessing:*

The peace of God, which passeth all understanding, keep your hearts and minds in the knowledge and love of God, and of his Son Jesus Christ our Lord; and the blessing of God Almighty, the Father, the Son, and the Holy Spirit, be among you, and remain with you always. **Amen.**

The Order for the Service of Marriage

† *The minister is enjoined diligently to instruct those requesting his offices for their prospective marriage in the Christian significance of the holy estate into which they seek to enter.*

† *All arrangements pertaining to the service of marriage shall be made in full consultation with the minister.*

† *This service may begin with a prelude, anthem, solo, or hymn. It may include a processional and recessional and be concluded with a postlude.*[1]

† *The congregation shall stand as the wedding procession begins.*

† *The Christian names of the bride and bridegroom may be used in place of "this man and this woman" in the first, third, and fourth paragraphs.*

† *When the Sacrament of the Lord's Supper is requested, this service should be provided at a time other than the service of marriage.*

† *At the time appointed, the persons to be married, having been qualified according to the laws of the state and the standards of the Church, standing together facing the minister, the man at the minister's left hand and the woman at the right hand, the minister shall say,*

Dearly beloved, we are gathered together here in the sight of God, and in the presence of these witnesses, to join together *this man and this woman* in holy matrimony; which is an honorable estate, instituted of God, and signifying unto us the mystical union which exists between Christ and his Church; which holy estate Christ adorned and beautified with his presence in Cana of Galilee. It is therefore not to be entered into unadvisedly, but reverently, discreetly, and in the fear of God. Into this holy estate these two persons come now to be joined. If any man can show just cause why they may not lawfully be joined together, let him now speak, or else hereafter forever hold his peace.

[1] Suggested music from *The Methodist Hymnal:*

Processional: Praise the Lord! ye heavens, adore him; For the beauty of the earth; Praise to the Lord, the Almighty; Praise, my soul, the King of heaven.

Recessional: Now thank we all our God; Joyful, joyful, we adore thee; God is love, his mercy brightens; Love divine, all loves excelling.

Prayers and hymns: May the grace of Christ our Savior; Blessed Jesus, at thy word; The King of love my Shepherd is; O perfect Love, all human thought transcending.

† *Addressing the persons to be married, the minister shall say,*

I require and charge you both, as you stand in the presence of God, before whom the secrets of all hearts are disclosed, that, having duly considered the holy covenant you are about to make, you do now declare before this company your pledge of faith, each to the other. Be well assured that if these solemn vows are kept inviolate, as God's Word demands, and if steadfastly you endeavor to do the will of your heavenly Father, God will bless your marriage, will grant you fulfillment in it, and will establish your home in peace.

† *Then shall the minister say to the man, using his Christian name,*

N., wilt thou have this woman to be thy wedded wife, to live together in the holy estate of matrimony? Wilt thou love her, comfort her, honor and keep her, in sickness and in health; and forsaking all other keep thee only unto her so long as ye both shall live?

† *The man shall answer,*

I will.

† *Then shall the minister say to the woman, using her Christian name,*

N., wilt thou have this man to be thy wedded husband, to live together in the holy estate of matrimony? Wilt thou love him, comfort him, honor and keep him, in sickness and in health; and forsaking all other keep thee only unto him so long as ye both shall live?

† *The woman shall answer,*

I will.

† *Then shall the minister say,*

Who giveth this woman to be married to this man?

† *The father of the woman, or whoever gives her in marriage, shall answer,*

I do.

† *Then, the minister, receiving the hand of the woman from her father or other sponsor, shall cause the man with his right hand to take the woman by her right hand, and say after him,*

I, N., take thee, N., to be my wedded wife, to have and to hold, from this day forward, for better, for worse, for richer, for poorer, in sickness and in health, to love and to cherish, till death us do part, according to God's holy ordinance; and thereto I pledge thee my faith.

† *Then shall they loose their hands; and the woman, with her right hand taking the man by his right hand, shall say after the minister,*

I, N., take thee, N., to be my wedded husband, to have and to hold, from this day forward, for better, for worse, for richer, for poorer, in sickness and in health, to love and to cherish, till death us do part, according to God's holy ordinance; and thereto I pledge thee my faith.

† *Then they may give to each other rings, or the man may give to the woman a ring, in this wise: the minister, taking the ring or rings, shall say,*

The wedding ring is the outward and visible sign of an inward and spiritual grace, signifying to all the uniting of this man and woman in holy matrimony, through the Church of Jesus Christ our Lord.

† *Then the minister may say,*

Let us pray.

Bless, O Lord, the giving of these rings, that they who wear them may abide in thy peace, and continue in thy favor; through Jesus Christ our Lord. **Amen.**

† *Or, if there be but one ring, the minister may say,*

Bless, O Lord, the giving of this ring, that he who gives it and she who wears it may abide forever in thy peace, and continue in thy favor; through Jesus Christ our Lord. **Amen.**

† *The minister shall then deliver the proper ring to the man to put upon the third finger of the woman's left hand. The man, holding the ring there, shall say after the minister,*

In token and pledge of our constant faith and abiding love, with this ring I thee wed, in the name of the Father, and of the Son, and of the Holy Spirit. Amen.

† *Then, if there is a second ring, the minister shall deliver it to the woman to put upon the third finger of the man's left hand; and the woman, holding the ring there, shall say after the minister,*

In token and pledge of our constant faith and abiding love, with this ring I thee wed, in the name of the Father, and of the Son, and of the Holy Spirit. Amen.

† *Then shall the minister join their right hands together and, with his hand on their united hands, shall say,*

Forasmuch as *N.* and *N.* have consented together in holy wedlock, and have witnessed the same before God and this company, and thereto have pledged their faith each to the other, and have declared the same by joining hands and by giving and receiving *rings;* I pronounce that they are husband and wife together, in the name of the Father, and of the Son, and of the Holy Spirit. Those whom God hath joined together, let not man put asunder. **Amen.**

† *Then shall the minister say,*
Let us pray.

† *Then shall the husband and wife kneel; the minister shall say,*
O eternal God, creator and preserver of all mankind, giver of all spiritual grace, the author of everlasting life: Send thy blessing upon this man and this woman, whom we bless in thy name; that they may surely perform and keep the vow and covenant between them made, and may ever remain in perfect love and peace together, and live according to thy laws.

Look graciously upon them, that they may love, honor, and cherish each other, and so live together in faithfulness and patience, in wisdom and true godliness, that their home may be a haven of blessing and a place of peace; through Jesus Christ our Lord. **Amen.**

† *Then the husband and wife, still kneeling, shall join with the minister and congregation in the Lord's Prayer, saying,*
Our Father, who art in heaven, hallowed be thy name. Thy kingdom come, thy will be done on earth as it is in heaven. Give us this day our daily bread. And forgive us our trespasses, as we forgive those who trespass against us. And lead us not into temptation, but deliver us from evil. For thine is the kingdom, and the power, and the glory, forever. Amen.

† *Then the minister shall give this blessing,*
God the Father, the Son, and the Holy Spirit bless, preserve, and keep you; the Lord graciously with his favor look upon you, and so fill you with all spiritual benediction and love that you may so live together in this life that in the world to come you may have life everlasting. **Amen.**

The Order for the Burial of the Dead

† *The death of a member of the church should be reported to the pastor as soon as possible, and arrangements for the funeral should be made in consultation with him.*

† *The pastor shall not accept an honorarium for this service when the deceased was a member of his parish.*

† *Funeral services of church members should be held in the sanctuary. The casket should be placed before the altar or the Lord's Table and remain closed.*

† *In the event of cremation the service may be adapted at the discretion of the minister.*

† *The service may begin and end with appropriate music selected in consultation with the minister.*

† *The minister shall begin the service by reading one or more of the following sentences; or the minister, meeting the body, and going before it, shall say one or more of the following sentences:*

Jesus said, "I am the resurrection and the life; he who believes in me, though he die, yet shall he live, and whosoever lives and believes in me shall never die."   *John 11:25-26*

The eternal God is your dwelling place, and underneath are the everlasting arms.   *Deuteronomy 33:27a*

The Lord is my light and my salvation; whom shall I fear? The Lord is the stronghold of my life; of whom shall I be afraid?   *Psalm 27:1*

Blessed be the Lord! for he has heard the voice of my supplications. The Lord is my strength and my shield; in him my heart trusts. *Psalm 28:6-7a*

For we know that if the earthly tent we live in is destroyed, we have a building from God, a house not made with hands, eternal in the heavens.
                                                          II Corinthians 5:1

† *Here a hymn may be sung, and then the minister shall say,*
Let us pray.

† *Here the minister may offer one or more of the following prayers:*
O God, the Lord of life, the conqueror of death, our help in every time of trouble, who dost not willingly grieve or afflict the children of men:

Comfort us who mourn, and give us grace, in the presence of death, to worship thee, that we may have sure hope of eternal life and be enabled to put our whole trust in thy goodness and mercy; through Jesus Christ our Lord. **Amen.**

Almighty God, our Father, from whom we come, and unto whom our spirits return: Thou hast been our dwelling place in all generations. Thou art our refuge and strength, a very present help in trouble. Grant us thy blessing in this hour, and enable us so to put our trust in thee that our spirits may grow calm and our hearts be comforted. Lift our eyes beyond the shadows of earth, and help us to see the light of eternity. So may we find grace and strength for this and every time of need; through Jesus Christ our Lord. **Amen.**

O God our Father, creator of all mankind, giver and preserver of all life: We confess to thee our slowness to accept death as part of thy plan for life. We confess our reluctance to commit to thee those whom we love. Restore our faith that we may come to trust in thy care and providence; through Jesus Christ our Lord. **Amen.**

O Jesus Christ our risen Lord, who in death hast gone before us: Grant us the assurance of thy presence, that we who are anxious and fearful in the face of death may confidently face the future, in the knowledge that thou hast prepared a place for all who love thee. **Amen.**

† *Here one or more of the following psalms may be read by the minister, or by the minister and people responsively or in unison. If the people participate, they shall stand for the psalm and remain standing for the Gloria Patri.*

The Lord is my shepherd;
   I shall not want.
He maketh me to lie down in green pastures:
   he leadeth me beside the still waters.
He restoreth my soul:
   he leadeth me in the paths of righteousness for his name's sake.
Yea, though I walk through the valley of the shadow of death, I will fear
   no evil:
   for thou art with me; thy rod and thy staff they comfort me.
Thou preparest a table before me in the presence of mine enemies:
   thou anointest my head with oil; my cup runneth over.

Surely goodness and mercy shall follow me all the days of my life:
and I will dwell in the house of the Lord for ever. *Psalm 23 KJV*

The Lord is my light and my salvation;
  whom shall I fear?
The Lord is the stronghold of my life;
  of whom shall I be afraid?
Though a host encamp against me,
  my heart shall not fear;
though war arise against me,
  yet I will be confident.
One thing have I asked of the Lord,
  that will I seek after;
that I may dwell in the house of the Lord
  all the days of my life,
to behold the beauty of the Lord,
  and to inquire in his temple.
For he will hide me in his shelter
  in the day of trouble;
  he will set me high upon a rock.
I believe that I shall see the goodness of the Lord
  in the land of the living!
Wait for the Lord;
  be strong, and let your heart take courage;
  yea, wait for the Lord. *From Psalm 27*

Lord, thou hast been our dwelling place
  in all generations.
Before the mountains were brought forth,
  or ever thou hadst formed the earth and the world,
  from everlasting to everlasting thou art God.
For a thousand years in thy sight,
  are but as yesterday when it is past,
  or as a watch in the night.
Thou dost sweep men away; they are like a dream,
  like grass which is renewed in the morning:
in the morning it flourishes and is renewed;
  in the evening it fades and withers.

So teach us to number our days
   that we may get a heart of wisdom.
Let thy work be manifest to thy servants,
   and thy glorious power to their children.
Let the favor of the Lord our God be upon us,
   and establish thou the work of our hands upon us,
   yea, the work of our hands establish thou it.

From Psalm 90

I lift up my eyes to the hills.
   From whence does my help come?
My help comes from the Lord,
   who made heaven and earth.
He will not let your foot be moved,
   he who keeps you will not slumber.
Behold, he who keeps Israel
   will neither slumber nor sleep.
The Lord is your keeper;
   the Lord is your shade on your right hand.
The sun shall not smite you by day,
   nor the moon by night.
The Lord will keep you from all evil;
   he will keep your life.
The Lord will keep
   your going out and your coming in
   from this time forth and for evermore.   *Psalm 121*

† *Then the people shall say or sing,*

Glory be to the Father, and to the Son, and to the Holy Ghost; as it was in the beginning, is now, and ever shall be, world without end. Amen.

† *Here the congregation may confess their faith according to the Apostles' Creed or another affirmation of faith.*

† *Here one or more of the following lessons from the Scriptures shall be read:*

"Let not your hearts be troubled; believe in God, believe also in me. In my Father's house are many rooms; if it were not so, would I have told you that I go to prepare a place for you? And when I go and prepare a place for you, I will come again and will take you to myself, that where I am you may be also. And you know the way where I am going."

Thomas said to him, "Lord, we do not know where you are going; how can we know the way?"

Jesus said to him, "I am the way, and the truth, and the life; no one comes to the Father, but by me. If you had known me, you would have known my Father also; henceforth you know him and have seen him.

"If you love me, you will keep my commandments. And I will pray the Father, and he will give you another Counselor, to be with you forever, even the Spirit of truth, whom the world cannot receive, because it neither sees him nor knows him; you know him, for he dwells with you, and will be in you.

"Peace I leave with you; my peace I give to you; not as the world gives do I give to you. Let not your hearts be troubled, neither let them be afraid." *John 14:1-7, 15-17, 27*

All who are led by the Spirit of God are sons of God. For you did not receive the spirit of slavery to fall back into fear, but you have received the spirit of sonship. When we cry, "Abba! Father!" it is the Spirit himself bearing witness with our spirit that we are children of God, and if children, then heirs, heirs of God and fellow heirs with Christ, provided we suffer with him in order that we may also be glorified with him.

I consider that the sufferings of this present time are not worth comparing with the glory that is to be revealed to us.

We know that in everything God works for good with those who love him, who are called according to his purpose.

What then shall we say to this? If God is for us, who is against us? Who shall separate us from the love of Christ? Shall tribulation, or distress, or persecution, or famine, or nakedness, or peril, or sword? No, in all these things we are more than conquerors through him who loved us. For I am sure that neither death, nor life, nor angels, nor principalities, nor things present, nor things to come, nor powers, nor height, nor depth, nor anything else in all creation, will be able to separate us from the love of God in Christ Jesus our Lord.

Romans 8:14-18, 28, 31, 35, 37-39

In fact Christ has been raised from the dead, the first fruits of those who have fallen asleep. For as by a man came death, by a man has come also the resurrection of the dead. For as in Adam all die, so also in Christ shall all be made alive.

But some one will ask, "How are the dead raised? With what kind of body do they come?" You foolish man! What you sow does not come to life unless it dies. But God gives it a body as he has chosen.

So is it with the resurrection of the dead. What is sown is perishable, what is raised is imperishable. It is sown in dishonor, it is raised in glory. It is sown in weakness, it is raised in power. It is sown a physical body, it is raised a spiritual body. If there is a physical body, there is also a spiritual body. Just as we have borne the image of the man of dust, we shall also bear the image of the man of heaven. I tell you this, brethren: flesh and blood cannot inherit the kingdom of God, nor does the perishable inherit the imperishable.

For this perishable nature must put on the imperishable, and this mortal nature must put on immortality. When the perishable puts on the imperishable, and the mortal puts on immortality, then shall come to pass the saying that is written: "Death is swallowed up in victory. O death, where is thy victory? O death, where is thy sting?" The sting of death is sin, and the power of sin is the law. But thanks be to God, who gives us the victory through our Lord Jesus Christ.

Therefore, my beloved brethren, be steadfast, immovable, always abounding in the work of the Lord, knowing that in the Lord your labor is not in vain.   *I Corinthians 15:20-22, 35-36, 38a, 42-44, 49-50, 53-58*

And I saw the holy city, new Jerusalem, coming down out of heaven from God, prepared as a bride adorned for her husband; and I heard a great voice from the throne saying, "Behold, the dwelling of God is with men. He will dwell with them, and they shall be his people, and God himself will be with them; he will wipe away every tear from their eyes, and death shall be no more, neither shall there be mourning nor crying nor pain any more, for the former things have passed away."

And he who sat upon the throne said, "Behold, I make all things new." Also he said, "Write this, for these words are trustworthy and true." And he said to me, "It is done! I am the Alpha and the Omega, the beginning and the end. To the thirsty I will give water without price from the fountain of the water of life. He who conquers shall have this heritage, and I will be his God and he shall be my son."   *Revelation 21:2-7*

Then he showed me the river of the water of life, bright as crystal, flowing from the throne of God and of the Lamb through the middle of the street of the city; also, on either side of the river, the tree of life with its twelve kinds of fruit, yielding its fruit each month; and the leaves of the tree were for the healing of the nations. There shall no more be anything accursed, but the throne of God and of the Lamb shall be in it, and his servants shall worship him; they shall see his face, and his name shall be on their foreheads. And night shall be no more; they need no light of lamp or sun, for the Lord God will be their light, and they shall reign for ever and ever. *Revelation 22:1-5*

For this reason I bow my knees before the Father, from whom every family in heaven and on earth is named, that according to the riches of his glory he may grant you to be strengthened with might through his Spirit in the inner man, and that Christ may dwell in your hearts through faith; that you, being rooted and grounded in love, may have power to comprehend with all the saints what is the breadth and length and height and depth, and to know the love of Christ which surpasses knowledge, that you may be filled with all the fulness of God.

Now to him who by the power at work within us is able to do far more abundantly than all we ask or think, to him be glory in the church and in Christ Jesus to all generations, for ever and ever. Amen.

Ephesians 3:14-21

† *Here may be sung a hymn or anthem.*

† *Then may follow a sermon, after which the minister may pray as he is moved, or may offer one or more of the following prayers:*

Eternal God, who committest to us the swift and solemn trust of life: Since we know not what a day may bring forth, but only that the hour for serving thee is always present, may we wake to the instant claims of thy holy will, not waiting for tomorrow, but yielding today. Consecrate with thy presence the way our feet may go; and the humblest work will shine, and the roughest places be made plain. Lift us above unrighteous anger and mistrust into faith and hope and love by a simple and steadfast reliance on thy sure will. In all things draw us to the mind of Christ, that thy lost image may be traced again, and that thou mayest own us at one with him and thee. **Amen.**

O God, who art the strength of thy saints, and who redeemest the souls of thy servants: We bless thy name for all those who have died in the Lord, and who now rest from their labors, having received the end of their faith, even the salvation of their souls. Especially we call to remembrance thy lovingkindness and thy tender mercies to this *thy servant.*

For all thy goodness that withheld not *his* portion in the joys of this earthly life, and for thy guiding hand along the way of *his* pilgrimage, we give thee thanks and praise. Especially we bless thee for thy grace that kindled in *his* heart the love of thy dear name, that enabled *him* to fight the good fight, to endure unto the end, and to obtain the victory, yea, to become more than conqueror, through him that loveth us. We magnify thy holy name that, *his* trials and temptations being ended, sickness and death being passed, with all the dangers and difficulties of this mortal life, *his* spirit is at home in thy presence, with whom dwelleth eternal peace. And grant, O Lord, we beseech thee, that we who rejoice in the triumph of thy saints may profit by their example, that becoming followers of their faith and patience, we also may enter with them into an inheritance incorruptible and undefiled, and that fadeth not away; through Jesus Christ our Lord. **Amen.**

Almighty God, the fountain of all life, who art our refuge and strength and our help in trouble: Enable us, we pray thee, to put our trust in thee, that we may obtain comfort, and find grace to help in this and every time of need; through Jesus Christ our Lord. **Amen.**

Remember thy servant, O Lord, according to the favor which thou bearest unto thy people, and grant that, increasing in knowledge and love of thee, *he* may go from strength to strength, in the life of perfect service in thy heavenly kingdom; through Jesus Christ our Lord, who liveth and reigneth with thee and the Holy Spirit ever, one God, world without end. **Amen.**

Father of spirits, we have joy at this time in all who have faithfully lived, and in all who have peacefully died. We thank thee for all fair memories and all living hopes; for the sacred ties that bind us to the unseen world; for the dear and holy dead who compass us as a cloud of witnesses, and make the distant heaven a home to our hearts. May we be followers of those who now inherit the promises; through Jesus Christ our Lord. **Amen.**

O Lord and Master, who thyself didst weep beside the grave, and art touched with the feeling of our sorrows: Fulfill now thy promise that thou wilt not leave thy people comfortless, but wilt come to them. Reveal thyself unto thy sorrowing servants, and cause them to hear thee say, I am the resurrection and the life. Help them, O Lord, to turn to thee with true discernment, and to abide in thee through living faith, that, finding now the comfort of thy presence, they may have also a sure confidence in thee for all that is to come; until the day break, and the shadows flee away. Hear us for thy great mercy's sake, O Jesus Christ our Lord. **Amen.**

O Thou who hast ordered this wondrous world, and who knowest all things in earth and heaven: So fill our hearts with trust in thee that, by night and by day, at all times and in all seasons, we may without fear commit those who are dear to us to thy never-failing love for this life and the life to come. **Amen.**

O Lord, we pray thee, give us thy strength, that we may live more bravely and faithfully for the sake of those who are no longer with us here upon earth; and grant us so to serve thee day by day that we may find eternal fellowship with them; through him who died and rose again for us all, Jesus Christ our Lord. **Amen.**

Almighty God, who art leading us through the changes of time to the rest and blessedness of eternity: Be thou near to comfort and uphold. Make us to know and feel that thy children are precious in thy sight, that they live evermore with thee, and that thy mercy endureth forever. Thankful for the life which thou hast given us for these seasons, we pray thy help now to resign it obediently unto thee. Assist us to return to the scenes of our daily life, to obey thy will with patience, and to bear our trials with fortitude and hope. And when the peace of death falls upon us, may we find our perfect rest in thee; through Jesus Christ our Lord. **Amen.**

† *For a child one or both of the following prayers may be used:*

O God, whose most dear Son did take little children into his arms and bless them: Give us grace, we beseech thee, to entrust the soul of this child to thy never-failing love and care, and bring us all to thy heavenly kingdom; through the same thy Son Jesus Christ our Lord. **Amen.**

O God, we pray that thou wilt keep in thy tender love the life of this child whom we hold in blessed memory. Help us who continue here to serve thee with constancy, trusting in thy promise of eternal life, that hereafter we may be united with thy blessed children in glory everlasting; through Jesus Christ our Lord. **Amen.**

† *Then the minister shall give this blessing:*

The peace of God, which passeth all understanding, keep your hearts and minds in the knowledge and love of God, and of his Son Jesus Christ our Lord; and the blessing of God Almighty, the Father, the Son, and the Holy Spirit, be among you, and remain with you always. **Amen.**

† *At the grave, when the people are assembled, the minister shall say one or more of the following sentences:*

Our help is in the name of the Lord, who made heaven and earth.

Psalm 124:8

As a father pities his children, so the Lord pities those who fear him.

Psalm 103:13

Say to those who are of a fearful heart, "Be strong, fear not! Behold, your God will come and save you." *From Isaiah 35:4*

The steadfast love of the Lord is from everlasting to everlasting upon those who fear him, and his righteousness to children's children.

Psalm 103:17

† *Then the minister may say,*

Forasmuch as the spirit of the departed has entered into the life immortal, we therefore commit *his* body to its resting place, but *his* spirit we commend to God, remembering how Jesus said upon the cross, "Father, into thy hands I commend my spirit."

† *Or the minister may say,*

Forasmuch as almighty God hath received unto himself the soul of our departed *brother,* we therefore tenderly commit *his* body to the ground, in the blessed hope that as *he* hath borne the image of the earthly so also *he* shall bear the image of the heavenly.

† *Or the minister may say,*

Forasmuch as the spirit of the departed hath returned to God who gave it, we therefore commit *his* body to the ground, earth to earth, ashes to ashes, dust to dust; looking for the general resurrection in the last day, and the life of the world to come, through our Lord Jesus Christ; at whose coming in glorious majesty to judge the world, the earth and the sea shall give up their dead; and the corruptible bodies of those who sleep in him shall be changed and made like unto his own glorious body; according to the mighty working whereby he is able to subdue all things unto himself.

† *Then may be said:*

I heard a voice from heaven, saying unto me:

Blessed are the dead who die in the Lord from henceforth: Yea, saith the Spirit, that they may rest from their labors; and their works do follow them.

Lord, have mercy upon us.

Christ, have mercy upon us.

Lord, have mercy upon us.

† *Here the minister and people may pray, saying,*

Our Father, who art in heaven, hallowed be thy name. Thy kingdom come, thy will be done on earth as it is in heaven. Give us this day our daily bread. And forgive us our trespasses, as we forgive those who trespass against us. And lead us not into temptation, but deliver us from evil. For thine is the kingdom, and the power, and the glory, forever. Amen.

† *Then the minister may offer one or more of the following prayers:*

Almighty God, with whom do live the spirits of those who depart hence in the Lord, and with whom the souls of the faithful after death are in strength and gladness: We give thee hearty thanks for the good examples of all those thy servants who, having finished their course in faith, do now rest from their labor. And we beseech thee that we, with all those who have finished their course in faith, may have our perfect consummation and bliss in thy eternal and everlasting glory; through Jesus Christ our Lord. **Amen.**

O merciful God, the Father of our Lord Jesus Christ, who is the resurrection and the life, in whom whosoever believeth shall live, though he die, and whosoever liveth and believeth in him shall not die eternally: We beseech thee, O Father, to raise us from the death of sin into the life of righteousness, that when we shall depart this life we may rest in him, and may receive that blessing which thy well-beloved Son shall pronounce to all that love and fear thee, saying, Come, ye blessed of my Father, receive the kingdom prepared for you from the foundation of the world. Grant this, we beseech thee, O merciful Father, through Jesus Christ our mediator and Redeemer. **Amen.**

O God of infinite compassion, who art the comforter of thy children: Look down in thy tender love and pity, we beseech thee, upon thy servants. In the stillness of our hearts we entreat for them thy sustaining grace. Be thou their stay, their strength, and their shield, that trusting in thee they may know thy presence near, and in the assurance of thy love be delivered out of their distresses; through Jesus Christ our Lord. **Amen.**

† *Then the minister may give one of these blessings:*

Now may the God of peace who brought again from the dead our Lord Jesus, the great shepherd of the sheep, by the blood of the eternal covenant, equip you with everything good that you may do his will, working in you that which is pleasing in his sight; through Jesus Christ, to whom be glory for ever and ever. **Amen.**

The grace of our Lord Jesus Christ and the love of God and the fellowship of the Holy Spirit be with you all. **Amen.**

The Order for the Ordination of Deacons

† *When the day appointed by the bishop is come, there shall be a sermon or exhortation declaring the duty and office of such as come to be admitted deacons, how necessary that order is in the Church of Christ, and also how the people ought to esteem them in their office; after which one of the elders shall present unto the bishop all who are to be ordained, and say,*

I present unto you *these persons* present to be ordained *deacons:*

† *Their names having been read aloud, the bishop shall say to the people,*

Brethren, *these are they* whom we purpose, God willing, this day to ordain *deacons.* For, after due examination, we find that *they are* lawfully called to this office and ministry and that *they are persons* meet for the same. But if there be any of you who knows any valid reason for which *any one of them* ought not to be received into this holy ministry, let him come forth in the name of God, and disclose what the impediment is.

† *If any impediment be alleged, the bishop shall desist from ordaining that person until he shall be found to be innocent.*

† *Then shall be read the collect:*

Almighty God, who by thy divine providence hast appointed divers orders of ministers in thy Church, and didst inspire thine apostles to choose into the order of deacons thy first martyr, St. Stephen, with others: Mercifully behold *these* thy *servants,* now called to the like office and administration; so replenish *them* with the truth of thy doctrine, and adorn *them* with innocency of life, that by both word and good example *they* may faithfully serve thee in this office, to the glory of thy name and the edification of thy Church; through the merits of our Savior Jesus Christ, who liveth and reigneth with thee and the Holy Spirit, one God, now and forever. **Amen.**

† *Then shall be read the Epistle:*

Deacons likewise must be serious; they must hold the mystery of the faith with a clear conscience. Those who serve well as deacons gain a good standing for themselves and also great confidence in the faith which is in Christ Jesus. *I Timothy 3:8a, 9, 13*

Look carefully then how you walk, not as unwise men but as wise, making the most of the time. Therefore do not be foolish, but understand

44

what the will of the Lord is. Be filled with the Spirit, always and for everything giving thanks in the name of our Lord Jesus Christ to God the Father. Be subject to one another out of reverence for Christ.

Ephesians 5:15-16a, 17, 18b, 20-21

Finally, be strong in the Lord and in the strength of his might. Put on the whole armor of God, that you may be able to stand against the wiles of the devil. For we are not contending against flesh and blood, but against the principalities, against the powers, against the world rulers of this present darkness, against the spiritual hosts of wickedness in the heavenly places. Therefore take the whole armor of God, that you may be able to withstand in the evil day, and having done all, to stand. Stand therefore, having girded your loins with truth, and having put on the breastplate of righteousness, and having shod your feet with the equipment of the gospel of peace; above all taking the shield of faith, with which you can quench all the flaming darts of the evil one. And take the helmet of salvation, and the sword of the Spirit, which is the word of God. Pray at all times in the Spirit, with all prayer and supplication. To that end keep alert with all perseverance, making supplication for all the saints.

Ephesians 6:10-18

† *Then the bishop, in the presence of the people, shall examine every one of those to be ordained, after this manner:*

Do you trust that you are inwardly moved by the Holy Spirit to take upon you the office of the ministry in the Church of Christ, to serve God for the promoting of his glory and the edifying of his people?

I trust so.

Do you unfeignedly believe the Scriptures of the Old and New Testaments?

I do believe them.

Will you diligently read and expound the same unto the people whom you shall be appointed to serve?

I will.

It appertains to the office of a deacon to conduct divine worship and to assist the elder in the administration of the Holy Communion, to read and expound the Holy Scriptures, to instruct the youth, and to baptize. And, furthermore, it is his office to search for the needy, that they may be visited and relieved. Will you do this gladly and willingly?

I will so do, by the help of God.

45

Will you apply all your diligence to frame and fashion your own *lives* and the lives of your *families* according to the teachings of Christ?

I will, the Lord being my helper.

Will you reverently heed them to whom the charge over you is committed, following with a glad mind and will their godly admonitions?

I will so do.

† *Here those to be ordained shall kneel, and the bishop, laying his hands upon the head of each severally, shall say,*

Take thou authority to execute the office of a deacon in the Church of God; in the name of the Father, and of the Son, and of the Holy Spirit. **Amen.**

† *Then the bishop shall deliver to every one of them the Bible, saying,*

Take thou authority to read the Holy Scriptures in the Church of God, and to preach the Word. **Amen.**

† *Then shall be read the Gospel:*

Let your loins be girded and your lamps burning, and be like men who are waiting for their master to come home from the marriage feast, so that they may open to him at once when he comes and knocks. Blessed are those servants whom the master finds awake when he comes; truly, I say to you, he will gird himself and have them sit at table, and he will come and serve them. If he comes in the second watch, or in the third, and finds them so, blessed are those servants! *Luke 12:35-38*

† *Then the bishop shall pray, saying,*

Almighty God, giver of all good things, who of thy great goodness hast vouchsafed to accept *these* thy *servants* into the office of deacon in thy Church: Make *them,* we beseech thee, O Lord, to be modest, humble, and constant in *their* ministration, and to have a ready will to observe all spiritual discipline; that *they,* continuing ever stable and strong in thy Son Jesus Christ, may so well behave *themselves* in this office that *they* may be found worthy to be called into the higher ministry in thy Church; through thy Son our Savior Jesus Christ, to whom be glory and honor, world without end. **Amen.**

Direct us, O Lord, in all our doings, with thy most gracious favor, and further us with thy continual help, that in all our works, begun, continued, and ended in thee, we may glorify thy holy name, and finally, by thy mercy, obtain everlasting life; through Jesus Christ our Lord. **Amen.**

† *Then the bishop may give this blessing:*

The peace of God, which passeth all understanding, keep your hearts and minds in the knowledge and love of God, and of his Son Jesus Christ our Lord; and the blessing of God Almighty, the Father, the Son, and the Holy Spirit, be among you, and remain with you always. **Amen.**

The Order for the Ordination of Elders

† *When the day appointed by the bishop is come, there shall be a sermon of exhortation declaring the duty and office of such as come to be admitted elders, how necessary that order is in the Church of Christ, and also how the people ought to esteem them in their office; after which one of the elders shall present unto the bishop all who are to be ordained, and say,*

I present unto you *these persons* present to be ordained *elders:*

† *Their names having been read aloud, the bishop shall say to the people,*

Brethren, *these are they* whom we purpose, God willing, this day to ordain *elders.* For, after due inquiry, we find that *they are* lawfully called to this office and ministry, and that *they are persons* meet for the same. But if there be any of you who knows any valid reason for which *any one of them* ought not to be received into this holy ministry, let him come forth in the name of God, and disclose what the impediment is.

† *If any impediment be alleged, the bishop shall desist from ordaining that person until he shall be found to be innocent.*

† *Then shall be read the collect:*

Almighty God, giver of all good things, who by thy Holy Spirit hast appointed divers orders of ministers in thy Church: Mercifully behold *these* thy *servants,* now called to the office of elder, and so replenish *them* with the truth of thy doctrine, and adorn *them* with innocency of life, that by both word and good example *they* may faithfully serve thee in this office, to the glory of thy name and the advancement of thy Church; through the merits of our Savior Jesus Christ, who liveth and reigneth with thee and the Holy Spirit, one God, world without end. **Amen.**

† *Then shall be read the Epistle and the Gospel:*

Of this gospel I was made a minister according to the gift of God's grace which was given me by the working of his power. To me, though I am the very least of all the saints, this grace was given, to preach to the Gentiles the unsearchable riches of Christ, and to make all men see what is the plan of the mystery hidden for ages in God who created all things. And his gifts were that some should be apostles, some prophets, some evangelists, some pastors and teachers, for the equipment of the saints, for the work of ministry, for building up the body of Christ, until we all attain to the unity of the faith and of the knowledge of the Son of God, to mature manhood, to the measure of the stature of the fulness of Christ. *Ephesians 3:7-9; 4:11-13*

Jesus said, "I am the door; if any one enters by me, he will be saved, and will go in and out and find pasture. The thief comes only to steal and kill and destroy; I came that they may have life, and have it abundantly. I am the good shepherd. The good shepherd lays down his life for the sheep. He who is a hireling and not a shepherd, whose own the sheep are not, sees the wolf coming and leaves the sheep and flees; and the wolf snatches them and scatters them. He flees because he is a hireling and cares nothing for the sheep. I am the good shepherd; I know my own and my own know me, as the Father knows me and I know the Father; and I lay down my life for the sheep. And I have other sheep, that are not of this fold; I must bring them also, and they will heed my voice. So there shall be one flock, one shepherd." *John 10:9-16*

† *Then the bishop shall say to the persons to be ordained elders,*
Dearly beloved, you have heard of what dignity and of how great importance is this office whereunto you are called. And now again we exhort you, in the name of our Lord Jesus Christ, that you are to be *messengers, watchmen,* and *stewards* of the Lord; to teach and to admonish, to feed and provide for the Lord's family; to seek for Christ's sheep that are dispersed abroad, and for his children who are in the midst of this evil world, that they may be saved through Christ forever.

Have always, therefore, in your remembrance how great a treasure is committed to your charge. For they unto whom you are to minister are the sheep of Christ, for whom he gave his life. The Church which you must serve is his Bride and his Body. And if it shall happen the Church, or any member thereof, do take any hurt or hindrance by reason of your negligence, you know the greatness of the fault. Wherefore see that you never cease your labor, your care, and your diligence until you have done all that lieth in you, according to your bounden duty, to bring all such as shall be committed to your charge unto perfectness in Christ.

Forasmuch, then, as your office is both of so great excellency and of so great difficulty, consider how you ought to forsake, as much as you can, all worldly cares, and be studious in learning the Scriptures, and in acquiring such knowledge and skill as may help you to declare the living Word of God.

We hope that you have weighed and pondered these things with *your-*

selves long before this time, and that you have clearly determined, by God's grace, to give *yourselves* wholly to this work whereunto it has pleased God to call you. Also that you will continually pray that the Holy Spirit may assist you to order your own *lives* and the lives of your *families* after the rule and doctrine of Christ, that you may grow riper and stronger in ministry and be godly and wholesome *examples* for the people to follow.

And now, that this congregation of Christ here assembled may also understand your purpose in these things, and that this your promise may the more move you to perform your duties, you shall answer plainly to these things which we, in the name of God and his Church, shall ask of you touching the same:

Do you believe in your heart that you are truly called, according to the will of our Lord Jesus Christ, to the ministry of elders?

I do so believe.

Are you persuaded that the Holy Scriptures contain all truth required for eternal salvation through faith in Jesus Christ? And are you determined out of the same Holy Scriptures so to instruct the people committed to your charge that they may enter into eternal life?

I am so persuaded and determined, by God's grace.

Will you give faithful diligence duly to minister the doctrine of Christ, the Sacraments, and the discipline of the Church, and in the spirit of Christ to defend the Church against all doctrine contrary to God's Word?

I will so do, by the help of the Lord.

Will you be diligent in prayer, in the reading of the Holy Scriptures, and in such studies as help to the knowledge of God and of his kingdom?

I will, the Lord being my helper.

Will you apply all your diligence to frame and fashion your own *lives* and the lives of your *families* according to the teachings of Christ?

I will, the Lord being my helper.

Will you maintain and set forward, as much as lieth in you, quietness, peace, and love among all Christian people, and especially among them that shall be committed to your charge?

I will so do, the Lord being my helper.

Will you reverently heed them to whom the charge over you is committed, following with a glad mind and will their godly admonitions?

I will so do.

† *Then the bishop shall say,*

Almighty God, our heavenly Father, who hath given you a good will to do all these things, grant also unto you wisdom and power to perform the same, that he may accomplish in you the good work which he hath begun, that you may be found blameless; through Jesus Christ our Lord. **Amen.**

† *Here those to be ordained elders shall kneel. The people shall be requested to make their earnest supplications in silent prayer to God for them. Silence shall be kept for a space, after which shall be said the* Veni, Creator Spiritus, *the bishop beginning, and all others responding:*

Come, Holy Ghost, our souls inspire,
And lighten with celestial fire.
Thou the anointing Spirit art,
Who dost thy sevenfold gifts impart.
Thy blessed unction from above
Is comfort, life, and fire of love.
Enable with perpetual light
The dullness of our blinded sight.
Anoint and cheer our soilèd face
With the abundance of thy grace.
Keep far our foes, give peace at home;
Where thou art guide, no ill can come.
Teach us to know the Father, Son,
And thee, of both to be but One;
That through the ages all along,
This may be our endless song:
Praise to thy eternal merit,
Father, Son, and Holy Spirit. Amen.

† *Then the bishop shall say,*

Let us pray.

Almighty God, our heavenly Father, we bless and magnify thy holy name for the gift of thy most dearly beloved Son Jesus Christ our Redeemer, and for all his apostles, prophets, evangelists, teachers, and pastors, whom he hath sent abroad into the world. For *these* here present whom thou hast called to the same holy office and ministry, we render unto thee our most hearty thanks. And now, O Lord, we humbly beseech thee to grant that by *these* thy *ministers,* and by those over whom *they* shall be appointed, thy holy name may be forever glorified, and thy blessed kingdom enlarged; through thy Son Jesus Christ our Lord, who liveth and reigneth with thee in the unity of the Holy Spirit, one God, world without end. **Amen.**

† *Those to be ordained still kneeling, the bishop and elders assisting shall lay their hands upon the head of each severally, the bishop saying,*

The Lord pour upon thee the Holy Spirit for the office and work of an elder in the Church of God, now committed unto thee by the authority of the Church through the imposition of our hands. And be thou a faithful dispenser of the Word of God, and of his holy Sacraments; in the name of the Father, and of the Son, and of the Holy Spirit. **Amen.**

† *Then the bishop shall deliver to every one of them the Bible, saying,*

Take thou authority as an elder in the Church to preach the Word of God, and to administer the holy Sacraments in the congregation. **Amen.**

† *Then the bishop shall pray, saying,*

Most merciful Father, we beseech thee to send upon *these* thy *servants* thy heavenly blessings, that *they* may be clothed with righteousness, and that thy Word spoken by *them* may never be spoken in vain. Grant also that we may have grace to receive what *they* shall deliver out of thy Word as the means of our salvation, and that in all our words and deeds we may seek thy glory, and the increase of thy kingdom; through Jesus Christ our Lord. **Amen.**

Direct us, O Lord, in all our doings, with thy most gracious favor, and further us with thy continual help, that in all our works, begun, continued, and ended in thee, we may glorify thy holy name, and finally, by thy mercy, obtain everlasting life; through Jesus Christ our Lord. **Amen.**

† *Then the bishop may give this blessing:*

The peace of God, which passeth all understanding, keep your hearts and minds in the knowledge and love of God, and of his Son Jesus Christ our Lord; and the blessing of God Almighty, the Father, the Son, and the Holy Spirit, be among you, and remain with you always. **Amen.**

† *If on the same day the order for deacon be given to some and that of elder to others, the deacons shall be presented first, and then the elders. The collect shall be said and the Epistle read, immediately after which they who are to be ordained deacons shall be examined and ordained as above described. Then, the Gospel having been read, they who are to be ordained elders shall likewise be examined and ordained.*

The Order for the Consecration of Bishops

† *When the time appointed for the consecration of bishops is come, the service shall begin with a hymn, after which the collect shall be read:*

Almighty God, who by thy Son Jesus Christ didst give to thy holy apostles, elders, and evangelists many excellent gifts, and didst charge them to feed thy flock: Give grace, we beseech thee, to all the ministers and pastors of thy Church, that they may diligently preach thy Word and duly administer the godly discipline thereof; and grant to the people that they may faithfully follow the same, that they may receive the crown of everlasting glory; through Jesus Christ our Lord. **Amen.**

† *Then an elder shall read the Epistle:*

And from Miletus he sent to Ephesus and called to him the elders of the church. And when they came to him, he said to them: "You yourselves know how I lived among you all the time from the first day that I set foot in Asia, serving the Lord with all humility and with tears and with trials which befell me; how I did not shrink from declaring to you anything that was profitable, and teaching you in public and from house to house, testifying both to Jews and to Greeks of repentance to God and of faith in our Lord Jesus Christ. And now, behold, I am going to Jerusalem, bound in the Spirit, not knowing what shall befall me there; except that the Holy Spirit testifies to me in every city that imprisonment and afflictions await me. But I do not account my life of any value nor as precious to myself, if only I may accomplish my course and the ministry which I received from the Lord Jesus, to testify to the gospel of the grace of God. Take heed to yourselves and to all the flock, in which the Holy Spirit has made you guardians, to feed the church of the Lord which he obtained with his own blood. I know that after my departure fierce wolves will come in among you, not sparing the flock; and from among your own selves will arise men speaking perverse things, to draw away the disciples after them. Therefore be alert, remembering that for three years I did not cease night or day to admonish every one with tears. And now I commend you to God and to the word of his grace, which is able to build you up and to give you the inheritance among all those who are sanctified."
From Acts 20:17-24, 28-32

† *Then an elder shall read the Gospel:*

When they had finished breakfast, Jesus said to Simon Peter, "Simon, son of John, do you love me more than these?" He said to him, "Yes, Lord; you know that I love you." He said to him, "Feed my lambs." A second time he said to him, "Simon, son of John, do you love me?" He said to him, "Yes, Lord; you know that I love you." He said to him, "Tend my sheep." He said to him the third time, "Simon, son of John, do you love me?" Peter was grieved because he said to him the third time, "Do you love me?" and he said to him, "Lord, you know everything; you know that I love you." Jesus said to him, "Feed my sheep."

John 21:15-17

And Jesus came and said to them, "All authority in heaven and on earth has been given to me. Go therefore and make disciples of all nations, baptizing them in the name of the Father and of the Son and of the Holy Spirit, teaching them to observe all that I have commanded you; and lo, I am with you always, to the close of the age." *Matthew 28:18-20*

† *Then each elected bishop shall be presented by two elders to the officiating bishop, the elders saying,*

We present unto you this elder chosen to be consecrated a bishop.

† *Then the bishop shall call upon the people present to pray, saying,*

Dearly beloved, it is written in the Gospel of St. Luke that our Savior Christ continued the whole night in prayer before he chose and sent forth his twelve apostles. It is also written in the Acts of the Apostles that the disciples who were at Antioch did fast and pray before they laid hands on Paul and Barnabas and sent them forth on their first mission to the Gentiles. Let us therefore, following the example of our Savior Christ and his apostles, give ourselves to prayer before we admit and send forth *this person* presented to us, to the work whereunto we trust the Holy Spirit hath called *him.*

† *Then the bishop shall pray, saying,*

Almighty God, giver of all good things, who by thy Holy Spirit hast appointed divers offices in thy Church: Graciously behold *this* thy *servant* now called to the office and ministry of a bishop. So replenish *him* with the truth of thy doctrine, and so adorn *him* with innocency of life, that by both word and deed *he* may faithfully serve thee in this office, to the glory of thy name and the edifying and well governing of thy Church; through the merits of our Savior Jesus Christ, who liveth and reigneth with thee and the Holy Spirit, one God, world without end. **Amen.**

† *Then the bishop shall say to the person or persons to be consecrated,*
Brother, forasmuch as the Holy Scriptures command that we should not be
hasty in admitting any person to government in the Church of Christ,
before you are admitted to this ministration, you will, in the fear of
God, give answer to these questions:

Are you persuaded that you are truly called to this ministration,
according to the will of our Lord Jesus Christ?

I am so persuaded.

Are you persuaded that the Holy Scriptures contain sufficiently all truth
required for eternal salvation through faith in Jesus Christ? And are
you determined out of the same Holy Scriptures so to instruct the people
committed to your charge that they may enter into eternal life?

I am so persuaded and determined, by God's grace.

Will you then faithfully exercise *yourself* in the Holy Scriptures, and call
upon God through study and prayer for the true understanding of the
same?

I will so do, by the help of God.

Are you ready with all faithful diligence to seek and to promote the truth
of Christ and to defend the Church against all doctrine contrary to God's
Word?

I am ready, the Lord being my helper.

Will you live soberly, righteously, and devoutly in this present world,
that you may show *yourself* in all things an example of good works unto
others, to the honor and glory of God?

I will so do, the Lord being my helper.

Will you show *yourself* gentle, and be merciful for Christ's sake to poor
and needy people, and to all strangers destitute of help?

I will, by the help of God.

Will you maintain and set forward, as much as lieth in you, quietness,
love, and peace among all men; and faithfully exercise such discipline
in the Church as shall be committed unto you?

I will so do, by the help of God.

Will you be faithful in ordaining and appointing others; and will you
ever seek to deal justly and kindly with your brethren of the ministry
over whom you are placed as chief pastor?

I will so do, by the help of God.

† *Then the bishop shall pray, saying,*

Almighty God, our heavenly Father, who hath given you a good will to do all these things, grant also unto you wisdom and power to perform the same, that he may accomplish in you the good work which he hath begun, that you may be found blameless; through Jesus Christ our Lord. **Amen.**

† *Then the persons to be consecrated bishops shall kneel. The people shall be requested to make their earnest supplications in silent prayer to God for them. Silence shall be kept for a space, after which shall be said the* Veni, Creator Spiritus, *the officiating bishop beginning, and all others responding:*

Come, Holy Ghost, our souls inspire,
And lighten with celestial fire.
Thou the anointing Spirit art,
Who dost thy sevenfold gifts impart.
Thy blessed unction from above
Is comfort, life, and fire of love.
Enable with perpetual light
The dullness of our blinded sight.
Anoint and cheer our soilèd face
With the abundance of thy grace.
Keep far our foes, give peace at home;
Where thou art guide, no ill can come.
Teach us to know the Father, Son,
And thee, of both to be but One;
That through the ages all along,
This may be our endless song:
Praise to thy eternal merit,
Father, Son, and Holy Spirit. Amen.

† *Then the bishop shall say,*

Let us pray.

Almighty and most merciful Father, who of thine infinite goodness hast given thine only and dearly beloved Son Jesus Christ to be our Redeemer, and hast made some apostles, some prophets, some evangelists, some pastors and teachers, to the edifying and making perfect of thy Church: Grant, we beseech thee, to *this* thy *servant* such grace that *he* may evermore be ready to spread abroad thy Gospel, the glad tidings of reconciliation with thee, and to use the authority given *him*, not to destruction, but to salvation; not to hurt, but to help; so that as *a* wise and faithful *servant*, giving to all their portion in due season, *he* may at last be received into everlasting joy; through Jesus Christ our Lord, who, with thee and the Holy Spirit, liveth and reigneth, one God, world without end. **Amen.**

† *The persons to be consecrated still kneeling, the bishops and elders assisting shall lay their hands upon the head of each severally, the officiating bishop saying,*

The Lord pour upon thee the Holy Spirit for the office and work of a bishop in the Church of God, now committed unto thee by the authority of the Church through the imposition of our hands, in the name of the Father, and of the Son, and of the Holy Spirit. And remember that thou stir up the grace of God which is in thee; for God hath not given us the spirit of fear, but of power, and of love, and of a sound mind. **Amen.**

† *Then the bishop shall deliver to each the Bible, saying,*

Give heed unto reading, exhortation, and teaching. Think upon the things contained in this Book. Be diligent in them, that the increase coming thereby may be manifest unto all men. Take heed unto thyself and to thy teaching; for by so doing thou shalt save both thyself and them that hear thee. Be to the flock of Christ a shepherd. Hold up the weak, heal the sick, bind up the broken, bring again the outcast, seek the lost; faithfully minister discipline, but forget not mercy; that the kingdom of God may come upon the earth and, when the chief Shepherd shall appear, that you may receive the never-fading crown of glory; through Jesus Christ our Lord. **Amen.**

† *Then the bishop shall pray, saying,*

Most merciful Father, we beseech thee to send down upon *this* thy *servant* thy heavenly blessing, and so endue *him* with thy Holy Spirit that *he,* preaching thy word, not only may be earnest to reprove, beseech, and rebuke with all patience and doctrine, but also may be to such as believe a wholesome example in word, in conversation, in love, in faith, in chastity, and in purity; that, faithfully fulfilling *his* course, at the latter day *he* may receive the crown of righteousness laid up by the Lord, the righteous judge, who liveth and reigneth with thee and the Holy Spirit, one God, world without end. **Amen.**

Direct us, O Lord, in all our doings, with thy most gracious favor, and further us with thy continual help, that in all our works, begun, continued, and ended in thee, we may glorify thy holy name, and finally, by thy mercy, obtain everlasting life; through Jesus Christ our Lord. **Amen.**

† *Then the bishop may give this blessing:*

The peace of God, which passeth all understanding, keep your hearts and minds in the knowledge and love of God, and of his Son Jesus Christ our Lord; and the blessing of God Almighty, the Father, the Son, and the Holy Spirit, be among you, and remain with you always. **Amen.**

II.

Aids for the
Ordering of Worship

THE CHRISTIAN YEAR

A LECTIONARY FOR PUBLIC WORSHIP

In addition to a psalm or other act of praise, two Scripture lessons may be read in each service of public worship: one from the Old Testament and one from the New, either Epistle or Gospel; but for the service of Holy Communion the two lessons are properly one from the Epistles and one from the Gospels, omitting an Old Testament lesson.

In the column headed "Acts of Praise," the first number refers to the Psalter, and the second number refers to a canticle or other act of praise.

The chapter and verse numbering of this Lectionary is that of the Revised Standard Version. The letter *a* after the number of a verse signifies the first major part of that verse; the letter *b*, the second major part; and the letter *c*, the third major part, etc.

Sundays are numbered as follows:

Advent Season: Four Sundays before Christmas Day, December 25, designated as Sundays *in* Advent.

Christmastide: Christmas Day, and one or two Sundays between December 25 and January 6, designated as Sundays *after* Christmas Day.

Epiphany Season: Four to nine Sundays between January 6, which is Epiphany Day, and the beginning of Lent, which depends upon the date of Easter Day, designated as Sundays *after* Epiphany Day.

Lenten Season: Six Sundays before Easter Day, designated as Sundays *in* Lent, of which the fifth may be called Passion Sunday and the sixth, Palm Sunday.

Eastertide: Easter Day and six other Sundays, designated as Sundays *after* Easter Day, of which the last may be called Ascension Sunday.

Pentecost Season: From eleven to sixteen Sundays beginning with Pentecost Sunday, the seventh Sunday after Easter Day, and continuing through the next to the last Sunday in August, designated as Sundays *after* Pentecost.

Kingdomtide: Thirteen or fourteen Sundays beginning the last Sunday in August and continuing until Advent, designated as Sundays *in* Kingdomtide.

	Acts of Praise [1]	Old Testament	Epistle	Gospel
ADVENT SEASON				
1st Sunday	1, 107	Mal. 3:1-7*b*	Rom. 13:8-14	Mark 13:33-37
2nd Sunday	23, 94	Isa. 11:1-10	I Thess. 5:1-11	Luke 1:26-35
3rd Sunday	32, 59	Isa. 62:10-12	I Cor. 4:1-5	Luke 3:2*b*-6
4th Sunday	31, 56	Isa. 7:10-14	Titus 2:11–3:7	Matt. 1:18-25
CHRISTMASTIDE				
Christmas Day	5, 102	Isa. 9:2, 6-7	Gal. 4:1-7	Luke 2:1-20
1st Sunday	2, 61	Isa. 42:1-9	I John 4:9-16	John 1:1-14
2nd Sunday	34, 67	Zech. 2:10-13	Heb. 1:1-12	Luke 2:21-32
EPIPHANY SEASON				
1st Sunday	24, 83	Isa. 60:1-3, 6*b*	Eph. 3:1-12	Matt. 2:1-12
2nd Sunday	10, 89	Isa. 49:8-13	Eph. 2:11-18	Matt. 5:14-20
3rd Sunday	16, 78	I Sam. 1:19*c*-28	II Cor. 4:1-6	Luke 2:39-52
4th Sunday	21, 85	Jonah 3:1-5	I Cor. 1:18-31	John 12:20-36*a*
5th Sunday	49, 58	Hos. 6:1-3	Col. 1:21-29	John 1:19-30
6th Sunday	50, 95	Jer. 10:1-7	Acts 8:26-35	John 4:7-26
7th Sunday	52, 98	Hab. 2:18-20; 3:2-4	I Peter 2:4-10	John 1:35-51
8th Sunday	47, 100	Lev. 19:1-2, 15-18	Eph. 4:17-32	Luke 10:25-37
9th Sunday	3, 101	Prov. 4:10-18	I Cor. 2:1-16	Mark 1:14-22
LENTEN SEASON				
Ash Wednesday	11, 62	Joel 2:12, 15-17	I Cor. 9:24-27	Matt. 6:16-21
1st Sunday	18, 88	Ezek. 33:7-16	I John 2:1-3, 15-17	Mark 1:9-12
2nd Sunday	40, 92	Exod. 33:18-23	Heb. 12:18-29	Matt. 17:1-9
3rd Sunday	41, 93	Amos 7:7-10, 14-16*a*	Rom. 6:15-23	Mark 10:17-27
4th Sunday	15, 82	Lamen. 3:22-26, 31-33	II Cor. 6:1-10	Luke 18:1-14
Passion Sunday	6, 87	Gen. 22:1-2, 9-13	Heb. 9:11-14	John 11:47-53
Palm Sunday	20, 81	Zech. 9:9-12	Phil. 2:5-11	Luke 19:29-40
Maundy Thursday	7, 96	Exod. 12:1, 3, 6-8, 11, 14, 25-27	I Cor. 11:23-26	Mark 14:17-25
Good Friday	6, 87	Isa. 52:13–53:12	Heb. 10:4-7, 10-23	Luke 23:33-38, 44-46
EASTERTIDE				
Easter Day	4, 106	Isa. 25:1, 7-9	Acts 13:26-33	Mark 16:1-7
1st Sunday	43, 55	Job 19:1, 23-27	I Cor. 15:12-22	John 20:19-31
2nd Sunday	42, 90	Isa. 12:1-6	Rom. 6:3-11	John 6:37-40

[1] First number refers to the Psalter; second number refers to a canticle or other act of praise.

	Acts of Praise	Old Testament	Epistle	Gospel
3rd Sunday	44, 95	Ezek. 34:11-16, 30-31	I Peter 2:19-25	John 10:11-16
4th Sunday	49, 101	Deut. 7:6-11	II Cor. 5:1-10	John 16:16-22
5th Sunday	36, 103	Deut. 10:12-15, 20–11:1	I John 5:1-5, 11	John 17:1-5
Ascension Sunday	29, 104	Dan. 7:9-10, 13-14	Eph. 1:15-23	Luke 24:44-53

PENTECOST SEASON

	Acts of Praise	Old Testament	Epistle	Gospel
Pentecost Sunday	30, 91	Jer. 31:31-34	Acts 2:1-8, 12-21	John 14:15-17, 25-27
1st Sunday	12, 89	Gen. 3:1-6, 22-23	Acts 3:1-7, 11-21	Matt. 11:2-6
2nd Sunday	2, 90	Gen. 9:8-15	Acts 4:8, 10-13, 18-20	Luke 10:1-11
3rd Sunday	3, 92	Gen. 28:10-22	Acts 9:22, 26-31	John 3:4-17
4th Sunday	5, 95	Gen. 45:4-11	Acts 15:1, 6-11	Matt. 16:13-19
5th Sunday	8, 96	Exod. 20:1-20	Acts 16:1-10	Luke 19:1-10
6th Sunday	9, 97	Num. 27:12-14a, 15-20, 22-23	Acts 18:24–19:6	John 10:1-10
7th Sunday	12, 98	Josh. 24:1-15, 24	Acts 17:21-31	Luke 8:4-15
8th Sunday	13, 99	Judges 7:2-7, 19-22	Acts 20:17-28, 32	Matt. 10:16-33
9th Sunday	14, 101	Ruth 1:1, 4-9, 16, 19a	Acts 28:16-20, 23-24, 30-31	Luke 15:1-10
10th Sunday	17, 102	I Sam. 9:15-17, 10:1	Romans 8:14-39	Luke 18:18-30
11th Sunday	20, 103	I Sam. 16:1-13	II Cor. 3:4-11, 17-18	Luke 11:1-4, 9-13
12th Sunday	19, 104	II Sam. 12:1-10, 13a	Eph. 3:13-21	Matthew 11:25-30
13th Sunday	21, 105	I Chron. 28:1-3, 5-10	Eph. 6:10-20	Matthew 20:20-28
14th Sunday	24, 107	II Chron. 6:1, 18-21	Eph. 4:1-8	John 2:1-11
15th Sunday	25, 108	II Kings 17:5-14, 18-23	Phil. 4:4-9, 19-20	Mark 14:3-9

KINGDOMTIDE

	Acts of Praise	Old Testament	Epistle	Gospel
1st Sunday	27, 57	I Chron. 29:10-18	Rev. 19:1, 4, 6-8	Matt. 25:31-40
2nd Sunday	28, 63	I Kings 18:21-39	I Tim. 6:6-19	Luke 16:10-15
3rd Sunday	33, 67	Isaiah 6:1-8	II Cor. 5:17–6:2	Mark 10:28-31
4th Sunday	35, 69	Obadiah 1:1-4, 15-17a, 21	Col. 3:1-15	Matt. 7:15-23
5th Sunday	37, 70	Nahum 1:1-8	Heb. 13:1-6	Matt. 18:15-22
6th Sunday	44, 71	Micah 6:1-4, 5d-8	Heb. 11:1-3, 6	Matt. 8:23-27
7th Sunday	38, 72	Ezek. 18:23-32	James 1:17-27	Luke 21:1-4
8th Sunday	39, 73	Amos 5:18-24	II Timothy 2:1-13	Matt. 25:14-30
9th Sunday	45, 74	Isa. 55:1-7	Philem. 1:1-3, 10-16	Luke 15:11-32

	Acts of Praise	Old Testament	Epistle	Gospel
10th Sunday	48, 75	Ezek. 37:1-6, 11-14	II John 1:3-4, 6 & III John 1:11	John 8:1-11
11th Sunday	52, 76	Zeph. 3:8-13	I John 2:24-25, 28-29; 3:1-2	Mark 6:31-44
12th Sunday	49, 77	Haggai 1:3-9; 2:2-3	II Peter 3:8-14	Matt. 7:24-29
13th Sunday	51, 78	Ezra 1:2-4; 3:10-13	Jude 1:17-21, 24-25	Luke 13:22-24, 34-35
14th Sunday	53, 84	Isa. 40:1-5	II Thess. 1:3-5, 11-12; 2:1-2, 13-15	Luke 17:20-25

SPECIAL DAYS

	Acts of Praise	Old Testament	Epistle	Gospel
Universal Bible Sunday	40, 68	Deut. 30:8-20	Romans 15:4-13	Luke 4:16-21
New Year's Day or Watch Night	27, 90	Eccl. 11:6-9; 12:13	Rev. 21:1-6a	Luke 9:57-62
Race Relations Sunday	20, 80	Gen. 1:1-3, 26-31	Acts 10:9-15, 34	Mark 3:31-35
Festival of the Christian Home	35, 105	Prov. 31:10-31	Eph. 5:25–6:4	Matt. 19:1-5, 10-14
Aldersgate Sunday	13, 62	Isa. 52:1-2, 7-12	Romans 5:1-11	Mark 12:28-34a
Ascension Day	8, 104	Dan. 7:9-10, 13-14	Eph. 1:15-23	Luke 24:44-53
Trinity Sunday	12, 108	Exod. 3:1-8b, 10-15	Romans 11:33-36	Matt. 28:16-20
Independence Day	42, 73	Deut. 1:5, 8-18	Gal. 5:13-15	John 8:31-36
Labor Day	2, 71	Amos 5:11-15	Col. 3:23-25	John 6:5-14, 26-27
Reformation Day	17, 101	Neh. 8:1-3, 5-8	Gal. 3:23-26	John 2:13-16
All Saints Day	3, 72	Isa. 51:11-16	Rev. 7:9-17	Matt. 5:1-12
World Order Sunday	43, 79	Micah 4:1-5	James 4:1-12	Matt. 5:43-48
Commitment Day	1, 98	Isa. 5:11-12, 20-24	I Cor. 3:16-17	Luke 21:23-26
Thanksgiving Day	22, 54	Deut. 8:7-18	II Cor. 9:6-12	Luke 12:16-31

A TABLE FOR EASTER DAY

A Table of the Days on Which Easter Day and Other Days Dependent on It Will Fall
A.D. 1964-2000

Year of Our Lord	Sundays After Epiphany	Ash Wednesday	Easter	Pentecost	Sundays After Pentecost	Sundays in Kingdomtide	First Sunday in Advent
1964	5	Feb. 12	Mar. 29	May 17	14	13	Nov. 29
1965	8	Mar. 3	Apr. 18	June 6	11	13	Nov. 28
1966	7	Feb. 23	Apr. 10	May 29	12	13	Nov. 27
1967	5	Feb. 8	Mar. 26	May 14	14	14	Dec. 3
1968	8	Feb. 28	Apr. 14	June 2	11	14	Dec. 1
1969	6	Feb. 19	Apr. 6	May 25	13	13	Nov. 30
1970	5	Feb. 11	Mar. 29	May 17	14	13	Nov. 29
1971	7	Feb. 24	Apr. 11	May 30	12	13	Nov. 28
1972	6	Feb. 16	Apr. 2	May 21	13	14	Dec. 3
1973	9	Mar. 7	Apr. 22	June 10	10	14	Dec. 2
1974	7	Feb. 27	Apr. 14	June 2	11	14	Dec. 1
1975	5	Feb. 12	Mar. 30	May 18	14	13	Nov. 30
1976	8	Mar. 3	Apr. 18	June 6	11	13	Nov. 28
1977	7	Feb. 23	Apr. 10	May 29	12	13	Nov. 27
1978	5	Feb. 8	Mar. 26	May 14	14	14	Dec. 3
1979	8	Feb. 28	Apr. 15	June 3	11	14	Dec. 2
1980	6	Feb. 20	Apr. 6	May 25	13	13	Nov. 30
1981	8	Mar. 4	Apr. 19	June 7	11	13	Nov. 29
1982	7	Feb. 24	Apr. 11	May 30	12	13	Nov. 28
1983	6	Feb. 16	Apr. 3	May 22	. 13	13	Nov. 27
1984	9	Mar. 7	Apr. 22	June 10	10	14	Dec. 2
1985	6	Feb. 20	Apr. 7	May 26	12	14	Dec. 1
1986	5	Feb. 12	Mar. 30	May 18	14	13	Nov. 30
1987	8	Mar. 4	Apr. 19	June 7	11	13	Nov. 29
1988	6	Feb. 17	Apr. 3	May 22	13	13	Nov. 27
1989	5	Feb. 8	Mar. 26	May 14	14	14	Dec. 3
1990	8	Feb. 28	Apr. 15	June 3	11	14	Dec. 2
1991	5	Feb. 13	Mar. 31	May 19	13	14	Dec. 1
1992	8	Mar. 4	Apr. 19	June 7	11	13	Nov. 29
1993	7	Feb. 24	Apr. 11	May 30	12	13	Nov. 28
1994	6	Feb. 16	Apr. 3	May 22	13	13	Nov. 27
1995	5	Mar. 1	Apr. 16	June 4	11	14	Dec. 3
1996	6	Feb. 21	Apr. 7	May 26	12	14	Dec. 1
1997	5	Feb. 12	Mar. 30	May 18	14	13	Nov. 30
1998	7	Feb. 25	Apr. 12	May 31	12	13	Nov. 29
1999	6	Feb. 17	Apr. 4	May 23	13	13	Nov. 28
2000	9	Mar. 8	Apr. 23	June 11	10	14	Dec. 3

ADVENT SEASON

The four Sundays preceding Christmas Day

COLOR: Purple

For additional materials see the section on General Aids to Worship.

Scripture Sentences or Calls to Worship

1

Lift up your heads, O gates! and be lifted up, O ancient doors! that the King of glory may come in. *Psalm 24:7*

2

The glory of the Lord shall be revealed, and all flesh shall see it together, for the mouth of the Lord has spoken. *Isaiah 40:5*

3

Prepare the way of the Lord, make straight in the desert a highway for our God. *Isaiah 40:3*

4

It is full time now for you to wake from sleep. For salvation is nearer to us now than when we first believed; the night is far gone, the day is at hand. Let us then cast off the works of darkness and put on the armor of light. *Romans 13:11-12*

5

It will be said on that day, "Lo, this is our God; we have waited for him, that he might save us. This is the Lord; we have waited for him; let us be glad and rejoice in his salvation." *Isaiah 25:9*

6

Sing and rejoice, O daughter of Zion; for lo, I come and I will dwell in the midst of you, says the Lord. And many nations shall join themselves to the Lord in that day, and shall be my people; and I will dwell in the midst of you. *Zechariah 2:10-11ab*

7

For it is the God who said, "Let light shine out of darkness," who has shone in our hearts to give the light of the knowledge of the glory of God in the face of Christ. *II Corinthians 4:6*

8

Minister: Praise be to God!

People: **Blessed be the Lord God, for he has visited and redeemed his people.**

Minister: Blessed is he who comes in the name of the Lord.

People: **Blessed be the name of the Lord.**

9

Minister: How beautiful upon the mountains are the feet of him who brings good tidings,

People: **Who publishes peace, who brings good tidings of good,**

Minister: Who publishes salvation,

People: **Who says to Zion, "Your God reigns."**

10

Minister: The Lord is in his holy temple.

People: **Let all the earth keep silence before him.**

Minister: Sing to the Lord a new song, his praise from the end of the earth!

People: **Show us thy steadfast love, O Lord, and grant us thy salvation.**

11

Minister: The Lord is near to all who call upon him in truth.

People: **O Lord, thou art our help and our deliverer: O come, let us worship and bow down.**

Invocations

1

O God, who didst prepare of old the minds and hearts of men for the coming of thy Son, and whose Spirit ever worketh to illumine our darkened lives with the light of the Gospel: Prepare now our minds and hearts, we beseech thee, that Christ may dwell in us, and ever reign in our thoughts and affections as the King of love, and the very Prince of Peace. Grant this, we pray thee, for his sake. **Amen.**

2

Almighty God, who in thy providence hast made all ages a preparation for the kingdom of thy Son: We beseech thee to make ready our hearts for the brightness of thy glory and the fulness of thy blessing in Jesus Christ our Lord. **Amen.**

3

O Thou who art the source of all existence and the light of all seeing: We remember with joy and awe that the world is thy creation, and that life is thy gift. Lift up our thoughts from the littleness of our own works to the greatness, the majesty, and the wonder of thine, and teach us so to behold thy glory that we may grow into thy likeness; through Jesus Christ our Lord. **Amen.**

4

O God, who in the days of old didst make thyself known to prophets and poets, and in the fulness of time didst reveal thyself in thy Son Jesus Christ: Help us to meditate upon the revelation of thyself which thou hast given, that thy constant love may become known to us, and that we may feel thy presence always with us; through the same Jesus Christ our Lord. **Amen.**

5

O God, who hast set before us the great hope that thy kingdom shall come on earth, and hast taught us to pray for its coming: Make us ever ready to thank thee for the signs of its dawning, and to pray and work for that perfect day when thy will shall be done on earth as it is in heaven; through Jesus Christ our Lord. **Amen.**

6

Most merciful God, who so loved the world as to give thine only begotten Son, that whosoever believeth in him should not perish, but have everlasting life: Grant unto us, we humbly pray thee, the precious gift of faith, that we may know that the Son of God is come, and may have power to overcome the world and gain a blessed immortality; through Jesus Christ our Lord. **Amen.**

Collects

Prayers 2 and 3 are appropriate for Bible Sunday, the second Sunday in Advent.

1

O almighty God, who hast taught us that the night is far spent and the day is at hand: Grant that we may ever be found watching for the coming of thy Son; save us from undue love of the world, that we may wait with patient hope for the day of the Lord, and so abide in him, that when he shall appear we may not be ashamed; through Jesus Christ our Lord. **Amen.**

2

Blessed Lord, who hast caused all holy Scriptures to be written for our learning: Grant that we may in such wise hear them, read, mark, learn, and inwardly digest them, that by patience, and comfort of thy holy Word, we may embrace and ever hold fast the blessed hope of everlasting life, which thou hast given us in our Savior Jesus Christ. **Amen.**

3

O Lord God, heavenly Father, we beseech thee so to rule and guide us by thy Holy Spirit that we may hear and receive thy holy Word with our whole heart; that through thy Word we may be sanctified, and may learn to place all our trust and hope in Jesus Christ thy Son, and following him may be led safely through all evil, until through thy grace we come to everlasting life; through the same Jesus Christ thy Son our Lord. **Amen.**

4

Bestow thy light upon us, O Lord, that, being rid of the darkness of our hearts, we may attain unto the true light; through Jesus Christ, who is the light of the world. **Amen.**

5

O Lord, raise up, we pray thee, thy power, and come among us, and with great might succor us; that, whereas, through our sins and wickedness, we are sorely hindered in running the race that is set before us, thy bountiful grace and mercy may speedily help and deliver us; through Jesus Christ our Lord, to whom, with thee and the Holy Ghost, be honor and glory, world without end. **Amen.**

6

Almighty and everlasting God, who art the brightness of faithful souls and the desire of all nations: So fill the world with thy glory and show thyself by the radiance of thy light that all the peoples of the earth may be subject unto thee; through Jesus Christ our Lord. **Amen.**

The Advent Antiphons

O Wisdom proceeding from the mouth of the highest, reaching from eternity to eternity and disposing all things with strength and sweetness:

Come, teach us the way of knowledge.

O Lord and leader of Israel, who didst appear to Moses in the burning bush and didst deliver the law to him on Sinai:

Come redeem us by thine outstretched arm.

O Root of Jesse, who standest as an ensign of the people; before whom kings open not their mouths; to whom the nations shall pray:

Come and deliver us, make no tarrying.

O Key of David and Scepter of Israel, who openest and none shutteth, who shuttest and none openeth:

Come and release from prison those who sit in darkness and in the shadow of death.

O Dayspring, splendor of eternal light and sun of righteousness:

Come and enlighten those that sit in darkness and in the shadow of death.

O King of nations, their desire and the cornerstone that binds them in one:

Come and save man whom thou formedst of clay.

O Emmanuel, our King and lawgiver, the expectation and Savior of the nations:

Come and save us, O Lord our God.

CHRISTMASTIDE

Usually two Sundays

COLOR: White

For additional materials see the section on General Aids to Worship.

CHRISTMAS

An Order of Worship for Christmas Day

† *Let the people be in silent meditation and prayer upon entering the sanctuary.*

PRELUDE

PROCESSIONAL HYMN † *The people standing.*

SCRIPTURE SENTENCES, OR CALL TO WORSHIP

Minister: Glory to God in the highest.

People: **And on earth peace, good will toward men.**

Minister: Behold, I bring you good tidings of great joy, which shall be to all people.

People: **Glory be to God on high.**

Minister: For unto you is born this day in the city of David a Savior, which is Christ the Lord.

People: **Glory to God in the highest, and on earth peace, good will toward men.**

INVOCATION † *By the minister, the people seated and bowed, or kneeling.*

Let us pray.

O Lord our God, most merciful and mighty: Fill our hearts with joy and our tongues with praise as this day we keep the festival of our Savior's birth. Let the Holy Spirit come upon us as we approach the mystery of his appearing in the flesh as a little child. Stir up in our hearts the precious gift of faith, that he may be born anew in us, and that his presence may shed abroad in our hearts the light of heavenly joy and peace. Grant this, O God, we beseech thee, for the love of Christ thy Son, our only Savior. **Amen.**

COLLECT † *To be said by all.*

O God, who hast given us grace at this time to celebrate the birth of our Savior Jesus Christ: We laud and magnify thy glorious name for the countless blessings which he hath brought unto us, and we beseech thee to grant that we may ever set forth thy praise in joyful obedience to thy will; through the same Jesus Christ our Lord. Amen.

THE LORD'S PRAYER

ANTHEM

CANTICLE † *To be said by all, responsively or in unison, the people standing; after which shall be said or sung the* Gloria Patri.

Blessed be the Lord God of Israel;

for he hath visited and redeemed his people;

and hath raised up an horn of salvation for us,

in the house of his servant David;

as he spake by the mouth of his holy prophets,

which have been since the world began;

that we should be saved from our enemies,

and from the hand of all that hate us;

to perform the mercy promised to our fathers,

and to remember his holy covenant;

the oath which he sware to our forefather Abraham,

that he would grant unto us;

that we being delivered out of the hand of our enemies

might serve him without fear;

in holiness and righteousness before him,

all the days of our life.

And thou, child, shalt be called the prophet of the Highest:

for thou shalt go before the face of the Lord, to prepare his ways;

to give knowledge of salvation unto his people

by the remission of their sins,

through the tender mercy of our God;

whereby the dayspring from on high hath visited us;

to give light to them that sit in darkness and in the shadow of death,
to guide our feet into the way of peace.

Luke 1:68-79 KJV

THE SCRIPTURE LESSONS

AFFIRMATION OF FAITH † *The people standing; after which may be sung a doxology.*

THE PASTORAL PRAYER † *The people seated and bowed, or kneeling.*

THE CHRISTMAS OFFERING

† *Here parish notices may be given.*

† *The minister may read Scripture sentences before the offering is received. An anthem may be sung during the receiving of the offering. Following the presentation of the offering a prayer of dedication may be said or sung.*

† *At the discretion of the minister, the offertory and prayers may follow the sermon.*

HYMN † *The people standing.*

THE SERMON

INVITATION TO CHRISTIAN DISCIPLESHIP

HYMN † *The people standing.*

BENEDICTION † *The people may be seated for silent prayer.*

POSTLUDE

Scripture Sentences or Calls to Worship

1

The grace of God has appeared for the salvation of all men. *Titus 2:11*

2

God so loved the world that he gave his only Son, that whoever believes in him should not perish but have eternal life. *John 3:16*

3

Thanks be to God for his inexpressible gift! *II Corinthians 9:15*

4

Behold, I bring you good news of a great joy which will come to all the people; for to you is born this day in the city of David a Savior, who is Christ the Lord. *Luke 2:10*

5

Glory to God in the highest, and on earth peace among men with whom he is pleased! *Luke 2:14*

6

In the beginning was the Word, and the Word was with God, and the Word was God. *John 1:1*

7

And the Word became flesh and dwelt among us, full of grace and truth. *John 1:14*

8

Minister: Behold, I bring you good news of a great joy which will come to all the people; for to you is born this day a Savior, who is Christ the Lord.

People: **O come, let us adore him, Christ the Lord.**

9

Minister: The Lord has made known his victory.

People: **He has revealed his vindication in the sight of the nations.**

Minister: It is the God who said, "Let light shine out of darkness," who has shone in our hearts.

People: **To give the light of the knowledge of the glory of God in the face of Christ.**

Invocations

1

O God our Father, who hast brought us again to the glad season when we commemorate the birth of thy Son Jesus Christ our Lord: Grant that his Spirit may be born anew in our hearts this day and that we may joyfully welcome him to reign over us. Open our ears that we may hear again the angelic chorus of old. Open our lips that we too may sing with uplifted hearts, Glory to God in the highest, and on earth peace, good will toward men. **Amen.**

2

O Lord God, whose chosen dwelling is the heart of the lowly: We give thee thanks that thou didst reveal thyself in the holy child Jesus, thereby sanctifying all childhood in him. We beseech thee to make us humble in faith and love, that we may know the joy of the Gospel that is hidden from the wise and prudent and revealed unto babes. This we ask in his name, who, wearing our mortal flesh, grew in wisdom and in favor with God and man. **Amen.**

3

O almighty God, who by the birth of thy holy child Jesus hast given us a great light to dawn upon our darkness: Grant, we pray thee, that in his light we may see light. Bestow upon us, we beseech thee, that most excellent Christmas gift of charity to all men, that so the likeness of thy Son may be formed in us, and that we may have the ever brightening hope of everlasting life; through Jesus Christ our Lord. **Amen.**

4

O God of grace, who at this time didst give Jesus Christ to be our Savior: We beseech thee to overcome our darkness with his light, our selfishness with his love, our indolence and cowardice with his steadfast devotion, that we may live ever as in thy presence, and perform faithfully our appointed tasks, and finally come to everlasting life; through the same Jesus Christ our Lord. **Amen.**

5

O God, to whom glory is sung in the highest, while on earth peace is proclaimed to men of good will: Grant that good will to us thy servants, cleanse us from all our sins, and give perpetual peace to us and to all people; through thy mercy, O God, who art blessed, and dost govern all things, world without end. **Amen.**

6

O God our Father, who didst send forth thy Son to be King of kings and Prince of Peace: Grant that all the kingdoms of this world may become the kingdom of Christ, and learn of him the way of peace. Send forth among all men the spirit of good will and reconciliation. Let those who are offended forgive, and those who have offended repent, so that all thy children may live together as one family, praising thee and blessing thee for the great redemption which thou hast wrought for us; through Jesus Christ our Lord. **Amen.**

7

Send, O God, into the darkness of this troubled world the light of thy Son. Let the star of thy hope touch the minds of all men with the bright beams of mercy and truth; and so direct our steps that we may ever walk in the way revealed to us, as the shepherds of Bethlehem walked with joy to the manger where he dwelt, who now and ever reigns in our hearts, Jesus Christ our Lord. **Amen.**

8

Almighty God, we invoke thee, the fountain of everlasting light, and entreat thee to send forth thy truth unto our hearts, and to pour upon us the glory of thy brightness; through Christ our Lord. **Amen.**

Collects

1

O God, who makest us glad with the yearly remembrance of the birth of thine only Son Jesus Christ: Grant that as we joyfully receive him for our Redeemer, so we may with sure confidence behold him when he shall come to be our judge, who liveth and reigneth with thee and the Holy Ghost, one God, world without end. **Amen.**

2

Eternal God, who by the birth of thy beloved Son Jesus Christ didst give thyself to mankind: Grant that, being born in our hearts, he may save us from all our sins, and restore within us the image and likeness of our creator, to whom be everlasting praise and glory, world without end. **Amen.**

3

O Father, who hast declared thy love to men by the birth of the holy child at Bethlehem: Help us to welcome him with gladness and to make room for him in our common days, so that we may live at peace with one another and in good will with all thy family; through Jesus Christ our Lord. **Amen.**

4

Almighty God, who hast given us thine only begotten Son to take our nature upon him, and as at this time to be born of a pure virgin: Grant that we, being born again, and made thy children by adoption and grace, may daily be renewed by thy Holy Spirit; through the same our Lord Jesus Christ, who liveth and reigneth with thee and the same Spirit ever, one God, world without end. **Amen.**

THE CLOSING YEAR

For a Watch Night service, or for the first Sunday of the year, see An Order of Worship for Such as Would Enter into or Renew Their Covenant with God, pp. 382-88.

Scripture Sentences or Calls to Worship

1

Lord, thou hast been our dwelling place in all generations. From everlasting to everlasting, thou art God. *Psalm 90:1, 2c*

2

The heavens will perish, but thou dost endure; they will all wear out like a garment. Thou changest them like raiment, and they pass away; but thou art the same, and thy years have no end. *Psalm 102:26-27*

3

But do not ignore this one fact, beloved, that with the Lord one day is as a thousand years, and a thousand years as one day. *II Peter 3:8*

4

God will be our guide for ever. *Psalm 48:14c*

5

Let the favor of the Lord our God be upon us, and establish thou the work of our hands upon us, yea, the work of our hands establish thou it. *Psalm 90:17*

6

Minister: The Lord has been mindful of us; he will bless us.

People: **He will bless those who fear the Lord, both small and great.**

Minister: Let us thank the Lord for his steadfast love;

People: **And for his wonderful works to the sons of men!**

Invocations

1

Almighty God, who hast been the dwelling place of thy people in all generations, and who in thy mercy hast brought us to the close of another year: We praise thee for all the way by which thou hast led us, and we humbly beseech thee to continue to us thy lovingkindness. Help us to cast our weakness on thy strength, that amid all the changes of time we may rest on thine unchanging love; through Jesus Christ our Lord. **Amen.**

2

Almighty and most merciful Father, who hast given us grace in times past, and hast mercifully brought us to see the end of another year: Grant that we may continue to grow in grace and in the knowledge of thy dear Son. Lead us forward by thy Spirit from strength to strength, that we may more perfectly serve thee. Stir up the gift that is in us. Increase our faith as thou dost increase our years; the longer we are suffered to abide on earth, the better may our service be, the more willing our obedience, the more consistent our daily lives, the more complete our devotion to thee. Grant this our prayer, O gracious Father, which we offer in the name of Jesus Christ thy Son our Lord. **Amen.**

3

As we keep holy time, O Lord of our life, under the deepening shadows of the closing year, we thank thee for all that it has brought to us of mercy and truth, for the lights that have ruled our day and cheered our night, for thy Being and our natures, for thy providence and our faith, for thy dear Son and the grace by which we are his disciples, for the law which upholds and the love which comforts our world; through Jesus Christ our Lord. **Amen.**

Collect

O Thou eternal God, who art ever the same: Grant us so to pass through the coming year with faithful hearts that we may be able in all things to please thee; through Jesus Christ our Lord. **Amen.**

THE OPENING YEAR

Scripture Sentences or Calls to Worship

1

He who sat upon the throne said, "Behold, I make all things new."
Revelation 21:5

2

Be strong and of good courage. *Deuteronomy 31:6a*

3

Behold, I have set before you an open door, which no one is able to shut.
Revelation 3:8

4

So teach us to number our days that we may get a heart of wisdom.
Psalm 90:12

5

Cast away from you all the transgressions which you have committed against me, and get yourselves a new heart and a new spirit! *Ezekiel 18:31*

6

I will be with you; I will not fail you or forsake you. *Joshua 1:5bc*

7

Minister: Sing to the Lord a new song, his praise from the end of the earth!

People: **Sing to the Lord, bless his name; tell of his salvation from day to day.**

Minister: Declare his glory among the nations, his marvelous works among all the peoples!

People: **Honor and majesty are before him; strength and beauty are in his sanctuary.**

8

Minister: He who sat upon the throne said, "Behold, I make all things new."

People: **Our help is in the name of the Lord, who made heaven and earth.**

Minister: Let days speak, and many years teach wisdom.

People: **The counsel of the Lord stands forever, the thoughts of his heart to all generations.**

Invocations

1

Everliving God, by whose mercy we have come to the gateway of another year: Grant that we may enter it with humble and grateful hearts; and confirm our resolution, we beseech thee, to walk more closely in thy way, and labor more faithfully in thy service, according to the teaching and example of thy Son our Lord. Let not the errors and offenses of the past cling to us, but pardon and set us free, that with purer purpose and a better hope we may renew our vows in thy presence, and set forth under the guidance of thy Spirit, to travel in the path which shineth more and more unto the perfect day of thy heavenly kingdom. **Amen.**

2

O Thou who art from everlasting to everlasting, without beginning or end of days: Replenish us with heavenly grace, at the beginning of this year, that we may be enabled to accept all its duties, to perform all its labors, to welcome all its mercies, to meet all its trials, and to advance through all it holds in store for us, with cheerful courage and a constant mind. O Lord, suffer us not to be separated from thee, either by joy or sorrow, or by any sin or weakness of our own; but have compassion upon us, and forgive us, and keep us in the strong confidence of thine eternal love in Jesus Christ; that as thou hast called us to immortality through him, so we may pass the remainder of our years in the power of an endless life; and to thy name shall be all the praise. **Amen.**

Collects

1

O almighty God, who alone art without variableness or shadow of turning, and hast safely brought us through the changes of time to the beginning of another year: We beseech thee to pardon the sins we have committed in the year which is past, and to give us grace that we may spend the remainder of our days to thy honor and glory; through Jesus Christ our Lord. **Amen.**

2

Eternal God, who makest all things new, and abidest forever the same: Grant us to begin this year in thy faith, and to continue it in thy favor; that, being guided in all our doings and guarded all our days, we may spend our lives in thy service, and finally by thy grace attain the glory of everlasting life; through Jesus Christ our Lord. **Amen.**

EPIPHANY SEASON

Four to Nine Sundays

COLOR: First Sunday, white; thereafter, green

For additional materials see the section on General Aids to Worship.

Scripture Sentences or Calls to Worship

1

Arise, shine; for your light has come, and the glory of the Lord has risen upon you.   *Isaiah 60:1*

2

And I have other sheep, that are not of this fold; I must bring them also, and they will heed my voice. So there shall be one flock, one shepherd.   *John 10:16*

3

Nations shall come to your light, and kings to the brightness of your rising.   *Isaiah 60:3*

4

They shall bring gold and frankincense, and shall proclaim the praise of the Lord.   *Isaiah 60:6b*

5

The Lord has made known his victory, he has revealed his vindication in the sight of the nations.   *Psalm 98:2*

6

We have the prophetic word made more sure. You will do well to pay attention to this as to a lamp shining in a dark place, until the day dawns and the morning star rises in your hearts.   *II Peter 1:19*

7

And men will come from east and west, and from north and south, and sit at table in the kingdom of God.   *Luke 13:29*

8

Then he said to his disciples, "The harvest is plentiful, but the laborers are few; pray therefore the Lord of the harvest to send out laborers into his harvest." *Matthew 9:37-38*

9

Minister: O magnify the Lord with me, and let us exalt his name together!

People: **For with thee is the fountain of life; in thy light do we see light.**

Minister: Light dawns for the righteous, and joy for the upright in heart.

People: **From the rising of the sun to its setting the name of the Lord is to be praised!**

10

Minister: It is good that one should wait quietly for the salvation of the Lord.

People: **The friendship of the Lord is for those who fear him, and he makes known to them his covenant.**

Minister: God is our refuge and strength, a very present help in trouble.

People: **We will lift up our voices in praise unto God, our strength and our Redeemer.**

11

Minister: Blessed be the name of God for ever and ever, to whom belong wisdom and might.

People: **He gives wisdom to the wise and knowledge to those who have understanding.**

Minister: Seek the Lord while he may be found, call upon him while he is near.

People: **For great is the Lord, and greatly to be praised.**

12

Minister: The Lord is near to all who call upon him.

People: **He fulfills the desire of all who fear him.**

Minister: The Lord has made known his victory.

People: **Our help is in the name of the Lord.**

13

Minister: Praise is due to thee, O God, in Zion; and to thee shall vows be performed.

People: **I was glad when they said to me, "Let us go to the house of the Lord!"**

Minister: Enter his gates with thanksgiving, and his courts with praise!

People: **For the Lord is good; his steadfast love endures for ever, and his faithfulness to all generations.**

14

Minister: The law of the Lord is perfect, reviving the soul.

People: **The testimony of the Lord is sure, making wise the simple.**

Minister: The precepts of the Lord are right, rejoicing the heart.

People: **The commandment of the Lord is pure, enlightening the eyes.**

15

Minister: God is light and in him is no darkness at all.

People: **O send out thy light and thy truth; let them lead me.**

Minister: Sing to the Lord, all the earth! Tell of his salvation from day to day.

People: **Declare his glory among the nations, his marvelous works among all peoples.**

Invocations

1

Almighty and everlasting God, the radiance of faithful souls, who didst bring the nations to thy light and kings to the brightness of thy rising: Fill, we beseech thee, the world with thy glory, and show thyself unto all the nations; through him who is the true light and the bright and morning star, even Jesus Christ thy Son our Lord. **Amen.**

2

From the rising of the sun to the going down of the same, thy name, O God, shall be great among the gentiles; and in every place incense shall be offered unto thy name, and a pure offering; for thy name shall be great among the nations; through Jesus Christ our Lord. **Amen.**

3

O Thou who art the true sun of the world, ever rising, and never going down, who by thy most wholesome appearing and light dost nourish and make joyful all things in heaven and in earth: We beseech thee mercifully to shine into our hearts, that the night and darkness of sin and the mists of error on every side may be driven away, and that all our life long we may walk without stumbling as children of the light and the day. **Amen.**

4

O God our Father, give to the Church a new vision and a new charity, new wisdom and fresh understanding, the revival of her brightness and the renewal of her unity; that the eternal message of thy Son, undefiled by the traditions of men, may be hailed as the good news of the new age; through him who maketh all things new, Jesus Christ our Lord. **Amen.**

5

O almighty God, who hast built thy Church upon the foundation of the apostles and prophets, Jesus Christ himself being the head cornerstone: Grant us so to be joined together in unity of spirit by their doctrine, that we may be made a holy temple acceptable unto thee; through the same Jesus Christ our Lord. **Amen.**

Collects

1

O Lord, we beseech thee mercifully to receive the prayers of thy people who call upon thee; and grant that they may both perceive and know what things they ought to do, and also may have grace and power faithfully to fulfill the same; through Jesus Christ our Lord. **Amen.**

2

O Lord, who seest that all hearts are empty except thou fill them, and all desires balked except they crave after thee: Give us light and grace to seek and find thee, that we may be thine and thou mayest be ours for ever. **Amen.**

3

Almighty and everlasting God, who dost govern all things in heaven and earth: Mercifully hear the supplications of thy people, and grant us thy peace all the days of our life; through Jesus Christ our Lord. **Amen.**

4

Almighty and everlasting God, mercifully look upon our infirmities, and in all dangers and necessities stretch forth thy right hand to help and defend us; through Jesus Christ our Lord. **Amen.**

5

O Lord God, who seest that we put not our trust in anything that we do: Mercifully grant that by thy power we may be defended against all adversity; through Jesus Christ our Lord. **Amen.**

6

Master of men, who hast given us work to do: Give us strength to do it with gladness and singleness of heart; and when it is done grant us a place in thy kingdom; through Jesus Christ our Lord. **Amen.**

7

O Thou who didst command thine apostles to go into all the world, and to preach the Gospel to every creature: Let thy name be great among the nations from the rising up of the sun unto the going down of the same. **Amen.**

8

O Lord, who hast taught us that all our doings without charity are worth nothing: Send thy Holy Spirit, and pour into our hearts that most excellent gift of charity, the very bond of peace and of all virtues, without which whosoever liveth is counted dead before thee. Grant this for the sake of thine only Son Jesus Christ. **Amen.**

9

O God, who knowest us to be set in the midst of so many and great dangers, that by reason of the frailty of our nature we cannot always stand upright: Grant to us such strength and protection, as may support us in all dangers, and carry us through all temptations; through Jesus Christ our Lord. **Amen.**

Prayers of Petition and Intercession

FOR THE CHURCH

1

O God, our heavenly Father, who didst manifest thy love by sending thine only Son into the world that all might live through him: Pour thy Spirit upon thy Church, that it may fulfill his command to preach the Gospel to every creature; send forth, we beseech thee, laborers into thy harvest; defend them in all dangers and temptations; give them grace to bear faithful witness unto thee; endue them with zeal and love, that they may turn many to righteousness; through the same thy Son Jesus Christ our Lord. **Amen.**

2

Almighty and everlasting God, who in the days of old didst cause thy Word to grow mightily and prevail: We praise and magnify thy holy name for the manifestation of thy presence in this our day, and we beseech thee to pour out thy Spirit upon the Church, that thy way may be known upon the earth and thy saving health among all nations; through Jesus Christ our Lord. **Amen.**

3

O God, the Father of our Lord Jesus Christ our only Savior, the Prince of Peace: Give us grace seriously to lay to heart the great dangers we are in by our unhappy divisions. Take away all hatred and prejudice, and whatsoever else may hinder us from godly union and concord: that as there is but one Body and one Spirit, and one hope of our calling, one Lord, one Faith, one Baptism, one God and Father of us all, so we may be all of one heart and of one soul, united in one holy bond of truth and peace, of faith and charity, and may with one mind and one mouth glorify thee; through Jesus Christ our Lord. **Amen.**

FOR MISSIONS AND MISSIONARIES

4

O God, who by thy Son Jesus Christ has commanded us to go into all the world and preach the Gospel to every creature: Make us faithful and obedient to do thy holy will. Give us compassion for all who are unaware of thee in all the world. Send forth, we beseech thee, laborers into thy harvest. Protect and guide them wherever they go. Give them patience, love, and a right judgment in all things, and give them fruit for their labors; through Jesus Christ our Lord. **Amen.**

5

O God, who willest that all men should be saved and come to the knowledge of the truth: Prosper, we pray thee, our brethren who labor in distant lands (especially those whom we now name before thee). Protect them in all perils by land and sea; support them in loneliness and in the hour of trial; give them grace to bear faithful witness unto thee; and endue them with burning zeal and love, that they may turn many to righteousness, and finally obtain a crown of glory; through Jesus Christ our Lord. **Amen.**

6

O God, who hast made of one blood all nations of men for to dwell on the face of the whole earth, and didst send thy blessed Son to preach peace to them that are afar off and to them that are nigh: Grant that all men everywhere may seek after thee and find thee. Bring the nations into thy fold, pour out thy Spirit upon all flesh, and hasten thy kingdom; through the same thy Son Jesus Christ our Lord. **Amen.**

RACE RELATIONS DAY

7

O God, who hast made man in thine own likeness, and who dost love all whom thou hast made; teach us the unity of thy family and the breadth of thy love. By the example of thy Son Jesus Christ our Savior enable us to enter into the fellowship of the whole human family; and forbid that, from pride of race or hardness of heart, we should despise any for whom he died, or injure any in whom he lives; through the same Jesus Christ our Lord. **Amen.**

BROTHERHOOD DAY

8

Almighty God, we who are members of different races and faiths desire to recognize together thy fatherhood and our kinship. In our differences, we find that many of our hopes, our fears, our aspirations are one. Thou art our Father and we are thy children.

We are heartily sorry for the mists of fear, envy, hatred, suspicion, and greed which have blinded our eyes and thrust us asunder. May the light that comes from thee scatter those mists, cleanse our hearts and give health to our spirits, teach us to put away all bitterness and to walk together in the ways of human friendship.

Open our eyes to see that, as nature abounds in variation, so differences in human beings make for richness in the common life. May we give honor where honor is due—regardless of race, color, or circumstance. Deepen our respect for unlikeness and our eagerness to understand one another. Through the deeper unities of the spirit in sympathy, insight and co-operation may we transcend our differences. May we gladly share with one another our best gifts and together seek for a humane world fashioned for good under thy guidance. **Amen.**

A Litany for Missions

Let us pray.

Blessed be the Lord God for his tender mercy, whereby the dayspring from on high hath visited us,

to give light to them that sit in darkness and in the shadow of death, to guide our feet into the way of peace.

Jesus said: "They shall come from the east, and from the west, and from the north, and from the south, and shall sit down in the kingdom of God."

Thanks be to thee, O Christ, for thy holy Gospel.

Other sheep I have, which are not of this fold: them also I must bring, and they shall hear my voice; and there shall be one fold, and one shepherd.

Thanks be to thee, O Christ, for thy holy promise.

Go ye therefore, and teach all nations, baptizing them in the name of the Father, and of the Son, and of the Holy Spirit; teaching them to observe all things whatsoever I have commanded you.

Thanks be to thee, O Christ, for thy holy Word.

Ye shall receive power after that the Holy Spirit is come upon you: and ye shall be witnesses unto me both in Jerusalem, and in all Judea, and in Samaria, and unto the uttermost part of the earth.

Thanks be to thee, O Christ, for thy Holy Spirit.

We beseech thee to hear us, O Lord, that thou wouldst stir up the hearts of thy faithful people to greater obedience, and unite thy Church to face the world's great need, that thou wouldst send forth laborers into thy harvest.

Hear us, we beseech thee.

That those who have gone forth may be supported by thy presence, guided by thy counsel, and filled with thy power,

Hear us, we beseech thee.

Accept the devotion of our hearts, until we all come in the unity of the faith, and of the knowledge of thee, unto a perfect man, unto the measure of the stature of thy fulness. Amen.

LENTEN SEASON

Six Sundays

COLOR: Purple

For additional materials see the section on General Aids to Worship.

An Order of Worship for Ash Wednesday

† *Let the people be in silent meditation and prayer upon entering the sanctuary.*

† *Let the service of worship begin at the time appointed.*

PRELUDE

SCRIPTURE SENTENCES, OR CALL TO WORSHIP † *The people standing.*

> *Minister:* "Rend your hearts and not your garments," says the Lord. Return to the Lord your God.
>
> *People:* **For he is gracious and merciful, slow to anger and abounding in steadfast love.**
>
> *Minister:* With what shall I come before the Lord, and bow myself before God on high?
>
> *People:* **He has showed you, O man, what is good; and what does the Lord require of you, but to do justice, and to love kindness, and to walk humbly with your God?**

HYMN † *The people standing.*

INVOCATION † *By the minister, the people seated and bowed, or kneeling.*

Let us pray.

Almighty and everlasting God, who hatest nothing that thou hast made, and dost forgive the sins of those who are penitent: Create and make in us new and contrite hearts, that we, truly lamenting our sins and acknowledging our wickedness, may obtain of thee, the God of all mercy, perfect remission and forgiveness; through Jesus Christ our Lord. **Amen.**

CALL TO CONFESSION   † *The minister.*

Let the wicked forsake his way, and the unrighteous man his thoughts: and let him return unto the Lord, and he will have mercy upon him; and to our God, for he will abundantly pardon.

The sacrifices of God are a broken spirit: a broken and a contrite heart, O God, thou wilt not despise.

If we confess our sins, he is faithful and just to forgive us our sins, and to cleanse us from all unrighteousness.

PRAYER OF CONFESSION   † *To be said by all, the minister first saying,*

Let us pray.

Almighty God, Father of our Lord Jesus Christ, maker of all things, judge of all men: We acknowledge and bewail our manifold sins and wickedness, which we from time to time most grievously have committed by thought, word, and deed, against thy divine majesty. We do earnestly repent, and are heartily sorry for these our misdoings; the remembrance of them is grievous unto us. Have mercy upon us, have mercy upon us, most merciful Father. For thy Son our Lord Jesus Christ's sake, forgive us all that is past; and grant that we may ever hereafter serve and please thee in newness of life, to the honor and glory of thy name; through Jesus Christ our Lord. Amen.

THE LORD'S PRAYER

ANTHEM OR HYMN

THE PSALTER   † *To be said by all, responsively or in unison, the people standing; then shall be said or sung the* Gloria Patri.

Out of the depths I cry to thee, O Lord!

Lord, hear my voice!

Let thy ears be attentive

to the voice of my supplications.

If thou, O Lord, shouldst mark iniquities,

Lord, who could stand?

But there is forgiveness with thee,

that thou mayest be feared.

I wait for the Lord, my soul waits,

and in his word I hope.

My soul waits for the Lord more than watchmen for the morning,

more than watchmen for the morning.

O Israel, hope in the Lord! For with the Lord there is steadfast love,
and with him is plenteous redemption.

And he will redeem Israel
from all his iniquities. *Psalm 130*

THE SCRIPTURE LESSONS

AFFIRMATION OF FAITH † *To be said by all, the people standing; then may be sung a doxology.*

THE PASTORAL PRAYER † *The people seated and bowed, or kneeling.*

OFFERTORY

† *At the discretion of the minister, the offertory and prayers may follow the sermon.*

THE SERMON

AN INVITATION TO CHRISTIAN DISCIPLESHIP

PRAYER † *To be said by all, the minister first saying,*

Let us pray.

Almighty God, who hast taught us in the life and teaching of thy Son the way of true blessedness, and hast shown us in his suffering and death that the path of love may lead to a cross: Give us grace to learn these hard lessons, to take up our cross and follow Christ, in strength, patience, and constancy of faith; through the same thy Son Jesus Christ our Lord. Amen.

HYMN OF DEDICATION † *The people standing.*

BENEDICTION † *The people may be seated for silent prayer.*

POSTLUDE

Scripture Sentences or Calls to Worship

1

Come, let us walk in the light of the Lord, that he may teach us his ways and that we may walk in his paths. *Isaiah 2:5, 3c*

2

Seek the Lord while he may be found, call upon him while he is near; let the wicked forsake his way, and the unrighteous man his thoughts; let him return to the Lord. *Isaiah 55:6-7*

3

Draw near to God and he will draw near to you. *James 4:8*

4

Humble yourselves before the Lord and he will exalt you. *James 4:10*

5

Rend your hearts and not your garments. Return to the Lord, your God, for he is gracious and merciful, slow to anger, and abounding in steadfast love, and repents of evil. *Joel 2:13*

6

In returning and rest you shall be saved; in quietness and in trust shall be your strength. *Isaiah 30:15bc*

7

Watch and pray that you may not enter into temptation; the spirit indeed is willing, but the flesh is weak. *Matthew 26:41*

8

Beloved, let us cleanse ourselves from every defilement of body and spirit, and make holiness perfect in the fear of God. *II Corinthians 7:1*

9

For thus says the high and lofty One who inhabits eternity, whose name is Holy: "I dwell in the high and holy place, and also with him who is of a contrite and humble spirit, to revive the spirit of the humble, and to revive the heart of the contrite." *Isaiah 57:15*

10

Minister: Let us test and examine our ways, and return to the Lord!

People: **God has blessed us; let all the ends of the earth fear him!**

Minister: Seek the Lord while he may be found, call upon him while he is near; let the wicked forsake his way, and the unrighteous man his thoughts; let him return to the Lord.

People: **The sacrifice acceptable to God is a broken spirit; a broken and contrite heart, O God, thou wilt not despise.**

11

Minister: O magnify the Lord with me, and let us exalt his name together.

People: **Blessed be the Lord, the God of Israel, who alone does wondrous things. Blessed be his glorious name for ever; may his glory fill the whole earth!**

Minister: Come, let us return to the Lord, that we may live before him.

People: **Behold, the dwelling of God is with men. He will dwell with them, and they shall be his people, and God himself will be with them.**

12

Minister: The Lord is merciful and gracious, slow to anger and abounding in steadfast love.

People: **He does not deal with us according to our sins, nor requite us according to our iniquities.**

Minister: What shall I render to the Lord for all his bounty to me?

People: **I will lift up the cup of salvation and call on the name of the Lord.**

13

Minister: Draw near to God and he will draw near to you.

People: **The Lord is near to all who call upon him, to all who call upon him in truth.**

Minister: Let not loyalty and faithfulness forsake you; write them on the tablet of your heart.

People: **God is light and in him is no darkness at all. If we walk in the light, we have fellowship with one another.**

14

Minister: O magnify the Lord with me, and let us exalt his name together!

People: **Our help is in the name of the Lord, who made heaven and earth.**

Invocations

1

O God our Father, who hast led us apart from the busy world into the quiet of thy house: Grant us grace to worship thee in spirit and in truth, to the comfort of our souls and the upbuilding of every good purpose and holy desire. Enable us to do more perfectly the work to which thou hast called us, that we may not fear the coming of night, when we shall resign into thy hands the tasks which thou hast committed to us. So may we worship thee not with our lips only at this hour, but in word and deed all the days of our lives; through Jesus Christ our Lord. **Amen.**

2

O merciful Father, who in compassion for thy sinful children didst send thy Son Jesus Christ to be the Savior of the world: Grant us grace to feel and to lament our share of the evil which made it needful for him to suffer and to die for our salvation. Help us by self-denial, prayer, and meditation to prepare our hearts for deeper penitence and a better life. And give us a true longing to be free from sin, through the deliverance wrought by Jesus Christ our only Redeemer. **Amen.**

3

Give ear, O Lord, unto our prayer, and attend to the voice of our supplications. Teach us thy way, O Lord: we will walk in thy truth. Unite our hearts to fear thy name. We will praise thee, O Lord our God, with all our heart; and we will glorify thy name for evermore: for great is thy mercy toward us. **Amen.**

4

We beseech thee, almighty God, mercifully to look upon thy people; that by thy great goodness they may be governed and preserved evermore, both in body and soul; through Jesus Christ our Lord. **Amen.**

Collects

1

Almighty God, who seest that we have no power of ourselves to help ourselves: Keep us, both outwardly in our bodies and inwardly in our souls, that we may be defended from all adversities which may happen to the body, and from all evil thoughts which may hurt the soul; through Jesus Christ our Lord. **Amen.**

2

Almighty God, who hast given thine only Son to be unto us both a sacrifice for sin, and also an example of godly life: Give us grace that we may always most thankfully receive that his inestimable benefit, and also daily endeavor ourselves to follow the blessed steps of his most holy life; through the same thy Son Jesus Christ our Lord. **Amen.**

3

O God, who by thy Word dost marvelously work out the reconciliation of mankind: Grant, we beseech thee, that following the example of our blessed Lord, and walking in such a way as thou dost choose, we may be subjected to thee with all our hearts, and united to each other in holy love; through Jesus Christ our Lord. **Amen.**

4

Almighty God, who through thy Son dost continually prompt us to conform our wills to thine: Grant that we may love the thing which thou desirest for us, and find thy commandments in the purified wishes of our hearts; through Jesus Christ our Lord. **Amen.**

5

Grant us, O Lord, in all our ways of life thy help, in all our perplexities of thought thy counsel, in all our dangers of temptations thy protection, and in all our sorrows of heart thy peace; through Jesus Christ our Lord. **Amen.**

6

O God, beneath whose eyes every heart trembles, and all consciences are afraid: Be merciful to us, and heal the wounds of all, that as not one of us is free from fault, so not one may be shut out from pardon; through Jesus Christ our Lord. **Amen.**

7

Almighty and merciful God, who willest not the souls of sinners to perish, but their faults: Restrain the anger which we deserve, and pour out upon us the clemency which we entreat, that through thy mercy we may pass from mourning into joy; through Jesus Christ our Lord. **Amen.**

8

O Savior of the world, who by thy cross and precious blood hast redeemed us: Save us and help us, we humbly beseech thee, O Lord. **Amen.**

9

Grant, O Father, that as we move in the world of men, they may take knowledge of us that we have been with thy Son Jesus Christ. **Amen.**

Prayers of Petition

1

O Lord our God, teach us temperance and self-control, that we may live unto the spirit and be mindful of all that Jesus endured and sacrificed for our sakes, and how he was made perfect through sufferings; and help us so to keep the fast that thou hast chosen, that we may loose the bands of wickedness, undo the heavy burdens, and let the oppressed go free; through the grace of Christ Jesus our crucified and risen Savior. **Amen.**

2

O Lord of all good life, we pray thee to purify our lives. Help us each day to know more of thee, and by the power of thy Spirit use us to show forth thyself to others. Make us humble, brave, and loving; make us ready for adventure. We do not ask that thou wilt keep us safe, but keep us ever loyal to the example of our Lord and Savior Jesus Christ. **Amen.**

3

O almighty God, we thank thee for all thy blessings and all thy mercies which thou in thy love hast bestowed upon us. Do thou continue thy care for us. Help us to live as thine obedient and dutiful children. Let us never forget who thou art, and whose we are; and grant to every member of this house strength and courage for the battle of life; for the sake of Jesus Christ our Lord. **Amen.**

PASSION SUNDAY
Fifth Sunday in Lent

Invocation

Forbid, O God, that we should forget, amid our earthly comforts, the pains and mortal anguish that our Lord Jesus endured for our salvation. Grant us this day a true vision of all that he suffered: his betrayal, his lonely agony, his false trial, his mocking and scourging, the torture of the cross; that, remembering his sufferings and death, we may give ourselves wholly to thee; through the same Jesus Christ our only Lord and Savior. **Amen.**

Collect

O God, who by the passion of thy blessed Son hast made the instrument of shameful death to be unto us the means of life and peace: Grant us so to glory in the cross of Christ that we may gladly suffer shame and loss; for the sake of the same thy Son our Lord. **Amen.**

Prayers of Petition and Intercession

1

O Lord our God, who didst deliver thy Son our Savior Jesus Christ even to death upon the cross for our salvation: Mercifully grant us the help of thy Holy Spirit that we, being cleansed from our sin and confirmed in thy faith, may worthily praise thee for those mighty acts whereby thou hast redeemed us to thyself and made us heirs of everlasting life; through Jesus Christ our Lord. **Amen.**

2

O almighty God, who in Jesus Christ didst conquer tears by crying, pain by suffering, and death by dying: Mercifully grant that we who commemorate his passion, being always obedient to thy holy will, may by thy grace receive that life which triumphs over sin and death; through the same Jesus Christ our Lord. **Amen.**

PALM SUNDAY

Sunday Before Easter

Scripture Sentences or Calls to Worship

1

Blessed be he who comes in the name of the Lord!   *Matthew 21:9b*

2

God has highly exalted him and bestowed on him the name which is above every name.   *Philippians 2:9*

3

Behold my servant, whom I uphold, my chosen, in whom my soul delights; I have put my spirit upon him.   *Isaiah 42:1ab*

98

4

The kingdom of the world has become the kingdom of our Lord and of his Christ. *Revelation 11:15b*

5

Minister: Rejoice greatly, O daughter of Zion! Shout aloud, O daughter of Jerusalem! Lo, your king comes to you.

People: **Triumphant and victorious is he.**

Minister: His dominion shall be from sea to sea,

People: **And from the river to the ends of the earth.**

6

Minister: And the disciples began to rejoice and praise God, saying, Hosanna!

People: **Hosanna to the son of David!**

Minister: Blessed is the King who comes in the name of the Lord!

People: **Blessed be the kingdom of our father David that is coming!**

Minister: Hosanna!

People: **Hosanna in the highest!**

Invocations

1

Our Father, as on this day we keep the special memory of our Redeemer's entry into Jerusalem: Grant, we beseech thee, that now and ever he may triumph in our hearts. Let the King of grace and glory enter in, and let us lay ourselves and all we are in full and joyful homage before him; through the same Jesus Christ our Lord. **Amen.**

2

O God, we praise thee for the Master, who rode in triumph into the city of his fathers. We thank thee that he came not as a conqueror to destroy but as a Messiah to save, and that he appealed to human hearts with the glory of love. In the spirit of praise and worship we ask that every knee shall bow, and every tongue confess that Jesus Christ is Lord, to the glory of God the Father. **Amen.**

3

Come, O Christ, and reign among us, in love and joy and peace; extend thine empire over human hearts; let the burning vision of thy beauty shine out before the eyes of the world; hasten the consummation of thy kingdom in which love shall be the only king. **Amen.**

4

O King of men, Master of our lives, enter into thy glory by the cross, to whom all authority is given, both in heaven and on earth: We acknowledge thy sovereignty over every realm of life. Come, O Lord; enter into thy kingdom; subdue the world by the might of thy love. **Amen.**

Collect

Almighty and everlasting God, who, of thy tender love toward mankind, hast sent thy Son our Savior Jesus Christ to take upon him our flesh, and to suffer death upon the cross, that all mankind should follow the example of his great humility: Mercifully grant that we may both follow the example of his patience and also be made partakers of his resurrection; through the same Jesus Christ our Lord. **Amen.**

HOLY WEEK

Scripture Sentences or Calls to Worship

1

It is the Spirit himself bearing witness with our spirit that we are children of God, and if children, then heirs, heirs of God and fellow heirs with Christ, provided we suffer with him in order that we may also be glorified with him.   *Romans 8:16-17*

2

Let us run with perseverance the race that is set before us, looking to Jesus the pioneer and perfecter of our faith, who for the joy that was set before him endured the cross, despising the shame, and is seated at the right hand of the throne of God.   *Hebrews 12:1b-2*

3

Is it nothing to you, all you who pass by? Look and see if there is any sorrow like my sorrow. *Lamentations 1:12ab*

4

If any man would come after me, let him deny himself and take up his cross and follow me. For whoever would save his life will lose it; and whoever loses his life for my sake and the gospel's will save it.

Mark 8:34b-35

5

Minister: Christ himself bore our sins in his body on the tree,

People: **That we might die to sin and live to righteousness.**

Collects for Holy Week

MONDAY

Grant, we beseech thee, almighty God, that we, who in so many occasions of adversity, by reason of our frailty are found wanting, may yet, through the passion and intercession of thine only begotten Son, be continually refreshed; who liveth and reigneth with thee, in the unity of the Holy Spirit, world without end. **Amen.**

TUESDAY

Almighty, everlasting God, grant us so perfectly to follow the passion of our Lord, that we may obtain the help and pardon of his all-sufficient grace; through him who liveth and reigneth with thee, in the unity of the Holy Spirit, world without end. **Amen.**

WEDNESDAY

Assist us mercifully with thy help, O Lord God of our salvation, that we may enter with joy upon the meditation of those mighty acts through which thou hast given unto us life and immortality; through Jesus Christ our Lord. **Amen.**

MAUNDY THURSDAY

O God, who by the example of thy Son our Savior Jesus Christ hast taught us the greatness of true humility, and dost call us to watch with him in his passion: Give us grace to serve one another in all lowliness, and to enter into the fellowship of his sufferings; in his name and for his sake. **Amen.**

GOOD FRIDAY

Almighty God, we beseech thee graciously to behold this thy family, for which our Lord Jesus Christ was content to be betrayed and given into the hands of wicked men, and to suffer death upon the cross; who now liveth and reigneth with thee and the Holy Spirit ever, one God, world without end. **Amen.**

EASTER EVEN

Grant us, O Lord, that, as we are baptized into the death of thy blessed Son our Savior Jesus Christ, so by continual mortifying of our corrupt affections we may be buried with him, and that through the grave and gate of death we may pass to our joyful resurrection; for his merits who died, and was buried, and arose again for us, thy Son Jesus Christ our Lord. **Amen.**

MAUNDY THURSDAY

The Sacrament of the Lord's Supper

Collect

Almighty Father, whose dear Son, on the night before he suffered, did institute the Sacrament of his body and blood: Mercifully grant that we may thankfully receive the same in remembrance of him, who in these holy mysteries giveth us a pledge of life eternal; the same thy Son Jesus Christ our Lord, who now liveth and reigneth with thee and the Holy Spirit ever, one God, world without end. **Amen.**

GOOD FRIDAY

COLOR: Black

An Order of Worship for Good Friday

A Three-Hour Service of Devotion

This order of worship is for use on Good Friday from twelve o'clock noon to three o'clock—the traditional hours for the commemoration of the crucifixion of our Lord.

† *Let the people be in silent meditation and prayer upon entering the sanctuary.*

PRELUDE

HYMN † *The people standing.*

SCRIPTURE SENTENCES, OR CALL TO WORSHIP † *The people standing.*

Minister: Is it nothing to you, all ye that pass by?

People: **Behold, and see if there be any sorrow like unto his sorrow.**

Minister: God commendeth his love toward us, in that, while we were yet sinners, Christ died for us.

People: **Behold the Lamb of God, which taketh away the sin of the world. Amen.**

INVOCATION † *By the minister, the people seated and bowed, or kneeling.*

Let us pray.

O God our Father, we come beseeching thee mercifully to guide us in these our meditations, supplications, and prayers, and to dispose the minds and hearts of all men toward the attainment of everlasting salvation; through Jesus Christ our Lord. **Amen.**

COLLECT FOR GOOD FRIDAY † *To be said by all.*

Almighty God, we beseech thee graciously to behold this thy family, for which our Lord Jesus Christ was content to be betrayed, and given up into the hands of wicked men, and to suffer death upon the cross; who now liveth and reigneth with thee and the Holy Spirit ever, one God, world without end. Amen.

Minister: O Lord, open thou our lips.

People: **And our mouth shall show forth thy praise.**

Minister: Praise ye the Lord.

People: **The Lord's name be praised.**

ANTHEM

PRAYER OF CONFESSION † *The minister beginning, the people responding.*

Let us pray.

O God, in this hour of solemn remembrance we acknowledge with sorrow and shame that our sins are such as sent our blessed Lord to the cross.

Lord, have mercy upon us.

We confess with penitence that we have been slow to accept that forgiveness of sins and cleansing from all unrighteousness which by his death he sealed for us as the free gift of God.

Lord, have mercy upon us.

We have not always entered into the fellowship of his sufferings, and have charged thee with indifference to sorrow and pain.

Lord, have mercy upon us. Amen.

WORDS OF FORGIVENESS † *The minister.*

Hear these words from Scripture:

The Lord is gracious and merciful, slow to anger and abounding in steadfast love. *Psalm 145:8*

THE LORD'S PRAYER † *To be said by all.*

HYMN † *The people standing.*

The First Word

"Father, forgive them; for they know not what they do." *Luke 23:34a*

HYMN † *The people standing.*

SILENT MEDITATION † *Here let the people be seated.*

PRAYERS † *The minister.*

Let us pray.

Almighty and everlasting God, grant us so to celebrate the mysteries of our Lord's passion, that we, obtaining pardon through his precious blood, may come with joy to the commemoration of that sacrifice by which thou hast been pleased to redeem us; through the same thy Son our Savior Jesus Christ. **Amen.**

† *To be said by all.*

> **O Lord, we beseech thee, absolve thy people from their offenses, that through thy bountiful goodness, we may be delivered from the bonds of those sins which by our frailty we have committed. Grant this, O heavenly Father, for the sake of Jesus Christ, our blessed Lord and Savior. Amen.**

ANTHEM

The Second Word

"Today you will be with me in Paradise."   *Luke 23:43*

HYMN † *The people standing.*

SILENT MEDITATION † *Here let the people be seated.*

PRAYERS † *The minister.*

Let us pray.

O Lord, we beseech thee, mercifully hear our prayers, and spare all those who confess their sins unto thee, that they whose consciences by sin are accused, by thy merciful pardon may be absolved; through Christ our Lord. **Amen.**

† *To be said by all.*

> **O Thou who art love, and who seest all the suffering, injustice, and misery which reign in this world: Have pity, we implore thee, on the work of thy hands. Look mercifully upon the poor, the oppressed, and all who are heavy-laden with error, labor, and sorrow. Fill our hearts with deep compassion for those who suffer, and hasten the coming of thy kingdom of justice and truth; through Jesus Christ our Lord. Amen.**

The Third Word

"Woman, behold your son! . . . Behold your mother!"   *John 19:26-27*

HYMN † *The people standing.*

SILENT MEDITATION † *Here let the people be seated.*

PRAYERS † *The minister.*

Let us pray.

Infinite and eternal Spirit, our God and our Father, author of all good, and never far from any of thy children: We draw near to thee that in fellowship with thee we may receive of thy Spirit. May all the bonds of love and ties of friendship be made stronger and sweeter through him who in his mortal agony was not unmindful that we need one another's love, even Jesus Christ our Lord. **Amen.**

† *To be said by all.*

O eternal God, who alone makest men to be of one mind in a house: Help us, the members of this household, faithfully to fulfill our duties to thee and to each other. Put far from us all unkind thoughts, anger, and evil speaking. Give us tender hearts, full of affection and sympathy toward all. Grant us grace to feel the sorrows and trials of others as our own, and to bear patiently with their imperfections. Preserve us from selfishness, and grant that, day by day, walking in love, we may grow up into the likeness of thy Son Jesus Christ our Lord. Amen.

The Fourth Word

"My God, my God, why hast thou forsaken me?"   *Matthew 27:46b*

Hymn † *The people standing.*

Silent Meditation † *Here let the people be seated.*

Prayers † *The minister.*

Let us pray.

O almighty God, who art a most strong tower to all those who put their trust in thee, to whom all things in heaven in earth and under the earth do bow and obey: Be now and evermore our defense, and make us know and feel that there is none other name under heaven given to man in whom and through whom we may receive health and salvation, but only the name of thy Son our Lord Jesus Christ. **Amen.**

† *To be said by all.*

Thou knowest, Lord, the secrets of our hearts; shut not thy merciful ears to our prayer; but spare us, Lord most holy, O God most mighty, O holy and merciful Savior, thou most worthy judge eternal, suffer us not, at our last hour, for any pains of death, to fall from thee. May we not feel forsaken of thee, or shut out from thy love; but save us in all our mortal strife; through Jesus Christ our Lord. Amen.

Anthem

The Fifth Word

"I thirst."   *John 19:28*

Hymn † *The people standing.*

Silent Meditation † *Here let the people be seated.*

Prayers † *The minister.*

Let us pray.

Almighty God, whose most dear Son went not up to joy but first he suffered pain, and entered not into glory before he was crucified: Mercifully grant that we, walking in the way of the cross, may find it none other than the way of life and peace; through Jesus Christ our Lord. **Amen.**

† *To be said by all.*

O Lord, increase our faith, renew our courage, and by thy spirit make us victors over the things that beset us by giving our utmost to the highest. May thy blessing rest upon all who give cups of cold water to others because they belong to Christ. Show us that in every woe thou art still with us, that in every sorrow thou art still loving us, even unto the uttermost. And may our faith stand firm in thy faithfulness; through Jesus Christ our Lord. Amen.

The Sixth Word

"It is finished."   *John 19:30*

Hymn † *The people standing.*

Silent Meditation † *Here let the people be seated.*

Prayers † *The minister.*

Let us pray.

Thou forgiver of sin, healer of sorrow, vanquisher of death: Draw us unto thyself, who art our salvation and our all-conquering hope. Make us citizens of thy kingdom, men of invincible good will, builders of a world where righteousness shall reign and the law of love shall triumph over hate and strife. Hasten the day when thou shalt take unto thyself thy great power and reign. Increase in us true devotion unto thyself; nourish us with all goodness; and of thy great mercy keep us steadfast; through Jesus Christ our Lord. **Amen.**

† *To be said by all.*

Almighty God, we thank thee for the good examples of all those thy servants who, having finished their course in faith, do now rest from their labors. And we beseech thee that we, with all those who are departed in the true faith of thy holy name, may have our perfect consummation and bliss in thy eternal and everlasting glory; through Jesus Christ our Lord. Amen.

The Seventh Word

"Father, into thy hands I commit my spirit!" *Luke 23:46*

HYMN † *The people standing.*

SILENT MEDITATION † *Here let the people be seated.*

ANTHEM

PRAYERS † *The minister.*

Let us pray.

O Father of mercies, whose beloved Son was, as on this day, crucified for us, the just for the unjust, to bring us to thee: Give grace, we beseech thee, to every member of this family to look in faith upon that cross, and to crucify himself upon it to every impure desire and unchristian temper. May we learn in humble devotion to our Master's service to deny ourselves daily, for his sake, and for one another's sake, that we may follow him. Remove from us every corrupt and unfaithful affection. May we never be afraid to do right and never dare to do wrong. And so out of the good treasure of the heart may we ever be bringing forth good things to the praise and glory of thy name; through Jesus Christ our Lord. **Amen.**

† *To be said by all.*

O Lord, our heavenly Father, we offer and present unto thee ourselves, our souls and bodies, to be a reasonable, holy, and living sacrifice unto thee. Take us as we are and make us more fit for thy service. Use us for thyself and for the edification of thy Church. We are not our own, but thine, bought with a price; therefore claim us as thy right, keep us as thy charge, and use us as thou wilt, to the glory of thy holy name and the good of our fellow men; through Jesus Christ our Lord. Amen.

HYMN † *The people standing.*

PRAYER † *By the minister, the people seated and bowed, or kneeling.*

BENEDICTION † *The people may remain seated for silent prayer.*

POSTLUDE

† *The offerings for this service may be received at the door as the worshipers leave.*

† *Those who find it necessary to leave the service before its close should leave during the singing of the hymns.*

An Order of Worship for Good Friday Evening

† *Let the people be in silent meditation and prayer upon entering the sanctuary.*

† *Let the service of worship begin at the time appointed.*

PRELUDE

HYMN † *The people standing.*

SCRIPTURE SENTENCES, OR CALL TO WORSHIP † *The people standing.*

Minister: God so loved the world that he gave his only Son, that whoever believes in him should not perish but have eternal life.

People: **Christ also died for sins once for all, the righteous for the unrighteous, that he might bring us to God.**

Minister: God did not spare his own Son but gave him up for us all.

People: **Greater love has no man than this, that a man lay down his life for his friends.**

INVOCATION † *By the minister, the people seated and bowed, or kneeling.*

Let us pray.

Almighty and most merciful God, whose will is that all men should be saved, and who didst give thy Son our Lord Jesus Christ to be the expiation for the sins of the whole world: We bow in adoration before thy throne and praise thee for this thine unspeakable gift. **Amen.**

ASCRIPTION † *To be said by all.*

To him who loves us and has freed us from our sins by his blood and made us a kingdom, priests to his God and Father, to him be glory and dominion for ever and ever. Worthy is the Lamb who was slain, to receive power and wealth and wisdom and might and honor and glory and blessing! Amen. *Revelation 1:5b-6; 5:12b*

ANTHEM

THE REPROACHES † *The people seated and bowed, or kneeling; the minister beginning, the people responding.*

O my people, what have I done unto thee, or wherein have I wearied thee? Testify against me. Because I brought thee forth out of the land of Egypt, thou hast prepared a cross for thy Savior.

O God, holy and mighty, have mercy upon us.

Because I led thee through the desert forty years, and fed thee with manna, and brought thee to a land exceeding good, thou has prepared a cross for thy Savior.

O God, holy and mighty, have mercy upon us.

Before thee I opened the sea: and thou hast opened my side with a spear. I went before thee in a pillar of cloud: and thou hast brought me to the judgment hall of Pilate.

O God, holy and mighty, have mercy upon us.

I fed thee with manna in the desert: and thou hast beaten me with blows and stripes. I made thee to drink the water of salvation from the rock: and thou hast made me to drink gall and vinegar.

O God, holy and mighty, have mercy upon us.

I gave thee a royal scepter: and thou hast given my head a crown of thorns. I lifted thee up with great power: and thou hast hung me upon the gibbet of the cross.

O God, holy and mighty, have mercy upon us.

THE LESSON FROM THE NEW TESTAMENT

ADORATION AT THE CROSS † *The people bowed or kneeling; the minister beginning, the people singing the responses.*

Far be it from me to glory except in the cross of our Lord Jesus Christ, by which the world has been crucified to me, and I to the world.

Galatians 6:14

> **In the cross of Christ I glory,**
> **Towering o'er the wrecks of time;**
> **All the light of sacred story**
> **Gathers round its head sublime.**

He himself bore our sins in his body on the tree.   *I Peter 2:24a*

> **O love divine, what hast thou done!**
> **The incarnate God hath died for me!**
> **The Father's coeternal Son**
> **Bore all my sins upon the tree!**
> **The Son of God for me hath died:**
> **My Lord, my love, is crucified.**

You know that you were ransomed from the futile ways inherited from your fathers, not with perishable things such as silver or gold, but with

the precious blood of Christ, like that of a lamb without blemish or
spot.   *I Peter 1:18-19*

> **O sacred Head, now wounded,**
>   **With grief and shame weighed down,**
> **Now scornfully surrounded**
>   **With thorns, thine only crown;**
> **How pale thou art with anguish,**
>   **With sore abuse and scorn!**
> **How does that visage languish**
>   **Which once was bright as morn!**

Christ also died for sins once for all, the righteous for the unrighteous,
that he might bring us to God.   *I Peter 3:18a*

> **See, from his head, his hands, his feet,**
> **Sorrow and love flow mingled down:**
> **Did e'er such love and sorrow meet,**
> **Or thorns compose so rich a crown?**

We see Jesus, who for a little while was made lower than the angels,
crowned with glory and honor because of the suffering of death.

Hebrews 2:9a

> **Ask ye what great thing I know**
> **That delights and stirs me so?**
> **What the high reward I win?**
> **Whose the name I glory in?**
>   **Jesus Christ, the Crucified.**
>
> **Who defeats my fiercest foes?**
> **Who consoles my saddest woes?**
> **Who revives my fainting heart,**
> **Healing all its hidden smart?**
>   **Jesus Christ, the Crucified.**
>
> **Who is life in life to me?**
> **Who the death of death will be?**
> **Who will place me on his right,**
> **With the countless hosts of light?**
>   **Jesus Christ, the Crucified.**

† *Here let the people stand.*

This is that great thing I know;
This delights and stirs me so:
Faith in him who died to save,
Him who triumphed o'er the grave,
Jesus Christ, the Crucified.

INTERCESSION † *To be said by all, the people seated and bowed, or kneeling.*

O merciful God, who hast made all men, and hatest nothing that thou hast made, and willest not the death of a sinner, but rather that he should be converted and live: Have mercy upon all who do not know thee, or who deny the faith of Christ crucified. Take from them all ignorance, hardness of heart, and contempt of thy Word; and so bring them home, blessed Lord, to thy fold, that we may be made one flock under one shepherd, Jesus Christ our Lord, who liveth and reigneth with thee and the Holy Spirit, one God, world without end. Amen.

THE LORD'S PRAYER

OFFERTORY

† *At the discretion of the minister, the offertory and prayers may follow the sermon.*

HYMN † *The people standing.*

THE SERMON

PRAYER † *By the minister, the people seated and bowed, or kneeling.*

AN INVITATION TO CHRISTIAN DISCIPLESHIP

HYMN † *The people standing.*

BENEDICTION † *The people may be seated for silent prayer.*

POSTLUDE

EASTERTIDE

Seven Sundays

COLOR: White

For additional materials see the section on General Aids to Worship.

EASTER DAY

Scripture Sentences or Calls to Worship

1

Christ is risen! Hallelujah!

2

But in fact Christ has been raised from the dead, the first fruits of those who have fallen asleep. *I Corinthians 15:20*

3

Break forth together into singing, you waste places of Jerusalem; for the Lord has comforted his people. *Isaiah 52:9ab*

4

Minister: The Lord is risen!

People: **The Lord is risen indeed!**

5

Minister: Blessed be the God and Father of our Lord Jesus Christ! By his great mercy we have been born anew to a living hope through the resurrection of Jesus Christ from the dead.

People: **We have an inheritance which is imperishable, undefiled, and unfading.**

Minister: Sing praises to the Lord, for he has done gloriously!

People: **Sing for joy, O heavens, and exult, O earth; for the Lord has comforted his people.**

Minister: Hallelujah! For the Lord our God the Almighty reigns. The kingdom of the world has become the kingdom of our Lord

113

and of his Christ, and he shall reign for ever and ever, King of kings and Lord of lords. Hallelujah!

People: **Thanks be to God, who gives us the victory.**

Invocations

1

Almighty, God, who through thine only Son hast overcome death, and opened unto us the gate of everlasting life: Grant, we beseech thee, that we who celebrate our Lord's resurrection may by the renewing of thy Spirit arise from the death of sin to the life of righteousness; through the same Jesus Christ our Lord. **Amen.**

2

O Thou, who makest the stars and turnest the shadow of death into the morning: On this day of days we meet to render thee, our Lord and King, the tribute of our praise: for the resurrection of the springtime, for the everlasting hopes that rise within the human heart, and for the Gospel which has brought life and immortality to light. Receive our thanksgiving, reveal thy presence, and send into our hearts the Spirit of the risen Christ. **Amen.**

Collects

1

O God, who for our redemption didst give thine only begotten Son to the death of the cross, and by his glorious resurrection hast delivered us from the power of our enemy: Grant us so to die daily to sin that we may evermore live with him in the joy of his resurrection; through Jesus Christ our Lord. **Amen.**

2

Almighty God, who hast brought again from the dead our Lord Jesus, the glorious Prince of Peace: Grant us power, we beseech thee, to rise with him to newness of life, that we may overcome the world with the wisdom of faith, and have part at last in the resurrection of the just. **Amen.**

3

O Lord God Almighty, whose blessed Son our Savior Jesus Christ did on the third day rise triumphant over death: Raise us, we beseech thee, from the death of sin unto the life of righteousness, that we may seek those things which are above, where he sitteth on thy right hand in glory; and this we pray for the sake of the same thy Son Jesus Christ our Lord. **Amen.**

SIX SUNDAYS AFTER EASTER

Scripture Sentences or Calls to Worship

1

Sing for joy, O heavens, and exult, O earth; break forth, O mountains into singing! For the Lord has comforted his people, and will have compassion on his afflicted. *Isaiah 49:13*

2

The ransomed of the Lord shall return, and come to Zion with singing, with everlasting joy upon their heads; they shall obtain joy and gladness, and sorrow and sighing shall flee away. *Isaiah 35:10*

3

We have this as a sure and steadfast anchor of the soul, a hope that enters into the inner shrine behind the curtain, where Jesus has gone as a forerunner on our behalf. *Hebrews 6:19-20a*

4

If there is a physical body, there is also a spiritual body. Just as we have borne the image of the man of dust, we shall also bear the image of the man of heaven. *I Corinthians 15:44b, 49*

5

Praise the Lord! Praise the Lord from the heavens, praise him in the heights! His glory is above earth and heaven. *Psalm 148:1, 13b*

6

If then you have been raised with Christ, seek the things that are above, where Christ is, seated at the right hand of God. *Colossians 3:1*

7

Trust in him at all times, O people; pour out your heart before him.

Psalm 62:8a

8

Set your minds on things that are above, not on things that are on earth.

Colossians 3:2

9

Where the Spirit of the Lord is, there is freedom.   *II Corinthians 3:17b*

10

Since then we have a great high priest who has passed through the heavens, Jesus the Son of God, let us hold fast our confession.

Hebrews 4:14

11

It is good to give thanks to the Lord, to sing praises to thy name, O Most High; to declare thy steadfast love in the morning, and thy faithfulness by night.   *Psalm 92:1-2*

12

Minister: There is one God and Father of us all, who is above all and through all and in you all.

People: **For all who are led by the spirit of God are sons of God.**

Minister: Come, walk in the way of the Lord with songs of gladness and joy.

People: **The Lord is near to all who call upon him, to all who call upon him in truth.**

13

Minister: O magnify the Lord with me, and let us exalt his name together!

People: **Sing praises to God, sing praises unto the Lord!**

Minister: As thy name, O God, so thy praise reaches to the ends of the earth.

People: **This is God, our God for ever and ever. He will be our guide forever.**

14

Minister: Honor and majesty are before him; strength and beauty are in his sanctuary.

People: **Let us test and examine our ways, and return to the Lord! Let us lift up our hearts and hands to God in heaven.**

Minister: Ascribe to the Lord the glory due his name; bring an offering, and come into his courts.

People: **Blessed be the Lord God of Israel, for he has visited and redeemed his people, and has raised up a horn of salvation for us.**

15

Minister: Lift up your hearts.

People: **We lift them up unto the Lord.**

Minister: Let us worship and give thanks unto him.

People: **He is the way, the truth, and the life; both now and for evermore.**

16

Minister: I was glad when they said to me, "Let us go to the house of the Lord."

People: **Let me hear what God the Lord will speak, for he will speak peace to his people.**

Minister: Peace, peace, to the far and to the near, says the Lord.

People: **Blessed are the peacemakers, for they shall be called sons of God.**

17

Minister: Since then we have a great high priest who has passed through the heavens, Jesus the Son of God,

People: **Let us with confidence draw near to the throne of grace, that we may receive mercy and find grace to help in time of need.**

Minister: Give unto the Lord glory and strength.

People: **To him who sits upon the throne and to the Lamb be blessing and honor and glory and might for ever and ever.**

Invocations

1

O God, who art the source of all true joy: Grant us a vision of our risen Lord, that we may know the peace which passeth understanding, which the world can neither give nor take away, and that pure joy which shall make radiant all our duty and our toil; through the same Jesus Christ our Lord. **Amen.**

2

O Thou who hast ordered this wondrous world, and who knowest all things in earth and heaven: So fill our hearts with trust in thee that by night and day, at all times and in all seasons, we may without fear commit all that we have and hope to be to thy never-failing love, for this life and the life to come; through Jesus Christ our Lord. **Amen.**

3

O God our Father, renew our spirits and draw our hearts to thyself, that our work may not be to us a burden but a delight; and give us such love to thee as may sweeten all our obedience. Help us that we may serve thee with the cheerfulness and gladness of children, delighting ourselves in thee and rejoicing in all that is to the honor of thy name; through Jesus Christ our Lord. **Amen.**

4

Lord of life and love, help us to worship thee in the holiness of beauty, that some beauty of holiness may appear in us. Quiet our souls in thy presence with the stillness of a wise trust. Lift us above dark moods, and the shadow of sin, that we may find thy will for our lives; through Jesus Christ our Lord. **Amen.**

5

O God, who through the grace of thy Holy Spirit dost pour the gift of love into the hearts of thy faithful people: Grant us health, both of mind and body, that we may love thee with our whole strength, and with glad hearts may perform those things which are pleasing unto thee; through Jesus Christ our Lord. **Amen.**

6

O Lord, whose wondrous birth meaneth nothing unless we be born again, whose death and sacrifice nothing unless we die unto sin, whose resurrection nothing if thou be risen alone: Raise and exalt us, O Savior, both now to the estate of grace and hereafter to the state of glory; where with the Father and the Holy Spirit thou livest and reignest, God for ever and ever. **Amen.**

7

Thou brightness of God's glory and express image of his person, whom death could not conquer nor the tomb imprison: As thou hast shared our mortal frailty in the flesh, help us to share thine immortal triumph in the spirit. Let no shadow of the grave affright us and no fear of darkness turn our hearts from thee. Reveal thyself to us this day as the first and the last, the living one, our Savior and Lord. **Amen.**

Collects

1

O God, who through the resurrection of Jesus Christ hast freed us from the power of darkness and brought us into the kingdom of thy love: Grant, we beseech thee that, as by his death he has recalled us into life, so by his abiding presence he may bring us to the joys eternal; through him who for our sakes died and rose again, and is ever with us in power, the same thy Son Jesus Christ our Lord. **Amen.**

2

O almighty God, who alone canst order the unruly wills and affections of sinful men: Grant unto thy people, that they may love the thing which thou dost command, and desire that which thou dost promise; that so, among the sundry and manifold changes of the world, our hearts may surely there be fixed, where true joys are to be found; through Jesus Christ our Lord. **Amen.**

3

Almighty God, who showest to them that are in error the light of thy truth, to the intent that they may return into the way of righteousness: Grant unto all those who are admitted into the fellowship of Christ's religion, that they may avoid those things that are contrary to their profession, and follow all such things as are agreeable to the same; through our Lord Jesus Christ. **Amen.**

4

Almighty and everlasting God, who dost govern all things in heaven and earth: Mercifully hear the supplications of thy people, and grant us thy peace all the days of our life; through Jesus Christ our Lord. **Amen.**

5

Almighty and everlasting God, who hast given us the faith of Christ for a light to our feet amid the darkness of this world: Have pity upon all who, by doubting or denying it, are gone astray from the path of safety; bring home the truth to their hearts, and grant them to receive it; through the same Jesus Christ our Lord and Savior. **Amen.**

6

O Lord Jesus Christ, who art the eternal Wisdom of the Father: We beseech thee to assist us by thy heavenly grace, that we may be blessed in our work this day, and above all things may attain the knowledge of thee, whom to know is life eternal; and that according to thy most holy example, we may ever be found going about among our fellow men, doing good, healing the sick and preaching the Gospel of the kingdom of heaven; through Jesus Christ our Lord. **Amen.**

The Emmaus Litany

An Office for Eastertide

Let us pray.

By the love with which thou didst draw near to thy disciples as they went to Emmaus and talked together of thy passion, draw near and join thyself to us, and give us a knowledge of thyself.

Hear us, blessed Lord.

By the mercy with which at first their eyes were holden that they should not know thee, be merciful to those who are slow of heart to believe.

Hear us, blessed Lord.

By the compassion with which, amid the joy of thy resurrection, thou didst seek them out who were sad, console the fainthearted who have not yet learned to rejoice in thee.

Hear us, blessed Lord.

By the patience with which, beginning at Moses, thou didst expound unto them in all the Scriptures the things concerning thyself, open thou our understanding and insight.

Hear us, our Lord and Savior.

By the fire with which thou didst make their hearts to burn within them, as thou didst talk with them by the way, opening to them the

Scriptures, inflame with devotion every heart that is not always burning with the love of thee, and consume with zeal those that thou hast kindled.

Hear us, our Lord and Savior.

By the wisdom with which thou didst make as though thou wouldest have gone farther, thus inviting them to constrain thee to tarry with them, may no soul thou desirest to bless suffer thee to depart until it hath received from thee the blessing which thou art waiting to give.

Hear us, our Lord and Savior.

By the loyalty with which thou didst go in and tarry with thy disciples when the day was far spent, fulfill in every soul that loveth thee that word of thine which saith, I will come in to him, and will sup with him, and he with me.

Hear us, Jesus Christ our Lord.

By the blessing wherewith thou didst manifest thyself to thy disciples in the breaking of bread, let every act of thine, whether of nature or of grace, be to us a Sacrament, opening the eyes of our faith, that we may know thee.

Hear us, Jesus Christ our Lord.

By the power whereby thou didst vanish out of their sight, that their faith in the mystery of thy resurrection might be increased, strengthen and confirm his faith in us.

Hear us, Jesus Christ our Lord.

O blessed Jesus, who, when the doors were shut where the disciples were assembled, didst come and stand in the midst and say, "Peace be unto you": May no fear ever place a barrier between our souls and thee, or hinder us from that peace which the world cannot give.

May the peace which thou gavest to thine apostles, sending them forth in thy Father's name as thou thyself wast sent, be also upon us, and remain with us always. Amen.

ROGATION OR RURAL LIFE SUNDAY

Fifth Sunday after Easter

Prayers

1

O Lord, from whom all good things do come: Grant to us, thy humble servants, that by thy holy inspiration we may think those things that are good, and by thy merciful guiding may perform the same; through our Lord Jesus Christ. **Amen.**

2

O God, who hast placed us as thy children in a world thou hast created for us: Give us thankful hearts as we work and as we pray. We praise thee for the day of light and life, for the night which brings rest and sleep, and for the ordered course of nature, seedtime and harvest, which thou hast given us. We bless thee that thou hast given us the joy of children, the wisdom of old men. We thank thee for all holy and humble men of heart, for the love of God and man which shines forth in commonplace lives, and above all for the vision of thyself, in loneliness and in fellowship, in Sacrament and in prayer; for these and all other benefits we praise and glorify thy name, now and for evermore. **Amen.**

ASCENSION DAY

Fortieth day after Easter

Collect

Almighty God, whose blessed Son our Savior Jesus Christ ascended far above all heavens, that he might fill all things: Mercifully give us faith to perceive that according to his promise he abideth with his Church on earth, even unto the end of the world; through the same thy Son Jesus Christ our Lord. **Amen.**

FESTIVAL OF THE CHRISTIAN HOME [1]

Second Sunday in May

For additional material see the section for Home and Kindred.

Invocation

Almighty God, our heavenly Father, who settest the solitary in families: We commend to thy continual care the homes in which thy people dwell. Put far from them, we beseech thee, every root of bitterness, the desire of vainglory, and the pride of life. Fill them with faith, virtue, knowledge, temperance, patience, godliness. Knit together in constant affection those who, in holy wedlock, have been made one. Turn the hearts of the fathers to the children, and the hearts of the children to the fathers; and so kindle charity among us all, that we may ever have for each other kindly affection and brotherly love; through Jesus Christ our Lord. **Amen.**

Collect

Most merciful Father, who hast willed that thy children should dwell in homes and families: We praise thy name for every simple sanctity of home, and all the joys of family love and comradeship. Enable us, of thy great mercy, so to open unto thee the doors of our abodes that thou thyself mayest dwell therein, and thy blessing may rest continually upon them; through Jesus Christ our Lord. **Amen.**

Prayers of Petition and Intercession

1

O God our Father, we pray thee to regard with thy lovingkindness the homes of our country, that marriage may be held in due honor, and that husbands and wives may live faithfully together, in honor preferring one another. We pray that the members of every family may be rich in mutual understanding and forbearance, in courtesy and kindness, bearing one another's burdens, and so fulfilling the law of thy blessed Son Jesus Christ our Lord. **Amen.**

[1] Sometimes in Pentecost Season.

2

O eternal God, who alone makest men to be of one mind in a house: Help us faithfully to fulfill our duties as members of our several households. Put far from us all unkind thoughts, anger and evil speaking. Give us tender hearts, full of affection and sympathy toward all. Grant us grace to feel the sorrows and trials of others as our own, and to bear patiently with their imperfections. Preserve us from selfishness, and grant that, day by day, walking in love, we may grow up into the likeness of thy blessed Son; through the same thy Son Jesus Christ our Lord. **Amen.**

CHURCH LOYALTY SUNDAY [2]

Invocation

Almighty God, giver of every good and perfect gift: Teach us to render unto thee all that we have and all that we are, that we may praise thee, not with our lips only, but with our whole lives, turning the duties, the sorrows, and the joys of all our days into a living sacrifice unto thee; through Jesus Christ our Lord. **Amen.**

Collect

Almighty and everlasting God, by whose mercy we come to this high hour in the life of the Church: Regard us with thy favor, and further us with thy continual help, as with devoted minds we consecrate our fellowship of faith to thee and thy kingdom; through Jesus Christ our Lord. **Amen.**

Prayers of Petition and Intercession

1

Almighty God, grant us thy gift of loyalty. For our homes give us love and obedience; for our country, sacrifice and service; for our church, reverence and devotion; and in everything make us true to thee; through thy Son our Savior Jesus Christ our Lord. **Amen.**

---

[2] Sometimes at another season.

2

O God, who in thine infinite love didst send thy Son to bring light to all that are in darkness: Fill us with thine own love for men; and, since thou hast entrusted to us both the knowledge of thy truth and the gifts of thy bounty, help us in all things to be good stewards; through Jesus Christ our Lord. **Amen.**

PENTECOST SEASON

Eleven to Sixteen Sundays

COLOR: Red

For additional materials see the section on General Aids to Worship.

PENTECOST OR WHITSUNDAY

Scripture Sentences or Calls to Worship

1

And it shall come to pass afterward, that I will pour out my spirit on all flesh; your sons and your daughters shall prophesy, your old men shall dream dreams, and your young men shall see visions.   *Joel 2:28*

2

God did not give us a spirit of timidity but a spirit of power and love and self-control.   *II Timothy 1:7*

3

God's love has been poured into our hearts through the Holy Spirit which has been given to us.   *Romans 5:5b*

4

Minister: And in the last days it shall come to pass, God declares, that I will pour out my Spirit on all flesh,

People: **And your sons and your daughters shall prophesy, and your young men shall see visions, and your old men shall dream dreams.**

Minister: When the day of Pentecost had come, they were all gathered together in one place.

People: **And suddenly a sound came from heaven like the rush of a mighty wind, and it filled all the house where they were sitting.**

Minister: And there appeared unto them tongues as of fire, distributed and resting on each of them,

People: **And they were all filled with the Holy Spirit.**

5

Minister: You shall receive power when the Holy Spirit has come upon you; and you shall be my witnesses,

People: **In Jerusalem and in all Judea and Samaria and to the end of the earth.**

Minister: And they were all filled with the Holy Spirit

People: **And spoke the word of God with boldness.**

6

Minister: Now the Lord is the Spirit,

People: **And where the spirit of the Lord is, there is freedom.**

Invocations

1

Grant, we beseech thee, merciful God, that thy Church, being gathered together in unity by thy Holy Spirit, may manifest thy power among all peoples, to the glory of thy name; through Jesus Christ our Lord, who liveth and reigneth with thee and the same Spirit, one God, world without end. **Amen.**

2

O eternal God, the Father of spirits and the lover of souls, who didst send thy Holy Spirit upon thy Church on the day of Pentecost, and hast promised that he shall abide with it forever: Let that same Spirit lead us into all truth, defend us from all sin, enrich us with his gifts, refresh us with his comfort, rule our hearts in all things, and lead us in the way everlasting; through Jesus Christ our Lord, who with thee and the same Spirit liveth and reigneth, one God, world without end. **Amen.**

Collects

1

O God, who at this time didst teach the hearts of thy faithful people, by sending them the light of thy Holy Spirit: Grant us by the same Spirit to have a right judgment in all things, and evermore to rejoice in his holy comfort; through the merits of Christ Jesus our Savior, who liveth and reigneth with thee, in the unity of the same Spirit, one God, world without end. **Amen.**

2

O God, who at this time didst send down thy Holy Spirit from above upon thine apostles, and dost evermore send him to renew thine image in our souls: Mercifully grant that by the working of his grace we may be saved from sin and may glorify thee; through the merits and mediation of thy Son our Savior Jesus Christ, who liveth and reigneth with thee in the unity of the same Spirit, one God, world without end. **Amen.**

3

O God, who in the exaltation of thy Son Jesus Christ dost sanctify thy universal Church: Shed abroad in every race and nation the gift of his Spirit, that the work wrought by his power at the first preaching of the Gospel may be extended throughout the whole world; through the same our Lord Jesus Christ, who liveth and reigneth with thee in the unity of the same Spirit now and ever. **Amen.**

4

O God, the protector of all that trust in thee, without whom nothing is strong, nothing is holy: Increase and multiply upon us thy mercy, that, thou being our ruler and guide, we may so pass through things temporal that we finally lose not the things eternal. Grant this, O heavenly Father, for the sake of Jesus Christ our Lord. **Amen.**

Prayers of Petition and Intercession

1

We beseech thee, O Lord, to remember thine holy Church on earth: teach us to love thy house above all dwellings; thy Scriptures above all books; thy Sacraments above all gifts; the communion of saints above all company; and grant that, as one family, we may give thanks and adore thy glorious name; through Jesus Christ our Lord. **Amen.**

2

O God, who didst send the Holy Spirit to enkindle the zeal of Christ's followers waiting in Jerusalem for his promised gift: We beseech thee to pour the same inspiration on thy people here assembled, and on the

Church of Christ throughout the world. Revive the power of the Gospel in our hearts, that it may be to us a sacred trust for the blessing of mankind. Enable thy Church to spread the good news of salvation, so that all nations may hear it in their own tongue, and welcome it into their own life. Protect, encourage, and bless all missionaries of the cross, and prosper their word and work, so that Jesus, being lifted up, may draw all men unto him, and the kingdoms of the world may become the kingdom of our Lord and of his Christ. **Amen.**

3

Almighty God our heavenly Father, send, we beseech thee, thy Holy Spirit into our hearts, that we may be directed and controlled according to thy will, led into all truth, defended from all sin, and enriched in all grace; through Jesus Christ our Lord. **Amen.**

A Canticle for Pentecost

VENI, CREATOR SPIRITUS

Come, Holy Ghost, our souls inspire,
 And lighten with celestial fire.
Thou the anointing Spirit art,
 Who dost thy sevenfold gifts impart.
Thy blessed unction from above
 Is comfort, life, and fire of love.
Enable with perpetual light
 The dullness of our blinded sight.
Anoint and cheer our soilèd face
 With the abundance of thy grace.
Keep far our foes, give peace at home;
 Where thou art guide, no ill can come.
Teach us to know the Father, Son,
 And thee, of both to be but One;
That through the ages all along,
 This may be our endless song:
Praise to thy eternal merit,
 Father, Son, and Holy Spirit. Amen.

TRINITY SUNDAY

First Sunday After Pentecost

COLOR: White

Scripture Sentences or Calls to Worship

1

Canst thou by searching find out God? Canst thou find out the Almighty unto perfection? *Job 11:7 KJV*

2

No man has ever seen God; if we love one another, God abides in us and his love is perfected in us. *I John 4:12*

3

God is love, and he who abides in love abides in God, and God abides in him. *I John 4:16*

4

Minister: Enter his gates with thanksgiving, and his courts with praise!

People: **Give thanks to him, bless his name! For the Lord is good.**

Minister: Know that the Lord is, God! It is he that made us and we are his.

People: **We are his people and the sheep of his pasture.**

5

Minister: Worship the Lord in holy array: tremble before him, all the earth.

People: **Holy, holy, holy is the Lord of hosts; the whole earth is full of his glory.**

Minister: Holy, holy, holy is the Lord God Almighty, who was and is and is to come.

People: **O Lord God, great and mighty is thy name, and to thee we ascribe all honor and glory, Father, Son, and Holy Spirit.**

Invocations

1

Almighty God, whose glory the heavens are telling, whose power the earth and sea declare, and whose greatness is revealed in all feeling and thinking creatures everywhere: To thee belong glory, honor, dominion, and power, now and forever, world without end. **Amen.**

2

Almighty and everlasting God, thou lover of peace and concord, who hast called us in Christ to love and unity: We pray thee so to rule our hearts by thy Holy Spirit that we, being delivered by the true fear of God from all fear of man, may evermore serve thee in righteousness, mercy, humility, and gentleness toward each other; through thy dear Son Jesus Christ our Lord. **Amen.**

Collects

1

Almighty and everlasting God, who hast given unto us thy servants grace, by the confession of a true faith, to acknowledge the glory of the eternal Trinity, and in the power of the divine majesty to worship the unity: We beseech thee to keep us steadfast in this faith, and evermore defend us from all adversities; who livest and reignest, one God, world without end. **Amen.**

2

Almighty and everlasting God, who hast revealed thyself as Father, Son, and Holy Spirit, and dost ever live and reign in the perfect unity of love: Grant that we may always hold firmly and joyfully to this faith, and, living in praise of thy divine majesty, may finally be one in thee; who art three persons in one God, world without end. **Amen.**

Prayers of Petition and Intercession

1

O Thou in whose hand are the hearts of thy creatures, shed abroad thy peace upon the world. By the might of thy Holy Spirit quench the pride, anger, and greediness which cause man to strive against man, and people against people. Lead all nations in the ways of mutual help and good will, and hasten the time when the earth shall confess thee indeed for its Savior and King; through Jesus Christ our Lord. **Amen.**

2

O most Holy Spirit, give thy strength unto all who are tried by any special temptation. Help them to stand fast in thee, that they may be able to bear it; for the sake of Jesus Christ our Lord and Savior. **Amen.**

3

O merciful God, bless thy Church throughout all the world, and all those who love thee in sincerity, although they follow not with us in all things. Heal all strife, divisions, and discord, and make us all thine in willing devotion as we are all thine by redemption and grace; through Jesus Christ our Lord. **Amen.**

4

O God most high, the only ruler: Grant, we beseech thee, to all who rule over us the inspiration of thy Holy Spirit, that as they labor faithfully for our country, they may also advance thy kingdom upon earth; through Jesus Christ our Lord. **Amen.**

SUNDAYS AFTER PENTECOST

COLOR: Red

Scripture Sentences or Calls to Worship

1

But the hour is coming, and now is, when the true worshipers will worship the Father in spirit and truth, for such the Father seeks to worship him. God is spirit, and those who worship him must worship in spirit and truth.   *John 4:23-24*

2

By this we know that we abide in him and he in us, because he has given us of his own Spirit.   *I John 4:13*

3

The wind blows where it wills, and you hear the sound of it, but you do not know whence it comes or whither it goes; so it is with every one who is born of the Spirit.   *John 3:8*

4

God's love has been poured into our hearts through the Holy Spirit which has been given to us.
Romans 5:5b

5

Then he said to his disciples, "The harvest is plentiful, but the laborers are few; pray therefore the Lord of the harvest to send out laborers into his harvest."
Matthew 9:37-38

6

I tell you, many will come from east and west and sit at table with Abraham, Isaac, and Jacob in the kingdom of heaven.
Matthew 8:11

7

The steadfast love of the Lord never ceases, his mercies never come to an end; they are new every morning; great is thy faithfulness. "The Lord is my portion," says my soul, "therefore I will hope in him."
Lamentations 3:22-24

8

Whither shall I go from thy Spirit? Or whither shall I flee from thy presence? If I ascend to heaven, thou art there! If I make my bed in Sheol, thou art there! If I take the wings of the morning and dwell in the uttermost parts of the sea, even there thy hand shall lead me, and thy right hand shall hold me.
Psalm 139:7-10

9

Agree with God, and be at peace; thereby good will come to you. Then you will delight yourself in the Almighty, and lift up your face to God.
Job 22:21, 26

10

It is the spirit that gives life, the flesh is of no avail; the words that I have spoken to you are spirit and life.
John 6:63

11

Do not be deceived; God is not mocked, for whatever a man sows, that he will also reap. For he who sows to his own flesh will from the flesh reap corruption; but he who sows to the Spirit will from the Spirit reap eternal life.
Galatians 6:7-8

12

Minister: Come and see what God has done.

People: **His work is honorable and glorious, and his righteousness endureth forever.**

Minister: Let us test and examine our ways, and return to the Lord!

People: **Let us lift up our hearts and hands to God in heaven.**

13

Minister: I will bless the Lord at all times; his praise shall continually be in my mouth. My soul makes its boast in the Lord; let the afflicted hear and be glad. O magnify the Lord with me, and let us exalt his name together!

People: **For with him is the fountain of life; in his light do we see light.**

14

Minister: This is the day which the Lord has made; let us rejoice and be glad in it.

People: **This is none other than the house of God and this is the gate of heaven.**

Minister: The hour is coming, and now is, when the true worshipers will worship the Father in spirit and truth, for such the Father seeks to worship him.

People: **Enter his gates with thanksgiving, and his courts with praise! Give thanks to him, bless his name!**

15

Minister: God is light and in him is no darkness at all.

People: **If we walk in the light, as he is in the light, we have fellowship with one another.**

Minister: O magnify the Lord with me, and let us exalt his name together!

People: **For with thee is the fountain of life; in thy light do we see light.**

16

Minister: In the midst of the congregation I will praise thee.

People: **Rejoice in the Lord, O you righteous, and give thanks to his holy name!**

Minister: I will extol thee, my God and King, and bless thy name for ever and ever.

People: **Great is the Lord, and greatly to be praised, and his greatness is unsearchable.**

17

Minister: The Lord reigns; let the earth rejoice.

People: **I will be glad and exult in thee, I will sing praise to thy name, O Most High.**

Minister: Thine, O Lord, is the greatness, and the power, and the glory, and the victory, and the majesty; for all that is in the heavens and in the earth is thine; thine is the kingdom, O Lord, and thou art exalted as head above all.

People: **Because thy steadfast love is better than life, my lips will praise thee.**

18

Minister: It is good to give thanks to the Lord, to sing praises to thy name, O Most High;

People: **To declare thy steadfast love in the morning, and thy faithfulness by night.**

Minister: Bless our God, O peoples, let the sound of his praise be heard.

People: **My lips will shout for joy, when I sing praises to thee; my soul also, which thou hast rescued.**

19

Minister: The Lord is in his holy temple;

People: **Let all the earth keep silence before him.**

Minister: O come, let us worship and bow down.

People: **Let us kneel before the Lord, our maker!**

20

Minister: Let us thank the Lord for his steadfast love, for his wonderful works to the sons of men!

People: **The Lord is good to all, and his compassion is over all that he has made.**

Minister: Blessed be the Lord, the God of Israel, who alone does wondrous things.

People: **Blessed be his glorious name for ever; may his glory fill the whole earth!**

21

Minister: May those who love thy salvation say continually, "Great is the Lord!"

People: **Yea, our heart is glad in him, because we trust in his holy name.**

Minister: Let us make a joyful noise to him with songs of praise!

People: **We praise thee, O God; we acknowledge thee to be the Lord.**

22

Minister: The Lord is near to all who call upon him, to all who call upon him in truth.

People: **O Thou who hearest prayer! To thee shall all flesh come on account of sins.**

Invocations

1

Our heavenly Father, we thy humble children invoke thy blessing upon us in this hour of worship. We adore thee, whose name is love, whose nature is compassion, whose presence is joy, whose Word is truth, whose spirit is goodness, whose holiness is beauty, whose will is peace, whose service is perfect freedom, and in knowledge of whom standeth our eternal life. Unto thee be all honor and all glory; through Jesus Christ our Lord. **Amen.**

2

Almighty and everlasting God, in whom we live and move and have our being, who hast created us for thyself, so that our hearts are restless until they find rest in thee: Grant unto us such purity of heart and strength of purpose, that no selfish passion may hinder us from knowing thy will, and no weakness from doing it. In thy light may we see life clearly, and in thy service find perfect freedom; through Jesus Christ our Lord. **Amen.**

3

O Thou eternal God, speak to each of us the word that we need, and let thy word abide with us until it hath wrought in us thy holy will. Cleanse, quicken, and refresh our hearts; direct and increase our faith; and grant that we, by our worship at this time, may be enabled to see thee more clearly, to love thee more fully, and to serve thee more perfectly; through Jesus Christ our Lord. **Amen.**

4

O Lord our God, great, eternal, wonderful in glory, who keepest covenant and promise for those that love thee with their whole hearts, who art the life of all, the help of those who flee unto thee, the hope of those who cry unto thee: Cleanse us from our sins, and from every thought displeasing to thy goodness, that with a pure heart and a clean mind, with perfect love and calm hope, we may venture confidently and fearlessly to pray unto thee; through Jesus Christ our Lord. **Amen.**

5

Almighty and everlasting God, who hast built thy Church upon the foundation of the apostles and prophets, Jesus Christ himself being the chief cornerstone: We pray thee to inspire the Church universal with the spirit of truth, unity, and concord; and grant that all who confess thy holy name may abide in thy truth and live in unity and godly love; through Jesus Christ our Lord. **Amen.**

6

O God, author of eternal light, do thou shed forth continual day upon us who watch for thee; that our lips may praise thee, our lives may bless thee, and our meditations may glorify thee; through Christ our Lord. **Amen.**

7

O Lord our God, who art always more ready to bestow thy good gifts upon us than we are to seek them, and art willing to give more than we desire or deserve: Help us so to seek that we may truly find, so to ask that we may joyfully receive, so to knock that the door of thy mercy may be opened unto us; through Jesus Christ our Lord. **Amen.**

8

O Lord, our heavenly Father, at the beginning of another week we come to thee for help and light. Grant, we beseech thee, that we may hallow this day of rest to thy service, and find in thee all peace and strength. Quicken our devotion that we may serve thee in spirit and in truth, and lay a good foundation for our coming work. Be with us in all the public services of thy day, that we may join in them with heart and soul, and receive the blessing which thou hast promised to all who sincerely pray to thee and faithfully hear thy Word. This we ask for the sake of Jesus Christ our Lord. **Amen.**

9

O God, who givest us not only the day for labor and the night for rest, but also the peace of this blessed day: Grant, we beseech thee, that its quiet may be profitable to us in heavenly things, and refresh and strengthen us to finish the work which thou hast given us to do; through Jesus Christ our Lord. **Amen.**

Collects

1

O God, the strength of all those who put their trust in thee: Mercifully accept our prayers; and because, through the weakness of our mortal nature, we can do no good thing without thee, grant us the help of thy grace, that in keeping thy commandments we may please thee, both in will and deed; through Jesus Christ our Lord. **Amen.**

2

O Lord, who never failest to help and govern those whom thou dost bring up in thy steadfast fear and love: Keep us, we beseech thee, under the protection of thy good providence, and make us to have a perpetual fear and love of thy holy name; through Jesus Christ our Lord. **Amen.**

3

O Lord, we beseech thee mercifully to hear us; and grant that we, to whom thou hast given a hearty desire to pray, may by thy mighty aid be defended and comforted in all dangers and adversities; through Jesus Christ our Lord. **Amen.**

4

Grant, O Lord, we beseech thee, that the course of this world may be so peaceably ordered by thy governance, that the Church may joyfully serve thee in all godly quietness; through Jesus Christ our Lord. **Amen.**

5

O God, who hast prepared for those who love thee such good things as pass man's understanding: Pour into our hearts such love toward thee, that we, loving thee above all things, may obtain thy promises, which exceed all that we can desire; through Jesus Christ our Lord. **Amen.**

6

Lord of all power and might, who art the author and giver of all good things: Graft in our hearts the love of thy name, increase in us true religion, nourish us with all goodness, and of thy great mercy keep us in the same; through Jesus Christ our Lord. **Amen.**

7

O God, whose never-failing providence ordereth all things both in heaven and earth: We humbly beseech thee to put away from us all hurtful things, and to give us those things which are profitable for us; through Jesus Christ our Lord. **Amen.**

8

Grant to us, Lord, we beseech thee, the spirit to think and do always such things as are right; that we, who cannot do anything that is good without thee, may by thee be enabled to live according to thy will; through Jesus Christ our Lord. **Amen.**

9

Let thy merciful ears, O Lord, be open to the prayers of thy humble servants; and, that they may obtain their petitions, make them to ask such things as shall please thee; through Jesus Christ our Lord. **Amen.**

10

O God, who declarest thy almighty power chiefly in showing mercy and pity: Mercifully grant unto us such a measure of thy grace, that we, running the way of thy commandments, may obtain thy gracious promises, and be made partakers of thy heavenly treasure; through Jesus Christ our Lord. **Amen.**

11

Almighty and everlasting God, who art always more ready to hear than we to pray, and art wont to give more than either we desire or deserve: Pour down upon us the abundance of thy mercy, forgiving us those things whereof our conscience is afraid, and giving us those good things which we are not worthy to ask, but through the merits and mediation of Jesus Christ thy Son our Lord. **Amen.**

12

Almighty and merciful God, of whose only gift it cometh that thy faithful people do unto thee true and laudable service: Grant, we beseech thee, that we may so faithfully serve thee in this life that we fail not finally to attain thy heavenly promise; through the merits of Jesus Christ our Lord. **Amen.**

13

Almighty and everlasting God, give unto us the increase of faith, hope, and charity; and, that we may obtain that which thou dost promise, make us to love that which thou dost command; through Jesus Christ our Lord. **Amen.**

14

Keep, we beseech thee, O Lord, thy Church with thy perpetual mercy; and because the frailty of man without thee cannot but fall, keep us ever by thy help from all things hurtful, and lead us to all things profitable to our salvation; through Jesus Christ our Lord. **Amen.**

15

O Lord, we beseech thee, let thy continual pity cleanse and defend thy Church; and, because it cannot continue in safety without thy succor, preserve it evermore by thy help and goodness; through Jesus Christ our Lord. **Amen.**

16

O God, who hast taught us to keep all thy heavenly commandments by loving thee and our neighbor: Grant us the spirit of peace and grace, that we may be both devoted to thee with our whole heart and united to each other with a pure will; through Jesus Christ our Lord. **Amen.**

17

O Lord our God, grant us grace to desire thee with our whole heart, that desiring thee we may find thee, and finding thee we may love thee, and loving thee we may rejoice in thee forever; through Jesus Christ our Lord. **Amen.**

18

O God, who art a hiding place from the wind and a shelter from the storm: Help us to turn from the tumult and clamor of the world to the calm of thy great assurance; through Jesus Christ our Lord. **Amen.**

Prayers of Petition and Intercession

1

Most merciful Father, we beseech thee to send thy heavenly blessings upon this thy Church, that all its members may dwell together in unity and brotherly love. Keep far from us all self-will and discord. Endue thy ministers with righteousness, and enable them faithfully to fulfill their ministry, to bring again the outcasts, and to seek the lost. And grant to us so to receive their ministrations, and to use thy means of grace, that in all our words and deeds we may seek thy glory and the advancement of thy kingdom; through Jesus Christ our Lord. **Amen.**

2

O Thou eternal, in whose appointment our life standeth, and who hast committed our work to us, we would commit our cares to thee. We thank thee that we are thy children, and that thou hast assured us that, while we are intent upon thy will, thou wilt heed our wants. More and more fill us with that compassion for others' troubles which comes from forgetfulness of our own; with the charity of them that know their own unworthiness; and the glad hope of the children of eternity. And unto thee, the beginning and the end, Lord of the living, refuge of the dying, be thanks and praise for ever. **Amen.**

3

O Thou almighty one, who art the one God and Father of all, who hast breathed thine own Spirit into thy children, and made them to be members of one family: We bring to thee, in our common prayer, the burdens of each who bows with us, and of all, throughout the world, who stand in need of thy succor and grace. Give us love above all gifts, that we may be delivered from all blindness and prejudice, and from whatever else would turn over hearts from one another and from thee. Fill us with that most excellent grace of charity, which suffereth long and is kind, which thinketh no evil, but only good. And create in our hearts, we beseech thee, such a sincere love of one another, that we may be children of our Father in heaven and true followers of Christ our Lord. **Amen.**

4

Almighty Father, we beseech thee to hear us, as we pray for the friendless and the lonely, the tempted and the unbelieving. Be merciful to those who suffer, in body or in mind, to those who are in danger or distress, and who have suffered loss. Let thy love surround the infirm and the aged. Be especially near to those who are passing through the valley of death. May they find eternal rest, and light at evening time; through Jesus Christ our Lord. **Amen.**

5

O Lord God, who dwellest on high and yet delightest to have thy habitation in the hearts of men; and who hast built thy Church as a city upon a hill, and hast founded it upon the apostles and prophets, Jesus Christ being the chief cornerstone: Make us to be a spiritual building fit for the indwelling of thy Holy Spirit, grounding us in faith, building us up in hope, and perfecting us in charity, that we, joined in union with the Church militant on earth, may enter into thy Church triumphant in heaven; through Jesus Christ our Lord. **Amen.**

6

God of all comfort, we commend to thy mercy all those upon whom any cross or tribulation is laid; the nations who are afflicted with famine, pestilence, or war; those of our brethren who suffer persecution for the sake of the Gospel; all such as are in danger by sea or land; and all persons oppressed with poverty, sickness, or any infirmity of body or sorrow of mind. We pray particularly for the sick and afflicted members of this church, and for those who desire to be remembered in our prayers (and for any such known only to ourselves, whom we name in our hearts before thee). May it please thee to show them thy fatherly kindness in the midst of affliction, that their hearts may turn unto thee, and receive perfect consolation and healing, and deliverance from their troubles; for Christ's sake. **Amen.**

7

Almighty Father, who art afflicted in the afflictions of thy people and art full of compassion and tender mercy, hear us as we pray for those who suffer:

For all who are handicapped in the race of life through no fault of their own; for the defective and the delicate; and all who are permanently injured;

For those whose livelihood is insecure; the overworked, the hungry, and the destitute; for those who have been downtrodden, ruined, and driven to despair;

For little children, whose surroundings hide from them thy love and beauty; for all the fatherless and motherless;

For those who have to bear their burdens alone, and for all who have lost those whom they love;

For those who are in doubt and anguish of soul; for those who are oversensitive and afraid;

For those whose suffering is unrelieved by the knowledge of thy love;

For those who suffer through their own wrongdoing.

Set free, O Lord, the souls of thy servants from all restlessness and anxiety; give us that peace and power which flow from thee; and keep us in all perplexities and distresses, in all griefs and grievances, from any fear or faithlessness; that, being upheld by thy strength and stayed on the rock of thy faithfulness, through storm and stress we may abide in thee. **Amen.**

MEMORIAL DAY

Prayers of Petition and Intercession

1

O God, our heavenly Father, we bless thee again for the remembrance of this day, when, by thy providence, and by the might of thine arm, thou madest wars to cease; accept our praise and thanksgiving. As on this day we remember before thee all those who fought and died that we might live, accept our gratitude, and make us, we humbly beseech thee, more worthy of their sacrifice even unto death, and help us to follow more closely in the steps of thy blessed Son, that at last we with them may stand in thy presence; to whom all praise, thanksgiving, honor, and power be ascribed, world without end. **Amen.**

2

We bless thy holy name, O God, for all thy servants who, having finished their course, do now rest from their labors. Give us grace, we beseech thee, to follow the example of their steadfastness and faithfulness, to thy honor and glory; through Christ Jesus our Lord. **Amen.**

3

In remembrance of those who made the great sacrifice, O God, make us better men and women, and give peace in our time; through Jesus Christ thy Son our Savior. **Amen.**

4

O eternal Lord God, who holdest all souls in life: Vouchsafe, to thy whole Church in heaven and on earth, thy light and thy peace; and grant that we, following the good examples of those who have served thee here and are now at rest, may at the last enter with them into thine unending joy; through Jesus Christ our Lord. **Amen.**

A Litany for Memorial Day

O God the Father, almighty and everlasting, from whom we have come and unto whom we go,

> **have mercy upon us.**

O God the Son, captain of the souls of men, who hast brought life and immortality to light,

> **have mercy upon us.**

O God the Holy Spirit, the comforter, who dost take of the things of Christ and show them unto men,

> **have mercy upon us.**

Let us give thanks unto God:

For the land of our birth with all its chartered liberties, for all the wonder of our country's story,

> **we praise thee, O God.**

144

For leaders in nation and state, and those who in days past and in these present times have labored for the commonwealth,

we praise thee, O God.

For those who in all times and places have been true and brave, and in the world's common ways have lived upright lives and ministered to their fellows,

we praise thee, O God.

For those who served their country in her hour of need, and especially those who gave even their lives,

we praise thee, O God.

O almighty God and most merciful Father, whose nature and whose name is love, as we give thee thanks for the courage and the strength vouchsafed to these thy servants, we would remember before thee those who mourn them as their kindred. Look in mercy upon them; and as this day brings them memories of those whom they have lost, may it also bring them consolations from thee, quickening in them the sense of communion with the world unseen, and confirming their assurance of that great day when thou shalt restore to them their own in the very presence of our Lord and Savior Jesus Christ. **Amen.**

STUDENT DAY

Second Sunday in June

Scripture Sentences or Call to Worship

Minister: One thing have I asked of the Lord, that will I seek after; to behold the beauty of the Lord, and to inquire in his temple.

People: **Send out thy light and thy truth; let them lead me, let them bring me to thy holy hill.**

Minister: Let us worship the Lord in holy array.

People: **Let us worship him in spirit and truth.**

Invocation

O Christ, to whom all authority is given both in heaven and earth: Transform our wills and our understanding, cleanse our hearts and enlighten our minds; that, our thoughts and desires being made obedient to thy pure and holy law, we may grow up in all things unto thee, and present ourselves a living sacrifice, to the praise and glory of thy name, who livest and reignest with the Father and the Holy Spirit, now and ever. **Amen.**

Collect

Eternal God, the light of the minds that know thee, the joy of the hearts that love thee, and the strength of the wills that serve thee: Grant us so to know thee that we may truly love thee, and so to love thee that we may fully serve thee, to the honor and glory of thy holy name. **Amen.**

Prayers of Petition and Intercession

1

O Thou only wise God, in whom are all the treasures of wisdom and knowledge: We beseech thee to illumine all universities, colleges, and schools with the light that cometh from above, that those who teach may be taught of thee, and those who learn may be led by thy Spirit; and that by the increase of knowledge thy truth may be confirmed, and thy glory manifested; through Jesus Christ the living Word. **Amen.**

2

O God, who didst reveal thy Son Jesus Christ to wise men of old: Grant us to welcome the revelation of wisdom and science through which in our own day thou dost make thy works known among men. Reveal thyself again to men of learning, that through their work the world may come to know thee anew, and may offer new gifts and treasures to the glory of thy name, who art evermore revealed in thy Son Jesus Christ our Lord. **Amen.**

INDEPENDENCE DAY

Scripture Sentences or Call to Worship

Minister: Blessed is the nation whose God is the Lord, and the people whom he has chosen as his heritage!

People: **Righteousness exalts a nation, but sin is a reproach to any people.**

Minister: You shall bless the Lord your God for the good land he has given you.

People: **Our soul waits for the Lord; he is our help and shield.**

Invocation

Be gracious unto us, O Lord, and bless us. Stretch forth the right hand of thy protection to guard our country, that we, being devoted to thy service, may ever be defended by thy power; through Jesus Christ our Lord. **Amen.**

Collect

Almighty God, ruler of all the peoples of the earth: Forgive, we beseech thee, our shortcomings as a nation; purify our hearts to see and love the truth; give wisdom to our counselors and steadfastness to our people; and bring us at last to that fair city of peace whose foundations are mercy, justice, and good will, and whose builder and maker thou art; through Jesus Christ our Lord. **Amen.**

Prayer of Petition and Intercession

Almighty God, who hast given us this good land for our heritage: We humbly beseech thee that we may always prove ourselves a people mindful of thy favor and glad to do thy will. Bless our land with honorable industry, sound learning, and pure manners. Save us from violence, discord, and confusion, from pride and arrogance, and from every evil way. Defend our liberties, and fashion into one united people the multitudes brought hither out of many kindreds and tongues. Endue with the spirit of wisdom those to whom in thy name we entrust the authority of government, that there may be justice and peace at home, and that through obedience to thy law, we may show forth thy praise among the nations of the earth. In the time of prosperity, fill our hearts with thankfulness, and in the day of trouble, suffer not our trust in thee to fail; all which we ask through Jesus Christ our Lord. **Amen.**

KINGDOMTIDE

Thirteen or fourteen Sundays, beginning with the last Sunday in August

COLOR: Green

For additional materials see the section on General Aids to Worship.

Scripture Sentences or Calls to Worship

1

O sing to the Lord a new song; sing to the Lord, all the earth: for he comes, for he comes to judge the earth. He will judge the world with righteousness, and the peoples with his truth.   *Psalm 96:1, 13*

2

Thus says the Lord: "Let not the wise man glory in his wisdom, let not the mighty man glory in his might, let not the rich man glory in his riches; but let him who glories glory in this, that he understands and knows me, that I am the Lord who practice kindness, justice, and righteousness in the earth; for in these things I delight, says the Lord."

Jeremiah 9:23-24

3

Let justice roll down like waters, and righteousness like an everflowing stream.   *Amos 5:24*

4

Choose this day whom you will serve; but as for me and my house, we will serve the Lord.   *From Joshua 24:15*

5

The Lord our God we will serve, and his voice we will obey.

Joshua 24:24

6

The kingdom of God does not mean food and drink but righteousness and peace and joy in the Holy Spirit.   *Romans 14:17*

7

Blessed are those who hunger and thirst for righteousness, for they shall be satisfied.   *Matthew 5:6*

8

Behold, all souls are mine; the soul of the father as well as the soul of the son is mine.   *Ezekiel 18:4*

9

All thy works shall give thanks to thee, O Lord, and all thy saints shall bless thee! They shall speak of the glory of thy kingdom, and tell of thy power.   *Psalm 145:10-11*

10

Therefore, since we are surrounded by so great a cloud of witnesses, let us also lay aside every weight, and sin which clings so closely, and let us run with perseverance the race that is set before us.   *Hebrews 12:1*

11

Those who are wise shall shine like the brightness of the firmament; and those who turn many to righteousness, like the stars for ever and ever.   *Daniel 12:3*

12

The earth is the Lord's and the fulness thereof, the world and those who dwell therein.   *Psalm 24:1*

13

Let them thank the Lord for his steadfast love, for his wonderful works to the sons of men!   *Psalm 107:8*

14

Thou crownest the year with thy bounty. The pastures of the wilderness drip, the valleys deck themselves with grain, they shout and sing together for joy.   *Psalm 65:11a, 12a, 13bc*

15

I will send down the showers in their season; they shall be showers of blessing. And the trees of the field shall yield their fruit, and the earth shall yield its increase, and they shall be secure in their land; and they shall know that I am the Lord.   *Ezekiel 34:26b-27a*

16

Minister: Make a joyful noise to the Lord, all the lands! Serve the Lord with gladness! Come into his presence with singing!

People: **Know that the Lord is God! It is he that made us, and we are his; we are his people, and the sheep of his pasture.**

Minister: Enter his gates with thanksgiving, and his courts with praise! Give thanks to him and bless his name!

People: **For the Lord is good; his steadfast love endures for ever, and his faithfulness to all generations.**

17

Minister: Let us test and examine our ways, and return to the Lord!

People: **Let us lift up our hearts to God.**

Minister: With what shall I come before the Lord, and bow myself before God on high?

People: **He has showed you, O man, what is good; and what does the Lord require of you but to do justice, and to love kindness, and to walk humbly with your God?**

18

Minister: Behold, I stand at the door and knock; if anyone hears my voice and opens the door, I will come in.

People: **Come to me, all who labor and are heavy-laden, and I will give you rest.**

Minister: The hour is coming, and now is, when the true worshipers will worship the Father in spirit and truth.

People: **For such the Father seeks to worship him.**

19

Minister: Blessed be the name of God for ever and ever, to whom belong wisdom and might.

People: **He gives wisdom to the wise and knowledge to those who have understanding.**

Minister: Seek the Lord while he may be found, call upon him while he is near.

People: **Great is the Lord, and greatly to be praised.**

20

Minister: Trust in the Lord.

People: **The Lord God is an everlasting rock.**

Minister: Worship the Lord in holy array.

People: **Blessed be God, because he has not rejected our prayer or removed his steadfast love from us!**

21

Minister: Trust in the Lord, and do good.

People: **May the Lord give strength to his people!**

Minister: O taste and see that the Lord is good!

People: **God is our refuge and strength.**

Invocations

1

Great art thou, O Lord, and greatly to be praised; great is thy power and thy wisdom is infinite. Thee would we praise without ceasing. Thou callest us to delight in thy praise, for thou hast made us for thyself, and our hearts are restless till they rest in thee; to whom with the Son and the Holy Ghost all glory, praise, and honor be ascribed both now and evermore. **Amen.**

2

Almighty God, from whom all thoughts of truth and peace proceed: Kindle, we pray thee, in the hearts of all men the true love of peace, and guide with thy pure and peaceable wisdom those who take counsel for the nations of the earth, that in tranquillity thy kingdom may grow, till the earth is filled with the knowledge of thy love; through Jesus Christ our Lord. **Amen.**

3

We give thee humble thanks, most merciful Father, that thou dost graciously hear the prayers of thy servants who call upon thee, and hast done for us great things whereof we rejoice; through Jesus Christ our Lord. **Amen.**

4

Almighty and merciful God, to whom the light and the darkness are both alike, and without whom nothing befalls thy children: Strengthen us to meet all the experiences of life with a steadfast and undaunted heart; help us to go on our way bravely whether it be rough or smooth and, when the mists hide thy face, to continue patiently till they are dispersed by the sun of thy unchanging love; through Jesus Christ our Lord. **Amen.**

5

O Holy Spirit of God, abide with us: inspire all our thoughts, pervade our imaginations, suggest all our decisions, order all our doings. Be with us in our silence and in our speech, in our haste and in our leisure, in company and in solitude, in the freshness of the morning and in the weariness of the evening; and give us grace at all times humbly to rejoice in thy mysterious companionship; through Jesus Christ our Lord. **Amen.**

6

O Lord, open thou our lips and purify our hearts, that we may worthily magnify thy holy name. Help us to be reverent in thought, word, and act, and to worship thee now and always in the faith and spirit of Jesus Christ our Lord. **Amen.**

7

Almighty God, who hast given unto thy Son Jesus Christ a kingdom, that all peoples, nations, and languages should serve him: Make us loyal followers of our living Lord, that we may always hear his word, obey his commands, and live in his Spirit; and hasten the day when every knee shall bow and every tongue confess that he is Lord; to thine eternal glory. **Amen.**

8

Almighty God our Father, grant, we beseech thee, a great outpouring of thy Holy Spirit upon thy people, so as to cause a deep and widespread revival of a living faith in Christ, working by love, and bringing forth the fruits of the Spirit, love of humanity, joy in sacrifice, and fraternity in righteousness; through Jesus Christ our Lord. **Amen.**

9

O Thou who art the light of the world, the desire of all nations, and the shepherd of our souls: Let thy light shine in the darkness, that all the ends of the earth may see thy salvation; by the lifting up of thy cross gather the peoples to thine obedience, so that there may be one flock, one shepherd, one holy kingdom of righteousness and peace, one God and Father of us all, above all, and through all, and in all. **Amen.**

10

O Lord our God, we cried unto thee in trouble, and thou didst hear us; we put our trust in thee, and were not confounded. Thou hast turned our heaviness into joy, and guided us with gladness; therefore will we praise thee with all our heart, and give thanks unto thy holy name forever. Hear us and accept us; for the sake of Jesus Christ our Lord. **Amen.**

11

O God, age after age the living seek thee, and find that of thy faithfulness there is no end. Our fathers in their pilgrimage walked by thy guidance, and rested on thy compassion: still to their children be thou the cloud by day, the fire by night. O thou sole source of peace and righteousness! take now the veil from every heart; and join us in one communion with thy prophets and saints who have trusted in thee, and were not ashamed; through Jesus Christ our Lord. **Amen.**

Collects

1

O God, by whom the meek are guided in judgment, and light riseth up in darkness for the godly: Grant us, in all doubts and uncertainties, the grace to ask what thou wouldst have us to do, that the spirit of wisdom may save us from all false choices, and that in thy light we may see light and in thy straight path may not stumble; through Jesus Christ our Lord. **Amen.**

2

Almighty God, who has created man in thine own image: Grant us grace fearlessly to contend against evil, and to make no peace with oppression; and, that we may reverently use our freedom, help us to employ it in the maintenance of justice among men and nations to the glory of thy holy name; through Jesus Christ our Lord. **Amen.**

3

O almighty and most merciful God, of thy bountiful goodness keep us, we beseech thee, from all things that may hurt us; that we, being ready both in body and soul, may cheerfully accomplish those things which thou commandest; through Jesus Christ our Lord. **Amen.**

4

Lord, we beseech thee to keep thy household the Church in continual godliness, that through thy protection it may be free from all adversities, and devoutly given to serve thee in good works, to the glory of thy name; through Jesus Christ our Lord. **Amen.**

5

O God, our refuge and strength, who art the author of all godliness: Be ready, we beseech thee, to hear the devout prayers of thy Church; and grant that those things which we ask faithfully we may obtain effectually; through Jesus Christ our Lord. **Amen.**

6

Thou hast showed us, O Lord, what is good; enable us, we beseech thee, to perform what thou dost require, even to do justly, to love mercy, and to walk humbly with our God. **Amen.**

7

O heavenly Father, in whom we live and move and have our being: We humbly pray thee so to guide and govern us by thy Holy Spirit that in all the cares and occupations of our daily life we may remember that we are ever walking in thy sight; for thine own name's sake. **Amen.**

8

O God, who art the author of truth, of beauty, and of goodness: Inspire, we pray thee, all who enrich the lives of the people, all artists and poets, dramatists and musicians, that our common life may be made radiant with the beauty of him in whom thy fulness dwelt, even Jesus Christ our Lord. **Amen.**

9

O God, who hast joined together divers nations in the confession of thy name: Grant us both to will and to do what thou commandest, that thy people, being called to an eternal inheritance, may hold the same faith in their hearts, and show the same godliness in their lives; through Jesus Christ our Lord. **Amen.**

10

Almighty God, our heavenly Father: Guide, we beseech thee, the nations of the world into the way of justice and truth, and establish among them that peace which is the fruit of righteousness, that they may become the kingdom of our Lord and Savior Jesus Christ. **Amen.**

11

O God, who art the author of peace and lover of concord, in knowledge of whom standeth our eternal life, whose service is perfect freedom: Defend us thy humble servants in all assaults of our enemies; that we, surely trusting in thy defense, may not fear the power of any adversaries; through the might of Jesus Christ our Lord. **Amen.**

12

O Thou holy one who inhabitest eternity: Visit us with the inward vision of thy glory, that we may bow our hearts before thee, and obtain that grace which thou hast promised to the lowly; through Jesus Christ our Savior. **Amen.**

13

Almighty God, who in a world of change hast placed eternity in our hearts and hast given us power to discern good from evil: Grant us sincerity that we may persistently seek the things that endure, refusing those which perish, and that, amid things vanishing and deceptive, we may see the truth steadily, follow the light faithfully, and grow ever richer in that love which is the life of men; through Jesus Christ our Lord. **Amen.**

14

O Lord, who hast promised that whatsoever is done unto the least of thy brethren thou wilt receive as done unto thee: Give us grace, we humbly beseech thee, to be ever willing and ready, as thou dost enable us, to minister to the necessities of our fellow men; in thine own name we pray. **Amen.**

LABOR SUNDAY

First Sunday in September

Prayers

1

O God, who movest in love unceasing, and dost give to each man his appointed work: Help us steadfastly, and as in thy sight, to fulfill the duties of our calling, that when our Lord shall take account of us, we may be found faithful in that which is least, and enter into his eternal joy. **Amen.**

2

O God, we thank thee for the sweet refreshment of sleep and for the glory and vigor of the new day. As we set our faces once more toward our daily work, we pray thee for strength sufficient for our tasks. May Christ's spirit of duty and service ennoble all we do. Uphold us by the consciousness that our work is useful work and a blessing to all. If there has been anything in our work harmful to others and dishonorable to ourselves, reveal it to our inner eye with such clearness that we shall hate it and put it away, though it be at a loss to ourselves. When we work with others, help us to regard them, not as servants to our will, but as brothers equal to us in human dignity, and equally worthy of their full reward. May there be nothing in this day's work of which we shall be ashamed when the sun has set, nor in the eventide of our life when our task is done and we go to meet thy face. **Amen.**

3

O God, who in thy providence hast appointed to every man his work: We humbly beseech thee to put away all strife and contention between those who are engaged in the labors of industry and those who employ their labor. Deliver them from all greed and covetousness, and grant that they, seeking only that which is just and equal, may live and work in brotherly union and concord, to thy glory, their own well-being, and the prosperity of their country; through Jesus Christ our Lord. **Amen.**

4

O God, who hast taught us that we are members one of another: Remove, we beseech thee, from among us all distrust and bitterness in industrial disputes; and grant that, seeking what is just and equal, and caring for the needs of others, we may live and work together in unity and love; through Jesus Christ our Lord. **Amen.**

5

O Lord and heavenly Father, we commend to thy care and protection the men and women of this land who are suffering distress and anxiety through lack of work. Strengthen and support them, we beseech thee; and so prepare the counsels of those who govern our industries that thy people may be set free from want and fear to work in peace and security, for the relief of their necessities, and the well-being of this realm; through Jesus Christ our Lord. **Amen.**

OPENING OF SCHOOL

Usually in September

Prayers

1

Almighty God, we beseech thee, with thy gracious favor to behold our universities, colleges, and schools, that knowledge may be increased among us, and all good learning flourish and abound. Bless all who teach and all who learn; and grant that in humility of heart they may ever look unto thee, who art the fountain of all wisdom; through Jesus Christ our Lord. **Amen.**

2

Bless, we pray thee, O Father, the children and youth of this nation, returning to their schools and colleges. May thy Holy Spirit enlighten their minds, purify their vision, and strengthen their wills; that being taught of thee they may learn to follow in the steps of him who grew in wisdom and stature, and in favor with God and man; through the same Jesus Christ our Lord. **Amen.**

CHRISTIAN EDUCATION SUNDAY

(Formerly called Rally Day)

Usually in September

Prayer

Almighty God, our heavenly Father, who has committed to thy holy Church the care and nurture of thy children: Enlighten with thy wisdom those who teach and those who learn, that, rejoicing in the knowledge of thy truth, they may worship thee and serve thee from generation to generation; through Jesus Christ our Lord. **Amen.**

REFORMATION SUNDAY

Last Sunday in October

Prayers

1

O gracious Father, we humbly beseech thee for thy holy Church universal, that thou wouldst be pleased to fill it with all truth, in all peace. Where it is corrupt, purify it; where it is in error, direct it; where in any thing it is amiss, reform it. Where it is right, establish it; where it is in want, provide for it; where it is divided, reunite it; for the sake of him who died and rose again, and ever liveth to make intercession for us, Jesus Christ thy Son our Lord. **Amen.**

2

Almighty God, whose Son Jesus Christ came to cast fire upon the earth: Grant that by the prayers of thy faithful people a fire of burning zeal may be kindled and pass from heart to heart, that the light of thy Church may shine forth bright and clear; through the same thy Son Jesus Christ our Lord. **Amen.**

3

O Lord Jesus Christ, who biddest thy Church to bring all men to thyself: Make clear to each one of us his part in the task. Enlighten our minds with a vision of a more perfect society here on earth in which justice and right, peace and brotherhood shall reign according to thy will; and help us, O Lord, to do our part, that thy will may be done on earth as it is in heaven. **Amen.**

4

Almighty God, who of thy great mercy hast gathered us into thy Church: Grant that we may so honor thee, both in spirit and in outward form, that thy name may be glorified, and we may be true members of thy living fellowship; through Jesus Christ our Lord. **Amen.**

ALL SAINTS' DAY
November 1

Prayers

1

O King eternal, immortal, invisible, who in the righteousness of thy saints hast given us an example of godly life, and in their blessedness a glorious pledge of the hope of our calling: We beseech thee that, being compassed about with so great a cloud of witnesses, we may run with patience the race that is set before us, and with them receive the crown of glory that fadeth not away; through Jesus Christ our Lord. **Amen.**

2

O Lord our God, we praise thy holy name for the glorious company of the apostles, the goodly fellowship of the prophets, the noble army of martyrs, and for all who have served thee faithfully in thy holy Church throughout the world. We bless thee for all who by their speech, their writings, and their lives have enabled us to see more of the light of the knowledge of thy glory in the face of Jesus Christ; and for all who have helped and comforted, strengthened and encouraged us on our way. For all whom thou hast called to be saints, and through whom thou dost manifest the riches of thy grace, we praise thee, O God; and we beseech thee that with them, and with all the host of thy redeemed, we may perfectly praise thee in thy heavenly kingdom; through Jesus Christ our Lord. **Amen.**

3

Almighty God, who holdest in thy hand the souls of the righteous: We give thanks and praise for all the generations of the faithful who have served thee in godliness and love, and who dwell forever in thy presence. We bless thee for all who have enriched the world with truth and beauty, who have labored in the service of their fellows, and devoted themselves to thee and thy Church. We bless thee for all near and dear to us, for our fathers and mothers, our brothers and sisters, for those who have helped and defended and loved and cherished us. Grant that all the good we have seen and known in them may continue to inspire and guide us, that we may always love them and hallow their memory, and that when we have fulfilled our time on earth, we may have part with them in thy heavenly kingdom; through Jesus Christ our Lord. **Amen.**

An Order of Worship for All Saints' Day

SCRIPTURE SENTENCES

Minister: I beheld, and, lo, a great multitude, which no man could number, of all nations, and kindreds, and peoples, and tongues, stood before the throne, and before the Lamb, clothed with white robes, and palms in their hands; and cried with a loud voice, saying,

People: **Salvation to our God who sits upon the throne, and unto the Lamb.**

Minister: And all the angels stood round about the throne, and about the elders and the four living creatures, and fell before the throne on their faces, and worshiped God, saying,

People: **Amen: blessing, and glory, and wisdom, and thanksgiving, and honor, and power, and might be unto our God for ever and ever. Amen.**

HYMN "Come let us join our friends above" (Charles Wesley)

† *Here let the people stand and remain standing through the* Te Deum.

THE TE DEUM † *To be said by all responsively.*

We praise thee, O God; we acknowledge thee to be the Lord.

All the earth doth worship thee, the Father everlasting.

To thee all angels cry aloud; the heavens, and all the powers therein;

to thee cherubim and seraphim continually do cry.

Holy, holy, holy, Lord God of Sabaoth;

heaven and earth are full of the majesty of thy glory.

The glorious company of the apostles praise thee.

The goodly fellowship of the prophets praise thee.

The noble army of martyrs praise thee.

The holy Church throughout all the world doth acknowledge thee;

the Father, of an infinite majesty;

thine adorable, true, and only Son; also the Holy Ghost, the Comforter.

Thou art the King of glory, O Christ.

Thou art the everlasting Son of the Father.

When thou tookest upon thee to deliver man,

thou didst humble thyself to be born of a virgin.

When thou hadst overcome the sharpness of death,

thou didst open the kingdom of heaven to all believers.

Thou sittest at the right hand of God,

in the glory of the Father.

We believe that thou shalt come to be our judge.

We therefore pray thee, help thy servants, whom thou hast redeemed with thy precious blood.

Make them to be numbered with thy saints,

in glory everlasting.

THE SCRIPTURE LESSONS

THE SERMON

† *Here the minister shall say,*

The Lord be with you.

People: **And with thy spirit.**

Minister: Let us pray.

O almighty God, who hast knit together thine elect in one communion and fellowship, in the mystical body of thy Son Christ our Lord: Grant us grace so to follow thy blessed saints in all virtuous and godly living, that we may come to those unspeakable joys which thou hast prepared for those who unfeignedly love thee; through the same thy Son Jesus Christ our Lord. Amen.

HYMN "For All the Saints" (William W. How)

BENEDICTION † *The people may be seated for silent prayer.*

VETERAN'S DAY
November 11

Prayers

1

O almighty God, we turn to thee in the time of trouble. Direct the course of our world; lead the nations into likemindedness and fellowship;

prosper all counsels which make for the establishment and maintenance of rightful and abiding peace; through Jesus Christ our Lord. **Amen.**

2

Almighty God, we pray thee for the coming of thy kingdom of righteousness and peace. In the midst of a changing social order, may faith in thee and obedience to the teachings of thy dear Son prevail, to build a new life of love in which the ills of this present time may disappear and the glad day of brotherhood and mutual service may dawn. Strengthen thy Church in its labors for the happiness and welfare of all people, that they may find in thee their salvation and their peace; through Jesus Christ our Lord. **Amen.**

3

O God, who through thy prophets of old hast foretold a day when the armaments of war shall be beaten into the implements of peace: Hasten, we beseech thee, the fulfillment of thy most sure promise. Still the tumult of the nations, and set at naught the peoples that delight in war, that we may be speedily delivered from our present confusion into the order and righteousness of thy kingdom; through Jesus Christ our Lord. **Amen.**

THANKSGIVING DAY

An Order of Worship for Thanksgiving Day

† *Let the service of worship begin at the time appointed. Let the people be in silent meditation and prayer upon entering the sanctuary.*

PRELUDE

PROCESSIONAL HYMN † *The people standing. If there be no processional, let the first hymn follow the call to worship.*

CALL TO WORSHIP

Minister: God be merciful unto us, and bless us,

People: **And cause his face to shine upon us.**

Minister: Let us worship the Lord in the beauty of holiness.

People: **Let us worship him in spirit and in truth.**

INVOCATION † *By the minister, the people seated and bowed, or kneeling.*

Let us pray.

Most gracious God, by whose appointment the seasons come and go, and who makest the fruits of the earth to minister to the needs of men: We offer thee our thanksgivings that thou hast brought us through the circuit of another year, and that according to thy promise seedtime and harvest have not failed. At the remembrance of thy bounty we offer unto thee the sacrifices of our thanksgiving, and pray that thou wilt feed our souls with the bread of life; through Jesus Christ our Lord. **Amen.**

PRAYER OF THANKSGIVING † *Here let the people unite with the minister, saying,*

O God, we praise thee, we give thanks to thee for thy bountiful providence, for all the blessings and all the hopes of life. Above all we praise and adore thee for thine unspeakable gift in thine only Son our Lord and Savior Jesus Christ. Let the memory of thy goodness, we beseech thee, fill our hearts with joy and thankfulness to thee; through Jesus Christ our Lord. Amen.

THE LORD'S PRAYER

Our Father, who art in heaven, hallowed be thy name. Thy kingdom come, thy will be done on earth as it is in heaven. Give us this day our daily bread. And forgive us our trespasses, as we forgive those who trespass against us. And lead us not into temptation, but deliver us from evil. For thine is the kingdom, and the power, and the glory, forever. Amen.

THE PSALTER OR OTHER ACT OF PRAISE † *To be read responsively or in unison, the people standing; then shall be sung the* Gloria Patri.

† *Here let the people be seated.*

LITANY OF THANKSGIVING AND INTERCESSION † *The minister beginning, the people responding.*

Let us pray.

For all thy blessings in creation, for the beauty of earth and sea and sky, for thy manifold works, and the wisdom with which thou hast made them all,

we thank thee, O God.

For the happiness of our earthly life, for peaceful homes and healthful days, for our powers of mind and body, for faithful friends, for the joy of loving and being loved,

we thank thee, O God.

For the revelation of thy love and for newness of life in our Savior, for the blessings brought to us by thy holy Church, and for our fellowship with thee in Christ,

we thank thee, O God.

That it may please thee to strengthen and encourage all those who by reason of temptation, hardness of circumstances, or personal loss find it difficult to be thankful and to praise thy holy name,

we humbly beseech thee, our Father.

That it may please thee to solace all who have lost those whom they most loved, to uphold all who are sick and suffering, to protect such as have lost the kindly light of reason, and to supply the needs of the blind, the deaf, and the mute,

we humbly beseech thee, our Father.

That it may please thee to inspire all who are seeking to improve the conditions of our industrial life, and to give courage and devotion to all who do the work of every day, and to restore ordered prosperity and peace to our world,

we humbly beseech thee, our Father.

That it may please thee to bless with wisdom and courage thy servant the President of the United States, and all who bear with him the responsibility of the nation, and to give thy guidance and blessing to all the councils of the people,

we humbly beseech thee, our Father.

That it may please thee to direct the minds of all to whom thou hast committed the responsibility of leadership in the nations of the world. Give to them a vision of truth and justice, that by their counsel all nations and peoples may work together in true brotherhood, and thy Church may serve thee in unity and peace; through Jesus Christ our Lord,

we humbly beseech thee, our Father. Amen.

ANTHEM

THE SCRIPTURE LESSONS

AFFIRMATION OF FAITH † *The people standing; then may be sung a doxology.*

PASTORAL PRAYER † *The people seated and bowed, or kneeling.*

OFFERTORY

† *Here parish notices may be given.*

† *The minister may read Scripture sentences before the offering is received. An anthem may be sung during the receiving of the offering. Following the presentation of the offering a prayer of dedication may be said or sung.*

† *At the discretion of the minister, the offertory and prayers may follow the sermon.*

HYMN † *The people standing.*

THE THANKSGIVING SERMON

AN INVITATION TO CHRISTIAN DISCIPLESHIP

HYMN † *The people standing.*

BENEDICTION

POSTLUDE † *The people may be seated for silent prayer.*

GENERAL AIDS
TO WORSHIP

FOR USE IN CORPORATE WORSHIP

Prayers for Use on Entering the Church

1

Almighty God, unto whom all hearts are open, all desires known, and from whom no secrets are hid: Cleanse the thoughts of our hearts by the inspiration of thy Holy Spirit, that we may perfectly love thee, and worthily magnify thy holy name; through Christ our Lord. **Amen.**

2

O God, who makest us glad with the weekly remembrance of the glorious resurrection of thy Son our Lord: Vouchsafe us this day such blessing through our worship of thee, that the days to come may be spent in thy service; through the same Jesus Christ our Lord. **Amen.**

3

O God of peace, who hast taught us that in returning and rest we shall be saved, in quietness and confidence shall be our strength: By the might of thy Spirit, lift us, we pray thee, to thy presence, where we may be still and know that thou art God; through Jesus Christ our Lord. **Amen.**

4

O almighty God, who alone canst order the unruly wills and affections of sinful men: Grant unto thy people, that they may love the thing which thou commandest, and desire that which thou dost promise; that among the sundry and manifold changes of the world, our hearts may surely there be fixed, where true joys are to be found; through Jesus Christ our Lord. **Amen.**

5

Let thy merciful ears, O Lord, be open to the prayers of thy humble servants; and, that they may obtain their petitions, make them to ask such things as shall please thee; through Jesus Christ our Lord. **Amen.**

Prayers with the Choir

Minister: The Lord be with you.

Choir: **And with thy spirit.**

Minister: Let us pray.

† *Then shall follow one of these prayers, or other prayer by the minister or member of the choir:*

1

O almighty God, who art worthy to be praised and to be held in reverence by all those who stand before thee: Pour out upon us, we pray thee, thy redeeming and sanctifying Spirit, that we, being cleansed from sin, may worship thee with unfeigned joy; grant that all our praises, begun and ended in thee, may make thy name glorious; through Jesus Christ our Lord. **Amen.**

2

Almighty God, at whose right hand are pleasures for evermore: We pray that as redeemed and forgiven children we may evermore rejoice in singing thy praises. Grant, we beseech thee, that what we sing with our lips we may believe in our hearts, and what we believe in our hearts we may practice in our lives; so that being doers of the Word and not hearers only, we may obtain everlasting life; through Jesus Christ our Lord. **Amen.**

3

Most merciful and gracious God, who art the strength of all who put their trust in thee: Prepare us now to worship thee in spirit and in truth, with all reverence and godly fear. Quicken our devotion, that with holy gladness we may show forth thy most worthy praise, to the end that those who worship here may humbly receive thy Word, steadfastly cling to it, and obediently perform all such good works as thou dost appoint for us to do, that thereby we may manifest that thankfulness which we owe to thee for thy redeeming love; through Jesus Christ our Lord. **Amen.**

4

O God, before whose throne the whole family of heaven and earth bow down in ceaseless adoration: Accept, we pray thee, the praises which we offer thee this day. Make us to know the joy of thy salvation, that with glad hearts we may proclaim thy Word in such wise that the sorrowing may be comforted, the faint in heart made strong, the wayward restored to ways of life and peace, and thy saving health be made known to all nations; through Jesus Christ our Lord. **Amen.**

Scripture Sentences or Calls to Worship

1

This is the day which the Lord has made; let us rejoice and be glad in it.

Psalm 118:24

2

The hour is coming, and now is, when the true worshipers will worship the Father in spirit and truth, for such the Father seeks to worship him. God is spirit, and those who worship him must worship him in spirit and truth.

John 4:23-24

3

The Lord is good to those who wait for him, to the soul that seeks him. It is good that one should wait quietly for the salvation of the Lord.

Lamentations 3:25-26

4

"If with all your hearts ye truly seek me, ye shall surely find me"; thus saith our God. Draw nigh to God, and he will draw nigh to you. Humble yourselves before the Lord, and he will lift you up.

From Deuteronomy 4:29; James 4:8, 10

5

Dearly beloved, we are come together in the presence of almighty God, and of the whole company of heaven, to make humble confession of our sins unto him; to set forth his most worthy praise; to hear his most holy Word; to declare our faith in him; to ask, for ourselves and all men, those things which are necessary for the body and the soul; to offer unto him the service of our lives; and to receive his blessing.

Wherefore, let us invoke God's presence with us now.

or

Wherefore, let us rejoice and offer unto God our praises.

Invocations

1

Almighty God, unto whom all hearts are open, all desires known, and from whom no secrets are hid: Cleanse the thoughts of our hearts by the inspiration of thy Holy Spirit, that we may perfectly love thee, and worthily magnify thy holy name; through Christ our Lord. **Amen.**

2

Almighty God, from whom every good prayer cometh, and who pourest out on all who desire it the spirit of grace and supplication: Deliver us, when we draw nigh to thee, from coldness of heart and wanderings of mind, that, with steadfast thoughts and kindled affections, we may worship thee in spirit and in truth; through Jesus Christ our Lord. **Amen.**

3

O God, the King eternal, who dividest the day from the darkness, and turnest the shadow of death into the morning: Drive far off from us all wrong desires; incline our hearts to keep thy law; and guide our feet into the way of peace, that having done thy will with cheerfulness while it was day, we may, when the night cometh, rejoice to give thee thanks; through Jesus Christ our Lord. **Amen.**

4

O Lord God, who hast bidden the light to shine out of darkness, and who hast again wakened us to praise thy goodness and ask for thy grace: Accept now the sacrifice of our worship and thanksgiving. Make us to be children of the light and of the day, and heirs of thine everlasting inheritance. Remember, O God, thy whole Church, our brethren in every land. Pour out the riches of thy mercy, so that we, being redeemed, and steadfast in faith, may ever praise thy wonderful and holy name; through Jesus Christ our Lord. **Amen.**

5

Almighty God, who hast given a day of rest to thy people, and, through thy Spirit in the Church, hast consecrated the first day of the week to be a perpetual memorial of thy Son's resurrection: Grant that we may so use thy gift that, refreshed and strengthened in soul and body, we may serve thee faithfully all the days of our life; through the same Jesus Christ our Lord. **Amen.**

6

Almighty God, purify our hearts from every vain and sinful thought; prepare our souls to worship thee this day acceptably, with reverence and godly fear. Set our affection on things above, and give us grace to receive thy Word into good and honest hearts, so that we may rise to newness of life; through Jesus Christ our Lord. **Amen.**

7

Grant, O Lord, that all who worship within this place may present their bodies a living sacrifice, holy, acceptable unto thee; and that they may themselves be temples of the Holy Spirit wherein thou wilt dwell for evermore. **Amen.**

8

Regard, O Lord, the supplication of thy servants, and grant that thy Word, which shall be read and preached in this place, may have such acceptance that it may never be spoken in vain. Grant also that the people may have grace to hear and receive what shall be delivered out of thy most holy Word as the means of their salvation, that in all their words and deeds they may seek the glory and the increase of thy kingdom; through Jesus Christ our Lord. **Amen.**

9

O God, to whom belong adoration and praise: Prepare us, through the active presence of thy Spirit, to come before thee worthily and to ask of thee rightly; enlighten our understanding; purify our every desire; quicken our wills into instant obedience to thy Word; strengthen every right purpose; direct this hour of worship to the magnifying of thy name, and to the enduring good of us thy children and servants; through Jesus Christ our Lord. **Amen.**

10

Almighty God, author of eternal light: Illumine our hearts by the light of thy grace, that our lips may praise thee, that our lives may bless thee, that our worship may glorify thee; through Jesus Christ our Lord. **Amen.**

11

O God, from whom all holy desires, all good counsels, and all just works do proceed: Give unto thy servants that peace which the world cannot give; that our hearts may be set to obey thy commandments, and also that by thee we, being defended from the fear of our enemies, may pass our time in rest and quietness; through the merits of Jesus Christ our Savior. **Amen.**

12

Almighty God, our heavenly Father: Receive us in this evening hour as we offer ourselves anew to thee in body, soul, and spirit. Let not thy holy day pass except it leave its benediction with us. Give to us the still and quiet heart. Speak to us thy truth, that we may glorify thee; through Jesus Christ our Lord. **Amen.**

13

Blessed be thou, O Lord our God, ruler of the world, by whose law the shadows of evening fall and the gates of morn are opened. In wisdom thou hast established the changes of times and seasons, and ordered the ways of the stars in their heavenly courses. Creator of heaven and earth, O living God, rule thou over us for ever. Blessed be thou, O Lord, for the day and its work and for the night and its rest. **Amen.**

Prayers of Confession

1

Have mercy upon us, O God, according to thy lovingkindness; according to the multitude of thy tender mercies blot out our transgressions. Wash us thoroughly from our iniquities, and cleanse us from our sins. For we acknowledge our transgressions, and our sin is ever before us. Create in us clean hearts, O God, and renew a right spirit within us; through Jesus Christ our Lord. **Amen.**

2

O Thou who art of purer eyes than to behold evil, if thou shouldest mark iniquities, who should stand? Enter not into judgment with thy servants, for in thy sight shall no man living be justified; for thou knowest our foolishness, and our sins are not hid from thee. But thou, O Lord, art full of compassion and gracious, slow to anger and plenteous in mercy; there is forgiveness with thee, that thou mayest be obeyed. Cleanse us from secret faults; keep back thy servants also from presumptuous sins; deliver us from all our transgressions; draw nigh unto our souls and redeem them, and purge away our sins; through Jesus Christ our Lord. **Amen.**

3

Almighty and most merciful Father, we have erred and strayed from thy ways like lost sheep. We have followed too much the devices and desires of our own hearts. We have offended against thy holy laws. We have left undone those things which we ought to have done, and we have done those things which we ought not to have done. But thou, O Lord, have mercy upon us. Spare thou those, O God, who confess their faults. Restore thou those who are penitent, according to thy promises declared unto mankind in Christ Jesus our Lord. And grant, O most merciful Father, for his sake, that we may hereafter live a godly, righteous, and sober life; to the glory of thy holy name. **Amen.**

4

Almighty God, Father of our Lord Jesus Christ, maker of all things, judge of all men: We acknowledge and bewail our manifold sins and wickedness, which we from time to time most grievously have committed by thought, word, and deed, against thy divine majesty. We do earnestly repent, and are heartily sorry for these our misdoings; the remembrance of them is grievous unto us. Have mercy upon us, most merciful Father. For thy Son our Lord Jesus Christ's sake, forgive us all that is past; and grant that we may ever hereafter serve and please thee in newness of life, to the honor and glory of thy name; through Jesus Christ our Lord. **Amen.**

5

Our heavenly Father, who by thy love hast made us, and through thy love hast kept us, and in thy love wouldst make us perfect: We humbly confess that we have not loved thee with all our heart and soul and mind and strength, and that we have not loved one another as Christ hath loved us. Thy life is within our souls, but our selfishness hath hindered thee. We have not lived by faith. We have resisted thy Spirit. We have neglected thine inspirations.

Forgive what we have been; help us to amend what we are; and in thy Spirit direct what we shall be, that thou mayest come into the full glory of thy creation, in us and in all men; through Jesus Christ our Lord. **Amen.**

6

Almighty and most merciful God, who knowest the thoughts of our hearts: We confess that we have sinned against thee, and done evil in thy sight. We have transgressed thy holy laws; we have neglected thy Word and ordinances. Forgive us, O Lord, we beseech thee; and give us grace and power to put away all hurtful things, that, being delivered from the bondage of sin, we may bring forth fruit worthy of repentance, and henceforth may ever walk in thy holy ways; through Jesus Christ our Lord. **Amen.**

7

O holy and merciful God, we confess that we have not always taken upon ourselves with joy the yoke of obedience, nor been willing to seek and to do thy perfect will. We have not loved thee with all our heart and mind and soul and strength, neither have we loved our neighbors as ourselves. Thou hast called to us in the need of our fellows, and we have passed unheeding on our way. In the pride of our hearts, and our unwillingness to repent, we have turned away from the cross of Christ, and have grieved thy Holy Spirit. **Amen.**

8

O God, our heavenly Father, we have sinned against thee and are not worthy to be called thy children. We have forsaken thy way, and walked in the light of our own eyes. We have not loved thee with our whole heart. We have not loved our neighbor as ourselves. We have not had in us the mind of Christ. We have grieved thy Holy Spirit. We have been conformed to this world which passeth away. We have not endured as seeing him who is invisible. Forgive us, we beseech thee, most merciful Father, and renew us again in the strength of thy grace; through Jesus Christ our Lord. **Amen.**

9

Almighty and eternal God, who searchest the hearts of men: We acknowledge and confess that we have sinned against thee in thought, word, and deed; that we have not loved thee with all our heart and soul, with all our mind and strength; and that we have not loved our neighbors as ourselves. Forgive us our transgressions and help us to amend our ways; and of thine eternal goodness direct what we shall be, so that we may henceforth walk in the way of thy commandments, and do those things which are worthy in thy sight; through Jesus Christ our Lord. **Amen.**

10

Almighty God, who art rich in mercy to all those who call upon thee: Hear us, we beseech thee, as we confess our sins before thee. In the presence of thy love and our neighbor's need, we acknowledge our disobedience and ingratitude, our pride and willfulness, our heedlessness and indifference. We confess that we are not worthy to be called thy children; yet do thou in mercy keep us as thine own. Grant us true repentance, and forgive us all our sins; through Jesus Christ our Lord. **Amen.**

11

Most merciful Father, we have done little to forward thy kingdom in this world, to foster the brotherhood of man, and to establish love as the law of life. We have allowed self to blind us, pains to embitter us. We have forgotten that whatsoever is done to one of the least of thy children is done unto thee. Pardon our shortcomings; forgive our neglect; give us a pure heart intent on pleasing thee. Help us in all our seeking to seek first thy kingdom and thy righteousness. And make us to come, as came thy Son Jesus Christ, not to be ministered unto, but to minister. All which we ask through Jesus Christ our Lord. **Amen.**

12

Almighty and most merciful God, our heavenly Father: We confess that we have grievously sinned against thee in thought, in word, and in deed. We have come short of thy glory; we have broken the unity of thy holy Church; and we have turned every one of us aside from the way of life. Yet do thou, O most merciful Father, hear us when we call upon thee with penitent hearts. Pardon our sins, and grant us thy peace. Confirm us in all goodness, that we may serve thee with a quiet mind, and bring us to the life everlasting; through Jesus Christ our Lord. **Amen.**

13

O Lord, holy and righteous God,
we acknowledge before thee that we do not fear thee
and that we do not love thee above all things.
We do not delight in prayer, nor take pleasure in thy Word.
We do not really love our neighbor;
we lack the conscience that should accompany our Christian profession.
Our hearts are divided, crossed by doubts and guilty desires.
We accuse ourselves before thee, O God,
we implore thee, whose nature and whose name is love,
to forgive us, and in forgiving, to heal us
so that in our lives something will finally be changed. **Amen.**

Words of Assurance

1

For as the heavens are high above the earth, so great is his steadfast love toward those who fear him; as far as the east is from the west, so far does he remove our transgressions from us.   *Psalm 103:11-12*

2

As a father pities his children, so the Lord pities those who fear him. ·
Psalm 103:13

3

The Lord is gracious and merciful, slow to anger and abounding in steadfast love.   *Psalm 145:8*

4

This is the message we have heard from him and proclaim to you, that God is light and in him is no darkness at all. If we walk in the light, as he is in the light, we have fellowship with one another, and the blood of Jesus his Son cleanses us from all sin.   *I John 1:5, 7*

5

Jesus said: "Him who comes to me I will not cast out."   *John 6:37b*

6

If we confess our sins, he is faithful and just, and will forgive our sins and cleanse us from all unrighteousness.   *I John 1:9*

7

Your sins are forgiven for his sake.   *I John 2:12b*

8

Come to me, all who labor and are heavy-laden, and I will give you rest.
Matthew 11:28

9

For God so loved the world that he gave his only Son, that whoever believes in him should not perish but have eternal life.   *John 3:16*

10

The sacrifice acceptable to God is a broken spirit; a broken and contrite heart, O God, thou wilt not despise.   *Psalm 51:17*

11

The saying is sure and worthy of full acceptance, that Christ Jesus came into the world to save sinners.   *I Timothy 1:15*

12

There is therefore now no condemnation for those who are in Christ Jesus, who walk not according to the flesh but according to the Spirit.
Romans 8:1, 4b

13

The Lord is my light and my salvation; whom shall I fear? The Lord is the stronghold of my life; of whom shall I be afraid?   *Psalm 27:1*

14

For he will hide me in his shelter in the day of trouble; he will conceal me under the cover of his tent.   *Psalm 27:5ab*

15

Wait for the Lord; be strong, and let your heart take courage; yea, wait for the Lord!   *Psalm 27:14*

16

The Lord is near to the brokenhearted, and saves the crushed in spirit.
Psalm 34:18

17

The Lord redeems the life of his servants; none of those who take refuge in him will be condemned.   *Psalm 34:22*

18

Trust in the Lord, and do good; and he will give you the desires of your heart.   *Psalm 37:3a, 4b*

19

Ask, and it will be given you; seek and you will find; knock, and it will be opened to you. For every one who asks receives, and he who seeks finds, and to him who knocks it will be opened.   *Matthew 7:7-8*

20

And my God will supply every need of yours according to his riches in glory in Christ Jesus.   *Philippians 4:19*

21

Who is like unto God, who pardons iniquity and passes over transgression? He does not retain his anger for ever because he delights in steadfast love. He will again have compassion upon us, he will tread our iniquities under foot. He will cast all our sins into the depths of the sea.

From Micah 7:18-19

Prayers for Pardon and Forgiveness

1

May the almighty and merciful God grant us pardon, forgiveness, and remission of our sins; through Jesus Christ our Lord. **Amen.**

2

May almighty God, who caused light to shine out of darkness, shine in our hearts, cleansing us from all our sins, and restoring us to the light of the knowledge of his glory in the face of Jesus Christ our Lord. **Amen.**

3

Grant, we beseech thee, merciful Lord, to thy faithful people pardon and peace, that they may be cleansed from all their sins, and serve thee with a quiet mind; through Jesus Christ our Lord. **Amen.**

4

May the almighty and merciful Lord grant us remission of all our sins, true repentance, amendment of life, and the grace and consolation of his Holy Spirit. **Amen.**

5

O Lord, we beseech thee, absolve thy people from their offenses, that through thy bountiful goodness we may be delivered from the bonds of those sins which by our frailty we have committed. Grant this, O heavenly Father, for the sake of Jesus Christ, our blessed Lord and Savior. **Amen.**

6

O Lord, we beseech thee, mercifully hear our prayers, and spare all those who confess their sins unto thee, that they whose consciences by sin are accused, by thy merciful pardon may be absolved; through Christ our Lord. **Amen.**

7

O God, forgive those who repent of their sins, that returning from the path of error to the way of righteousness they may retain in fulness what thy grace hath given, and may enjoy forever what thy mercy hath restored; through Jesus Christ our Lord. **Amen.**

8

Grant, we beseech thee, almighty God, that we who are burdened with the consciousness of our guilt may by thy mercy be forgiven, that being cleansed from sin we may be clothed in thy righteousness, and worthily rejoice in the joy of thy saints; through Jesus Christ our Lord. **Amen.**

9

Almighty God, our heavenly Father, who of thy great mercy hast promised forgiveness of sins to all them that with hearty repentance and true faith turn unto thee: Have mercy upon us; pardon and deliver us from all our sins; confirm and strengthen us in all goodness; and bring us to everlasting life; through Jesus Christ our Lord. **Amen.**

10

O Lord God, there is none like unto thee, in the heavens or upon the earth; yet hast thou promised to hear the cry of those who call upon thee; wherefore have respect unto the supplications of thy servants, and hearken unto the prayer that they make before thee; and, however they may have sinned, yet hear thou in heaven, thy dwelling place; and when thou hearest, Lord, forgive. **Amen.**

11

Almighty God, the Father of our Lord Jesus Christ, who desirest not the death of a sinner, but rather that he may turn from his wickedness and live, and who dost pardon and absolve all them that truly repent and unfeignedly believe thy holy Gospel: Grant us true repentance and thy Holy Spirit, we beseech thee, that those things may please thee which we do at this present, and that the rest of our life hereafter may be pure and holy, so that at the last we may come to thy eternal joy; through Jesus Christ our Lord. **Amen.**

Affirmations of Faith

THE APOSTLES' CREED

1

Minister: Let us unite in this historic confession of the Christian faith:

Minister and People: I believe in God the Father Almighty, maker of heaven and earth;

And in Jesus Christ his only Son our Lord: who was conceived by the Holy Spirit,[1] born of the Virgin Mary, suffered under Pontius Pilate, was crucified, dead, and buried;[2] the third day he rose from the dead; he ascended into heaven, and sitteth at the right hand of God the Father Almighty; from thence he shall come to judge the quick and the dead.

I believe in the Holy Spirit, the holy catholic Church, the communion of saints, the forgiveness of sins, the resurrection of the body, and the life everlasting. **Amen.**

THE NICENE CREED

2

Minister: Let us unite in this historic confession of the Christian faith:

Minister and People: I believe in one God: the Father Almighty, maker of heaven and earth, and of all things visible and invisible;

And in one Lord Jesus Christ, the only begotten Son of God: begotten of the Father before all worlds, God of God, Light of Light, very God of very God, begotten, not made, being of one substance with the Father, through whom all things were made; who for us men and for our salvation came down from heaven, and was incarnate by the Holy Ghost of the Virgin Mary, and was made man, and was crucified also for us under Pontius Pilate; he suffered and was buried, and the third day he rose again according to the Scriptures, and ascended into heaven, and sitteth on the right hand of the Father; and he shall come again with glory, to judge both the quick and the dead; whose kingdom shall have no end.

And I believe in the Holy Ghost, the Lord, the giver of life, who proceedeth from the Father and the Son, who with the Father and the Son together is worshiped and glorified, who spake by the prophets. And I believe in one holy catholic and apostolic Church. I acknowledge one

[1] Or Holy Ghost.
[2] Traditional use of this creed includes these words: "He descended into hell."

baptism for the remission of sins. And I look for the resurrection of the dead, and the life of the world to come. **Amen.**

A MODERN AFFIRMATION

3

Minister: Where the Spirit of the Lord is, there is the one true Church, apostolic and universal, whose holy faith let us now declare:

Minister and People: We believe in God the Father, infinite in wisdom, power and love, whose mercy is over all his works, and whose will is ever directed to his children's good.

We believe in Jesus Christ, Son of God and Son of man, the gift of the Father's unfailing grace, the ground of our hope, and the promise of our deliverance from sin and death.

We believe in the Holy Spirit as the divine presence in our lives, whereby we are kept in perpetual remembrance of the truth of Christ, and find strength and help in time of need.

We believe that this faith should manifest itself in the service of love as set forth in the example of our blessed Lord, to the end that the kingdom of God may come upon the earth. **Amen.**

THE KOREAN CREED

4

Minister: Where the Spirit of the Lord is, there is the one true Church, apostolic and universal, whose holy faith let us now declare:

Minister and People: We believe in the one God, maker and ruler of all things, Father of all men, the source of all goodness and beauty, all truth and love.

We believe in Jesus Christ, God manifest in the flesh, our teacher, example, and Redeemer, the Savior of the world.

We believe in the Holy Spirit, God present with us for guidance, for comfort, and for strength.

We believe in the forgiveness of sins, in the life of love and prayer, and in grace equal to every need.

We believe in the Word of God contained in the Old and New Testaments as the sufficient rule both of faith and of practice.

We believe in the Church as the fellowship for worship and for service of all who are united to the living Lord.

We believe in the kingdom of God as the divine rule in human society, and in the brotherhood of man under the fatherhood of God.

We believe in the final triumph of righteousness, and in the life everlasting. **Amen.**

A CREED IN THE WORDS OF ST. JOHN

5

Minister: Where the Spirit of the Lord is, there is the one true Church, apostolic and universal, whose holy faith let us now declare:

Minister and People: We believe that God is Spirit, and they that worship him must worship him in spirit and in truth.

We believe that God is Light, and that if we walk in the light, as he is in the light, we have fellowship one with another.

We believe that God is Love, and that everyone that loveth is born of God and knoweth God.

We believe that Jesus Christ is the Son of God, and that God hath given to us eternal life, and this life is in his Son.

We believe that he is the Resurrection and the Life, and that whosoever believeth on him, though he were dead, yet shall he live.

We believe that we are children of God, and that he hath given us of his Spirit.

We believe that if we confess our sins, he is faithful and just to forgive us our sins, and to cleanse us from all uncleanness.

We believe that the world passeth away and the lust thereof, but he that doeth the will of God abideth forever. **Amen.**

Prayers of Thanksgiving

1

Almighty God, Father of all mercies, we thine unworthy servants do give thee most humble and hearty thanks for all thy goodness and loving-kindness to us, and to all men. We bless thee for our creation, preservation, and all the blessings of this life, but above all for thine inestimable love in the redemption of the world by our Lord Jesus Christ, for the means of grace, and for the hope of glory. And we beseech thee, give us that due sense of all thy mercies, that our hearts may be unfeignedly thankful, and that we may show forth thy praise, not only with our lips, but in our lives, by giving up ourselves to thy service and by walking before thee in holiness and righteousness all our days; through Jesus Christ our Lord, to whom, with thee and the Holy Spirit, be all honor and glory, world without end. **Amen.**

2

Almighty God, whose mercy is over all thy works: We praise thee for the blessings which have been brought to mankind by thy holy Church throughout the world. We bless thee for the grace of thy Sacraments; for our fellowship in Christ with thee, and with one another; for the teaching of the Scriptures and for the preaching of thy Word. We thank thee for the holy example of thy saints in all ages; for thy servants departed this life in thy faith and fear, and for the memory and example of all that has been true and good in their lives. And we humbly beseech thee that we may be numbered with them in the great company of the redeemed in heaven; through Jesus Christ our Lord. **Amen.**

3

O God of love, we yield thee thanks for whatsoever thou hast given us richly to enjoy, for health and vigor, for the love and care of home, for joys of friendship, and for every good gift of happiness and strength. We praise thee for all thy servants who by their example and encouragement have helped us on our way, and for every vision of thyself which thou hast ever given us in Sacrament or prayer; and we humbly beseech thee that all these thy benefits we may use in thy service and to the glory of thy holy name; through Jesus Christ thy Son our Lord. **Amen.**

4

Almighty and most merciful God, we give thanks to thee for the light of another day, for the work we have to do, and for the strength to do it. Guide us, we pray thee, by thy truth; uphold us by thy power; and purify us by the continual indwelling of thy spirit. Grant that in every circumstance we may grow in wisdom, and, knowing the things that belong to our peace, obtain strength to persevere; through Jesus Christ our Lord. **Amen.**

5

Almighty God, who didst send thy Son Jesus Christ to be the light of the world, that all who follow him might not walk in darkness, but have the light of life: We praise thee for the Gospel of thy love to men, for the word of salvation to all people, and for the revelation of thy glory among the nations. We bless thee for the faithful of every age who have borne their witness to thy truth, for the labors of those who first brought the Gospel to this land, and for all who have gone forth to distant lands as ambassadors of Christ. We thank thee for the growth of thy Church through all the world; and we beseech thee to hasten the fulfillment of thy promise that the kingdoms of men shall become the kingdom of our Lord and Savior Jesus Christ; to whom, with thee, O Father, and the Holy Spirit, be the glory for ever and ever. **Amen.**

6

Almighty and most merciful Father, from whom cometh down every good and perfect gift: We yield thee praise and thanks for all thy mercies. Thy goodness hath created us, thy bounty hath sustained us, thy fatherly discipline hath chastened us, thy patience hath borne with us, thy love hath redeemed us. Give us a heart to love and serve thee, and enable us to show our thankfulness for all thy goodness and mercy by giving up ourselves to thy service, and cheerfully submitting in all things to thy blessed will. **Amen.**

7

O Lord our God, the author and giver of all good things: We thank thee for all thy mercies, and for thy loving care over all thy creatures. We bless thee for the gift of life, for thy protection round about us, for thy guiding hand upon us, and for the tokens of thy love within us. We thank thee for friendship and duty, for good hopes and precious memories, for the joys that cheer us, and the trials that teach us to trust in thee. Most of all we thank thee for the saving knowledge of thy Son our Savior; for the living presence of thy Spirit, the comforter; for thy Church, the body of Christ; for the ministry of Word and Sacrament, and all the means of grace.

In all these things, O heavenly Father, make us wise unto a right use of thy benefits, that we may render an acceptable thanksgiving unto thee all the days of our life; through Jesus Christ our Lord. **Amen.**

8

O almighty God, who crownest the year with thy goodness: We praise thee that thou hast ever fulfilled thy promise to men, that, while earth remaineth, seedtime and harvest shall not cease. We bless thee for the order and constancy of nature, for the beauty of earth and sky and sea, and for the providence that year by year supplies our need. We thank thee for thy blessing upon the work of those who plowed the soil and sowed the seed, and have now gathered in the fruits of the earth. And with our thanksgiving for these temporal mercies, accept our praise, O God, for the eternal riches of thy grace in Christ our Lord; to whom, with thee, O Father, and the Holy Spirit, be all glory and honor and worship, for ever and ever. **Amen.**

Prayers of Petition and Intercession

FOR ALL CONDITIONS OF MEN

1

O God, the creator and preserver of all mankind; we humbly beseech thee for all sorts and conditions of men; that thou wouldst be pleased to make thy ways known unto them, thy saving health unto all nations. More especially we pray for thy holy Church universal, that it may be so guided and governed by thy good Spirit, that all who profess and call themselves Christians may be led into the way of truth, and hold the faith in unity of spirit, in the bond of peace, and in righteousness of life. Finally, we commend to thy fatherly goodness all those who are in any way afflicted or distressed in mind, body, or estate; that it may please thee to comfort and relieve them according to their several necessities, giving them patience under their suffering, and a happy issue out of all their afflictions. And this we ask for Jesus Christ's sake. **Amen.**

FOR THE CHURCH

2

O God our Father, we pray for thy Church, which is set today amid the perplexities of a changing order, and face to face with new tasks. Baptize her afresh in the life-giving spirit of Jesus! Bestow upon her a great responsiveness to duty, a swifter compassion with suffering, and an utter loyalty to the will of God. Help her to proclaim boldly the coming of the kingdom of God. Put upon her lips the ancient Gospel of her Lord. Fill her with the prophets' scorn of tyranny, and with a Christlike tenderness for the heavy-laden and downtrodden. Bid her cease from seeking her own life, lest she lose it. Make her valiant to give up her life to humanity, that, like her crucified Lord, she may mount by the path of the cross to a higher glory; through the same Jesus Christ our Lord. **Amen.**

3

O God, who hast built thy Church upon the foundation of the apostles and prophets, Jesus Christ himself being the chief cornerstone: Save the community of thy people from cowardly surrender to the world, from rendering unto Caesar what belongs to thee, and from forgetting the eternal Gospel amid the temporal pressures of our troubled days.

For the unity of the Church we pray, and for her fellowship across the embittered lines of race and nation; and to her growth in grace, her building in love, her enlargement in service, her increase in wisdom, faith, charity, and power, we dedicate our lives; through Jesus Christ our Lord. **Amen.**

FOR CHURCH UNION

4

O Lord Jesus Christ, who didst pray that thy Church might be one even as thou and the Father are one: Make us who profess one Lord, one faith, and one Baptism, to be of one heart and of one mind. Deliver us from blindness and prejudice, from intolerance and evil-speaking, that, joined in one holy bond of faith and charity, we, whom thou hast reconciled to thyself, may be reconciled to one another, and so make thy praise glorious; through the same thy Son Jesus Christ our Lord, who with the Father and the Holy Spirit liveth and reigneth ever, one God, world without end. **Amen.**

FOR THE UNITY OF GOD'S PEOPLE

5

O almighty God, who didst send thy Son Jesus Christ to break down every middle wall of partition, and who didst create in him one new man by reconciling all men to thyself in one body through the cross: Hear us, we beseech thee, who maintain old walls, and build new ones, so separating ourselves one from the other and bringing the cross to open shame. Remove far from us, we pray thee, all false pride and worldly ambition, that being kindly affectioned one toward another, and in honor preferring one another, we may worship thee in spirit and in truth, one people of God; to the glory of thy holy name. **Amen.**

FOR THE CHURCH THROUGHOUT THE WORLD

6

Father of all, who hast declared thy love to all men: Hear us as we bring their needs to thee in prayer.

We pray for thy Church throughout the world. Enlighten her ministers with the knowledge and understanding of thy word. Send down thy grace upon all her congregations. Deliver her from false doctrine. Manifest more and more her unity, and clothe her with the beauty of holiness and peace. (Especially we ask thy blessing upon every good work carried on in this congregation.) Reveal and establish thy glory among the nations. Send the light of thy Gospel to the dark places of the earth; call back to thy fold those who have wandered from thee. And bring in speedily the full victory of thine everlasting kingdom.

Pour forth thy Spirit upon all flesh, that discord and strife may be brought to a perpetual end. Deliver men everywhere from all contempt for others not of their race or color, condition or creed. Quicken by thy Gospel the sense of brotherhood among all peoples, and bring them to true unity of spirit, in the bond of peace. **Amen.**

FOR MISSIONS

7

O Thou who art the light and the life of the world: Have compassion, we pray thee, upon those who are sitting in darkness and in the shadow of death; and, as thou didst at the first, by the preaching of thine apostles, cause the light of thy Gospel to shine throughout the world; be pleased to make thy ways known upon earth, thy saving health unto all nations. Bless thy servants who have gone into hard fields and unto distant lands to proclaim the message of salvation. Endue them with thy Holy Spirit, enrich them with thy heavenly grace, prosper them in all their labors, and give them souls as their reward; through Jesus Christ our Lord. **Amen.**

FOR THOSE WHO LABOR IN THE GOSPEL

8

Increase, O God, the faith and zeal of all thy people, that they may more earnestly desire, and more diligently seek, the salvation of their fellow men, through the message of thy love in Jesus Christ our Lord. Send forth a mighty call unto thy servants who labor in the Gospel, granting unto them a heart of love, sincerity of speech, and the power of the Holy Spirit, that they may persuade men to forsake sin and return unto thee. And so bless and favor the work of thine evangelists, that multitudes may be brought from the kingdom of evil into the kingdom of thy dear Son our Savior Jesus Christ. **Amen.**

FOR THOSE WHO GIVE THEMSELVES TO SERVICE

9

O Lord, our heavenly Father, who by thy blessed Son hast taught us that thou art love: We beseech thee graciously to bless all those who, following in his steps, give themselves to the service of their fellow men. Grant unto them clear vision to perceive those things which in our social order are amiss; give them true judgment, courage, and perseverance to help those that suffer wrong, and endue them with unfailing love to minister to the poor, the suffering, and the friendless. Make us aware of our kinship one with another as thy children, that we may strive wisely to order all things among us according to thy will; for the sake of him who laid down his own life for us, thy Son our Savior Jesus Christ. **Amen.**

FOR SINGLENESS OF HEART

10

Almighty God, our heavenly Father, who declarest thy glory and showest forth thy handiwork in the heavens and in the earth: Deliver us, we beseech thee, in our several callings from the service of mammon, that we may do the work which thou givest us to do in truth, in beauty, and in righteousness, with singleness of heart as thy servants, and to the benefit of our fellow men; for the sake of him who came among us as one that serveth, thy Son Jesus Christ our Lord. **Amen.**

FOR THE PRESIDENT AND OTHERS IN AUTHORITY

11

O Lord, our heavenly Father, whose glory is in all the world, and who dost from thy throne behold all the dwellers upon earth: Most heartily we beseech thee, with thy favor to behold and bless thy servants, *the President of the United States, the governor of this state,* and all others who bear rule throughout the world. Grant them wisdom and strength to know and to do thy will. Fill them with the love of truth and righteousness. So rule their hearts and prosper their endeavors, that law and order, justice and peace may everywhere prevail, to the honor of thy holy name; through Jesus Christ our Lord. **Amen.**

FOR OUR LEADERS

12

O God, almighty Father, King of kings and Lord of all our rulers: Grant that the hearts and minds of all our leaders, statesmen, judges, men of learning, and men of wealth, may be so filled with the love of thy laws, and of that which is righteous and life-giving, that they may be worthy stewards of thy good and perfect gifts; through Jesus Christ our Lord. **Amen.**

FOR LEADERS IN THE CITY

13

Guide, O Lord, we pray thee, the mayors and chief officers of our cities, with all others who share in the ordering of our community life. Give strength, honor, and charity to all our fellow citizens, that they and we may do our work, seeking not the good of any party or faction but of all people. Sustain us by a vision of freedom and a peaceful and happy city; through Jesus Christ our Lord. **Amen.**

FOR CONGRESS

14

O Thou, who dost govern the world in righteousness, and whose judgments are true and righteous altogether: Grant, we beseech thee, that those who rule over us and who legislate for us may be of one mind to establish justice and promote the welfare of all our people. Endow all members of Congress with a right understanding, pure purposes, and sound speech. Enable them to rise above all self-seeking and party zeal to the nobler concerns of public good and human brotherhood. Cleanse our public life of every evil; subdue in our nation all that is harmful; and make us a disciplined and devoted people, that we may do thy will on earth as it is done in heaven; even through Jesus Christ our Lord. **Amen.**

FOR COURTS OF JUSTICE

15

Almighty God, who sittest in the throne judging right: We humbly beseech thee to bless the courts of justice and the magistrates in all this land, and give unto them the spirit of wisdom and understanding, that they may discern the truth, and impartially administer the law in the fear of thee alone; through him who shall come to be our judge, thy Son our Savior Jesus Christ. **Amen.**

FOR THOSE WHO ARE RESPONSIBLE FOR GOVERNMENT

16

Almighty God, who alone givest wisdom and understanding: Inspire, we pray thee, the minds of all to whom thou hast committed the responsibility of government and leadership in the nations of the world. Give to them the vision of truth and justice, that by their counsel all nations and peoples may work together in true brotherhood, and thy Church may serve thee in unity and peace; through Jesus Christ our Lord. **Amen.**

FOR CIVIC RIGHTEOUSNESS

17

O God, thou great governor of all the world: We pray for all who hold public office and power, and for the life, welfare, and virtue of the people who are in their hands. Strengthen the sense of duty in our political life. Grant that the servants of the state may feel ever more deeply that any diversion of their public powers for private ends is a betrayal of their country. Purge our cities, states, and nation of the deep causes of corruption which have so often made sin profitable and uprightness hard. Breathe a new spirit into all our nation. Give our leaders new vision and set their hearts on fire with large resolves. Raise up a new generation of public men with the faith and daring of the kingdom of God in their hearts, who will enlist for life in a holy warfare for the freedom and the rights of all people. **Amen.**

FOR NATIONAL POLICY IN THE LIGHT OF FAITH

18

Teach us, O Lord, to see every question of national policy in the light of our faith; that we may check in ourselves and in others every temper which makes for war, all ungenerous judgments, all promptings of self-assurance, all presumptuous claims; and grant that, being ever ready to recognize the needs and aspirations of other nations, we may with patience do whatsoever in us lies to remove suspicions and misunderstandings; and to honor all men in Jesus Christ our Lord. **Amen.**

FOR OUR COUNTRY

19

Almighty God, our heavenly Father, bless our country that it may be a blessing to the world. Keep us from hypocrisy in feeling or action. Grant us sound government and just laws, good education and a clean press, simplicity and justice in our relations with one another, and, above all, a spirit of service which will abolish pride of place and inequality of opportunity; through Jesus Christ our Lord. **Amen.**

FOR THE PEOPLE OF THIS CITY

20

O God, who hast taught us to live in the cities of this world as knowing our citizenship to be in heaven: Bless the people of this city, and guide with thy heavenly wisdom those who bear office in the same; that they may ever keep before their eyes the vision of that city which hath foundations, whose builder and maker is God; through Jesus Christ our Lord. **Amen.**

FOR THE PEOPLE OF THIS LAND

21

O God, who hast mercifully guided our forefathers to build a new world in this broad land, and who didst give them faith to believe that these varied peoples might become one nation, indivisible, with liberty and justice for all: So implant within our hearts, we beseech thee, the desire to do thy holy will, that we may not fail them or thee, and that being always open to thy gracious demands, we may so serve thee in this present time, that thou canst here show thy favor to the generations yet to come; in the name of Jesus Christ our Lord, and for his sake. **Amen.**

FOR ALL RACES AND KINDREDS OF MEN

22

O God, who art the hope of all the ends of the earth, the God of the spirits of all flesh: We beseech thee to hear our humble intercession for all races and kindreds of men, that thou will turn all hearts unto thyself. Remove from our minds hatred, prejudice, and contempt for those who are not of our own race or color, class or creed, that, departing from everything that estranges and divides, we may by thee be brought into unity of spirit, in the bond of peace. **Amen.**

FOR THE CONCORD OF THE NATIONS

23

O almighty God, the refuge of all them that put their trust in thee: We turn to thee in this time of trouble. Direct the course of his world, we humbly beseech thee, in accordance with thy holy will; take away whatsoever hinders the nations from unity and concord; prosper all counsels which make for the restoration of a rightful and abiding peace. This we ask for thy mercy's sake; through Jesus Christ our Lord. **Amen.**

FOR PEACE

24

Eternal God, in whose perfect kingdom no sword is drawn but the sword of righteousness, and no strength known but the strength of love: So guide and inspire, we pray thee, the work of all who seek thy kingdom at home and abroad, that all peoples may seek and find their security, not in force of arms, but in the perfect love that casteth out fear, and in the fellowship revealed to us by thy Son Jesus Christ our Lord. **Amen.**

FOR JUSTICE AND PEACE

25

O God, the King of righteousness, lead us, we pray thee, in ways of justice and peace; inspire us to break down all tyranny and oppression, to gain for every man his due reward, and from every man his due service, that each may live for all and all may care for each; in Jesus Christ our Lord. **Amen.**

26

Almighty Father, who by thy Son Jesus Christ has sanctified labor to the welfare of mankind: Prosper, we pray thee, the industries of this land, and all those who are engaged therein; that, shielded in all their temptations and dangers, and receiving a due reward of their labors, they may praise thee by living according to thy will; through Jesus Christ our Lord. **Amen.**

27

O God, who hast made us messengers of peace in a world of strife, and messengers of strife in a world of false peace: Make strong our hands, make clear our voices, give us humility with firmness and insight with passion, that we may fight not to conquer but to redeem; through Jesus Christ our Lord. **Amen.**

FOR ALL NATIONS

28

O Lord our God, who dost will for all nations such good things as pass man's understanding: Shape the desires and deeds of thy people in accordance with thy purpose for the world, that, seeking first thy kingdom and righteousness, we may be good citizens of our country, and set forth the true welfare of mankind; through thy Son our Lord Jesus Christ, to whom with thee and the Holy Spirit be all honor and glory, world without end. **Amen.**

FOR PROTECTION FROM WAR

29

O God, who hast made of one blood all the nations of the earth, and hast set the bounds of their habitation that they might seek after thee and find thee: Mercifully hear our supplications, and remove from us the menace of war. Guide the rulers with thy counsel and restrain the passions of the people, so that bloodshed may be averted and peace be preserved. And, by the pouring forth of thy Spirit upon all flesh, quicken the sense of our common brotherhood; bring the nations into a new bond of fellowship; and hasten the time when the kingdoms of this world shall become the kingdom of our Lord and Savior Jesus Christ. **Amen.**

ATOMIC POWER

30

Almighty and merciful God, without whom all things hasten to destruction and fall into nothingness: Look, we beseech thee, upon thy family of nations and men, to which thou hast committed power in trust for their mutual health and comfort. Save us and help us, O Lord, lest we abuse thy gift and make it our misery and ruin. Draw all men unto thee in thy kingdom of righteousness and truth; uproot our enmities, heal our divisions, cast out our fears; and renew our faith in thine unchanging purpose of good will and peace on earth; for the love of Jesus Christ our Lord. **Amen.**

FOR THE SPACE AGE

31

Almighty God, whose creative hand we discern in the vastness of the oceans, the strength of the hills, and the unimaginable reaches of space: Grant that as we delve more deeply into the mysteries of the world which thou hast made, we may never forget thy loving purpose for us and for all men, lest we perish in ignorance of the things belonging to our peace; in the name of Jesus Christ our Lord. **Amen.**

FOR RECONCILIATION

32

O God, who hast given us the grace to be the instruments of love in its work of healing and judgment, who hast commissioned us to proclaim forgiveness and condemnation, deliverance to the captive and captivity to the proud: Give us the patience of those who understand, and the impatience of those who love, that the might of thy gentleness may work through us, and the mercy of thy wrath may speak through us; in the name of Jesus Christ and for his sake. **Amen.**

A GENERAL INTERCESSION

33

O God, at whose word man goeth forth unto his work and to his labor until the evening: Be merciful to all whose duties are difficult or burdensome, and comfort them concerning their toil. Shield from bodily accident and harm the workmen at their work. Protect the efforts of sober and honest industry, and suffer not the hire of the laborers to be kept back. Incline the hearts of employers and of those whom they employ to mutual forbearance, fairness, and good will. Give the spirit of grace and of a sound mind to all in places of authority. Bless all those who labor in works of mercy and schools of good learning. Care for all aged persons and all little children, the sick and the afflicted, and those who travel by land, by sea, or by air. Remember all who by reason of weakness are overtasked, or because of poverty are forgotten. Let the sorrowful sighing of the prisoners come before thee, and according to the greatness of thy power preserve thou those that draw nigh unto death. Give ear unto our prayer, O merciful and gracious Father, for the love of thy dear Son our Savior Jesus Christ. **Amen.**

A GENERAL INTERCESSION

34

We pray, O blessed God, for thy holy and universal Church, that thou wouldest deepen her life, and increase and perfect her witness to thee in the world.

We pray for all nations, that to each may be given the blessings of Christian light and truth, a right mind, and just counsels. Grant peace on earth and good will among men, that all may employ thy good gifts of order and liberty to the welfare of mankind and to thy glory. Guide and strengthen the president and all others in authority, and continue thy favor to our beloved land.

Let thy blessing rest, O Lord, upon our common life, that our spirit be disciplined and earnest. Grant that our homes be holy, our work honorable, and our pleasures and enjoyments pure. Guard and save us from every selfish use of the liberty in which we stand. Bless our just and lawful undertakings, and grant that in time of prosperity we may not forget thee, nor in time of adversity think ourselves forgotten of thee.

Into thy hands, O Father, we commit the sick, the sorrowful, the lonely, the tempted, that they may know thy healing and sanctifying power, and obtain the victory of faith; through Jesus Christ thy Son. **Amen.**

FOR CHURCH, LAND, AND WORLD

35

Remember, O Lord, thy Church upon earth; deepen her influence and extend her power for good, till the kingdoms of this world become the kingdom of our Lord and of his Christ.

We pray for our beloved land: for our leaders and governors, and for all who have part in public service. Make them pure in motive, wise in counsel, and strong in action, doing right in the fear of thy holy name.

Father in heaven, look down in mercy upon our distraught and fevered world; forgive the mistaken ambitions, the selfish passions, and the presumptuous claims of men; remove all suspicion and bitterness from among the nations, and bring them to peace and concord by the redeeming love of Christ.

Have mercy, O Lord, upon those who are passing through sore trial: the poor, the sick, the anxious, the oppressed, those who are in danger from the fury of the elements or from the violence of men. Inspire in us and in our fellow men the will to help our suffering brethren. Heal, protect, and strengthen them according to their need. Comfort those in sorrow with the comfort which is in Christ Jesus our Lord.

We pray for our own dear ones, wheresoever they are, that, surrounded by thy love, they may be kept in health and joy, and abide in safety and peace; through Jesus Christ our Lord. **Amen.**

FOR CHURCH, STATE, AND WORLD

36

Let us pray for a new spirit in the Church:

By this shall all men know that we are his disciples, if we have love one to another.

God our shepherd, give to the Church a new vision and a new love, new wisdom and fresh understanding, the revival of her brightness and the renewal of her unity, that the eternal message of thy Son, undefiled by the traditions of men, may be hailed as the good news of the new age; through him who maketh all things new, Jesus Christ our Lord. **Amen.**

Let us pray for a new spirit in the state:

194

Thou shalt wipe away all tears from their eyes: for the former things are passed away.

God our ruler, give to every state the dawning spirit of human brotherhood, a new respect for man and for woman, new loyalty in service and charity, new happiness in work and justice in reward, that our homes may be restored in thee, our cities rebuilt, and all the world may reflect the radiance of that new Jerusalem whose river is the water of life, and whose light is the Lamb that was slain and now liveth for evermore. **Amen.**

Let us pray for a new spirit in the world:

Unto the Father of our Lord Jesus Christ, of whom the whole family in heaven and earth is named.

God our Father, give to the nations of the world a new heart of comradeship, the old man of ignorance and cruelty being done away, and the new man put on, renewed in knowledge, to strengthen and to serve the brethren; that every people may bring its tribute of excellence to the common treasury, without fear, and without the lust of domination, and all the world may go forward in the new and living way which he hath consecrated for us, who now liveth and reigneth, with thee and the Spirit of truth, one God, world without end. **Amen.**

FOR GOD'S MERCY

37

Almighty God, the fountain of all wisdom, who knowest our necessities before we ask, and our ignorance in asking: We beseech thee to have compassion upon our infirmities; and those things, which for our unworthiness we dare not and for our blindness we cannot ask, vouchsafe to give us, for the worthiness of thy Son Jesus Christ our Lord. **Amen.**

Offertory Sentences and Prayers

1

Remember the words of the Lord Jesus, how he said, "It is more blessed to give than to receive." *From Acts 20:35*

2

Let your light so shine before men, that they may see your good works and give glory to your Father who is in heaven. *Matthew 5:16*

3

Every man shall give as he is able, according to the blessing of the Lord your God which he has given you. *Deuteronomy 16:17*

4

Do not neglect to do good and to share what you have, for such sacrifices are pleasing to God. *Hebrews 13:16*

5

He who sows sparingly will also reap sparingly, and he who sows bountifully will also reap bountifully. Each one must do as he has made up his mind, not reluctantly or under compulsion, for God loves a cheerful giver. *II Corinthians 9:6-7*

6

Offer to God a sacrifice of thanksgiving, and pay your vows to the Most High. *Psalm 50:14*

7

Not everyone who says to me, "Lord, Lord," shall enter the kingdom of heaven, but he who does the will of my Father who is in heaven.

Matthew 7:21

8

And the King will answer them, "Truly, I say to you, as you did it to one of the least of these my brethren, you did it to me." *Matthew 25:40*

9

So whatever you wish that men would do to you, do so to them; for this is the law and the prophets. *Matthew 7:12*

10

Blessed is he who considers the poor! The Lord delivers him in the day of trouble. *Psalm 41:1*

11

Therefore, I command you, You shall open wide your hand to your brother, to the needy and to the poor, in the land. *Deuteronomy 15:11*

12

If you have many possessions, make your gift from them in proportion; if few, do not be afraid to give according to the little you have. So you will be laying up a good treasure for yourself against the day of necessity.

Tobit 4:8-9

13

He who is kind to the poor lends to the Lord, and he will repay him for his deed.

Proverbs 19:17

14

So then, as we have opportunity, let us do good to all men, and especially to those who are of the household of faith.

Galatians 6:10

15

If any one has the world's goods and sees his brother in need, yet closes his heart against him, how does God's love abide in him? Let us not love in word or speech but in deed and in truth.

I John 3:17-18

16

Do not lay up for yourselves treasures on earth, where moth and rust consume and where thieves break in and steal, but lay up for yourselves treasures in heaven, where neither moth nor rust consumes and where thieves do not break in and steal. For where your treasure is, there will your heart be also.

Matthew 6:19-21

17

There is great gain in godliness with contentment; for we brought nothing into the world, and we cannot take anything out of the world.

I Timothy 6:6-7

18

Thine, O Lord, is the greatness, and the power, and the glory, and the victory, and the majesty; for all that is in the heavens and in the earth is thine; thine is the kingdom, O Lord, and thou art exalted as head above all.

I Chronicles 29:11

19

O Lord our God, send down upon us thy Holy Spirit, we beseech thee, to cleanse our hearts, to hallow our gifts, and to perfect the offering of ourselves to thee; through Jesus Christ our Lord. **Amen.**

20

Accept, O Lord, these offerings thy people make unto thee, and grant that the work to which they are devoted may prosper under thy guidance, to the glory of thy name; through Jesus Christ our Lord. **Amen.**

21

Accept these offerings, we beseech thee, O Lord, and mercifully direct and enable us by thy Holy Spirit, that all things which we do in thy name may be truly wrought in thee; through Jesus Christ our Lord. **Amen.**

22

O God, most merciful and gracious, of whose bounty we have all received: Accept this offering of thy people. Remember in thy love those who have brought it, and those for whom it is given, and so follow it with thy blessing that it may promote peace and good will among men, and advance the kingdom of our Lord and Savior Jesus Christ. **Amen.**

23

O God, of whose bounty we have all received: Accept this offering of thy people; and so follow it with thy blessing that it may promote peace and good will among men, and advance the kingdom of our Lord and Savior Jesus Christ. **Amen.**

24

Almighty God, whose loving hand hath given us all that we possess: Grant us grace that we may honor thee with our substance, and remembering the account which we must one day give, be faithful stewards of thy bounty; through Jesus Christ our Lord. **Amen.**

25

O God, who needest not to be enriched with any gifts that we may bring, yet who lovest the cheerful giver: Receive these our offerings which we present before thee, and with them ourselves, our souls and our bodies, as a living sacrifice, holy and acceptable to thee; through Jesus Christ our Lord. **Amen.**

26

Lord Jesus, who for our sake didst become poor, that by thy poverty we might become rich: Grant to thy people so to give of their substance as to acknowledge that they belong wholly to thee; for thine own sake. **Amen.**

27

Heavenly Father, giver of all good things, who hast taught us that it is more blessed to give than to receive: We dedicate these our offerings to the service of thy Church, humbly beseeching thee that all our gifts and energies may be consecrated to the extension of thy kingdom on earth; through Jesus Christ our Lord. **Amen.**

28

For the preservation of thy Church, O God; for the ordering of thy worship; for the due administration of thy Word and ordinances; for the maintenance of Christian fellowship and discipline; for the edification of believers, and the conversion of the world, we offer unto thee these gifts. Accept them, we beseech thee, in the name of Jesus Christ our Lord. **Amen.**

29

Eternal God, giver of every good and perfect gift, who seekest above all thy gifts to give thyself to us: Grant that, with these token gifts of our hands, we may more fully give ourselves in joyous obedience and service; through Jesus Christ our Lord. **Amen.**

30

Almighty God, the source of all our comfort and joy: Receive us and these our gifts as we dedicate them and ourselves anew unto thee. Consecrate for us the experience and resolves of this hour, and lead us in the way of true understanding and fruitful service; through Jesus Christ our Lord. **Amen.**

31

All that we have, we have of thee, Creator and preserver of mankind; accept these gifts which we now bring before thee; and help us to make the whole of life an offering, and every thought a prayer. We would seal this our worship in a renewed consecration of ourselves and our coming days to thy service; through Jesus Christ our Lord. **Amen.**

Versicles

† *These may be used to introduce Acts of Worship.*

BEFORE THE PSALTER OR ACT OF PRAISE

1

Minister: O Lord, open thou our lips.

People: **And our mouth shall show forth thy praise.**

Minister: Praise ye the Lord.

People: **The Lord's name be praised.**

2

Minister: O magnify the Lord with me.

People: **And let us exalt his name together.**

† *Here let the people stand.*

Minister: Let the people praise thee, O God.

People: **Yea, let all the people praise thee.**

BEFORE A LITANY OR PRAYER

3

Minister: Lord, have mercy upon us.

People: **Christ, have mercy upon us.**

Minister: Lord, have mercy upon us.

4

Minister: The Lord be with you.

People: **And with thy spirit.**

Minister: Let us pray.

† *Here let the people be seated and bowed.*

Minister: O Lord, show thy mercy upon us.

People: **And grant us thy salvation.**

Minister: O God, make clean our hearts within us.

People: **And take not thy Holy Spirit from us.**

5

Minister: The Lord be with you.

People: **And with thy spirit.**

Minister: Let us pray.

† *Here let the people be seated and bowed.*

Minister: O Lord, show thy mercy upon us.
People: **And grant us thy salvation.**
Minister: O Lord, save the nation.
People: **And mercifully hear us when we call upon thee.**
Minister: Endue thy ministers with righteousness.
People: **And make thy chosen people joyful.**
Minister: O Lord, save thy people.
People: **And bless thine inheritance.**
Minister: Give peace in our time, O Lord;
People: **Because there is none other that fighteth for us, but only thou, O God.**

BEFORE A SCRIPTURE LESSON

6

Minister: O Lord, open thou our eyes
People: **That we may behold wondrous things out of thy law.**

Salutations

† *These may be used to express greeting at the beginning of a service or before the sermon.*

1

In the name of the Father and of the Son and of the Holy Spirit.
Matthew 28:19

2

Grace to you and peace from God our Father and the Lord Jesus Christ.
Romans 1:7

3

Grace to you and peace from him who is and who was and who is to come.
Revelation 1:4b

4

Peace be to this house, in the name of the Father and of the Son and of the Holy Spirit.

201

Communion Table Dismissals

† *For use in the service of Holy Communion.*

1

Jesus said: "I am the bread of life; he who comes to me shall not hunger, and he who believes in me shall never thirst." *John 6:35*

Arise and go in peace, and may the bread of heaven nourish your soul unto everlasting life. **Amen.**

2

Jesus said: "I am the door; if any one enters by me, he will be saved, and will go in and out and find pasture." *John 10:9*

Arise and go in peace, and in his service may you find perfect freedom. **Amen.**

3

Jesus said: "I am the light of the world; he who follows me will not walk in darkness, but will have the light of life." *John 8:12*

Arise and go in peace, and may the light of the world shine on your pathway and in your heart forever. **Amen.**

4

Jesus said: "I am the way, and the truth, and the life; no one comes to the Father, but by me." *John 14:6*

Arise and go in peace, and may you ever walk in the way of life and truth. **Amen.**

5

Jesus said: "I am the vine, you are the branches. By this my Father is glorified, that you bear much fruit, and so prove to be my disciples." *John 15:5a, 8*

Arise and go in peace, and may the glory of your life be the fruits of the Spirit. **Amen.**

6

Jesus said: "I am the good shepherd; I know my own and my own know me. And I have other sheep, that are not of this fold; I must bring them also. So there shall be one flock, one shepherd." *John 10:14, 16*

Arise and go in peace, and may the voice of the good shepherd be your comfort in sorrow and your guide in happiness. **Amen.**

7

Jesus said: "I came that they may have life, and have it abundantly."

John 10:10b

Arise and go in peace, and may your abundant life in Christ overflow in deeds of love and service. **Amen.**

8

Jesus said: "You did not choose me, but I chose you and appointed you that you should go and bear fruit and that your fruit should abide."

John 15:16a

Arise and go in peace, and by your fruits may all men know that you are disciples of our Lord. **Amen.**

9

Jesus said: "You are the light of the world. Let your light so shine before men, that they may see your good works and give glory to your Father who is in heaven." *Matthew 5:14a, 16*

Arise and go in peace, and may the true light shine into your mind with the knowledge and love of God and of his Son Jesus Christ our Lord. **Amen.**

10

Jesus said: "If any man would come after me, let him deny himself and take up his cross and follow me. For whoever would save his life will lose it, and whoever loses his life for my sake will find it."

Matthew 16:24-25

Arise and go in peace, and by being spent in the service of Christ, may you find the source of rich and abundant life. **Amen.**

11

Jesus said: "Every one then who hears these words of mine and does them will be like a wise man who built his house upon the rock; and it did not fall." *From Matthew 7:24-25*

Arise and go in peace, and by faith in the true word of God may you have life everlasting. **Amen.**

12

Jesus said: "I have yet many things to say to you, but you cannot bear them now. When the Spirit of truth comes, he will guide you into all the truth." *John 16:12-13a*

Arise and go in peace, and may the Spirit of truth be your companion and guide forever. **Amen.**

Ascriptions of Glory

1

Now unto the King eternal, immortal, invisible, the only wise God, be honor and glory for ever and ever. **Amen.**   *I Timothy 1:17 KJV*

2

Now unto him that is able to do exceeding abundantly above all that we ask or think, according to the power that worketh in us, unto him be glory in the Church by Christ Jesus throughout all ages, world without end. **Amen.**   *Ephesians 3:20-21 KJV*

3

The God of all grace, who has called you to his eternal glory in Christ, will himself restore, establish, and strengthen you. To him be the dominion for ever and ever. **Amen.**   *I Peter 5:10-11*

4

Now unto him that is able to keep you from falling, and to present you faultless before the presence of his glory with exceeding joy: to the only wise God our Savior, be glory and majesty, dominion and power, both now and ever. **Amen.**   *Jude 1:24-25 KJV*

5

And now unto the blessed and only Sovereign, the King of kings and Lord of lords, who alone has immortality and dwells in unapproachable light, whom no man has ever seen or can see: to him be honor and eternal dominion. **Amen.**   *From I Timothy 6:15-16*

6

Thine, O Lord, is the greatness, and the power, and the glory, and the victory, and the majesty; for all that is in the heavens and in the earth is thine; thine is the kingdom, O Lord, and thou art exalted as head above all. **Amen.**   *I Chronicles 29:11*

7

To him who loves us and has freed us from our sins by his blood and made us a kingdom, priests to his God and Father: to him be glory and dominion for ever and ever. **Amen.**   *Revelation 1:5c-6*

8

To him who sits upon the throne and to the Lamb be blessing and honor and glory and might for ever and ever! **Amen.** *Revelation 5:13*

9

Blessing and glory and wisdom and thanksgiving and honor and power and might be to our God for ever and ever! **Amen.** *Revelation 7:12*

Benedictions

1

The grace of the Lord Jesus Christ and the love of God and the fellowship of the Holy Spirit be with you all. **Amen.** *II Corinthians 13:14*

2

The grace of the Lord Jesus Christ, and the love of God, and the communion of the Holy Ghost, be with you all. **Amen.**
II Corinthians 13:14 KJV

3

The Lord bless you and keep you: the Lord make his face to shine upon you, and be gracious to you: the Lord lift up his countenance upon you, and give you peace. **Amen.** *Numbers 6:24-26*

4

Now may the God of peace who brought again from the dead our Lord Jesus, the great shepherd of the sheep, by the blood of the eternal covenant, equip you with everything good that you may do his will, working in you that which is pleasing in his sight, through Jesus Christ: to whom be glory for ever and ever. **Amen.** *Hebrews 13:20-21*

5

And now may the blessing of God Almighty, Father, Son, and Holy Spirit, be among you and abide with you, now and evermore. **Amen.**

6

The peace of God, which passeth all understanding, keep your hearts and minds in the knowledge and love of God, and of his Son Jesus Christ our Lord; and the blessing of God Almighty, the Father, the Son, and the Holy Spirit, be among you, and remain with you always. **Amen.**

7

Unto God's gracious mercy and protection we commit you; and the blessing of God Almighty, the Father, the Son, and the Holy Spirit, be upon you, and remain with you always. **Amen.**

8

Now may our Lord Jesus Christ himself, and God our Father, who loved us and gave us eternal comfort and good hope through grace, comfort your hearts and establish them in every good work and word. **Amen.**

II Thessalonians 2:16-17

9

May the God of hope fill you with all joy and peace in believing, so that you may abound in hope by the power of the Holy Spirit. **Amen.**

From Romans 15:13

10

May the God of steadfastness and encouragement grant you to live in such harmony with one another, in accord with Christ Jesus, that together you may with one voice glorify the God and Father of our Lord Jesus Christ. **Amen.**

Romans 15:5-6

Prayers for Use Before Leaving the Church

1

Almighty God, who hast given us grace at this time with one accord to make our common supplications unto thee, and dost promise that, when two or three are gathered together in thy name, thou wilt grant their requests: Fulfill now, O Lord, the desires and petitions of thy servants, as may be most expedient for them, granting us in this world knowledge of thy truth, and in the world to come life everlasting. **Amen.**

2

Dismiss us now, O Lord, with thy blessing, and accompany us ever with thy grace, that we may henceforth live in peace, love, and holiness; through Jesus Christ our Lord. **Amen.**

3

O Lord God, Father Almighty, bless and sanctify this sacrifice of praise which has been offered unto thee to the honor and glory of thy name; through Jesus Christ our Lord. **Amen.**

4

Grant, O Lord, that what has been said with our lips we may believe in our hearts, and that what we believe in our hearts we may practice in our lives; through Jesus Christ our Lord. **Amen.**

5

Direct us, O Lord, in all our doings, with thy most gracious favor, and further us with thy continual help, that in all our works, begun, continued, and ended in thee, we may glorify thy holy name, and finally, by thy mercy, obtain everlasting life; through Jesus Christ our Lord. **Amen.**

6

Grant, we beseech thee, almighty God, that the words which we have heard this day with our outward ears may, through thy grace, be so grafted inwardly in our hearts, that they may bring forth in us the fruit of good living, to the honor and praise of thy name; through Jesus Christ our Lord. **Amen.**

7

Grant, O Lord, that the ears which have heard the voice of thy songs may be closed to the voice of clamor and dispute, that the eyes which have seen thy great love may also behold thy blessed hope, that the tongues which have sung thy praise may speak the truth, that the feet which have walked thy courts may walk in the light, and that the bodies which have partaken of thy living body may be restored in newness of life. Glory be to thee for thine unspeakable gift. **Amen.**

GENERAL PRAYERS

Litanies

A RECOLLECTION OF JESUS

1

Let us remember Jesus:

Who, though he was rich, yet for our sakes became poor and dwelt among us.

Who was content to be subject to his parents, the child of a poor man's home.

Who lived for nearly thirty years the common life, earning his living with his own hands and declining no humble tasks.

Whom the common people heard gladly, for he understood their ways.

May this mind be in us which was in Jesus Christ.

Let us remember Jesus:

Who was mighty in deed, healing the sick and the disordered, using for others the powers he would not invoke for himself.

Who refused to force men's allegiance.

Who was Master and Lord to his disciples, yet was among them as their companion and as one who served.

Whose meat was to do the will of the Father who sent him.

May this mind be in us which was in Jesus Christ.

Let us remember Jesus:

Who loved men, yet retired from them to pray, rose a great while before day, watched through a night, stayed in the wilderness, went up into a mountain, sought a garden.

Who, when he would help a tempted disciple, prayed for him.

Who prayed for the forgiveness of those who rejected him, and for the perfecting of those who received him.

Who observed good customs, but defied conventions which did not serve the purposes of God.

Who hated sin because he knew the cost of pride and selfishness, of cruelty, and impurity, to man, and still more to his Father in heaven.

May this mind be in us which was in Jesus Christ.

Let us remember Jesus:

Who believed in men to the last and never despaired of them.

Who through all disappointment never lost heart.

Who disregarded his own comfort and convenience, and thought first of others' needs, and, though he suffered long, was always kind.

Who, when he was reviled, reviled not again, and when he suffered, threatened not.

Who humbled himself and carried obedience to the point of death, even death on the cross, wherefore God has highly exalted him.

May this mind be in us which was in Jesus Christ.

Let us unite in prayer that Christ may dwell in our hearts.

O Christ, our only Savior, so come to dwell in us that we may go forth

with the light of thy hope in our eyes, and with thy faith and love in our hearts. Amen.

LITANY ON THE WILL OF GOD

2

Jesus said: "Not everyone who says to me, 'Lord, Lord,' shall enter the kingdom of heaven, but he who does the will of my Father who is in heaven. I have come not to do my own will, but the will of him who sent me."

It is the will of God:

To gather together in one all things in Christ, both which are in heaven and which are on earth.

That we should show forth his praises who called us out of the darkness into his marvelous light.

That we should believe in him and love him with all our heart, with all our mind, with all our soul, and with all our strength.

That we should worship him and put our whole trust in him all the days of our life.

Lord, have mercy upon us, and incline our hearts to do thy will.

Jesus said: "You are the salt of the earth, but if salt has lost its taste, how shall its saltness be restored?"

It is the will of God:

That we should endeavor to keep our bodies in health and strength, and our appetites and impulses under control, and everywhere and in all things be temperate and pure.

That we should train our minds to be true in our thinking and just in all our judging.

That we should be honest, truthful, and upright in thought, word, and deed.

That we should be diligent and faithful in our several callings, doing our daily work in all simplicity and integrity, and laboring only for the things which are just and good.

That speaking the truth in love, we should grow up together in all things unto him who is the head of the body, even Christ.

Lord, have mercy upon us, and incline our hearts to do thy will.

Jesus said: "You are the light of the world. Let your light so shine before men, that they may see your good works and give glory to your Father who is in heaven."

It is the will of God:

That we should not be anxious for the morrow, nor for our life, what we shall eat or what we shall drink, nor for the body what we shall put on.

That we should rule our spirits, bear with each other's infirmities, and, as much as in us lies, live peaceably with all men.

That we should live chiefly to minister to others' needs and not to seek only our own pleasure and gain.

That we should do what we can to take away the sin and sorrow of the world and to overcome evil with good.

Lord, have mercy upon us, and incline our hearts to do thy will.

Let us unite in prayer for grace to do God's will.

O Lord, we beseech thee mercifully to receive our prayers; and grant that we may both perceive and know what things we ought to do, and also may have grace and power faithfully to fulfill the same; through Jesus Christ our Lord. Amen.

A LITANY OF THE DIVINE WILL

3

Jesus said: "Whosoever shall do the will of God, the same is my brother, and sister, and mother."

Let us pray.

O God, who hast shown us thy eternal will in the life of Christ our Lord,

thy will be done on earth as it is in heaven.

O God, who art ever working in men's hearts by the operation of thy Spirit, to make us fellow workers with thy will,

thy will be done on earth as it is in heaven.

O God, who willest that all men should be saved, and come to the knowledge of thy truth,

thy will be done on earth as it is in heaven.

From all reliance on ourselves alone, from trying to limit the range of thy purposes, from doubts of thy mightiness in operation,

save us and help us, we humbly beseech thee, O Lord.

From all unwillingness to learn thy will, from clinging to our own plans and desires, from all want of faith that hinders self-commitment to thy guidance,

save us and help us, we humbly beseech thee, O Lord.

From cowardice in following thy leading, from ever suffering our own ambitions to cloud the vision of thy will for us, from trying to serve thee and escape the cost,

save us and help us, we humbly beseech thee, O Lord.

From weakness when we are faced with decisions, from overconfidence in making them, from acting without trying to learn thy will,

save us and help us, we humbly beseech thee, O Lord.

From shirking the responsibility of our place in the divine order, from fearing new truth and new ways of thought and life,

save us and help us, we humbly beseech thee, O Lord.

From seeking to set forward human progress, whether in the Church or in the world, by doing our own will instead of loyally asking to know thine,

save us and help us, we humbly beseech thee, O Lord. Amen.

A LITANY OF SELF-EXAMINATION

4

Let us pray.

O Lord, open thou our eyes, that we may see ourselves as thou seest us; in thy mercy show us the evil that is in us, and cleanse us by thy mighty power.

From irresolute purpose, from unchastened desires, and from a weak and wavering will,

good Lord, deliver us.

From slackness and indolence, from indifference to the treasures of knowledge, and a refusal to use the gifts with which thou hast endowed us,

good Lord, deliver us.

From low ideals of life, and from thoughtless disregard of the influence of our conduct,

good Lord, deliver us.

From pride and vanity and boasting, from self-assertion and self-seeking, and blindness to the common weal,

good Lord, deliver us.

From dislike of criticism and love of popularity, and from unreadiness to do our duty at whatever cost,

good Lord, deliver us.

From hastiness of speech and sullenness of temper, from readiness to think the worst of others, and from all unseemly and unworthy conversation,

good Lord, deliver us.

Let us pray together, saying,

Heavenly Father, blot out, we beseech thee, our past transgressions; forgive us our frequent negligence and ignorance; and lift us up to new energy of mind and devotion of heart, that we may have strength to persevere even to the end, through success and failure, through good report and evil report. This we ask in the name of Jesus Christ and for his sake. Amen.

LITANY OF CONFESSION

5

Let us humbly confess our sins to almighty God, our heavenly Father, praying that he will make us to know the faults we have not known, and that he will show us the harmful consequences of those things in us which we have not cared to control.

For deafness to thy call; for slothfulness in service; for indifference to the needs of others; for unwillingness to bear our brother's burden; for our faltering witness for thee;

Lord have mercy upon us.

For unguarded moments and sins of impulse; for anger and uncharitableness; for impatience and thoughtlessness which have wounded others;

Lord have mercy upon us.

For resentment under rebuke and the pride which hardens us against the truth; for slackness in self-discipline and complacency in unworthy habits;

Lord have mercy upon us.

In our waywardness and self-sufficiency; and in our utter need and helplessness;

Lord have mercy upon us.

Thou whose mercy is without measure, whose goodness never fails, grant us the forgiveness of what is past, and a perfect repentance of all our sins; that for the time to come we may with a pure spirit do thy will, O God, walking humbly with thee and charitably with all men. **Amen.**

A SUPPLICATION

6

Let us pray.

Be pleased, O Lord, to hear our humble supplication, and to keep us in thy way.

From indolence and weakness of purpose, from indifference, carelessness, and insincerity,

O Lord, deliver us.

From despondency and lack of faith, from cowardice and self-conceit,

O Lord, deliver us.

From dishonesty, extravagance, and debt, and all injustice to others,

O Lord, deliver us.

From all temptation to put pleasure above duty, and from all frailty of the flesh,

O Lord, deliver us.

In all times of ignorance or perplexity, in all times of mistake or misunderstanding,

help us, O Lord.

That we may love thee in our fellow men, and find thee in our work and prayers,

we beseech thee to hear us, O Lord.

O God, the protector of all that trust in thee, without whom nothing is strong, nothing is holy: Increase and multiply upon us thy mercy, that, thou being our ruler and guide, we may so pass through things temporal that we finally lose not the things eternal; through Jesus Christ our Lord, to whom with the Father and the Holy Spirit, one God, be honor, glory, dominion, and praise for ever and ever. **Amen.**

A LITANY OF REMEMBRANCE

7

Let us pray.

O God, who art the Father of all: Grant thy blessing upon us who are gathered here, and upon the multitudes of every name who are joined with us in one household of faith throughout the world.

We offer unto thee, O God, our thanksgiving, and come to pay our vows to the Most High.

We remember the fathers from the beginning of the world, and all who have wrought righteousness, even down to the present day.

Grant unto us, O God, that we may have our part and lot with all thy saints.

We remember all whom we love and who love us, both those who have fallen asleep and those whose presence still blesses us. Thanks be to thee for their benediction upon our lives.

Establish thou the work of their hands, and keep us in one spirit with them.

We remember those in distress, who suffer in body, mind, or estate, those who are in prison and in bonds. As bound with them, and as sufferers with them, we bear them in our hearts and pray for their relief.

Teach us and lead us through all life's ways to an awareness of thy love and care.

We remember our enemies, if there be any who have injured us or cherish hatred against us. We pray thee to turn their hearts, and ours, that we may live peaceably with all men. If there be any whom we have wronged, move us to make amends and to seek forgiveness at their hands; and may we freely forgive all who have wronged us.

Grant us grace to surrender ourselves wholly to thee, that we may find that inward peace which the world can neither give nor take away.

We remember the whole family of man, and pray thee that the spirits of all flesh may taste of thy grace, and that all the ends of the earth may see the salvation of our God.

May the faith that makes faithful, and hope that endures, and the love that triumphs be with us always; through Jesus Christ our Lord. Amen.

LITANY OF COMMEMORATION

8

Let us pray.

Almighty God, before whom do stand the living and the dead, we thy children, whose mortal life is but a hand's breadth, give thanks to thee for all those through whom thou hast blessed our pilgrimage,

thanks be to thee, O God.

For all lives that have quickened us, whose influence is a healing grace,

we praise thee, O Lord.

For the dear friends and kindred of our homes whose faces we see no more, but whose love is with us for ever,

we lift up thankful hearts.

For the teachers and companions of our childhood and youth, and for the members of our household of faith who worship thee now in heaven,

we lift up our hearts in gratitude and praise.

For those through whose sacrifice we live, our brethren who have given their life for our freedom among the nations,

we give thanks and will give thanks.

That we may hold them in continual remembrance, and ever think of them as with thee in that city whose gates are not shut by day and where there is no night,

we beseech thee to hear us, O God.

That we may now be dedicated to working for a world where labor is rewarded, fear dispelled, and the nations made one in the brotherhood of thy kingdom,

O Lord, save thy people and bless thine heritage. Day by day we magnify thee, and worship thy name, world without end. Amen.

LITANY OF INTERCESSION

9

The Lord be with you.

And with thy spirit.

Let us pray.

Almighty and ever-living God, who hast taught us to make prayer and supplication for all men: Hear us we humbly beseech thee:

That it may please thee to inspire continually the universal Church with the spirit of truth, unity, and concord;

hear us, we beseech thee, O Lord.

That it may please thee to grant that all they that confess thy holy name may agree in the truth of thy holy Word, and live in unity and godly love;

hear us, we beseech thee, O Lord.

That it may please thee to give thy heavenly grace to all pastors of thy flock that they may by their life and doctrine set forth thy true and living word, and faithfully administer thy holy Sacraments;

hear us, we beseech thee, O Lord.

That it may please thee to bless in their several callings all thy servants who are laboring for the building up of thy Church and the spread of thy Gospel; that they may be made worthy ministers unto thee, serving thee in holiness and righteousness;

hear us, we beseech thee, O Lord.

That it may please thee to lead all nations in the way of righteousness and peace; and so to direct all who bear authority that thy people may be justly and quietly governed;

hear us, we beseech thee, O Lord.

Let us pray together, saying,

Almighty God, the fountain of all wisdom, who knowest our necessities before we ask, and our ignorance in asking: We beseech thee to have compassion on our infirmities; and those things which for our unworthiness we dare not, and for our blindness we cannot ask, vouchsafe to give us, for the worthiness of thy Son Jesus Christ our Lord. Amen.

LITANY OF INTERCESSION

10

Let us pray for the members of Christ's Church throughout the world; for all ministers of the Gospel; and for all teachers, leaders, and office-bearers, that they may be good stewards of the manifold grace of God.

Lord, hear this prayer;

and let our cry come unto thee.

For Christian missions everywhere; for the careless and godless, and for all who live in ignorance or neglect of the love of God in Christ,

Lord, hear this prayer;

and let our cry come unto thee.

Let us pray that justice, truth, and love may prevail in human affairs, that strife and warfare may be no more, and that all classes and nations may dwell together as brethren.

Lord, hear this prayer;

and let our cry come unto thee.

Let us pray for schools, colleges, and universities, that those who grow in knowledge may dedicate their learning to the service of God and of their fellow men, remembering that from those to whom much is given much will be required.

Lord, hear this prayer;

and let our cry come unto thee.

Let us pray for all children, and especially those of our families and church schools, that they may early be led to put their trust in Jesus Christ as their Savior and acknowledge him as Lord and Master.

Lord, hear this prayer;

and let our cry come unto thee.

Let us pray for all who are suffering from sickness of body or mind, for those who draw near to the end of life, and for the doctors, nurses, and kinsfolk who minister to their necessities.

Lord, hear this prayer;

and let our cry come unto thee. Amen.

LITANY FOR PEACE

11

Let us pray.

Remember, O Lord, the peoples of the world divided into many nations and tongues; deliver us from every evil which obstructs thy saving purpose; and fulfill thy promises of old to establish thy kingdom of peace.

From the curse of war and all that begets it,

O Lord, deliver us.

From believing and speaking lies against other nations,

O Lord, deliver us.

From narrow loyalties and selfish isolation,

O Lord, deliver us.

From fear and distrust of other nations, from all false pride, vainglory, and self-conceit,

O Lord, deliver us.

From the lust of the mighty for riches, that drives peaceful peoples to slaughter,

O Lord, deliver us.

From putting our trust in the weapons of war, and from want of faith in the power of justice and good will,

O Lord, deliver us.

From every thought, word, and deed which divides the human family and separates us from the perfect realization of thy love,

O Lord, deliver us; unto thee we commit ourselves; use even us with our ignorance and frailty to accomplish thy holy will; and hasten the day when all shall dwell together in mutual helpfulness and love; for thine is the kingdom, the power, and the glory, for ever and ever. Amen.

Morning, Day, and Evening

IN THE MORNING

1

O God, who hast folded back the mantle of the night to clothe us in the golden glory of the day: Chase from our hearts all gloomy thoughts, and make us glad with the brightness of hope, that we may effectively aspire to unwon virtues; through Jesus Christ our Lord. **Amen.**

2

O God, we give thee hearty thanks for the rest of the past night and for the gift of a new day, with its opportunities of pleasing thee. Grant that we may so pass its hours in the perfect freedom of thy service, that at eventide we may again give thanks unto thee; through Jesus Christ our Lord. **Amen.**

3

O heavenly Father, in whom we live and move and have our being: We humbly pray thee so to guide and govern us by thy Holy Spirit, that in all the cares and occupations of our daily life we may never forget thee, but remember that we are ever walking in thy sight; for thine own name's sake. **Amen.**

4

O Lord, who hast brought us through the darkness of night to the light of morning, and who, by thy Holy Spirit, dost illumine the darkness of ignorance and sin: We beseech thee of thy lovingkindness to pour thy holy light into our souls, that we may be ever devoted to thee, by whose wisdom we were created, by whose mercy we were redeemed, and by whose providence we are governed; to the honor and glory of thy great name. **Amen.**

5

O Thou who art the true and only light, to whom darkness and light are both alike, and who yet sendest us alternate mercies of the darkness and the day: We beseech thee that as thou liftest the curtain of night from our abodes, thou wilt also take away the veil from our hearts. Rise with thy morning upon our souls; quicken all our labor and our prayer; and though all else declines, let the noontide of thy grace and peace remain. Make us to walk while it is yet day, in the steps of him who, with fewest hours, finished thy divinest work, even Jesus Christ thy Son our Lord. **Amen.**

6

Grant us, O Lord, to pass this day in gladness and peace, without stumbling and without stain; that, reaching the eventide victorious over all temptation, we may praise thee, the eternal God, who art blessed and dost govern all things, world without end. **Amen.**

7

O God, Lord of all power and might, preserver of all thy creatures: Keep us this day in health of body and soundness of mind, in purity of heart and cheerfulness of spirit, in contentment with our lot and charity with our neighbor; and further all our lawful undertakings with thy blessing. In our labor strengthen us; in our difficulties direct us; in our troubles comfort us; and supply all our needs according to the riches of thy grace in Christ Jesus our Lord. **Amen.**

THIS DAY

8

O God, who orderest the common things of the common day: Sanctify by thy presence, and aid the trivial round and routine tasks of thy servant whose hope is in thee, that least duties may be grandly done and all activities marked with the seal of thy righteousness; through Jesus Christ our Lord. **Amen.**

9

O God, the God of all goodness and grace, who art worthy of a greater love than we can either give or understand: Fill our hearts, we beseech thee, with such love toward thee that nothing may seem too hard for us to do or to suffer in obedience to thy will, that so we may become daily more like thee, and dwell more and more in the light of thy presence; through Jesus Christ our Lord. **Amen.**

10

Eternal God, who by the life of thy dear Son hast shown us that there is no minute of our own but we may be doing thy will: Help us to use our time aright, that howsoever we be engaged, in work or leisure or play, we may stand before thee with a pure conscience, acting, speaking, and thinking as in thy presence; through the same Jesus Christ our Lord. **Amen.**

11

O God, who hast commanded that no man should be idle, but that all should work to do the thing that is good: Grant that I may diligently do my duty in my daily work, improving those talents which thou hast given me, and doing only those things which can be done to thy honor and glory; who livest and reignest, God, world without end. **Amen.**

12

Almighty God, by whose will it is that we walk by faith and not by sight in the mysterious universe which thou hast created: Daily increase our faith in thee, that in the midst of things which pass man's understanding, we may never doubt thy fatherly love and providence; through Jesus Christ our Lord. **Amen.**

13

O God, renew our spirits by thy Holy Spirit, and draw our hearts this day unto thyself, that our work may not be a burden, but a delight; and give us such a mighty love to thee as may sweeten all our obedience. Let us not serve with the spirit of bondage as slaves, but with cheerfulness and gladness, as children, delighting ourselves in thee and rejoicing in thy wishes for the sake of Jesus Christ. **Amen.**

IN THE EVENING

14

O Lord Jesus Christ, who art the very bright sun of the world, ever rising, never going down: Shine, we beseech thee, upon our spirit, that the night of sin and error being driven away by thy inward light, we may walk without stumbling, as in the day. Grant this, O Lord, who livest and reignest with the Father and the Holy Ghost for evermore. **Amen.**

15

O God, who, by making the day to close with eventide, hast bestowed the gift of repose on thy weary children: Grant, we beseech thee, that while we enjoy these blessings of day and night, we may not fail to acknowledge thee, by whom the light and the darkness are alike made good. **Amen.**

16

O God, who hast drawn over weary day the restful veil of night: Wrap our consciences in heavenly peace. Lift from our hands our tasks, and all through the night bear in thy bosom the full weight of our burdens and sorrows, that in untroubled slumber we may press our weakness close to thy strength, and win new power for the morrow's duty from thee who givest thy beloved sleep. **Amen.**

17

O Lord our God, who alone makest us to dwell in safety: Refresh with quiet sleep this night those who are wearied with the labors of the day, and mercifully protect from harm all who put their trust in thee, that, lying down in peace to take our rest, we may fear no evil, but confidently give ourselves into thy holy keeping; through Jesus Christ our Lord. **Amen.**

18

Heavenly Father, who slumberest not nor sleepest: We commend to thy gracious care and keeping ourselves and all who belong to us. Lift from our minds the burdens of waking hours; visit our bodies with refreshing sleep; through the darkness keep us safe and undefiled. And wake us to meet tomorrow's duties in strength of body and vigor of mind, with peace in our souls and courage in our hearts; through Jesus Christ our Lord. **Amen.**

19

Lighten our darkness, we beseech thee, O Lord, and by thy great mercy defend us from all perils and dangers of this night; for the love of thine only Son our Savior Jesus Christ. **Amen.**

20

O God, with whom there is no darkness, but the night shineth as the day: Keep and defend us and all thy children in soul and body during the coming night. Make us to rest in the peace of a good conscience, in the faith of thy providence, in the comfort of thy love, and in the hope of a better life; through Jesus Christ our Lord. **Amen.**

21

Be present, O merciful God, and protect us through the silent hours of this night, so that we who are wearied by the work and the changes of this fleeting world may rest upon thy eternal changelessness; through Jesus Christ our Lord. **Amen.**

22

Watch thou, dear Lord, with those who wake, or watch, or weep tonight; and give thine angels charge over those who sleep. Tend thy sick ones, O Lord Christ. Rest thy weary ones. Bless thy dying ones. Soothe thy suffering ones. Pity thy afflicted ones. Shield thy joyous ones. This we ask for thy love's sake. **Amen.**

23

O Lord, support us all the day long of this troublous life, until the shadows lengthen, and the evening comes, and the busy world is hushed, and the fever of life is over, and our work is done. Then in thy mercy grant us a safe lodging, and a holy rest, and peace at the last; through Jesus Christ our Lord. **Amen.**

Home and Kindred

FOR FAMILY

1

O God our Father, as we begin this day, bestow upon our household that grace which shall keep us in the fellowship of the Christian way, and grant unto each one of us that guidance and control which shall maintain our hearts in peace with one another and with thee. Help and prosper us in the doing of our various duties; and defend us from inward evil and from outward harm so that when the day is ended it may leave us not in sorrow, strife, or shame, but in true unity and thankful rest; through Jesus Christ our Lord. **Amen.**

2

O heavenly Father, shed forth thy blessed Spirit richly on all the members of this household. Make each one of us an instrument in thy hands for good. Purify our hearts; strengthen our minds and bodies; fill us with mutual love. Let no pride, no self-conceit, no rivalry, no dispute spring up among us. Make us earnest and true, giving no just cause for offense; and may thy holy peace rest upon us this day and every day, cheering us in our work, and keeping us faithful; through Jesus Christ our Lord. **Amen.**

3

Shed the bright rays of thy light, O Father, upon this family and household, that every member, confident of thy guidance, may fulfill his daily duty with a gallant heart. Be close to us in time of stress and strain. May our courage and our hope never fail; may we be valiant in all peril; through Jesus Christ our Lord. **Amen.**

4

Visit, we beseech thee, most gracious Father, this family and household with thy protection. Let thy blessing descend and rest on all who belong to it. Guide us here, and hereafter bring us to thy glory; through Jesus Christ our Lord. **Amen.**

5

O God, we who are bound together in the tender ties of love, pray thee for a day of unclouded love. May no passing irritation rob us of our joy in one another. Forgive us if we have often been swift to see the human failings, and slow to feel the preciousness of those who are still the dearest comfort of our life. May there be no sharp words that wound and scar, and no rift that may grow into estrangement. Suffer us not to grieve those whom thou hast sent to us as the sweet ministers of love. May our eyes not be so holden by selfishness that we know thine angels only when they spread their wings to return to thee. **Amen.**

6

Lord, behold our family here assembled. We thank thee for this place in which we dwell; for the love that unites us; for the peace accorded us this day; for the hope with which we expect the morrow; for the health, the work, the food, and the bright skies that make our lives delightful; for our friends in all parts of the earth.

Give us courage, gaiety, and the quiet mind. Spare to us our friends; soften to us our enemies. Bless us, if it may be, in all our innocent endeavors. Give us ever the strength to encounter that which is to come, that we may be brave in peril, constant in tribulation, temperate in wrath, and, in all changes of fortune and down to the gates of death, loyal and loving one to another; through Jesus Christ our Lord. **Amen.**

7

We beseech thee, O Lord, to behold us, members of this household, with thy favor. Be patient with us still; suffer us a while longer to endure, and if it may be, help us to do better. Bless to us our extraordinary mercies. Go with each of us to rest; if any awake, temper to them the dark hours of watching; and when the day returns to us, call us up with morning faces and with morning hearts, eager to labor, eager to be happy—if happiness should be our portion—and, if the day be marked for sorrow, strong to endure it. **Amen.**

8

Deliver us, good Lord, from the excessive demands of business and social life that limit family relationships, from the insensitivity and harshness of judgment that prevent understanding, from domineering ways and selfish imposition of our will, from softness and indulgence mistaken for love. Bless us with wise and understanding hearts, that we may demand neither too much nor too little, and grant us such a measure of love that we may nurture our children to that fulness of manhood and womanhood which thou hast purposed for them; through Jesus Christ our Lord. **Amen.**

9

O Lord, we ask thee to bless and keep father and mother, and our brothers and sisters. Watch over them every day and night. Help us to try to help each other, and grant that we may all love and serve thee more and more, that at last we may come to live with thee in heaven; through Jesus Christ our Lord. **Amen.**

FOR THOSE WITHOUT FAMILY

10

O God, who settest the solitary in families, we pray for all who are without children or kin. Relate them in life with those who need their strength and love, and make them one in the fellowship of the Spirit, in the Church of thy dear Son. **Amen.**

FOR CHILDREN

11

Almighty God and heavenly Father, we thank thee for the children whom thou hast given us; give us grace to train them in thy faith, fear, and love, that as they advance in years they may grow in grace in the knowledge of our Lord Jesus Christ. **Amen.**

12

O heavenly Father, who long ago didst watch thy Son on earth grow in stature and in wisdom and in perfect love of thee: By his wondrous story and the teaching of his Church, so lead the children whom thou watchest now, that they may grow into his likeness, loving thee, obedient to thy will, and happy in thy house; through the same Jesus Christ our Lord. **Amen.**

13

Almighty and everlasting God, we make our humble supplications unto thee for our children. Let thy fatherly hand, we beseech thee, ever be over them. Let thy Holy Spirit ever be with them, and so lead them in the knowledge and obedience of thy Word, that they may have life abundantly; through our Lord Jesus Christ. **Amen.**

14

O Lord Jesus Christ, who didst take little children into thine arms and bless them: Bless, we beseech thee, all little children dear to us. Take them into the arms of thine everlasting mercy; keep them from all evil; and bring them into the company of those who ever behold the face of thy Father, who is in heaven; through the glory of thy holy name. **Amen.**

15

Almighty God, giver of all good things: Mercifully behold this thy child now going forth in thy name to school. So replenish *him* with the truth of thy doctrine and adorn *him* with innocency of life that both by word and good example *he* may faithfully serve thee to the glory of thy name and the edification of thy Church; through Jesus Christ our Lord. **Amen.**

FOR BIRTHDAYS OR BAPTISM

16

Watch over thy child, O Lord, as *his* days increase; bless and guide *him* wherever *he* may be. Strengthen *him* when *he* standeth; comfort *him* when discouraged or sorrowful; and in *his* heart may thy peace which passeth understanding abide all the days of *his* life; through Jesus Christ our Lord. **Amen.**

17

Eternal Father, the giver of life, who as on this day didst cause thy servant, *N.*, to be born into this world: We thank thee, O Lord, for all thy mercies vouchsafed to *him* from that time unto this present, humbly beseeching thee to continue thy gracious favor and protection unto *his* life's end. Assist *him* in every time of trial; shield *him* in danger; relieve and comfort *him* in trouble; succor *him* in temptation; defend *him* from the assaults of the enemy, that *his* days here may pass away in peace, and when *he* dies *he* may attain unto the everlasting rest that remaineth for thy people; through Jesus Christ our Lord. **Amen.**

ON JOINING THE CHURCH

18

Strengthen, O Lord, by thy Holy Spirit, thy *servant (child)* who is now about to take the vows of membership in the Church. Grant that *he* may confess thee boldly before men and may grow in the grace and knowledge of our Lord and Savior Jesus Christ, and be found worthy to be numbered among thy people; through the same Jesus Christ our Lord. **Amen.**

FOR A WEDDING

19

Lord God, giver of life and love, let thy blessing rest upon those whom thou hast drawn together in love. Build thou for them their home. Give them wisdom for life, and discretion in the guidance of their affairs; and may thy fatherly hand ever be over them, and thy Holy Spirit ever be with them; through Jesus Christ our Lord. **Amen.**

20

O God, our heavenly Father, from whom we come and to whom we belong, and whose mercy and steadfast love toward thy children are without end: We now commend to thy care and keeping *N.* and *N.*, whom thou hast here joined together in one. In thy bountiful goodness thou hast made them to know and love one another, and to entrust themselves each to the other throughout all the days of their lives.

Pour out upon them, we beseech thee, the riches of thy grace. Through all the changing scenes of life, in joy and gladness, in suffering and sorrow, bind them more closely to one another and to thee. Grant that, in continual increase of wisdom and understanding, of patience and for-bearance, and of mutual affection, they may walk with confident hearts down through the years.

And now let thy blessing be upon us their families and friends, and upon the Church whose sheltering wings are about us to protect us and redeem us. Undergird us all with thy great love, that we, obeying thy will and always being in safety under thy protection, may continually abide in thee, until at the end, beyond all shadows of our mortal night, we may behold the full glory of thy presence; through Jesus Christ our Lord, to whom with thee and the Holy Spirit be glory and praise, world without end. **Amen.**

FOR A WEDDING ANNIVERSARY

21

O God, our heavenly Father, on this anniversary of the day when we were made one in holy matrimony, we give thee heartfelt thanks for thy blessing upon us then, and for thy continual mercies until now. We thank thee that with the passing days thou hast increased and deepened our love for each other. We praise thee for all the joys of our home and family life. Renew thy blessings upon us now, we beseech thee, as we renew our vows of love and loyalty; and may thy Holy Spirit strengthen us that we may ever remain steadfast in our faith and in thy service; through Jesus Christ our Lord. **Amen.**

FOR ONE LEAVING HOME

22

O God, who art the strength and the protector of thy people: We humbly place in thy hands the member of this family who is today about to leave us and enter a new sphere of life and work. Keep and preserve *him,* O Lord, as it seemeth best to thy divine wisdom and love, in all health and safety, both of body and soul; through Jesus Christ our Lord. **Amen.**

23

We humbly commend to thy fatherly care, O Lord, thy servant about to leave this house and family, beseeching thee that thy grace and mercy may never fail *him.* Succor *him* in temptation, preserve *him* in danger, assist *him* in every good work, and further *him* continually in the right way. Grant, we beseech thee, thy presence with us while we are absent one from another. May our nearness to thee make and keep us always aware of our nearness to one another. In Jesus' name and for his sake, we pray. **Amen.**

FOR ABSENT ONES

24

Bless, O God, all the members of this our family and household, especially those who are absent from us. Guard and preserve them in their going out and their coming in; keep them free from sin and safe from danger; through Jesus Christ our Lord. **Amen.**

25

O Thou, who art present in every place and from whose love neither space nor distance can separate us, give us to know that those who are absent from each other are still present with thee; and grant that, though separated, we may realize our communion with one another in the fellowship of thy service, here and always; through Jesus Christ our Lord. **Amen.**

FOR HOME AND FAMILY

26

Be present with us, O Lord, in our daily lives, and grant to those who dwell in this house the strength and protection of thy continual help, that thou mayest be known as the master of the family and the defender of this house; through Jesus Christ our Lord. **Amen.**

27

Almighty God, who art the author of all goodness: Look down in mercy upon this family and household and bless all who belong to it, present or absent. Save and defend us in all dangers and adversities; give us all things that are needful to our souls and bodies; and bring us safely to thy heavenly kingdom; through Jesus Christ our Lord. **Amen.**

28

O God, who art perfect love: Grant that we who are born of thee, and eat of thy bread, may bear one another's burdens with sincere affection; that thy peace which passeth all understanding may keep our hearts and minds in Christ Jesus our Lord, who with thee and the Holy Ghost liveth and reigneth, one God, world without end. **Amen.**

29

O God our Father, we thank thee for our home and family: for love and forbearance, for friends and foes, for laughter enjoyed and sorrow shared, for the daily bread of thy bounty in good times and bad. Help us to be mindful of thy gifts and glad to show forth thy praise; through Jesus Christ our Lord. **Amen.**

30

Almighty God, who hast given us grace at this time with one accord to make our common supplications unto thee, and dost promise that, when two or three are gathered together in thy name, thou wilt grant their requests: Fulfill now, O Lord, the desires and petitions of thy servants, as may be most expedient for them, granting us in this world knowledge of thy truth, and in the world to come life everlasting. **Amen.**

Table Graces

THE WESLEY GRACES

1

Grace Before Meat

> Be present at our table, Lord;
> Be here and everywhere adored.
> These creatures bless, and grant that we
> May feast in Paradise with thee. **Amen.**

2

Alternate Form

> Be present at our table, Lord;
> Be here and everywhere adored.
> Thy mercies bless, and grant that we
> May feast in fellowship with thee. **Amen.**

3

Grace After Meat

> We thank thee, Lord, for this our food,
> But more because of Jesus' blood.
> Let manna to our souls be given,
> The Bread of Life, sent down from heaven. **Amen.**

———•———

4

> Let us with a gladsome mind
> Praise the Lord, for he is kind:

For his mercies shall endure,
Ever faithful, ever sure. **Amen.**

5   Bless these thy gifts, most gracious God,
From whom all goodness springs;
Make clean our hearts and feed our souls
With good and joyful things. **Amen.**

6   We thank thee, Father, for thy care
And for thy bounty everywhere;
For this and every other gift,
Our grateful hearts to thee we lift. **Amen.**

7   For health and strength and daily food,
We praise thy name, O Lord. **Amen.**

8   Heavenly Father, great and good,
We thank thee for this daily food.
Bless us even as we pray;
Guide and keep us through this day. **Amen.**

9   Father, for this noonday meal
We would speak the praise we feel,
Health and strength we have in thee;
Help us, Lord, to faithful be. **Amen.**

10   Gracious Giver of all good,
Thee we thank for rest and food;
Grant that all we do or say
In thy service be this day. **Amen.**

11

Our heavenly Father, accept our thanks for these and all thy gifts; help us to be worthy of thy love and care; through Jesus Christ our Lord. **Amen.**

12

O God our Father, who giveth food for the body and truth for the mind: So enlighten and nourish us that we may grow wise and strong to do thy will. **Amen.**

13

Almighty Giver of good, we thank thee for thy lovingkindness to us. Thou openest thy hand, and we are fed. Be at this table, we pray thee, and bless our gathering together; through Jesus Christ our Lord. **Amen.**

14

For this our daily bread, and for every good gift which comes from thee, we bless thy holy name; through Jesus Christ our Lord. **Amen.**

15

For these and all his blessings, God's holy name be praised; through Jesus Christ our Lord. **Amen.**

16

We bless thee, O God, for this food which betokens thy continued care over us; we acknowledge this gift, and thy love which prompts it, and pray for fidelity to use our strength in doing thy good pleasure; through Jesus Christ our Lord. **Amen.**

17

This food, which thou hast already blessed in the giving, do thou, O God, further bless in our partaking, that it may redound to thy glory; through Jesus Christ our Lord. **Amen.**

18

Lord, make us truly grateful for the blessings of this day, and keep us thine evermore. **Amen.**

19

Our Father, we bless thee for this food and for all the expressions of thy goodness to us. Give us grace this day to do thy will; through Jesus Christ our Lord. **Amen.**

20

May the peace and blessing of God descend upon us as we receive of his bounty; and may our hearts be filled with love and praise unto him who does all things well. **Amen.**

21

We thank thee, our heavenly Father, for thy care over us, and pray that thou wilt bless this food to our use. **Amen.**

22

Bless, O Lord, this food to our use, and us in thy service; through Jesus Christ our Lord. **Amen.**

23

Give us grateful hearts, our Father, for all thy mercies, and make us mindful of the needs of others; through Jesus Christ our Lord. **Amen.**

24

Thanks be to thee, O Lord, for these and all the blessings which thou dost so generously provide. We thank thee in the name of Christ. **Amen.**

25

With gratitude we acknowledge before thee, O God, these gifts and all the benefits of thy grace. Help us to live for thy glory; through Jesus Christ our Lord. **Amen.**

26

Accept, O Father, our humble thanks for this our daily food; and as it adds strength to our bodies, may it give us power to render better service to thee; through Jesus Christ our Lord. **Amen.**

27

Almighty God, gracious Father of men, who openest thy hand and fillest the earth with good, and hast provided thy children sufficient to satisfy all our need: Teach us to render back to thee thy due thanksgiving, not only in words, but also in the manner of our living; through Jesus Christ our Lord. **Amen.**

28

The eyes of all look to thee, and thou givest them their food in due season. Thou openest thy hand, thou satisfiest the desire of every living thing. Great is the Lord, and greatly to be praised. **Amen.**

Psalm 145:15-16, 3a

29

Unto him who in the breaking of bread brought us near to God, be glory and praise, dominion and power, for ever and ever. **Amen.**

For the Sick and Sorrowing

IN TIME OF ILLNESS

1

O God my Father, hold me in thy keeping. Be with me when I am distressed by sickness and distraught by pain. Let me always trust thy lovingkindness. Restore to me, I pray thee, health and vigor, that I may again with gladness set my hands to the task of life. May my suffering teach me sympathy with all who suffer, and may every gift of life renewed send me forth with a thankful heart to do thy will; through Jesus Christ my Lord. **Amen.**

2

O loving Father, I commit myself with perfect trust into thy loving hands. Watch over me and protect me in my hour of weakness, and grant that as I become unconscious to earthly things my thoughts may be turned to thee. Bless and guide thy servants who shall tend me; give them such success that we may praise thee for thy goodness. And finally grant that I may so bear suffering with cheerful courage that I may be the means, under thy hand, of helping others in their time of trial; for Jesus Christ's sake. **Amen.**

3

O Thou who hast prepared a place for my soul: Prepare my soul for that place; prepare it with holiness; prepare it with desire; and even while it sojourneth upon earth, let it dwell in heaven with thee, beholding the beauty of thy countenance and glory of thy saints, now and for evermore. **Amen.**

4

Thou knowest, Lord, the secrets of our hearts; shut not thy merciful ears to our prayers; but spare us, Lord most holy, O God most mighty, O holy and merciful Savior, thou most worthy judge eternal, suffer us not at our last hour, for any pains of death, to fall from thee. **Amen.**

5

O Lord Jesus Christ, to whom the sick were brought that they might be healed, and who didst send none of them away without thy blessing: Look in pity upon all who come to thee for healing of body, mind, and soul; send them not away without thy blessing, but now and evermore grant them thy healing grace. **Amen.**

6

O Christ our Lord, who art the great physician: Grant unto all who are sick the aid of heavenly healing. Look upon all faithful people who are in need and who love to call upon thy name, and take their souls into thy keeping, and vouchsafe to deliver them from all sickness and infirmity. **Amen.**

7

O living Christ, make us conscious now of thy healing nearness. Touch our eyes that we may see thee; open our ears that we may hear thy voice; enter our hearts that we may know thy love. Overshadow our souls and bodies with thy presence, that we may partake of thy strength, thy love, and thy healing life. **Amen.**

8

O Lord, holy Father, by whose lovingkindness our souls and bodies are renewed: Mercifully look upon this thy servant, that, every cause of sickness being removed, *he* may be restored to soundness of health; through Jesus Christ our Lord. **Amen.**

9

Almighty and immortal God, giver of life and health: We beseech thee for thy servant, for whom we implore thy mercy, that by thy blessing upon *him* and upon those who minister to *him* of thy healing gifts, *he* may be restored to soundness of health, and give thanks to thee; through Jesus Christ our Lord. **Amen.**

10

O God, our refuge and strength, who art a very present help in trouble: Look graciously, we beseech thee, upon this thy servant. Send *him* patience and comfort in this time of *his* great distress; strengthen *him* with the consolations of thy Holy Spirit; enable *him* to rise above all pain and weakness; through Jesus Christ our Lord. **Amen.**

11

O Lord Jesus Christ, who didst show thy love by restoring to health the little ones who were brought to thee: Give thy blessing, we beseech thee, to the means now used for the healing of this thy child, that *he* may be restored to health and strength, and spared to a life of usefulness. **Amen.**

12

O God, whose dear Son Jesus Christ did heal children who were sick: Send thy help to this child. Help *him* to be quiet, and patient, and cheerful. Take away *his* pain, and make *him* well again, that *he* may grow in body, in mind, and in likeness to Jesus Christ our Lord. **Amen.**

FOR THOSE WHO CARE FOR THE SICK

13

Almighty God, our heavenly Father, who hast power over life and death, over health and sickness: Give strength, wisdom, and gentleness to all thy ministering servants, all physicians and surgeons, nurses and watchers by the sick, that, always bearing thy presence with them, they may not only heal but bless, and shine as lamps of hope in the darkest hours of distress and fear; through Jesus Christ our Lord. **Amen.**

14

O God, in whose dearly beloved Son men have seen the glory of self-sacrifice: Grant that all who are called to the sacred office of nursing and caring for the sick may ever remember his holy example, and show forth his unfailing tenderness in the beauty and compassion of their daily lives. **Amen.**

15

O Lord, the great healer and good physician of both body and soul: Bless with skill and power all doctors and nurses, whom thou hast called to minister to the sick and suffering in our hospitals, that they may exercise their art for the well-being of thy children, and to thy glory, who livest and reignest with the Father and the Holy Spirit, one God, world without end. **Amen.**

16

Almighty God, whose blessed Son Jesus Christ went about doing good and healing all manner of sickness and disease among the people: Grant to physicians, surgeons, and nurses wisdom, skill, sympathy, and patience, that they may continue his gracious work among us in all hospitals and infirmaries; prosper their work, O Lord, with thy continual blessing; through the same Jesus Christ our Lord. **Amen.**

THANKSGIVING FOR RESTORED HEALTH

17

Almighty God, the giver of every good gift: We thank thee for the health restored to thy servant. Thou has been with *him* in sickness; be with *him* still in health and joy. In the hour of returning gladness suffer us not to forget the days of darkness that are gone. Let us not be numbered among those who are quick to ask in time of trouble, but careless to show themselves thankful when mercy is bestowed. Be thou, O God, loved and obeyed with all our strength; through Jesus Christ our Lord. **Amen.**

FOR ALL WHO SUFFER

18

O Lord, who dost feel the pain of the world: Look down upon all sick and suffering persons; enfold them with thy love, that in the midst of pain they may find thy presence. To doctors and nurses grant tender hearts and healing hands; and give health again in body and soul, for thy tender mercy's sake. **Amen.**

19

O God our Father, have compassion, we pray thee, upon all those whose hearts are touched with sorrow, whose spirits are troubled or cast down within them. Remember those to whom the burdens of this life bring darkness of soul; have mercy upon all who suffer in body or mind from whatever cause. Let thy mercy rest upon them according as they hope in thee; for the sake of Jesus Christ, our burden-bearer and Redeemer. **Amen.**

20

We thank thee, O Father, for all who by brave endurance hallow suffering, for those who in their concern for others find no room for pity for themselves, and for those whose patience inspires courage in others. Grant, O loving Father, to all who are bound in the mysterious fellowship of suffering, an awareness of comradeship with others, and the knowledge of thy love; and give them thy peace which passeth all understanding. **Amen.**

21

O almighty and merciful Father, who art the help of the helpless, and who dost lift up those who fall: Look with mercy on all who are oppressed in mind, body, or estate; comfort and relieve them, according to their several necessities; give them patience under their sufferings, and a happy issue out of all their affliction. **Amen.**

22

Almighty and everlasting God, the comfort of the sorrowing, the strength of sufferers: Hear the prayers of those in any tribulation who cry out to thee, that all may rejoice to find thy mercy present with them in their afflictions; through Jesus Christ our Lord. **Amen.**

23

We ask thee not, O Lord, to rid us of pain; but grant in thy mercy that our pain may be free from waste, unfretted by rebellion against thy will, unsoiled by thought of ourselves, purified by love of our kind, and ennobled by devotion to thy kingdom; through the merits of thine only Son our Lord. **Amen.**

24

O God, gracious and merciful, full of compassion and of great kindness: We beseech thee of thy goodness to look upon all who are at this time poor, afflicted, sick, wounded, or bereaved. Comfort them in all their troubles with the sweetness of thy Holy Spirit; uphold them with thy sure promises; fill their souls with the knowledge of thy love; turn their sufferings into blessings, and for their affliction give them a far more exceeding weight of glory; through thy dear Son, who lived and died and rose again that we might have life, Jesus Christ our Lord. **Amen.**

FOR THE BLIND
25

O God, who hast sent thy Son to be the true light: Grant that they who cannot see the things of this world may be the more enlightened and comforted by his inward guidance. Cheer them in their blindness with the sense of thy presence, that, beholding thee with increasing love, they may be conformed to thy likeness, until they see thee as thou art, and awake to the full revelation of thy glory; through the same Jesus Christ our Lord. **Amen.**

FOR THOSE WHO MOURN
26

Most merciful God, the helper of all men: So strengthen us by thy power that our sorrow may be turned into joy, and we may continually glorify thy holy name; through Jesus Christ our Lord. **Amen.**

27

Almighty God, Father of mercies and giver of all comfort: Deal graciously, we pray thee, with all those who mourn, that, casting every care on thee, they may know the consolation of thy love; through Jesus Christ our Lord. **Amen.**

28

Almighty God, who hast taught us that those who mourn shall be comforted: Grant that in all our grief we may turn to thee; and, because our need is beyond the help of man, grant us the peace of thy consolation and the joy of thy love; through Jesus Christ our Lord. **Amen.**

29

Almighty God, who abidest always, and who art ever near to uphold and bless: Hear now our prayers for thy servants bowed down with grief. May they find strength and peace in thee. For all that has been gracious and helpful in days past we devoutly thank thee. Visit us with thy comfort, and be thou thyself our companion. Keep us mindful of the many good things which make life dear and sacred. May our hearts be united in a closer bond of love and sympathy, and give us strength to return to the duties of life with increased devotion and with purer and more earnest purpose. May we ever feel that the eternal God is our refuge, and that underneath are the everlasting arms; through Jesus Christ our Lord. **Amen.**

For Specific Groups and Persons

FOR TRAVELERS

1

O God, our heavenly Father, who art present in thy power in every place: Preserve, we beseech thee, all who travel by land, by water, or by air (especially those whom we remember before thee) ; surround them with thy loving care; protect them from every danger; and bring them in safety to their journey's end; through Jesus Christ our Lord. **Amen.**

2

Almighty God, giver of life and health, guide we beseech thee, with thy wisdom all who are striving to save from injury and death the travelers on our roads. Grant to those who drive along our highways consideration for others, and to those who walk on them or play beside them thoughtful caution and care, that so without fear or disaster we all may come safely to our journey's end, by thy mercy who carest for us; through Jesus Christ our Lord. **Amen.**

3

O Lord Jesus Christ, who on the sea didst teach thy disciples many heavenly things, and even in the storm didst come close to them saying, It is I, be not afraid: We pray thee to show the power of thy presence to thy children on the deep. Be thou the guide and guardian of all that sail the seas; who livest and reignest with the Father and the Holy Spirit, one God, world without end. **Amen.**

FOR THOSE ON HOLIDAY

4

Grant, O Lord, that we may so enjoy our holiday that our bodies may be strengthened, our minds renewed, and our energies quickened for the perfect freedom of thy service; through Jesus Christ our Lord. **Amen.**

FOR THOSE IN THE ARMED FORCES

5

O Lord God of hosts, stretch forth, we pray thee, thine almighty arm to strengthen the men and women of our armed forces. Keep them temperate in all things, that they may serve thee without stumbling and without stain. For their homes, give them steadfast loyalty through all the days of separation; for their Church, give them reverence and devotion; and grant that, returning with greater insight into thy purposes, they may lead us into greater service in thy kingdom; through Jesus Christ our Lord. **Amen.**

6

O Lord God, our Father, our Savior, our might: We commend to thy keeping all those who are venturing their lives on our behalf, that whether by life or by death they may win for the whole world the fruits of their sacrifice, and a holy peace; through Jesus Christ our Lord. **Amen.**

7

Look in thy mercy, we beseech thee, O Lord, on those who are called to tasks of special peril in the air or beneath the sea. Even there let thy hand lead them, and thy right hand hold them. Help them to do their duty with prudence and with fearlessness, confident that in life or in death the eternal God is their refuge, and underneath are the everlasting arms. Grant this for Jesus Christ's sake, thy Son our Lord. **Amen.**

FOR CHAPLAINS IN THE ARMED FORCES

8

Blessed Lord, who didst commission thy disciples to continue the work which the Father sent thee into the world to do, support, we beseech thee, with thy Holy Spirit, those who minister in the armed forces of our country. Give them grace to preach thy Gospel both by word and deed; strengthen them in temptation, and make them courageous amid the perils of their calling, that they may glorify thee before all men. And do thou hold them ever in thy gracious keeping. **Amen.**

IN REMEMBRANCE OF THOSE
WHO HAVE LAID DOWN THEIR LIVES

9

O God, in whom the generations of mankind live and move and have their being: We remember with gratitude all those who have laid down their lives in the service of their country. May no forgetfulness of ours make them to have perished as though they had never been. To the end that these dead shall not have died in vain, may we receive with fit humility the fruits of their sacrifice, and carry on to further fulfillment their dearest hope for this their land and ours; through Jesus Christ our Lord. **Amen.**

FOR THOSE SUFFERING UNDER WAR

10

O Lord God Almighty, who from thy throne dost behold all the dwellers upon earth: Look down with pity upon those on whom have fallen the miseries of war. Have compassion on the wounded and dying; comfort the brokenhearted; assuage the madness of the nations; make war to cease; give peace in our time, O Lord. We ask it in the name of him who is the Prince of Peace, even thy Son Jesus Christ our Lord. **Amen.**

FOR ALL WHO LABOR FOR PEACE

11

Almighty God and most merciful Father, who wouldest have the kingdoms of this world become the kingdom of thy Son Jesus Christ: Bestow thy blessing, we beseech thee, upon all who labor for peace and righteousness among the peoples; that the day may be hastened when war shall be no more, and thy holy will shall govern the nations upon earth; through the same Jesus Christ our Lord. **Amen.**

FOR MINISTERS OF THE GOSPEL

12

O almighty God, remember, we beseech thee, all those who as ministers and pastors fulfill their calling. Give them, we pray thee, great gifts and great holiness, that wisely and charitably, diligently and zealously, prudently and acceptably, they may be guides to the blind and comforters to the sad and weary, that they may strengthen the weak and confirm the strong, and that in all their actions and ministrations they may advance the good of souls and the honor of our Lord Jesus Christ. **Amen.**

13

Almighty God, who through thy Son didst send forth disciples to proclaim the coming of thy kingdom and to teach thy new commandment: Give to those who now stand in their succession such understanding of the mind of Christ that they may rightly interpret his teachings, and such fellowship with his compassion that in them he may renew his unceasing ministry of reconciliation; through Jesus Christ our Lord. **Amen.**

14

O spirit of the living God, who in days of old didst speak by prophets and apostles: Raise up in our day devout and learned men as pastors and teachers of the people, by whose ministry the Church may be quickened and thy kingdom advanced; through Jesus Christ our Lord. **Amen.**

15

O almighty God, who in thy mercy hast redeemed the world by the love of thy dear Son: Call many, we beseech thee, to the ministry of thy Church, so that by their labors thy light may shine in the darkness, and the kingdom of thy Son be hastened by the perfecting of thy people; through Jesus Christ our Lord. **Amen.**

16

Almighty and everlasting God, look mercifully upon thy servants everywhere who visit the poor and the suffering, the needy and the distressed, and those who are in prison; that, guarded by thy protection and kept by thy power, they may do their work with joy and patience; through Jesus Christ our Lord. **Amen.**

FOR MISSIONARIES AND TEACHERS

17

Most merciful Father, we beseech thee to send thy heavenly blessing upon thy servants, the missionaries and teachers of thy Church, that they may be clothed with righteousness, and that thy Word spoken by their mouth may have such success that it may never be spoken in vain; through Jesus Christ our Lord. **Amen.**

DURING AN ELECTION

18

Almighty God, the fountain of all wisdom: Guide and direct, we humbly beseech thee, the minds of all those who are called at this time to exercise the responsible duty of electing fit persons to serve in the government of this *nation (or of this state or city or town)*. Grant that the effect and right issue of their choice may promote thy glory and the welfare of this people; and to all those who shall be elected, give, we pray thee, the spirit of wisdom, courage, sympathy, and true godliness. And this we ask for the sake of our Lord and Savior Jesus Christ. **Amen.**

FOR THOSE WHO INFLUENCE OPINION

19

Almighty God, who hast proclaimed thine eternal truth by the voice of prophets and evangelists: Direct and bless, we beseech thee, those who in this our generation speak where many listen and write what many read; that they may do their part in making the heart of the people wise, its mind sound, and its will righteous; to the honor of Jesus Christ our Lord. **Amen.**

FOR A COMMITTEE MEETING

20

Bless, we beseech thee, O God, the work of this committee; grant to its members clarity of thought, evenness of temper, and willingness to persevere in thy service; through Jesus Christ our Lord. **Amen.**

21

O God, with whom a thousand years are as one day, and who hast called us, whose lives pass as a watch in the night, to thy service: Grant that we may so do our work that it shall not need to be undone. Stay, we beseech thee, the fever of our hearts, and help us to walk in the light of thine own eternity; through Jesus Christ our Lord. **Amen.**

FOR AN OFFICIAL BOARD MEETING

22

O God, who through thy blessed Son our Lord didst preside at the councils of the apostles: So direct our purposes and guide our deliberations, we beseech thee, that our thoughts, words, and actions in this meeting may be according to thy holy will; through the same Jesus Christ our Lord. **Amen.**

23

O Lord, whose apostle has taught us that as members of thy body we all have our part to play in the whole life of thy Church: We thank thee for this work which thou hast given us to do together; and we pray thee to give us grace to persevere in it, and through it to serve thee to thy honor and glory; through Jesus Christ our Lord. **Amen.**

24

O God, who hast entrusted to us the ministry of reconciliation: Help us to fulfill our responsibilities in thy name with wisdom, cheerfulness, and honesty; through Jesus Christ our Lord. **Amen.**

For Various Gifts and Graces

FOR FORGIVENESS

1

I confess to God Almighty, the Father, the Son, and the Holy Ghost, that I have sinned exceedingly in thought, word, and deed, through my own grievous fault.

Wherefore I pray God to have mercy upon me, forgive me my sins, and bring me to everlasting life; through Jesus Christ our Lord. **Amen.**

A PRAYER OF AUGUSTINE

2

O Thou, from whom to be turned is to fall, to whom to be turned is to rise, and in whom to stand is to abide for ever: Grant us in all our duties thy help, in all our perplexities thy guidance, in all our dangers thy protection, and in all our sorrows thy peace; through Jesus Christ our Lord. **Amen.**

A PRAYER OF THOMAS AQUINAS

3

Give me, O Lord, a steadfast heart, which no unworthy thought can drag downward; an unconquered heart, which no tribulation can wear out; an upright heart, which no unworthy purpose may tempt aside.

Bestow upon me also, O Lord my God, understanding to know thee, diligence to seek thee, wisdom to find thee, and a faithfulness that may finally embrace thee; through Jesus Christ our Lord. **Amen.**

A PRAYER OF IGNATIUS LOYOLA

4

Teach us, good Lord, to serve thee as thou deservest; to give and not to count the cost; to fight and not to heed the wounds; to toil and not to seek for rest; to labor and not to ask for any reward, save that of knowing that we do thy will; through Jesus Christ our Lord. **Amen.**

A PRAYER OF FRANCIS OF ASSISI

5

Lord, make us instruments of thy peace.
Where there is hatred, let us sow love;
where there is injury, pardon;
where there is discord, union;
where there is doubt, faith;
where there is despair, hope;
where there is darkness, light;
where there is sadness, joy;
for thy mercy and for thy truth's sake. **Amen.**

FROM ST. PATRICK'S BREASTPLATE

6

Christ be with me, Christ within me,
Christ before me, Christ beside me.
Christ to win me,
Christ to comfort and restore me,
Christ beneath me, Christ above me,
Christ in quiet, Christ in danger,
Christ in hearts of all that love me,
Christ in mouth of friend and stranger. **Amen.**

GOD BE IN MY HEAD

7

God be in my head,
　And in my understanding;
God be in mine eyes
　And in my looking;
God be in my mouth,
　And in my speaking;
God be in my heart,
　And in my thinking;
God be at mine end,
　And at my departing. **Amen.**

FOR SELF-SURRENDER

8

O God our Father, whose law is a law of liberty: Give us wisdom to use aright the freedom which thou hast given to us, by surrendering ourselves to thy service, knowing that, when we are thy willing bondsmen, then only are we truly free; for Jesus Christ's sake. **Amen.**

FOR ILLUMINATION

9

O God, whose Word is sharper than any two-edged sword, piercing both heart and conscience with many wounds: Let the sword of thy Spirit pierce us through, and grant that the wounds that are made by thy truth may be healed by thy love; through Jesus Christ our Lord. **Amen.**

10

O God, who makest the blind to see and the lame to walk, and who openest the prison to them that are bound: Let thy Word come to us, we beseech thee, with power to deliver us from blindness and prejudice, from evil habits, from the fear of man, and from every bondage in which we are taken, that we may walk at large in the way of thy statutes; through Jesus Christ our Lord. **Amen.**

FOR COURAGE

11

O Lord God, who hast called us thy servants to ventures of which we cannot see the ending, by paths as yet untrodden and through perils unknown: Give us faith to go out with good courage, not knowing whither we go, but only that thy hand is leading us and thy love supporting us; through Jesus Christ our Lord. **Amen.**

12

O God, who rulest the worlds from everlasting to everlasting: Speak to our hearts when courage fails, and men faint for fear, and the love of many grows cold, and there is distress of the nations upon the earth. Keep us resolute and steadfast in the things that cannot be shaken, abounding in hope and knowing that our labor is not in vain in thee. Restore our faith in the omnipotence of good; renew the love that never fails; and make us to lift up our eyes and behold, beyond the things which are seen and temporal, the things which are unseen and eternal; through Jesus Christ our Lord. **Amen.**

FOR AN ADVENTUROUS SPIRIT

13

O Thou who art heroic love: Keep alive in our hearts that adventurous spirit which makes men scorn the way of safety, so that thy will may be done. For so only, O Lord, shall we be worthy of those courageous souls, who in every age have ventured all in obedience to thy call, and for whom the trumpets have sounded on the farther shore; through Jesus Christ our Lord. **Amen.**

FOR FREEDOM FROM FEAR AND ANXIETY

14

O most loving Father, who willest us to give thanks for all things, to dread nothing but the loss of thee, and to cast all our care on thee who carest for us: Preserve us from faithless fears and worldly anxieties, and grant that no clouds of this mortal life may hide from us the light of that love which is immortal, and which thou hast manifested to us in thy Son Jesus Christ our Lord. **Amen.**

15

Almighty God, who dost perpetually visit us with thy strengthening Spirit, that we may serve thee without fear: Grant us by the same Spirit such love as may cast out all our fears. Deliver us, O Lord, from fear of our enemies and them that hate us, from fear of pain and poverty that we may yet know, from fear of nameless ills in an unknown future, from fear of our own weakness, and from dread of the mysteries which environ our little life; through Jesus Christ our Lord. **Amen.**

FOR PERSEVERANCE

16

O Lord God, when thou givest to thy servants to endeavor any great matter, grant us also to know that it is not the beginning, but the continuing of the same unto the end, until it be thoroughly finished, which yieldeth the true glory; through him who for the finishing of thy work laid down his life, our Redeemer Jesus Christ. **Amen.**

FOR STEADFASTNESS

17

Fix thou our steps, O Lord, that we stagger not at the uneven motions of the world, but go steadily on our way, neither censuring our journey by the weather we meet, nor turning aside for anything that befalls us; through Jesus Christ our Lord. **Amen.**

18

Set before our minds, O heavenly Father, the example of our Lord Jesus Christ, who when he was upon earth found joy in doing the will of him that sent him, and in finishing his work. When many are coming and going, and there is little quiet, give us grace to remember him who knew neither impatience of spirit nor confusion of work, but in the midst of all his labors kept a tranquil heart, at leisure from itself to serve and sympathize; through the same Jesus Christ our Lord. **Amen.**

FOR OUR DAY'S WORK

19

O God, who hast ordained that whatever is to be desired, should be sought by labor, and who, by thy blessing, bringest honest labor to good effect: Look with mercy upon all our work, studies, and endeavors. Grant us, O Lord, to design only what is lawful and right; afford us calmness of mind, and steadiness of purpose, that we may so do thy will in this short life, as to obtain happiness in the world to come; for the sake of Jesus Christ our Lord. **Amen.**

FOR LOYALTY TO TRUTH

20

Almighty God, who hast sent the Spirit of truth unto us to guide us into all truth: So rule our lives by thy power that we may be truthful in thought and word and deed. Arm us with such trust in the truth that is invisible, that we may ask no rest from its demands and have no fear in its service; through Jesus Christ our Lord. **Amen.**

TO SPEAK THE TRUTH IN LOVE

21

O Lord, grant all who contend for the faith never to injure it by clamor and impatience, but, speaking thy precious truth in love, so to present it that it may be loved, and that men may see in it thy goodness and beauty; through Jesus Christ our Lord. **Amen.**

FOR UNDERSTANDING

22

O God, who hast bound us together in this bundle of life: Give us grace to understand how our lives depend upon the courage, the industry, the honesty, and the integrity of our fellow men; that we may be mindful of their needs, grateful for their fidelity, and faithful in our responsibilities to them; through Jesus Christ our Lord. **Amen.**

23

Teach us, O Lord, to see other lands and peoples by the light of the faith we profess, that we may check in ourselves all ungenerous judgments, all presumptuous claims, that being ever ready to recognize the needs and rightful claims of other nations, we may do whatever in us lies to remove old hatreds and rivalries, and to hasten new understandings, that each may bring his tribute of excellence to the treasury of our common humanity; through Jesus Christ our Lord. **Amen.**

FOR RIGHTEOUS DISCONTENT

24

O God, who hast taught us the joy of serving thee and hast given us an earnest of the peace that passeth understanding: Fill us also with righteous discontent, that we may never be perfectly at rest while injustice is done to thy people, and thy children cry out in anguish. Grant us so to desire thy kingdom, as a pearl of great price, that we may discern the signs of its coming upon earth; through Jesus Christ our Lord. **Amen.**

FOR HUMILITY

25

O Thou high and lofty one that inhabitest eternity, whose name is holy, and who hast promised to dwell with those that are of a contrite and humble spirit: We pray thee to cleanse our hearts from every stain of pride and vainglory, that though the heaven of heavens cannot contain thee, yet thou wouldest consent to abide with us for ever; through Jesus Christ our Lord. **Amen.**

A Form for Family Prayer
or Worship in a Small Group

† *Scripture sentences or call to worship may be selected from the appropriate section for each season of the Christian Year or in the General Aids to Worship.*

† *Here an invocation, collect, or other prayer may be selected from the collection of prayers in the General Aids to Worship. Note especially:*
    1. *Invocations, pp. 168-71.*
    2. *For Morning, Day, and Evening, pp. 218-22.*

† *Then a psalm, canticle, or other act of praise may be read responsively or in unison. See Section III.*

† *Following the act of praise shall be said or sung the* Gloria Patri.

† *Here a Scripture lesson shall be read. It may be selected from the Lectionary, pp. 61-64. Either the Old Testament or the New Testament lesson may be used.*

† *Then the leader or other member of the group may offer prayer as moved, or there may be read one or more of the prayers which may be found in the General Aids to Worship. Note especially:*
    1. *Litanies, pp. 207-18.*
    2. *Home and Kindred, pp. 222-29.*
    3. *For Specific Groups and Persons, pp. 238-43.*
    4. *For Various Gifts and Graces, pp. 243-49.*

† *The service may include hymns from* The Methodist Hymnal, *as time and circumstances permit.*

III.

Acts of Praise

Great art thou, O Lord, and greatly to be praised; great is thy power, and thy wisdom infinite. And thee would man praise: man, a part of thy creation; man, who bears about him his mortality, the witness of his sins, even the witness that thou dost resist the proud. Yet man would praise thee, he who is part of thy creation. Thou awakest us to delight in praising thee; for thou has made us for thyself and our hearts are restless till they find rest in thee.

Grant, then, Lord, that I may know and understand whether first to call upon thee or to praise thee; whether first to know thee or to call upon thee. But who can call upon thee, not knowing thee? For he that knoweth thee not may call on thee as other than thou art. Or, is it rather, that we call on thee that we may know thee? But how shall they call on him in whom they have not believed? Or how shall they believe without a preacher?

Now, they shall praise the Lord who seek him, for those who seek shall find, and finding him shall praise him. Thee will I seek, O Lord, calling upon thee; and I will call upon thee believing in thee: for to us thou hast been preached. My faith, Lord, calls upon thee: that faith which thou hast given me, where-with thou hast inspired me, through the incarnation of thy Son, through the ministry of thy preacher.

Augustine, The Confessions, *Book I, Chapter 1*

THE PSALTER

1 BLESSED IS THE MAN

Blessed is the man who walks not in the counsel of the wicked,

nor stands in the way of sinners, nor sits in the seat of scoffers;

but his delight is in the law of the Lord,

and on his law he meditates day and night.

He is like a tree planted by streams of water,

that yields its fruit in its season,

and its leaf does not wither.

In all that he does, he prospers.

The wicked are not so,

but are like chaff which the wind drives away.

Therefore the wicked will not stand in the judgment,

nor sinners in the congregation of the righteous;

for the Lord knows the way of the righteous,

but the way of the wicked will perish.   *Psalm 1*

2 O LORD, HOW MAJESTIC IS THY NAME!

O Lord, our Lord, how majestic is thy name in all the earth!

Thou whose glory above the heavens is chanted by the mouth of babes and infants,

thou hast founded a bulwark because of thy foes,

to still the enemy and the avenger.

When I look at thy heavens, the work of thy fingers,

the moon and the stars which thou hast established;

what is man that thou art mindful of him,

and the son of man that thou dost care for him?

Yet thou hast made him little less than God,

and dost crown him with glory and honor.

Thou hast given him dominion over the works of thy hands;

thou hast put all things under his feet,

all sheep and oxen,

and also the beasts of the field,

the birds of the air, and the fish of the sea,

whatever passes along the paths of the sea.

O Lord, our Lord,

how majestic is thy name in all the earth!   *Psalm 8*

3 WHO SHALL DWELL ON THY HOLY HILL?

O Lord, who shall dwell on thy holy hill?

He who walks blamelessly, and does what is right, and speaks truth from his heart;

who does not slander with his tongue, and does no evil to his friend,

nor takes up a reproach against his neighbor;

in whose eyes a reprobate is despised,

but who honors those who fear the Lord;

who swears to his own hurt and does not change;

and does not take a bribe against the innocent.

He who does these things

shall never be moved.
Psalm 15:1b-4, 5bc

4 PRESERVE ME, O GOD

Preserve me, O God,

for in thee I take refuge.

I say to the Lord,

"Thou art my Lord; I have no good apart from thee."

The Lord is my chosen portion and my cup;

thou holdest my lot.

The lines have fallen for me in pleasant places;

yea, I have a goodly heritage.

I bless the Lord who gives me counsel;

in the night also my heart instructs me.

I keep the Lord always before me;

because he is at my right hand, I shall not be moved.

Therefore my heart is glad, and my soul rejoices;

my body also dwells secure.

Thou dost show me the path of life; in thy presence there is fulness of joy,

in thy right hand are pleasures for evermore. *Psalm 16:1-2, 5-9, 11*

5 THE GLORY OF GOD

The heavens are telling the glory of God;

and the firmament proclaims his handiwork.

Day to day pours forth speech,

and night to night declares knowledge.

There is no speech, nor are there words;

their voice is not heard;

yet their voice goes out through all the earth,

and their words to the end of the world.

In them he has set a tent for the sun, which comes forth like a bridegroom leaving his chamber,

and like a strong man runs its course with joy.

Its rising is from the end of the heavens, and its circuit to the end of them;

and there is nothing hid from its heat.

The law of the Lord is perfect, reviving the soul;

the testimony of the Lord is sure, making wise the simple;

the precepts of the Lord are right, rejoicing the heart;

the commandment of the Lord is pure, enlightening the eyes;

the fear of the Lord is clean, enduring for ever;

the ordinances of the Lord are true, and righteous altogether.

More to be desired are they than gold, even much fine gold;

sweeter also than honey and drippings of the honeycomb.

Moreover by them is thy servant warned;

in keeping them there is great reward.

But who can discern his errors?

Clear thou me from hidden faults.

Keep back thy servant also from presumptuous sins;

let them not have dominion over me!

Then I shall be blameless,

and innocent of great transgression.

Let the words of my mouth and the meditation of my heart be acceptable in thy sight,

O Lord, my rock and my redeemer.

Psalm 19

6 MY GOD, WHY HAST THOU FORSAKEN ME?

My God, my God, why hast thou forsaken me?

Why art thou so far from helping me?

O my God, I cry by day, but thou dost not answer;

and by night, but find no rest.

Yet thou art holy,

enthroned on the praises of Israel.

In thee our fathers trusted;

they trusted, and thou didst deliver them.

To thee they cried, and were saved;

in thee they trusted, and were not disappointed.

All who see me mock at me,

they make mouths at me, they wag their heads;

"He committed his cause to the Lord; let him deliver him,

let him rescue him, for he delights in him!"

They divide my garments among them,

and for my raiment they cast lots.

But thou, O Lord, be not far off!

O thou my help, hasten to my aid!

I will tell of thy name to my brethren;

in the midst of the congregation I will praise thee:

You who fear the Lord, praise him!

all you sons of Jacob, glorify him,

for he has not despised or abhorred the affliction of the afflicted;

and he has not hid his face from him, but has heard, when he cried to him.

From thee comes my praise in the great congregation;

my vows I will pay before those who fear him.

All the ends of the earth shall remember and turn to the Lord;

and all the families of the nations shall worship before him.

For dominion belongs to the Lord,

and he rules over the nations.

Psalm 22:1ab, 2-5, 7-8, 18-19, 22-23ab, 24-25, 27-28

7 THE LORD IS MY SHEPHERD

The Lord is my shepherd;

I shall not want.

He maketh me to lie down in green pastures:

he leadeth me beside the still waters.

He restoreth my soul:

he leadeth me in the paths of righteousness for his name's sake.

Yea, though I walk through the valley of the shadow of death, I will fear no evil:

for thou art with me; thy rod and thy staff they comfort me.

Thou preparest a table before me in the presence of mine enemies:

thou anointest my head with oil; my cup runneth over.

Surely goodness and mercy shall follow me all the days of my life:

and I will dwell in the house of the Lord for ever. *Psalm 23 KJV*

8 THE EARTH IS THE LORD'S

The earth is the Lord's and the fulness thereof,

the world and those who dwell therein;

for he has founded it upon the seas,

and established it upon the rivers.

Who shall ascend the hill of the Lord?

And who shall stand in his holy place?

He who has clean hands and a pure heart,

who does not lift up his soul to what is false, and does not swear deceitfully.

He will receive blessing from the Lord,

and vindication from the God of his salvation.

Such is the generation of those who seek him,

who seek the face of the God of Jacob.

Lift up your heads, O gates! and be lifted up, O ancient doors!

that the King of glory may come in.

Who is the King of glory?

The Lord, strong and mighty, the Lord, mighty in battle!

Lift up your heads, O gates! and be lifted up, O ancient doors!

that the King of glory may come in!

Who is this King of glory?

The Lord of hosts, he is the King of glory!   *Psalm 24*

9 IN THEE I TRUST

To thee, O Lord, I lift up my soul.

O my God, in thee I trust,

let me not be put to shame;

let not my enemies exult over me.

Make me to know thy ways, O Lord;

teach me thy paths.

Lead me in thy truth, and teach me,

for thou art the God of my salvation; for thee I wait all the day long.

Be mindful of thy mercy, O Lord, and of thy steadfast love,

for they have been from of old.

Remember not the sins of my youth, or my transgressions;

according to thy steadfast love remember me, for thy goodness' sake, O Lord!

Good and upright is the Lord;

therefore he instructs sinners in the way.

He leads the humble in what is right,

and teaches the humble his way.

All the paths of the Lord are steadfast love and faithfulness,

for those who keep his covenant and his testimonies.

For thy name's sake, O Lord,

pardon my guilt, for it is great.

Who is the man that fears the Lord?

Him will he instruct in the way that he should choose.

The friendship of the Lord is for those who fear him,

and he makes known to them his covenant.

May integrity and uprightness preserve me,

for I wait for thee.

Psalm 25:1-2, 4-12, 14, 21

10 THE LORD IS MY LIGHT

The Lord is my light and my salvation;

whom shall I fear?

The Lord is the stronghold of my life;

of whom shall I be afraid?

When evildoers assail me, uttering slanders against me,

my adversaries and foes, they shall stumble and fall.

Though a host encamp against me,

257

my heart shall not fear;

though war arise against me,

yet I will be confident.

One thing have I asked of the Lord,

that will I seek after;

that I may dwell in the house of the Lord all the days of my life,

to behold the beauty of the Lord, and to inquire in his temple.

For he will hide me in his shelter in the day of trouble;

he will set me high upon a rock.

And now my head shall be lifted up above my enemies round about me;

I will sing and make melody to the Lord.

Hear, O Lord, when I cry aloud,

be gracious to me and answer me!

Thou hast said, "Seek ye my face."

My heart says to thee, "Thy face, Lord, do I seek."

I believe that I shall see the goodness of the Lord in the land of the living!

Wait for the Lord; be strong, and let your heart take courage; yea, wait for the Lord!

Psalm 27:1-5a, 5c-6a, 6c-8, 13-14

11 GOD'S FORGIVING LOVE

Blessed is he whose transgression is forgiven,

whose sin is covered.

Blessed is the man to whom the Lord imputes no iniquity,

and in whose spirit there is no deceit.

When I declared not my sin, my body wasted away

through my groaning all day long.

I acknowledged my sin to thee,

and I did not hide my iniquity;

I said, "I will confess my transgressions to the Lord";

then thou didst forgive the guilt of my sin.

Therefore let every one who is godly offer prayer to thee;

at a time of distress, in the rush of great waters, they shall not reach him.

Thou art a hiding place for me, thou preservest me from trouble;

thou dost encompass me with deliverance.

I will instruct you and teach you the way you should go;

I will counsel you with my eye upon you.

Many are the pangs of the wicked;

but steadfast love surrounds him who trusts in the Lord.

Be glad in the Lord, and rejoice, O righteous,

and shout for joy, all you upright in heart! *Psalm 32:1-3, 5-8, 10-11*

12 REJOICE IN THE LORD!

Rejoice in the Lord, O you righteous!

Praise befits the upright.

For the word of the Lord is upright;

and all his work is done in faithfulness.

He loves righteousness and justice;

the earth is full of the steadfast love of the Lord.

By the word of the Lord the heavens were made,

and all their host by the breath of his mouth.

Let all the earth fear the Lord,

let all the inhabitants of the world stand in awe of him!

For he spoke, and it came to be;

he commanded, and it stood forth.

The Lord brings the counsel of the nations to nought;

he frustrates the plans of the peoples.

The counsel of the Lord stands for ever,

the thoughts of his heart to all generations.

Blessed is the nation whose God is the Lord,

the people whom he has chosen as his heritage!

The Lord looks down from heaven, he sees all the sons of men;

from where he sits enthroned he looks forth on all the inhabitants of the earth,

he who fashions the hearts of them all,

and observes all their deeds.

Our soul waits for the Lord;

he is our help and shield.

Yea, our heart is glad in him,

because we trust in his holy name.

Let thy steadfast love, O Lord, be upon us,

even as we hope in thee.

Psalm 33:1, 4-6, 8-15, 20-22

13 THE LORD IS GOOD

I will bless the Lord at all times;

his praise shall continually be in my mouth.

My soul makes its boast in the Lord;

let the afflicted hear and be glad.

O magnify the Lord with me,

and let us exalt his name together!

I sought the Lord, and he answered me,

and delivered me from all my fears.

Look to him, and be radiant;

so your faces shall never be ashamed.

This poor man cried, and the Lord heard him,

and saved him out of all his troubles.

The angel of the Lord encamps around those who fear him,

and delivers them.

O taste and see that the Lord is good!

Happy is the man who takes refuge in him!

Come, O sons, listen to me,

I will teach you the fear of the Lord.

What man is there who desires life,

and covets many days, that he may enjoy good?

Keep your tongue from evil, and your lips from speaking deceit.

Depart from evil, and do good; seek peace, and pursue it.

When the righteous cry for help, the Lord hears,

and delivers them out of all their troubles.

The Lord is near to the brokenhearted,

and saves the crushed in spirit.

The Lord redeems the life of his servants;

none of those who take refuge in him will be condemned.

Psalm 34:1-8, 11-14, 17-18, 22

14 TRUST IN THE LORD

Fret not yourself because of the wicked,

be not envious of the wrongdoers!

For they will soon fade like the grass,

and wither like the green herb.

Trust in the Lord, and do good;

so you will dwell in the land, and enjoy security.

Take delight in the Lord,

and he will give you the desires of your heart.

Commit your way to the Lord;

trust in him, and he will act.

He will bring forth your vindication as the light,

and your right as the noonday.

Fret not yourself over him who prospers in his way,

over the man who carries out evil devices!

For the wicked shall be cut off;

but those who wait for the Lord shall possess the land.

The steps of a man are from the Lord,

and he establishes him in whose way he delights;

though he fall, he shall not be cast headlong,

for the Lord is the stay of his hand.

Depart from evil, and do good;

so shall you abide for ever.

For the Lord loves justice; he will not forsake his saints.

The righteous shall be preserved for ever.

The salvation of the righteous is from the Lord;

he is their refuge in the time of trouble.

The Lord helps them and delivers them;

he delivers them from the wicked, and saves them, because they take refuge in him.

Psalm 37:1-6, 7bc, 9, 23-24, 27-28ab, 39-40

15 PRAISE TO OUR GOD

I waited patiently for the Lord;

he inclined to me and heard my cry.

He drew me up from the desolate pit, out of the miry bog,

and set my feet upon a rock, making my steps secure.

He put a new song in my mouth,

a song of praise to our God.

Many will see and fear,

and put their trust in the Lord.

Blessed is the man who makes the Lord his trust,

who does not turn to the proud, to those who go astray after false gods!

Thou hast multiplied, O Lord my God, thy wondrous deeds and thy thoughts toward us;

none can compare with thee!

Were I to proclaim and tell of them,

they would be more than can be numbered.

Sacrifice and offering thou dost not desire;

but thou hast given me an open ear.

Burnt offering and sin offering thou hast not required.

Then I said, "Lo, I come; in the roll of the book it is written of me;

I delight to do thy will, O my God;

thy law is within my heart."

I have told the glad news of deliverance in the great congregation;

lo, I have not restrained my lips, as thou knowest, O Lord.

I have not hid thy saving help within my heart,

I have spoken of thy faithfulness and thy salvation;

I have not concealed thy steadfast love

and thy faithfulness from the great congregation.

Do not thou, O Lord, withhold thy mercy from me,

let thy steadfast love and thy faithfulness ever preserve me!

Psalm 40:1-11

16 MY SOUL THIRSTS FOR GOD

As a hart longs for flowing streams,

so longs my soul for thee, O God.

My soul thirsts for God, for the living God.

When shall I come and behold the face of God?

My tears have been my food day and night,

while men say to me continually, "Where is your God?"

These things I remember, as I pour out my soul:

how I went with the throng, and led them in procession to the house of God, with glad shouts and songs of thanksgiving,

> a multitude keeping festival.

Why are you cast down, O my soul,

> and why are you disquieted within me?

Hope in God;

> for I shall again praise him, my help and my God.

My soul is cast down within me,

> therefore I remember thee from the land of Jordan and of Hermon, from Mount Mizar.

Deep calls to deep at the thunder of thy cataracts;

> all thy waves and thy billows have gone over me.

By day the Lord commands his steadfast love;

> and at night his song is with me, a prayer to the God of my life.

I say to God, my rock: "Why hast thou forgotten me?

> Why go I mourning because of the oppression of the enemy?"

As with a deadly wound in my body, my adversaries taunt me,

> while they say to me continually, "Where is thy God?"

Why are you cast down, O my soul,

> and why are you disquieted within me?

Hope in God;

> for I shall again praise him, my help and my God.   *Psalm 42*

17 GOD IS OUR REFUGE

God is our refuge and strength,

> a very present help in trouble.

Therefore we will not fear though the earth should change,

> though the mountains shake in the heart of the sea;

though its waters roar and foam,

> though the mountains tremble with its tumult.

There is a river whose streams make glad the city of God,

> the holy habitation of the Most High.

God is in the midst of her, she shall not be moved;

> God will help her right early.

The nations rage, the kingdoms totter;

> he utters his voice, the earth melts.

The Lord of hosts is with us;

> the God of Jacob is our refuge.

Come, behold the works of the Lord,

> how he has wrought desolations in the earth.

He makes wars cease to the end of the earth;

> he breaks the bow, and shatters the spear, he burns the chariots with fire!

"Be still, and know that I am God.

> I am exalted among the nations, I am exalted in the earth!"

The Lord of hosts is with us;

the God of Jacob is our refuge.

Psalm 46

18 A CLEAN HEART

Have mercy on me, O God, according to thy steadfast love;

according to thy abundant mercy blot out my transgressions.

Wash me thoroughly from my iniquity,

and cleanse me from my sin!

For I know my transgressions,

and my sin is ever before me.

Against thee, thee only, have I sinned,

and done that which is evil in thy sight,

so that thou art justified in thy sentence

and blameless in thy judgment.

Behold, thou desirest truth in the inward being;

therefore teach me wisdom in my secret heart.

Hide thy face from my sins,

and blot out all my iniquities.

Create in me a clean heart, O God,

and put a new and right spirit within me.

Cast me not away from thy presence,

and take not thy holy Spirit from me.

Restore to me the joy of thy salvation,

and uphold me with a willing spirit.

Then I will teach transgressors thy ways,

and sinners will return to thee.

Deliver me from bloodguiltiness, O God, thou God of my salvation,

and my tongue will sing aloud of thy deliverance.

O Lord, open thou my lips,

and my mouth shall show forth thy praise.

For thou hast no delight in sacrifice;

were I to give a burnt offering, thou wouldst not be pleased.

The sacrifice acceptable to God is a broken spirit;

a broken and contrite heart, O God, thou wilt not despise.

Psalm 51:1-4, 6, 9-17

19 GOD'S STEADFAST LOVE

Be merciful to me, O God, be merciful to me,

for in thee my soul takes refuge;

in the shadow of thy wings I will take refuge,

till the storms of destruction pass by.

I cry to God Most High,

to God who fulfills his purpose for me.

He will send from heaven and save me,

God will send forth his steadfast love and his faithfulness!

Be exalted, O God, above the heavens!

Let thy glory be over all the earth!

263

My heart is steadfast, O God, my heart is steadfast!

I will sing and make melody!

I will give thanks to thee, O Lord, among the peoples;

I will sing praises to thee among the nations.

For thy steadfast love is great to the heavens,

thy faithfulness to the clouds.

Be exalted, O God, above the heavens!

Let thy glory be over all the earth!

Psalm 57:1-3ac, 5, 7, 9-11

20 GOD IS MY ROCK AND MY SALVATION

For God alone my soul waits in silence;

from him comes my salvation.

He only is my rock and my salvation, my fortress;

I shall not be greatly moved.

For God alone my soul waits in silence,

for my hope is from him.

He only is my rock and my salvation, my fortress;

I shall not be shaken.

On God rests my deliverance and my honor;

my mighty rock, my refuge is God.

Trust in him at all times, O people;

pour out your heart before him; God is a refuge for us.

Once God has spoken; twice have I heard this:

that power belongs to God;

and that to thee, O Lord, belongs steadfast love.

For thou dost requite a man according to his work.

Psalm 62:1-2, 5-8, 11-12

21 THOU ART MY GOD

O God, thou art my God, I seek thee,

my soul thirsts for thee;

my flesh faints for thee,

as in a dry and weary land where no water is.

So I have looked upon thee in the sanctuary,

beholding thy power and glory.

Because thy steadfast love is better than life,

my lips will praise thee.

So I will bless thee as long as I live;

I will lift up my hands and call on thy name.

My soul is feasted as with marrow and fat,

and my mouth praises thee with joyful lips,

when I think of thee upon my bed,

and meditate on thee in the watches of the night;

for thou hast been my help,

and in the shadow of thy wings I sing for joy.

My soul clings to thee;

thy right hand upholds me.

Psalm 63:1-8

22 Praise Is Due to Thee, O God

Praise is due to thee, O God, in Zion;

and to thee shall vows be performed,

O thou who hearest prayer!

To thee shall all flesh come on account of sins.

When our transgressions prevail over us,

thou dost forgive them.

Blessed is he whom thou dost choose and bring near, to dwell in thy courts!

We shall be satisfied with the goodness of thy house, thy holy temple!

By dread deeds thou dost answer us with deliverance, O God of our salvation,

who art the hope of all the ends of the earth, and of the farthest seas;

who by thy strength hast established the mountains,

being girded with might;

who dost still the roaring of the seas,

the roaring of their waves, the tumult of the peoples;

so that those who dwell at earth's farthest bounds are afraid at thy signs;

thou makest the outgoings of the morning and the evening to shout for joy.

Thou visitest the earth and waterest it, thou greatly enrichest it;

thou providest their grain, for so thou hast prepared it.

Thou waterest its furrows abundantly, settling its ridges,

softening it with showers, and blessing its growth.

Thou crownest the year with thy bounty;

the hills gird themselves with joy,

the meadows clothe themselves with flocks,

the valleys deck themselves with grain, they shout and sing together for joy.

Psalm 65:1-9a, 9c-11a, 12b-13

23 May God Be Gracious

May God be gracious to us and bless us

and make his face to shine upon us,

that thy way may be known upon earth,

thy saving power among all nations.

Let the peoples praise thee, O God;

let all the peoples praise thee!

Let the nations be glad and sing for joy,

for thou dost judge the peoples with equity and guide the nations upon earth.

Let the peoples praise thee, O God;

let all the peoples praise thee!

The earth has yielded its increase;

God, our God, has blessed us.

God has blessed us;

let all the ends of the earth fear him! *Psalm 67*

24 MAY RIGHTEOUSNESS FLOURISH

Give the king thy justice, O God,

and thy righteousness to the royal son!

May he judge thy people with righteousness,

and thy poor with justice!

Let the mountains bear prosperity for the people,

and the hills, in righteousness!

May he defend the cause of the poor of the people,

give deliverance to the needy, and crush the oppressor!

May he live while the sun endures, and as long as the moon,

throughout all generations!

May he be like the rain that falls on the mown grass,

like showers that water the earth!

In his days may righteousness flourish,

and peace abound, till the moon be no more!

May he have dominion from sea to sea,

may all kings fall down before him, all nations serve him!

For he delivers the needy when he calls,

the poor and him who has no helper.

From oppression and violence he redeems their life;

and precious is their blood in his sight.

May his name endure for ever,

his fame continue as long as the sun!

Blessed be the Lord, the God of Israel,

who alone does wondrous things.

Blessed be his glorious name for ever;

may his glory fill the whole earth! Amen and Amen!

Psalm 72:1-8a, 11-12, 14, 17ab, 18-19

25 GOD IS GOOD

Truly God is good to the upright,

to those who are pure in heart.

But as for me, my feet had almost stumbled,

my steps had well nigh slipped.

For I was envious of the arrogant,

when I saw the prosperity of the wicked.

For they have no pangs;

their bodies are sound and sleek.

They are not in trouble as other men are;

they are not stricken like other men.

Therefore pride is their necklace;

> violence covers them as a garment.

They set their mouths against the heavens,

> and their tongue struts through the earth.

Therefore the people turn and praise them;

> and find no fault in them.

And they say, "How can God know?

> Is there knowledge in the Most High?"

Behold, these are the wicked;

> always at ease, they increase in riches.

All in vain have I kept my heart clean

> and washed my hands in innocence.

For all the day long I have been stricken,

> and chastened every morning.

If I had said, "I will speak thus,"

> I would have been untrue to the generation of thy children.

But when I thought how to understand this,

> it seemed to me a wearisome task,

until I went into the sanctuary of God;

> then I perceived their end.

Truly thou dost set them in slippery places;

> thou dost make them fall to ruin.

How they are destroyed in a moment,

> swept away utterly by terrors!

They are like a dream when one awakes,

> on awaking you despise their phantoms.

When my soul was embittered,

> when I was pricked in heart,

I was stupid and ignorant,

> I was like a beast toward thee.

Nevertheless I am continually with thee;

> thou dost hold my right hand.

Thou dost guide me with thy counsel,

> and afterward thou wilt receive me to glory.

Whom have I in heaven but thee?

> And there is nothing upon earth that I desire besides thee.

My flesh and my heart may fail,

> but God is the strength of my heart and my portion for ever.

Psalm 73:1-6, 9-26

26 How Lovely Is Thy Dwelling Place

How lovely is thy dwelling place,

> O Lord of hosts!

My soul longs, yea, faints for the courts of the Lord;

> my heart and flesh sing for joy to the living God.

Even the sparrow finds a home, and the swallow a nest for herself, where she may lay her young, at thy altars, **O Lord of hosts, my king and my God.**

Blessed are those who dwell in thy house,

ever singing thy praise!

Blessed are the men whose strength is in thee,

in whose heart are the highways to Zion.

O Lord God of hosts, hear my prayer;

give ear, O God of Jacob!

Behold our shield, O God;

look upon the face of thine anointed!

For a day in thy courts is better than a thousand elsewhere.

I would rather be a doorkeeper in the house of my God than dwell in the tents of wickedness.

For the Lord God is a sun and shield; he bestows favor and honor.

No good thing does the Lord withhold from those who walk uprightly.

O Lord of hosts,

blessed is the man who trusts in thee! *Psalm 84:1-5, 8-12*

27 THE ETERNITY OF GOD

Lord, thou hast been our dwelling place

in all generations.

Before the mountains were brought forth, or ever thou hadst formed the earth and the world,

from everlasting to everlasting thou art God.

Thou turnest man back to the dust,

and sayest, "Turn back, O children of men!"

For a thousand years in thy sight are but as yesterday when it is past,

or as a watch in the night.

Thou dost sweep men away; they are like a dream,

like grass which is renewed in the morning:

in the morning it flourishes and is renewed;

in the evening it fades and withers.

For we are consumed by thy anger;

by thy wrath we are overwhelmed.

Thou hast set our iniquities before thee,

our secret sins in the light of thy countenance.

For all our days pass away under thy wrath,

our years come to an end like a sigh.

The years of our life are threescore and ten,

or even by reason of strength fourscore;

yet their span is but toil and trouble;

they are soon gone, and we fly away.

Who considers the power of thy anger,

and thy wrath according to the fear of thee?

So teach us to number our days

that we may get a heart of wisdom.

Return, O Lord! how long?

Have pity on thy servants!

Satisfy us in the morning with thy steadfast love,

that we may rejoice and be glad all our days.

Make us glad as many days as thou hast afflicted us,

and as many years as we have seen evil.

Let thy work be manifest to thy servants,

and thy glorious power to their children.

Let the favor of the Lord our God be upon us,

and establish thou the work of our hands upon us, yea, the work of our hands establish thou it.

Psalm 90

28 THE SHADOW OF THE ALMIGHTY

He who dwells in the shelter of the Most High,

who abides in the shadow of the Almighty,

will say to the Lord, "My refuge and my fortress;

my God, in whom I trust."

For he will deliver you from the snare of the fowler

and from the deadly pestilence;

he will cover you with his pinions, and under his wings you will find refuge;

his faithfulness is a shield and buckler.

You will not fear the terror of the night,

nor the arrow that flies by day,

nor the pestilence that stalks in darkness,

nor the destruction that wastes at noonday.

A thousand may fall at your side, ten thousand at your right hand;

but it will not come near you.

You will only look with your eyes

and see the recompense of the wicked.

Because you have made the Lord your refuge,

the Most High your habitation,

no evil shall befall you,

no scourge come near your tent.

For he will give his angels charge of you

to guard you in all your ways.

On their hands they will bear you up,

lest you dash your foot against a stone.

When he calls to me, I will answer him;

I will be with him in trouble, I will rescue him and honor him.

With long life I will satisfy him,

and show him my salvation.

Psalm 91:1-12, 15-16

29 THE LORD REIGNS

The Lord reigns; he is robed in majesty;

the Lord is robed, he is girded with strength.

Yea, the world is established;

it shall never be moved;

thy throne is established from of old;

thou art from everlasting.

The floods have lifted up, O Lord, the floods have lifted up their voice,

the floods lift up their roaring.

Mightier than the thunders of many waters, mightier than the waves of the sea,

the Lord on high is mighty!

Thy decrees are very sure;

holiness befits thy house, O Lord, for evermore. *Psalm 93*

30 SING TO THE LORD A NEW SONG

O sing to the Lord a new song;

sing to the Lord, all the earth!

Sing to the Lord, bless his name;

tell of his salvation from day to day.

Declare his glory among the nations,

his marvelous works among all the peoples!

For great is the Lord, and greatly to be praised;

he is to be feared above all gods.

For all the gods of the peoples are idols;

but the Lord made the heavens.

Honor and majesty are before him;

strength and beauty are in his sanctuary.

Ascribe to the Lord, O families of the peoples,

ascribe to the Lord glory and strength!

Ascribe to the Lord the glory due his name;

bring an offering, and come into his courts!

Worship the Lord in holy array;

tremble before him, all the earth!

Say among the nations, "The Lord reigns!

Yea, the world is established, it shall never be moved;

he will judge the peoples with equity."

Let the heavens be glad, and let the earth rejoice;

let the sea roar, and all that fills it;

let the field exult, and everything in it!

Then shall all the trees of the wood sing for joy before the Lord,

for he comes, for he comes to judge the earth.

He will judge the world with righteousness,

and the peoples with his truth.

Psalm 96

31 LIGHT DAWNS FOR THE RIGHTEOUS

The Lord reigns; let the earth rejoice;

let the many coastlands be glad!

Clouds and thick darkness are round about him;

righteousness and justice are the foundation of his throne.

His lightnings lighten the world;

the earth sees and trembles.

The mountains melt like wax before the Lord,

before the Lord of all the earth.

The heavens proclaim his righteousness;

and all the peoples behold his glory.

For thou, O Lord, art most high over all the earth;

thou art exalted far above all gods.

The Lord loves those who hate evil;

he preserves the lives of his saints; he delivers them from the hand of the wicked.

Light dawns for the righteous,

and joy for the upright in heart.

Rejoice in the Lord, O you righteous,

and give thanks to his holy name!

Psalm 97:1-2, 4-6, 9-12

32 THE VICTORY OF OUR GOD

O sing to the Lord a new song, for he has done marvelous things!

His right hand and his holy arm have gotten him victory.

The Lord has made known his victory,

he has revealed his vindication in the sight of the nations.

He has remembered his steadfast love and faithfulness to the house of Israel.

All the ends of the earth have seen the victory of our God.

Make a joyful noise to the Lord, all the earth;

break forth into joyous song and sing praises!

Sing praises to the Lord with the lyre,

with the lyre and the sound of melody!

With trumpets and the sound of the horn

make a joyful noise before the King, the Lord!

Let the sea roar, and all that fills it;

the world and those who dwell in it!

Let the floods clap their hands;

let the hills sing for joy together before the Lord,

for he comes to judge the earth. He will judge the world with righteousness,

and the peoples with equity.

Psalm 98

33 HEAR MY PRAYER, O LORD

Hear my prayer, O Lord;

let my cry come to thee!

Do not hide thy face from me in the day of my distress!

Incline thy ear to me; answer me speedily in the day when I call!

My days are like an evening shadow;

I wither away like grass.

But thou, O Lord, art enthroned for ever;

thy name endures to all generations.

Let this be recorded for a generation to come,

so that a people yet unborn may praise the Lord:

that he looked down from his holy height,

from heaven the Lord looked at the earth,

to hear the groans of the prisoners,

to set free those who were doomed to die;

that men may declare in Zion the name of the Lord, and in Jerusalem his praise,

when peoples gather together, and kingdoms, to worship the Lord.

Of old thou didst lay the foundation of the earth,

and the heavens are the work of thy hands.

They will perish, but thou dost endure;

they will all wear out like a garment.

Thou changest them like raiment, and they pass away;

but thou art the same, and thy years have no end.

Psalm 102:1-2, 11-12, 18-22, 25-27

34 BLESS THE LORD

Bless the Lord, O my soul;

and all that is within me, bless his holy name!

Bless the Lord, O my soul,

and forget not all his benefits,

who forgives all your iniquity,

who heals all your diseases,

who redeems your life from the Pit,

who crowns you with steadfast love and mercy,

who satisfies you with good as long as you live

so that your youth is renewed like the eagle's.

The Lord works vindication and justice

for all who are oppressed.

He made known his ways to Moses,

his acts to the people of Israel.

Psalm 103:1-7

35 THE LORD IS MERCIFUL

The Lord is merciful and gracious,

slow to anger and abounding in steadfast love.

He will not always chide,

nor will he keep his anger for ever.

He does not deal with us according to our sins,

nor requite us according to our iniquities.

For as the heavens are high above the earth,

so great is his steadfast love toward those who fear him;

as far as the east is from the west,

so far does he remove our transgressions from us.

As a father pities his children,

so the Lord pities those who fear him.

For he knows our frame;

he remembers that we are dust.

As for man, his days are like grass;

he flourishes like a flower of the field;

for the wind passes over it, and it is gone,

and its place knows it no more.

But the steadfast love of the Lord is from everlasting to everlasting upon those who fear him,

and his righteousness to children's children,

to those who keep his covenant

and remember to do his commandments. *Psalm 103:8-18*

36 O GIVE THANKS

O give thanks to the Lord, for he is good;

for his steadfast love endures for ever!

Let the redeemed of the Lord say so,

whom he has redeemed from trouble

and gathered in from the lands, from the east and from the west,

from the north and from the south.

Some wandered in desert wastes,

finding no way to a city to dwell in;

hungry and thirsty,

their soul fainted within them.

Then they cried to the Lord in their trouble,

and he delivered them from their distress;

he led them by a straight way,

till they reached a city to dwell in.

Let them thank the Lord for his steadfast love,

> for his wonderful works to the sons of men!

For he satisfies him who is thirsty,

> and the hungry he fills with good things.

Let them thank the Lord for his steadfast love,

> for his wonderful works to the sons of men!

And let them offer sacrifices of thanksgiving,

> and tell of his deeds in songs of joy! *Psalm 107:1-9, 21-22*

37 PRAISE THE LORD

Praise the Lord. I will give thanks to the Lord with my whole heart,

> in the company of the upright, in the congregation.

Great are the works of the Lord,

> studied by all who have pleasure in them.

Full of honor and majesty is his work,

> and his righteousness endures for ever.

He has caused his wonderful works to be remembered;

> the Lord is gracious and merciful.

He provides food for those who fear him;

> he is ever mindful of his covenant.

He has shown his people the power of his works,

> in giving them the heritage of the nations.

The works of his hands are faithful and just;

> all his precepts are trustworthy,

they are established for ever and ever,

> to be performed with faithfulness and uprightness.

He sent redemption to his people;

> he has commanded his covenant for ever. *Psalm 111:1-9a*

38 I LOVE THE LORD

I love the Lord,

> because he has heard my voice and my supplications.

Because he inclined his ear to me,

> therefore I will call on him as long as I live.

The snares of death encompassed me;

> I suffered distress and anguish.

Then I called on the name of the Lord:

> "O Lord, I beseech thee, save my life!"

Gracious is the Lord, and righteous;

> our God is merciful.

The Lord preserves the simple;

> when I was brought low, he saved me.

Return, O my soul, to your rest;

for the Lord has dealt bountifully with you.

For thou hast delivered my soul from death,

my eyes from tears, my feet from stumbling;

I walk before the Lord

in the land of the living.

What shall I render to the Lord

for all his bounty to me?

I will lift up the cup of salvation

and call on the name of the Lord,

I will pay my vows to the Lord

in the presence of all his people.

Precious in the sight of the Lord is the death of his saints.

O Lord, I am thy servant, the son of thy handmaid. Thou hast loosed my bonds.

I will offer to thee the sacrifice of thanksgiving

and call on the name of the Lord.

I will pay my vows to the Lord, in the presence of all his people,

in the courts of the house of the Lord, in your midst, O Jerusalem. Praise the Lord!

Psalm 116:1-3a, 3c-9, 12-19

39 LET US REJOICE AND BE GLAD

O give thanks to the Lord, for he is good;

his steadfast love endures for ever!

Let those who fear the Lord say,

"His steadfast love endures for ever."

Out of my distress I called on the Lord;

the Lord answered me and set me free.

With the Lord on my side I do not fear.

What can man do to me?

It is better to take refuge in the Lord

than to put confidence in princes.

Open to me the gates of righteousness,

that I may enter through them and give thanks to the Lord.

This is the gate of the Lord;

the righteous shall enter through it.

I thank thee that thou hast answered me

and hast become my salvation.

The stone which the builders rejected

has become the chief cornerstone.

This is the Lord's doing;

it is marvelous in our eyes.

This is the day which the Lord has made;

let us rejoice and be glad in it.

Blessed be he who enters in the name of the Lord!

We bless you from the house of the Lord.

275

Thou art my God, and I will give thanks to thee;

thou art my God, I will extol thee.

O give thanks to the Lord, for he is good;

for his steadfast love endures for ever!

Psalm 118:1, 4-6, 8, 19-24, 26, 28-29

40 TEACH ME THY STATUTES

Blessed are those whose way is blameless,

who walk in the law of the Lord!

Blessed are those who keep his testimonies,

who seek him with their whole heart,

who also do no wrong,

but walk in his ways!

Thou hast commanded thy precepts to be kept diligently.

O that my ways may be steadfast in keeping thy statutes!

Then I shall not be put to shame,

having my eyes fixed on all thy commandments.

I will praise thee with an upright heart,

when I learn thy righteous ordinances.

I will observe thy statutes;

O forsake me not utterly!

How can a young man keep his way pure?

By guarding it according to thy word.

With my whole heart I seek thee;

let me not wander from thy commandments!

I have laid up thy word in my heart,

that I might not sin against thee.

Blessed be thou, O Lord;

teach me thy statutes!

With my lips I declare all the ordinances of thy mouth.

In the way of thy testimonies I delight as much as in all riches.

I will meditate on thy precepts,

and fix my eyes on thy ways.

I will delight in thy statutes;

I will not forget thy word.

Psalm 119:1-16

41 THY LAW IS MY DELIGHT

Teach me, O Lord, the way of thy statutes;

and I will keep it to the end.

Give me understanding, that I may keep thy law

and observe it with my whole heart.

Lead me in the path of thy commandments, for I delight in it.

Incline my heart to thy testimonies,
and not to gain!

Turn my eyes from looking at vanities;

and give me life in thy ways.

Confirm to thy servant thy promise,

which is for those who fear thee.

Turn away the reproach which I
dread;

for thy ordinances are good.

Behold, I long for thy precepts;

in thy righteousness give me life!

Let thy steadfast love come to me, O
Lord,

thy salvation according to thy
promise;

then shall I have an answer for those
who taunt me,

for I trust in thy word.

And take not the word of truth utterly out of my mouth,

for my hope is in thy ordinances.

I will keep thy law continually, for
ever and ever;

and I shall walk at liberty, for I
have sought thy precepts.

For I find my delight in thy commandments, which I love.

I revere thy commandments, and I
will meditate on thy statutes.

I long for thy salvation, O Lord,

and thy law is my delight.

Psalm 119:33-45, 47-48, 174

42 THE LORD IS YOUR KEEPER

I lift up my eyes to the hills.

From whence does my help come?

My help comes from the Lord,

who made heaven and earth.

He will not let your foot be moved,

he who keeps you will not slumber.

Behold, he who keeps Israel

will neither slumber nor sleep.

The Lord is your keeper;

the Lord is your shade on your
right hand.

The sun shall not smite you by day,

nor the moon by night.

The Lord will keep you from all evil;

he will keep your life.

The Lord will keep your going out
and your coming in

from this time forth and for evermore.   *Psalm 121*

43 PEACE BE WITHIN YOU

I was glad when they said to me,

"Let us go to the house of the
Lord!"

Our feet have been standing

within your gates, O Jerusalem!

Jerusalem, built as a city

which is bound firmly together,

to which the tribes go up, the tribes
of the Lord,

as was decreed for Israel, to give thanks to the name of the Lord.

There thrones for judgment were set,

the thrones of the house of David.

Pray for the peace of Jerusalem!

"May they prosper who love you!"

Peace be within your walls,

and security within your towers!"

For my brethren and companions' sake

I will say, "Peace be within you!"

For the sake of the house of the Lord our God,

I will seek your good. *Psalm 122*

44 WITH SHOUTS OF JOY

When the Lord restored the fortunes of Zion,

we were like those who dream.

Then our mouth was filled with laughter,

and our tongue with shouts of joy;

then they said among the nations, "The Lord has done great things for them."

The Lord has done great things for us; we are glad.

May those who sow in tears

reap with shouts of joy!

He that goes forth weeping, bearing the seed for sowing,

shall come home with shouts of joy, bringing his sheaves with him.

Psalm 126:1-3, 5-6

45 BY THE WATERS OF BABYLON

By the waters of Babylon, there we sat down and wept, when we remembered Zion.

On the willows there we hung up our lyres.

For there our captors required of us songs, and our tormentors, mirth, saying,

"Sing us one of the songs of Zion!"

How shall we sing the Lord's song in a foreign land?

If I forget you, O Jerusalem, let my right hand wither!

Let my tongue cleave to the roof of my mouth, if I do not remember you,

if I do not set Jerusalem above my highest joy! *Psalm 137:1-6*

46 THE GLORY OF THE LORD

I give thee thanks, O Lord, with my whole heart;

before the gods I sing thy praise;

I bow down toward thy holy temple and give thanks to thy name for thy steadfast love and thy faithfulness;

for thou hast exalted above everything thy name and thy word.

On the day I called, thou didst answer me,

my strength of soul thou didst increase.

All the kings of the earth shall praise thee, O Lord,

> for they have heard the words of thy mouth;

and they shall sing of the ways of the Lord,

> for great is the glory of the Lord.

For though the Lord is high, he regards the lowly;

> but the haughty he knows from afar.

Though I walk in the midst of trouble, thou dost preserve my life;

> thou dost stretch out thy hand against the wrath of my enemies, and thy right hand delivers me.

The Lord will fulfill his purpose for me;

> thy steadfast love, O Lord, endures for ever.   *Psalm 138:1-8b*

47 WHITHER SHALL I GO FROM THY SPIRIT?

O Lord, thou hast searched me and known me!

> Thou knowest when I sit down and when I rise up; thou discernest my thoughts from afar.

Thou searchest out my path and my lying down,

> and art acquainted with all my ways.

Even before a word is on my tongue,

> lo, O Lord, thou knowest it altogether.

Thou dost beset me behind and before,

> and layest thy hand upon me.

Such knowledge is too wonderful for me;

> it is high, I cannot attain it.

Whither shall I go from thy Spirit?

> Or whither shall I flee from thy presence?

If I ascend to heaven, thou art there!

> If I make my bed in Sheol, thou art there!

If I take the wings of the morning

> and dwell in the uttermost parts of the sea,

even there thy hand shall lead me,

> and thy right hand shall hold me.

If I say, "Let only darkness cover me,

> and the light about me be night,"

even the darkness is not dark to thee, the night is bright as the day;

> for darkness is as light with thee.

How precious to me are thy thoughts, O God!

> How vast is the sum of them!

If I would count them, they are more than the sand.

> When I awake, I am still with thee.

Search me, O God, and know my heart!

> Try me and know my thoughts!

And see if there be any wicked way in me,

and lead me in the way everlasting!

Psalm 139:1-12, 17-18, 23-24

48 WHEN MY SPIRIT IS FAINT

I cry with my voice to the Lord,

with my voice I make supplication to the Lord,

I pour out my complaint before him,

I tell my trouble before him.

When my spirit is faint, thou knowest my way!

In the path where I walk they have hidden a trap for me.

I look to the right and watch, but there is none who takes notice of me;

no refuge remains to me, no man cares for me.

I cry to thee, O Lord; I say, Thou art my refuge,

my portion in the land of the living.

Give heed to my cry;

for I am brought very low!

Deliver me from my persecutors;

for they are too strong for me!

Bring me out of prison,

that I may give thanks to thy name!

The righteous will surround me;

for thou wilt deal bountifully with me. *Psalm 142*

49 GREAT IS THE LORD

I will extol thee, my God and King,

and bless thy name for ever and ever.

Every day I will bless thee,

and praise thy name for ever and ever.

Great is the Lord, and greatly to be praised,

and his greatness is unsearchable.

One generation shall laud thy works to another,

and shall declare thy mighty acts.

On the glorious splendor of thy majesty,

and on thy wondrous works, I will meditate.

Men shall proclaim the might of thy terrible acts,

and I will declare thy greatness.

They shall pour forth the fame of thy abundant goodness,

and shall sing aloud of thy righteousness.

The Lord is gracious and merciful,

slow to anger and abounding in steadfast love.

The Lord is good to all,

and his compassion is over all that he has made.

All thy works shall give thanks to thee, O Lord,

and all thy saints shall bless thee!

They shall speak of the glory of thy kingdom, and tell of thy power, to make known to the sons of men thy mighty deeds, and the glorious splendor of thy kingdom.

Thy kingdom is an everlasting kingdom,

and thy dominion endures throughout all generations.

Psalm 145:1-13b

50 THE LORD IS FAITHFUL

The Lord is faithful in all his words,

and gracious in all his deeds.

The Lord upholds all who are falling,

and raises up all who are bowed down.

The eyes of all look to thee,

and thou givest them their food in due season.

Thou openest thy hand,

thou satisfiest the desire of every living thing.

The Lord is just in all his ways,

and kind in all his doings.

The Lord is near to all who call upon him,

to all who call upon him in truth.

He fulfills the desire of all who fear him,

he also hears their cry, and saves them.

The Lord preserves all who love him;

but all the wicked he will destroy.

My mouth will speak the praise of the Lord,

and let all flesh bless his holy name for ever and ever.

Psalm 145:13c-21

51 PRAISE THE LORD, O MY SOUL

Praise the Lord!

Praise the Lord, O my soul!

I will praise the Lord as long as I live;

I will sing praises to my God while I have being.

Put not your trust in princes,

in a son of man, in whom there is no help.

When his breath departs he returns to his earth;

on that very day his plans perish.

Happy is he whose help is the God of Jacob,

whose hope is in the Lord his God,

who made heaven and earth,

the sea, and all that is in them;

who keeps faith for ever;

who executes justice for the oppressed; who gives food to the hungry.

The Lord sets the prisoners free;

the Lord opens the eyes of the blind.

The Lord lifts up those who are bowed down;

the Lord loves the righteous.

The Lord watches over the sojourners, he upholds the widow and the fatherless;

but the way of the wicked he brings to ruin.

The Lord will reign for ever,

thy God, O Zion, to all generations. Praise the Lord!

Psalm 146

52 PRAISE THE LORD FROM THE HEAVENS

Praise the Lord! Praise the Lord from the heavens,

praise him in the heights!

Praise him, all his angels,

praise him, all his host!

Praise him, sun and moon,

praise him, you highest heavens!

Let them praise the name of the Lord!

For he commanded and they were created.

And he established them for ever and ever;

he fixed their bounds which cannot be passed.

Praise the Lord from the earth,

you sea monsters and all deeps,

fire and hail, snow and frost,

stormy wind fulfilling his command!

Mountains and all hills,

fruit trees and all cedars!

Beasts and all cattle,

creeping things and flying birds!

Kings of the earth and all peoples,

princes and all rulers of the earth!

Young men and maidens together,

old men and children!

Let them praise the name of the Lord,

for his name alone is exalted; his glory is above earth and heaven.

Psalm 148:1-3a, 4a, 5-13

53 PRAISE GOD IN HIS SANCTUARY

Praise the Lord! Praise God in his sanctuary;

praise him in his mighty firmament!

Praise him for his mighty deeds;

praise him according to his exceeding greatness!

Praise him with trumpet sound;

praise him with lute and harp!

Praise him with timbrel and dance;

praise him with strings and pipe!

Praise him with sounding cymbals;

praise him with loud clashing cymbals!

Let everything that breathes praise the Lord!

Praise the Lord! *Psalm 150*

CANTICLES AND OTHER ACTS OF PRAISE

54 O Come, Let Us Sing
Venite, exultemus

O come, let us sing unto the Lord;

let us heartily rejoice in the strength of our salvation.

Let us come before his presence with thanksgiving;

and show ourselves glad in him with psalms.

For the Lord is a great God;

and a great King above all gods.

In his hand are all the corners of the earth;

and the strength of the hills is his also.

The sea is his, and he made it;

and his hands prepared the dry land.

O come, let us worship and fall down,

and kneel before the Lord our maker.

For he is the Lord our God;

and we are the people of his pasture, and the sheep of his hand.

O worship the Lord in the beauty of holiness;

let the whole earth stand in awe of him.

For he cometh, for he cometh to judge the earth;

and with righteousness to judge the world, and the people with his truth.

Psalm 95:1-7; 96:9, 13 Coverdale

55 We Praise Thee, O God
Te Deum laudamus

We praise thee, O God; we acknowledge thee to be the Lord.

All the earth doth worship thee, the Father everlasting.

To thee all angels cry aloud; the heavens, and all the powers therein;

to thee cherubim and seraphim continually do cry.

Holy, holy, holy, Lord God of Sabaoth;

heaven and earth are full of the majesty of thy glory.

The glorious company of the apostles praise thee.

The goodly fellowship of the prophets praise thee.

The noble army of martyrs praise thee.

The holy Church throughout all the world doth acknowledge thee;

the Father, of an infinite majesty;

thine adorable, true, and only Son; also the Holy Ghost, the Comforter.

Thou art the King of glory, O Christ.

Thou art the everlasting Son of the Father.

When thou tookest upon thee to deliver man,

thou didst humble thyself to be born of a virgin.

When thou hadst overcome the sharpness of death,

thou didst open the kingdom of heaven to all believers.

Thou sittest at the right hand of God,

in the glory of the Father.

We believe that thou shalt come to be our judge.

We therefore pray thee, help thy servants, whom thou hast redeemed with thy precious blood.

Make them to be numbered with thy saints,

in glory everlasting.

O Lord, save thy people, and bless thine heritage.

Govern them, and lift them up for ever.

Day by day we magnify thee;

and we worship thy name ever, world without end.

Vouchsafe, O Lord, to keep us this day without sin.

O Lord, have mercy upon us, have mercy upon us.

O Lord, let thy mercy be upon us, as our trust is in thee.

O Lord, in thee have I trusted; let me never be confounded.

56 BLESSED BE THE LORD GOD OF ISRAEL

Benedictus

Blessed be the Lord God of Israel;

for he hath visited and redeemed his people;

and hath raised up a mighty salvation for us,

in the house of his servant David;

as he spake by the mouth of his holy prophets,

which have been since the world began;

that we should be saved from our enemies,

and from the hand of all that hate us;

to perform the mercy promised to our forefathers,

and to remember his holy covenant;

to perform the oath which he sware to our forefather Abraham,

that he would give us;

that we being delivered out of the hand of our enemies

might serve him without fear;

in holiness and righteousness before him,

> all the days of our life.

And thou, child, shalt be called the prophet of the Highest:

> for thou shalt go before the face of the Lord, to prepare his ways;

to give knowledge of salvation unto his people

> for the remission of their sins,

through the tender mercy of our God;

> whereby the dayspring from on high hath visited us;

to give light to them that sit in darkness, and in the shadow of death,

> and to guide our feet into the way of peace.

> > *Luke 1:68-79 Coverdale*

57 BLESSED ART THOU, O LORD
Benedictus es, Domine

Blessed art thou, O Lord God of our fathers:

> praised and exalted above all for ever.

Blessed art thou for the name of thy Majesty:

> praised and exalted above all for ever.

Blessed art thou in the temple of thy holiness:

> praised and exalted above all for ever.

Blessed art thou that beholdest the depths, and dwellest between the cherubim:

> praised and exalted above all for ever.

Blessed art thou on the glorious throne of thy kingdom:

> praised and exalted above all for ever.

Blessed art thou in the firmament of heaven:

> praised and exalted above all for ever.

> > *Song of the Three Young Men, 29-34 Coverdale*

58 O BE JOYFUL IN THE LORD
Jubilate Deo

O be joyful in the Lord, all ye lands:

> serve the Lord with gladness, and come before his presence with a song.

Be ye sure that the Lord he is God; it is he that hath made us, and not we ourselves;

> we are his people, and the sheep of his pasture.

O go your way into his gates with thanksgiving, and into his courts with praise;

> be thankful unto him, and speak good of his name.

For the Lord is gracious, his mercy is everlasting;

and his truth endureth from generation to generation.

Psalm 100 Coverdale

59 MY SOUL DOTH MAGNIFY THE LORD

Magnificat

My soul doth magnify the Lord,

and my spirit hath rejoiced in God my Savior.

For he hath regarded

the lowliness of his handmaiden.

For behold, from henceforth

all generations shall call me blessed.

For he that is mighty hath magnified me;

and holy is his name.

And his mercy is on them that fear him

throughout all generations.

He hath showed strength with his arm;

he hath scattered the proud in the imagination of their hearts.

He hath put down the mighty from their seat,

and hath exalted the humble and meek.

He hath filled the hungry with good things;

and the rich he hath sent empty away.

He remembering his mercy hath helped his servant Israel;

as he promised to our forefathers, Abraham and his seed, for ever.

Luke 1:46-55 Coverdale

60 IT IS A GOOD THING TO GIVE THANKS

Bonum est confiteri

It is a good thing to give thanks unto the Lord,

and to sing praises unto thy name, O Most Highest;

to tell of thy lovingkindness early in the morning,

and of thy truth in the night season;

upon an instrument of ten strings, and upon the lute;

upon a loud instrument, and upon the harp.

For thou, O Lord, hast made me glad through thy works;

and I will rejoice in giving praise for the operations of thy hands.

Psalm 92:1-4 Coverdale

61 LORD, NOW LETTEST THOU THY SERVANT

Nunc Dimittis

Lord, now lettest thou thy servant depart in peace,

according to thy word.

For mine eyes have seen

thy salvation,

which thou hast prepared

before the face of all people;

to be a light to lighten the Gentiles,

and to be the glory of thy people Israel.

Luke 2:29-32 Coverdale

62 OUT OF THE DEPTHS
De Profundis

Out of the deep have I called unto thee, O Lord;

Lord, hear my voice.

O let thine ears consider well

the voice of my complaint.

If thou, Lord, wilt be extreme to mark what is done amiss,

O Lord, who may abide it?

For there is mercy with thee;

therefore shalt thou be feared.

I look for the Lord; my soul doth wait for him;

in his word is my trust.

My soul fleeth unto the Lord before the morning watch;

I say, before the morning watch.

O Israel, trust in the Lord, for with the Lord there is mercy,

and with him is plenteous redemption.

And he shall redeem Israel

from all his sins.

Psalm 130 Coverdale

63 BLESS THE LORD, ALL WORKS OF THE LORD
Benedicite, omnia opera Domini

Bless the Lord, all works of the Lord,

sing praise to him and highly exalt him for ever.

Bless the Lord, sun and moon,

bless the Lord, stars of heaven.

Bless the Lord, winter cold and summer heat,

bless the Lord, nights and days.

Bless the Lord, lightnings and clouds,

sing praise to him and highly exalt him for ever.

Bless the Lord, all things that grow on the earth,

bless the Lord, seas and rivers.

Bless the Lord, all creatures that move in the waters,

bless the Lord, all birds of the air.

Bless the Lord, you sons of men,

bless the Lord, you who are holy and humble in heart.

Bless him, all who worship the Lord, the God of gods,

sing praise to him and give thanks to him, for his mercy endures for ever.

The Song of the Three Young Men, 35, 40-41, 45, 47, 51, 54, 56-58, 60, 65, 68

64 GLORY BE TO THE FATHER
Gloria Patri

Glory be to the Father, and to the Son, and to the Holy Ghost;

as it was in the beginning, is now, and ever shall be, world without end. Amen.

65 GLORY BE TO GOD ON HIGH
Gloria in Excelsis Deo

Glory be to God on high,

and on earth peace, good will toward men.

We praise thee, we bless thee, we worship thee,

we glorify thee, we give thanks to thee for thy great glory:

O Lord God, heavenly King,

God the Father Almighty.

O Lord, the only begotten Son, Jesus Christ:

O Lord God, Lamb of God, Son of the Father:

that takest away the sins of the world,

have mercy upon us.

Thou that takest away the sins of the world,

receive our prayer.

Thou that sittest at the right hand of God the Father,

have mercy upon us.

For thou only art holy; thou only art the Lord;

thou only, O Christ, with the Holy Ghost, art most high in the glory of God the Father. Amen.

66 GLORY BE TO GOD
Gloria Deo

God is spirit. They that worship him must worship him in spirit and in truth.

Glory be to God on high.

God is light. If we walk in the light, as he is in the light, we have fellowship one with another; and truly our fellowship is with the Father, and with his Son Jesus Christ.

Glory be to God on high.

God is power. They that wait upon the Lord shall renew their strength; they shall mount up with wings as eagles; they shall run and not be weary; and they shall walk and not faint.

Glory be to God on high.

God is love. Behold what manner of love the Father hath bestowed upon us, that we should be called the sons of God. Hereby perceive we the love of God, because he laid down his life for us.

Glory be to God on high.

From John 4:24; I John 1:7, 3b; Isaiah 40:31; I John 3:1a, 16a

67 THE BEATITUDES

Blessed are the poor in spirit,
  for theirs is the kingdom of heaven.
Blessed are those who mourn,
  for they shall be comforted.
Blessed are the meek,
  for they shall inherit the earth.
Blessed are those who hunger and thirst for righteousness,
  for they shall be satisfied.
Blessed are the merciful,
  for they shall obtain mercy.
Blessed are the pure in heart,
  for they shall see God.
Blessed are the peacemakers,
  for they shall be called sons of God.
Blessed are those who are persecuted for righteousness' sake,
  for theirs is the kingdom of heaven.

Blessed are you when men revile you and persecute you and utter all kinds of evil against you falsely on my account. Rejoice and be glad, for your reward is great in heaven, for so men persecuted the prophets who were before you.

Matthew 5:3-12

68 THE COMMANDMENTS

I

And God spoke all these words, saying,

"I am the Lord your God, who brought you out of the land of Egypt, out of the house of bondage.

"You shall have no other gods before me.

"You shall not make yourself a graven image, or any likeness of anything that is in heaven above, or that is in the earth beneath, or that is in the water under the earth; you shall not bow down to them or serve them; for I the Lord your God am a jealous God, visiting the iniquity of the fathers upon the children to the third and the fourth generation of those who hate me, but showing steadfast love to thousands of those who love me and keep my commandments."

Lord, have mercy upon us, and incline our hearts to keep thy law.

"You shall not take the name of the Lord your God in vain; for the Lord will not hold him guiltless who takes his name in vain.

"Remember the sabbath day, to keep it holy. Six days you shall labor, and do all your work; but the seventh day is a sabbath to the Lord your God; in it you shall not do any work, you, or your son, or your daughter, your manservant, or your maidservant, or your cattle, or the sojourner who is within your gates; for in six days the Lord made heaven and earth, the sea, and all that is in them, and rested the seventh day; therefore the Lord blessed the sabbath day and hallowed it."

Lord, have mercy upon us, and incline our hearts to keep thy law.

"Honor your father and your mother, that your days may be long in the land which the Lord your God gives you.

"You shall not kill.

"You shall not commit adultery.

"You shall not steal.

"You shall not bear false witness against your neighbor.

"You shall not covet your neighbor's house; you shall not covet your neighbor's wife, or his manservant, or his maidservant, or his ox, or his ass, or anything that is your neighbor's."

Lord, have mercy upon us, and write all these thy laws in our hearts, we beseech thee.

II

Hear what our Lord Jesus Christ says,

"Hear, O Israel: The Lord our God, the Lord is one; and you shall love the Lord your God with all your heart, and with all your soul, and with all your mind, and with all your strength. This is the great and first commandment. And a second is like it, You shall love your neighbor as yourself. On these two commandments depend all the law and the prophets."

Lord, have mercy upon us.

Christ, have mercy upon us.

Lord, have mercy upon us.

Exodus 20:1-17; Mark 12:29-30; Matthew 22:38-40

290

69 O Lord, Thou Art Great

O Lord, thou art great and glorious,

wonderful in strength, invincible.

Let all thy creatures serve thee,

for thou didst speak, and they were made,

thou didst send forth thy Spirit, and it formed them;

there is none that can resist thy voice.

For the mountains shall be shaken to their foundations with the waters;

at thy presence the rocks shall melt like wax.

But to those who fear thee, thou wilt continue to show mercy.

For every sacrifice as a fragrant offering is a small thing,

and all fat for burnt offerings to thee is a very little thing,

but he who fears the Lord shall be great for ever.   *Judith 16:13b-16*

70 The Lord Created Man

The Lord created man out of earth,

and turned him back to it again.

He gave to men a few days, a limited time,

but granted them authority over the things upon the earth.

He endowed them with strength like his own,

and made them in his own image.

He made for them tongue and eyes;

he gave them ears and a mind for thinking.

He filled them with knowledge and understanding,

and showed them good and evil.

He set his eye upon their hearts

to show them the majesty of his works.

And they will praise his holy name,

to proclaim the grandeur of his works.

He established with them an eternal covenant,

and showed them his judgments.

Their eyes saw his glorious majesty,

and their ears heard the glory of his voice.

And he said to them, "Beware of all unrighteousness."

And he gave commandment to each of them concerning his neighbor.

Their ways are always before him,

they will not be hid from his eyes.

Their iniquities are not hidden from him.

And all their sins are before the Lord.

Yet to those who repent he grants a return,

and he encourages those whose endurance is failing.

How great is the mercy of the Lord,

291

and his forgiveness for those who turn to him!

Ecclesiasticus 17:1-3, 6-10, 12-15, 20, 24, 29

71 LET US NOW PRAISE FAMOUS MEN

Let us now praise famous men,

and our fathers in their generations.

The Lord apportioned to them great glory,

his majesty from the beginning.

There were those who ruled in their kingdoms,

and were men renowned for their power,

giving counsel by their understanding,

and proclaiming prophecies;

leaders of the people in their deliberations,

wise in their words of instruction;

those who composed musical tunes,

and set forth verses in writing;

rich men furnished with resources,

living peaceably in their habitations—

all these were honored in their generations,

and were the glory of their times.

There are some of them who have left a name,

so that men declare their praise.

And there are some who have no memorial,

who have perished as though they had not lived.

But these were men of mercy,

whose righteous deeds have not been forgotten;

their prosperity will remain with their descendants,

and their inheritance to their children's children.

Their posterity will continue for ever.

And their glory will not be blotted out.

Their bodies were buried in peace.

And their name lives to all generations.

Peoples will declare their wisdom,

and the congregation proclaims their praise.

Ecclesiasticus 44:1-4ac, 5-9ab, 10-11, 13-15

72 THE SOULS OF THE RIGHTEOUS

The souls of the righteous are in the hand of God,

and no torment will ever touch them.

In the eyes of the foolish they seem to have died,

and their departure was thought to be an affliction,

and their going from us to be their destruction;

but they are at peace.

God created man for incorruption,

and made him in the image of his own eternity.

The righteous live for ever, and their reward is with the Lord;

the Most High takes care of them.

With his right hand he will cover them,

and with his arm he will shield them.

> *Wisdom of Solomon 3:1-3; 2:23; 5:15; 5:16b*

73 LISTEN, O KINGS

Listen, therefore, O kings, and understand;

learn, O judges of the ends of the earth.

Give ear, you that rule over multitudes,

and boast of many nations.

For your dominion was given you from the Lord.

And your sovereignty from the Most High,

who will search out your works

and inquire into your plans.

For the Lord of all will not stand in awe of any one,

nor show deference to greatness;

because he himself made both small and great,

and he takes thought for all alike.

To you then, O monarchs, my words are directed,

that you may learn wisdom and not transgress.

Therefore set your desire on my words;

long for them, and you will be instructed.

Wisdom is radiant and unfading,

and she is easily discerned by those who love her.

She hastens to make herself known to those who desire her,

she goes about seeking those worthy of her,

and she graciously appears to them in their paths,

and meets them in every thought.

The beginning of wisdom is the most sincere desire for instruction,

and concern for instruction is love of her,

and love of her is the keeping of her laws,

and giving heed to her laws is assurance of immortality.

> *Wisdom of Solomon 6:1-3, 7, 9, 11-12ab, 13, 16-18*

74 THE SONG OF DAVID

Blessed art thou, O Lord, the God of Israel

our father, for ever and ever.

Thine, O Lord, is the greatness, and the power, and the glory, and the victory, and the majesty;

> for all that is in the heavens and in the earth is thine;

thine is the kingdom, O Lord,

> and thou art exalted as head above all.

Both riches and honor come from thee,

> and thou rulest over all.

In thy hand are power and might;

> and in thy hand it is to make great and to give strength to all.

And now we thank thee, our God,

> and praise thy glorious name.

> *I Chronicles 29:10b-13*

75 HE MAKES NATIONS GREAT

With God are wisdom and might;

> he has counsel and understanding.

If he tears down, none can rebuild;

> if he shuts a man in, none can open.

If he withholds the waters, they dry up;

> if he sends them out, they overwhelm the land.

With him are strength and wisdom;

> the deceived and the deceiver are his.

He leads counselors away stripped,

> and judges he makes fools.

He looses the bonds of kings,

> and binds a waistcloth on their loins.

He leads priests away stripped,

> and overthrows the mighty.

He pours contempt on princes,

> and looses the belt of the strong.

He makes nations great, and he destroys them:

> he enlarges nations, and leads them away.

In his hand is the life of every living thing

> and the breath of all mankind.

> *Job 12:13-19, 21, 23, 10*

76 WHERE SHALL WISDOM BE FOUND?

Surely there is a mine for silver,

> and a place for gold which they refine.

But where shall wisdom be found?

> and where is the place of understanding?

Man does not know the way to it,

> and it is not found in the land of the living.

The deep says, "It is not in me,"

> and the sea says, "It is not with me."

It cannot be gotten for gold,

> and silver cannot be weighed as its price.

The topaz of Ethiopia cannot compare with it,

nor can it be valued in pure gold.

Whence then comes wisdom?

And where is the place of understanding?

God understands the way to it,

and he knows its place.

Behold, the fear of the Lord, that is wisdom;

and to depart from evil is understanding.

Job 28:1, 12-15, 19-20, 23, 28

77 THE GOODNESS OF WISDOM

Happy is the man who finds wisdom,

and the man who gets understanding,

for the gain from it is better than gain from silver

and its profit better than gold.

She is more precious than jewels,

and nothing you desire can compare with her.

Long life is in her right hand;

in her left hand are riches and honor.

Her ways are ways of pleasantness,

and all her paths are peace.

She is a tree of life to those who lay hold of her;

those who hold her fast are called happy.

The Lord by wisdom founded the earth;

by understanding he established the heavens. *Proverbs 3:13-19*

78 THE LORD CREATED WISDOM

Does not wisdom call?

Does not understanding raise her voice?

The Lord created me at the beginning of his work,

the first of his acts of old.

Ages ago I was set up, at the first,

before the beginning of the earth.

Before the mountains had been shaped,

before the hills, I was brought forth;

before he had made the earth with its fields,

or the first of the dust of the world.

When he established the heavens, I was there.

When he marked out the foundations of the earth, then I was beside him. .

And I was daily his delight,

rejoicing before him always,

rejoicing in his inhabited world

and delighting in the sons of men.

For he who finds me finds life

and obtains favor from the Lord.

Proverbs 8:1, 22-23, 25-27a,
29c-31, 35

79 THE LORD SHALL REIGN

It shall come to pass in the latter days

that the mountain of the house of the Lord

shall be established as the highest of the mountains,

and shall be raised above the hills;

and all the nations shall flow to it,

and many peoples shall come, and say:

"Come, let us go up to the mountain of the Lord,

to the house of the God of Jacob;

that he may teach us his ways

and that we may walk in his paths."

For out of Zion shall go forth the law,

and the word of the Lord from Jerusalem.

He shall judge between the nations,

and decide for many peoples;

and they shall beat their swords into plowshares,

and their spears into pruning hooks;

nation shall not lift up sword against nation,

neither shall they learn war any more.   *Isaiah 2:2-4*

80 THE LORD MY RIGHTEOUSNESS

There shall come forth a shoot from the stump of Jesse,

and a branch shall grow out of his roots.

And the Spirit of the Lord shall rest upon him,

the spirit of wisdom and understanding,

the spirit of counsel and might,

the spirit of knowledge and the fear of the Lord.

He shall not judge by what his eyes see,

or decide by what his ears hear;

but with righteousness he shall judge the poor,

and decide with equity for the meek of the earth.

Righteousness shall be the girdle of his waist

and faithfulness the girdle of his loins.

The wolf shall dwell with the lamb,

and the leopard shall lie down with the kid,

and the calf and the lion and the fatling together,

and a little child shall lead them.

They shall not hurt or destroy in all my holy mountain;

> for the earth shall be full of the knowledge of the Lord as the waters cover the sea.

> > *Isaiah 11:1-2, 3b-4b, 5-6, 9*

81 THE DESERT SHALL REJOICE

The wilderness and the dry land shall be glad,

> the desert shall rejoice and blossom;

like the crocus it shall blossom abundantly,

> and rejoice with joy and singing.

The glory of Lebanon shall be given to it,

> the majesty of Carmel and Sharon.

They shall see the glory of the Lord,

> the majesty of our God.

Say to those who are of a fearful heart,

> "Be strong, fear not! Behold, your God will come."

Then the eyes of the blind shall be opened,

> and the ears of the deaf unstopped;

then shall the lame man leap like a hart,

> and the tongue of the dumb sing for joy.

For waters shall break forth in the wilderness,

> and streams in the desert;

the burning sand shall become a pool,

> and the thirsty ground springs of water.

And a highway shall be there,

> and it shall be called the Holy Way.

And the ransomed of the Lord shall return,

> and come to Zion with singing;

they shall obtain joy and gladness,

> and sorrow and sighing shall flee away.

> > *Isaiah 35:1-2, 4ab, 5-7ab, 8ab, 10ab, de*

82 COMFORT MY PEOPLE

Comfort, comfort my people, says your God.

> Speak tenderly to Jerusalem, and cry to her that her warfare is ended,

that her iniquity is pardoned,

> that she has received from the Lord's hand double for all her sins.

A voice cries, "In the wilderness prepare the way of the Lord,

> make straight in the desert a highway for our God.

Every valley shall be lifted up,

> and every mountain and hill be made low;

the uneven ground shall become level,

> and the rough places a plain.

And the glory of the Lord shall be revealed,

and all flesh shall see it together."

Isaiah 40:1-5ab

83 BEHOLD YOUR GOD

Get you up to a high mountain, O Zion, herald of good tidings;

lift up your voice with strength, O Jerusalem.

Lift it up, fear not;

say to the cities of Judah, "Behold your God!"

Behold, the Lord God comes with might, and his arm rules for him;

behold, his reward is with him, and his recompense before him.

He will feed his flock like a shepherd,

he will gather the lambs in his arms,

he will carry them in his bosom,

and gently lead those that are with young. *Isaiah 40:9-11*

84 THE SOVEREIGNTY OF GOD

Who has measured the waters in the hollow of his hand

and marked off the heavens with a span,

enclosed the dust of the earth in a measure

and weighed the mountains in scales?

Who has directed the Spirit of the Lord,

or as his counselor has instructed him?

Whom did he consult for his enlightenment,

and who showed him the way of understanding?

All the nations are as nothing before him,

they are accounted by him as less than nothing and emptiness.

Have you not known? Have you not heard? The Lord is the everlasting God,

the Creator of the ends of the earth.

He does not faint or grow weary,

his understanding is unsearchable.

He gives power to the faint,

and to him who has no might he increases strength.

Even youths shall faint and be weary,

and young men shall fall exhausted;

but they who wait for the Lord shall renew their strength,

they shall mount up with wings like eagles,

they shall run and not be weary,

they shall walk and not faint.

Isaiah 40:12-14ad, 17, 28-31

85 BEHOLD MY SERVANT

Behold my servant, whom I uphold,
my chosen, in whom my soul delights;

I have put my spirit upon him,
he will bring forth justice to the nations.

He will not cry or lift up his voice,
or make it heard in the street;

a bruised reed he will not break,
and a dimly burning wick he will not quench.

He will not fail or be discouraged
till he has established justice in the earth.

Thus says God, the Lord,
who created the heavens and stretched them out,

who spread forth the earth and what comes from it,
who gives breath to the people upon it and spirit to those who walk in it:

"I am the Lord, I have called you in righteousness,
I have taken you by the hand and kept you;

I have given you as a covenant to the people, a light to the nations,
to open the eyes that are blind,

to bring out the prisoners from the dungeon,
from the prison those who sit in darkness." *Isaiah 42:1-3ab, 4a, 5-7*

86 GOOD TIDINGS

How beautiful upon the mountains
are the feet of him who brings good tidings,

who publishes peace, who brings good tidings of good,
who publishes salvation, who says to Zion, "Your God reigns."

Break forth together into singing,
you waste places of Jerusalem;

for the Lord has comforted his people,
he has redeemed Jerusalem.

The Lord has bared his holy arm
before the eyes of all the nations;

and all the ends of the earth shall see
the salvation of our God.

And you shall know that I, the Lord, am your Savior
and your Redeemer, the Mighty One of Jacob.

Violence shall no more be heard in your land,
devastation or destruction within your borders;

you shall call your walls Salvation,
and your gates Praise.

The sun shall be no more your light by day,
nor for brightness shall the moon give light to you by night;

but the Lord will be your everlasting light,
and your God will be your glory.

Isaiah 52:7, 9-10; 60:16b, 18-19

87 THE SUFFERING SERVANT

I

Who has believed what we have heard?

And to whom has the arm of the Lord been revealed?

For he grew up before him like a young plant,

and like a root out of dry ground;

he had no form or comeliness that we should look at him,

and no beauty that we should desire him.

He was despised and rejected by men;

a man of sorrows, and acquainted with grief;

and as one from whom men hide their faces

he was despised, and we esteemed him not.

Surely he has borne our griefs and carried our sorrows;

yet we esteemed him stricken, smitten by God, and afflicted.

But he was wounded for our transgressions,

he was bruised for our iniquities;

upon him was the chastisement that made us whole,

and with his stripes we are healed.

II

All we like sheep have gone astray;

we have turned every one to his own way;

and the Lord has laid on him the iniquity of us all.

He was oppressed, and he was afflicted, yet he opened not his mouth;

like a lamb that is led to the slaughter,

and like a sheep that before its shearers is dumb, so he opened not his mouth.

By oppression and judgment he was taken away;

and as for his generation, who considered that he was cut off out of the land of the living, stricken for the transgression of my people?

And they made his grave with the wicked

and with a rich man in his death,

although he had done no violence,

and there was no deceit in his mouth.

Yet it was the will of the Lord to bruise him;

he has put him to grief;

when he makes himself an offering for sin,

he shall see his offspring, he shall prolong his days;

the will of the Lord shall prosper in his hand;

he shall see the fruit of the travail of his soul and be satisfied;

by his knowledge shall the righteous one, my servant, make many to be accounted righteous;

and he shall bear their iniquities.

Therefore I will divide him a portion with the great,

and he shall divide the spoil with the strong;

because he poured out his soul to death,

and was numbered with the transgressors;

yet he bore the sin of many,

and made intercession for the transgressors. *Isaiah 53:1-12*

88 SEEK THE LORD

Seek the Lord while he may be found,

call upon him while he is near;

let the wicked forsake his way,

and the unrighteous man his thoughts;

let him return to the Lord, that he may have mercy on him,

and to our God, for he will abundantly pardon.

For my thoughts are not your thoughts,

neither are your ways my ways, says the Lord.

For as the heavens are higher than the earth,

so are my ways higher than your ways and my thoughts than your thoughts.

For as the rain and the snow come down from heaven,

and return not thither but water the earth,

making it bring forth and sprout,

giving seed to the sower and bread to the eater,

so shall my word be that goes forth from my mouth;

it shall not return to me empty,

but it shall accomplish that which I purpose,

and prosper in the thing for which I sent it. *Isaiah 55:6-13*

89 I WILL GREATLY REJOICE

I will greatly rejoice in the Lord,

my soul shall exult in my God;

for he has clothed me with the garments of salvation,

he has covered me with the robe of righteousness,

as a bridegroom decks himself with a garland,

and as a bride adorns herself with her jewels.

For as the earth brings forth its shoots,

and as a garden causes what is sown in it to spring up,

so the Lord God will cause righteousness and praise

to spring forth before all the nations. *Isaiah 61:10-11*

90 BEHOLD, I CREATE

For behold, I create new heavens and a new earth;

> and the former things shall not be remembered or come into mind.

But be glad and rejoice for ever in that which I create;

> for behold, I create Jerusalem a rejoicing, and her people a joy.

I will rejoice in Jerusalem, and be glad in my people;

> no more shall be heard in it the sound of weeping and the cry of distress.

They shall build houses and inhabit them;

> they shall plant vineyards and eat their fruit.

They shall not build and another inhabit;

> they shall not plant and another eat;

for like the days of a tree shall the days of my people be,

> and my chosen shall long enjoy the work of their hands.

They shall not labor in vain,

> or bear children for calamity;

for they shall be the offspring of the blessed of the Lord,

> and their children with them.

Before they call I will answer,

> while they are yet speaking I will hear.

The wolf and the lamb shall feed together,

> the lion shall eat straw like the ox;

and dust shall be the serpent's food.

> They shall not hurt or destroy in all my holy mountain, says the Lord.   *Isaiah 65:17-19, 21-25*

91 THE NEW COVENANT

Behold, the days are coming, says the Lord, when I will make a new covenant with the house of Israel and the house of Judah, not like the covenant which I made with their fathers when I took them by the hand to bring them out of the land of Egypt. But this is the covenant which I will make with the house of Israel after those days, says the Lord: I will put my law within them, and I will write it upon their hearts; and I will be their God, and they shall be my people. And no longer shall each man teach his neighbor and each his brother, saying, "Know the Lord," for they shall all know me, from the least of them to the greatest, says the Lord; for I will forgive their iniquity, and I will remember their sin no more.   *Jeremiah 31:31-32a, 33-34*

92 THE MERCIES OF GOD

My soul is bereft of peace,

   I have forgotten what happiness is;

so I say, "Gone is my glory,

   and my expectation from the Lord."

Remember my affliction and my bitterness,

   the wormwood and the gall!

My soul continually thinks of it,

   and is bowed down within me.

But this I call to mind,

   and therefore I have hope:

The steadfast love of the Lord never ceases,

   his mercies never come to an end;

they are new every morning;

   great is thy faithfulness.

"The Lord is my portion," says my soul,

   "therefore I will hope in him!"

The Lord is good to those who wait for him,

   to the soul that seeks him.

It is good that one should wait quietly

   for the salvation of the Lord.

                     Lamentations 3:17-26

93 YET I WILL REJOICE

Though the fig tree do not blossom,

   nor fruit be on the vines,

the produce of the olive fail

   and the fields yield no food,

the flock be cut off from the fold

   and there be no herd in the stalls,

yet I will rejoice in the Lord,

   I will joy in the God of my salvation. *Habakkuk 3:17-18*

94 IN THE BEGINNING WAS THE WORD

In the beginning was the Word, and the Word was with God, and the Word was God. He was in the beginning with God; all things were made through him, and without him was not anything made that was made. In him was life, and the life was the light of men. The light shines in the darkness, and the darkness has not overcome it.

The true light that enlightens every man was coming into the world. He was in the world, and the world was made through him, yet the world knew him not. He came to his own home, and his own people received him not. But to all who received him, who believed in his name, he gave power to become children of God; who were born, not of blood nor of the will of the flesh nor of the will of man, but of God.

And the Word became flesh and dwelt among us, full of grace and truth; we have beheld his glory, glory as of the only Son from the Father. And from his fulness have we all received, grace upon grace. For the law was given through Moses; grace and truth came through Jesus Christ. No one has ever seen God; the only Son, who is in the bosom of the Father, he has made him known.

John 1:1-5, 9-14, 16-18

95 GOD SO LOVED THE WORLD

God so loved the world that he gave his only Son, that whoever believes in him should not perish but have eternal life. For God sent the Son into the world, not to condemn the world, but that the world might be saved through him.

And this is the judgment, that the light has come into the world, and men loved darkness rather than light, because their deeds were evil. For every one who does evil hates the light, and does not come to the light, lest his deeds should be exposed. But he who does what is true comes to the light, that it may be clearly seen that his deeds have been wrought in God. *John 3:16-17, 19-21*

96 THE TRUE VINE

Abide in me, and I in you. As the branch cannot bear fruit by itself, unless it abides in the vine, neither can you, unless you abide in me. I am the vine, you are the branches. He who abides in me, and I in him, he it is that bears much fruit, for apart from me you can do nothing. If a man does not abide in me, he is cast forth as a branch and withers; and the branches are gathered, thrown into the fire and burned. If you abide in me, and my words abide in you, ask whatever you will, and it shall be done for you. By this my Father is glorified, that you bear much fruit, and so prove to be my disciples. As the Father has loved me, so have I loved you; abide in my love. If you keep my commandments, you will abide in my love, just as I have kept my Father's commandments and abide in his love. These things I have spoken to you, that my joy may be in you, and that your joy may be full. *John 15:4-11*

97 THE LOVE OF CHRIST

If God is for us, who is against us?

He who did not spare his own Son but gave him up for us all, will he not also give us all things with him?

Who shall separate us from the love of Christ?

Shall tribulation, or distress, or persecution, or famine, or nakedness, or peril, or sword?

No, in all these things we are more than conquerors through him who loved us.

For I am sure that neither death, nor life, nor angels, nor principalities, nor things present, nor things to come, nor powers, nor height, nor depth, nor anything else in all creation, will be able to separate us from the love of God in Christ Jesus our Lord. *Romans 8:31b-32, 35, 37-39*

98 SPIRITUAL WORSHIP

I appeal to you therefore, brethren, by the mercies of God, to present your bodies as a living sacrifice, holy and acceptable to God, which is your spiritual worship. Do not be conformed to this world but be transformed by the renewal of your mind, that you may prove what is the will of God, what is good and acceptable and perfect.

Let love be genuine; hate what is evil, hold fast to what is good; love one another with brotherly affection; outdo one another in showing honor. Never flag in zeal, be aglow with the Spirit, serve the Lord. Rejoice in your hope, be patient in tribulation, be constant in prayer. Contribute to the needs of the saints, practice hospitality.

Bless those who persecute you; bless and do not curse them. Rejoice with those who rejoice, weep with those who weep. Live in harmony with one another; do not be haughty, but associate with the lowly; never be conceited. Repay no one evil for evil, but take thought for what is noble in the sight of all. Do not be overcome by evil, but overcome evil with good.

Romans 12:1-2, 9-17, 21

99 THE WAY OF LOVE

If I speak in the tongues of men and of angels, but have not love, I am a noisy gong or a clanging cymbal. And if I have prophetic powers, and understand all mysteries and all knowledge, and if I have all faith, so as to remove mountains, but have not love, I am nothing. If I give away all I have, and if I deliver my body to be burned, but have not love, I gain nothing.

Love is patient and kind; love is not jealous or boastful; it is not arrogant or rude. Love does not insist on its own way; it is not irritable or resentful; it does not rejoice at wrong, but rejoices in the right. Love bears all things, believes all things, hopes all things, endures all things.

Love never ends; as for prophecy, it will pass away; as for tongues, they will cease; as for knowledge, it will pass away. For our knowledge is imperfect and our prophecy is imperfect; but when the perfect comes, the imperfect will pass away. When I was a child, I spoke like a child, I thought like a child, I reasoned like a child; when I became a man, I gave up childish ways. For now we see in a mirror dimly, but then face to face. Now I know in part; then I shall understand fully, even as I have been fully understood. So faith, hope, love abide, these three; but the greatest of these is love. *I Corinthians 13*

100 THE MINISTRY OF GRACE

Therefore, having this ministry by the mercy of God, we do not lose heart. We have renounced disgraceful, underhanded ways; we refuse to practice cunning or to tamper with God's word, but by the open statement of the truth we would commend ourselves to every man's conscience in the sight of God.

But we have this treasure in earthen vessels, to show that the transcendent power belongs to God and not to us. We are afflicted in every way, but not crushed; perplexed, but not driven to despair; persecuted, but not forsaken, struck down, but not destroyed; always carrying in the body the death of Jesus, so that the life of Jesus may also be manifested in our bodies. For while we live we are always being given up to death for Jesus' sake, so that the life of Jesus may be manifested in our mortal flesh. So death is at work in us, but life in you.

So we do not lose heart. Though our outer nature is wasting away, our inner nature is being renewed every day. For this slight momentary affliction is preparing for us an eternal weight of glory beyond all comparison, because we look not to the things that are seen but to the things that are unseen; for the things that are seen are transient, but the things that are unseen are eternal.

II Corinthians 4:1-2, 7-12, 16-18

101 BY GRACE YOU HAVE BEEN SAVED

And you he made alive, when you were dead through the trespasses and sins in which you once walked, following the course of this world. But God, who is rich in mercy, out of the great love with which he loved us, even when we were dead through our trespasses, made us alive together with Christ, and raised us up with him, and made us sit with him in the heavenly places in Christ Jesus, that in the coming ages he might show the immeasurable riches of his grace.

For by grace you have been saved through faith; and this is not your own doing, it is the gift of God—not because of works, lest any man should boast. For we are his workmanship, created in Christ Jesus for good works, which God prepared beforehand, that we should walk in them. *From Ephesians 2:1-2a, 4-10*

102 THE MIND OF CHRIST

So if there is any encouragement in Christ, any incentive of love, any participation in the Spirit, any affection and sympathy, complete my joy by being of the same mind, having the same love, being in full accord and of one mind. Do nothing from selfishness or conceit, but in humility count others better than yourselves. Let each of you look not only to his own interests, but also to the interest of others. Have this mind among yourselves, which you have in

Christ Jesus, who, though he was in the form of God, did not count equality with God a thing to be grasped, but emptied himself, taking the form of a servant, being born in the likeness of men. And being found in human form he humbled himself and became obedient unto death, even death on a cross. Therefore God has highly exalted him and bestowed on him the name which is above every name, that at the name of Jesus every knee should bow, in heaven and on earth and under the earth, and every tongue confess that Jesus Christ is Lord, to the glory of God the Father.   *Philippians 2:1-11*

103 THE NEW LIFE IN CHRIST

He has delivered us from the dominion of darkness and transferred us to the kingdom of his beloved Son, in whom we have redemption, the forgiveness of sins.

He is the image of the invisible God, the first-born of all creation; for in him all things were created, in heaven and on earth, visible and invisible, whether thrones or dominions or principalities or authorities—all things were created through him and for him. He is before all things, and in him all things hold together. He is the head of the body, the church; he is the beginning, the first-born from the dead, that in everything he might be preeminent. For in him all the fulness of God was pleased to dwell, and through him to reconcile to himself all things, whether on earth or in heaven, making peace by the blood of his cross.   *Colossians 1:13-20*

104 WE HAVE BEEN BORN ANEW

Blessed be the God and Father of our Lord Jesus Christ! By his great mercy we have been born anew to a living hope through the resurrection of Jesus Christ from the dead, and to an inheritance which is imperishable, undefiled, and unfading, kept in heaven for you, who by God's power are guarded through faith for a salvation ready to be revealed in the last time. In this you rejoice, though now for a little while you may have to suffer various trials, so that the genuineness of your faith, more precious than gold which though perishable is tested by fire, may rebound to praise and glory and honor at the revelation of Jesus Christ. Without having seen him you love him; though you do not now see him you believe in him and rejoice with unutterable and exalted joy.
                                                            I Peter 1:3-8

105 GOD IS LOVE

Beloved, let us love one another; for love is of God, and he who loves is born of God and knows God. He who does not love does not know God; for God is love. In this the love of God was made manifest among us, that God sent his only Son into the world, so that we might live through him. In this is love, not that we loved God but that he loved us and sent his Son to be the expiation for our sins. Beloved, if God so loved us, we also ought to love one another. No man has ever seen God; if we love one another, God abides in us and his love is perfected in us.

We love, because he first loved us. If any one says, "I love God," and hates his brother, he is a liar; for he who does not love his brother whom he has seen, cannot love God whom he has not seen. And this commandment we have from him, that he who loves God should love his brother also.   *I John 4:7-12, 19-21*

106 CHRIST OUR PASSOVER

Christ our paschal lamb, has been sacrificed. Let us, therefore, celebrate the festival,

not with the old leaven, the leaven of malice and evil, but with the unleavened bread of sincerity and truth.

For we know that Christ being raised from the dead will never die again; death no longer has dominion over him.

The death he died he died to sin, once for all, but the life he lives he lives to God.

So you also must consider yourselves dead to sin and alive to God in Christ Jesus.

Christ has been raised from the dead, the first fruits of those who have fallen asleep.

For as by a man came death, by a man has come also the resurrection of the dead.

For as in Adam all die, so also in Christ shall all be made alive.

I Corinthians 5:7b-8; Romans 6:9-11; I Corinthians 15:20-22

107 I MAKE ALL THINGS NEW

Then I saw a new heaven and a new earth; for the first heaven and the first earth had passed away, and the sea was no more. And I saw the holy city, new Jerusalem, coming down out of heaven from God, prepared as a bride adorned for her husband; and I heard a great voice from the throne saying, "Behold, the dwelling of God is with men. He will dwell with them, and they shall be his people, and God himself will be with them; he will wipe away every tear from their eyes, and death shall be no more, neither shall there be mourning nor crying nor pain any more, for the former things have passed away."

And he who sat upon the throne said, "Behold, I make all things new." Also he said, "Write this, for these words are trustworthy and true." And he said to me, "It is done! I am the Alpha and the Omega, the beginning and the end."

And I saw no temple in the city, for its temple is the Lord God the Almighty and the Lamb. And the city has no need of sun or moon to shine upon it, for the glory of God is its light, and its lamp is the Lamb. By its light shall the nations walk; and the kings of the earth shall bring their glory into it, and its gates shall never be shut by day—and there shall be no night there; they shall bring into it the glory and the honor of the nations.

Revelation 21:1-6a, 22-26

108 The Lord God Almighty

Holy, holy, holy is the Lord God Almighty, who was and is and is to come!

Great and wonderful are thy deeds, O Lord God the Almighty!

Just and true are thy ways, O King of the ages!

Who shall not fear and glorify thy name, O Lord? For thou alone art holy.

Worthy art thou, our Lord and God, to receive glory and honor and power: for thou didst create all things, and by thy will they existed and were created.

Worthy is the Lamb who was slain, to receive power and wealth and wisdom and might and honor and glory and blessing!

Blessing and glory and wisdom and thanksgiving and honor and power and might be to our God for ever and ever!

To him who sits upon the throne and to the Lamb be blessing and honor and glory and might for ever and ever!

We give thanks to thee, Lord God Almighty, who art and who was, that thou hast taken thy great power and begun to reign.

Hallelujah! For the Lord our God the Almighty reigns. Let us rejoice and exult and give him the glory.

Revelation 4:8; 15:3-4a; 4:11; 5:12; 7:12; 5:13; 11:17; 19:6b-7a

109 A Canticle of Conquest Over Death

O Lord, thou art my God; I will exalt thee, I will praise thy name;

for thou hast done wonderful things, plans formed of old, faithful and sure.

For thou hast been a stronghold to the poor, a stronghold to the needy in his distress,

a shelter from the storm and a shade from the heat; for the blast of the ruthless is like a storm against a wall.

And he will destroy on this mountain the covering that is cast over all peoples,

the veil that is spread over all nations.

He will swallow up death for ever, and the Lord God will wipe away tears from all faces,

and the reproach of his people he will take away from all the earth; for the Lord has spoken.

It will be said on that day, "Lo, this is our God; we have waited for him, that he might save us.

This is the Lord; we have waited for him; let us be glad and rejoice in his salvation."

Thou dost keep him in perfect peace, whose mind is stayed on thee, because he trusts in thee.

Trust in the Lord for ever, for the Lord God is an everlasting rock.

Isaiah 25:1, 4, 7-9; 26:3-4

110 A Canticle of the Church

Arise, shine; for your light has come,

and the glory of the Lord has risen upon you.

For behold, darkness shall cover the earth,

and thick darkness the peoples;

But the Lord will arise upon you,

and his glory will be seen upon you.

And nations shall come to your light,

and kings to the brightness of your rising.

The abundance of the sea shall be turned to you,

the wealth of the nations shall come to you.

Your gates shall be open continually;

day and night they shall not be shut;

Violence shall no more be heard in your land,

devastation or destruction within your borders;

you shall call your walls Salvation,

and your gates Praise.

The sun shall be no more your light by day,

nor for brightness shall the moon give light to you by night;

but the Lord will be your everlasting light,

and your God will be your glory.

Your sun shall no more go down,

nor your moon withdraw itself;

for the Lord will be your everlasting light,

and your days of mourning shall be ended.

Isaiah 60:1-3, 5bc, 11ab, 18-20

111 A CANTICLE OF MISSIONS

Have mercy upon us, O Lord, the God of all, and show us thy salvation.

Send thy fear upon the nations who have not known thy name,

that they may know that there is none beside thee, and that they also may tell forth all thy wonders.

Lift up thy hand over the strange nations, and let them see thy mighty power.

Even as thou hast been sanctified amongst us in their sight, so be thou magnified in them before our eyes.

And let them know thee as we also have known thee, and that there is no God but only thou, O Lord.

Renew thy signs, and work great wonders: strengthen thine arm, and make glorious thy right hand.

Haste the time, and bring near the end, and let all declare thy mighty works.

Gather together all the tribes of Jacob, and take them for thine inheritance as in former days.

Have mercy upon thy people who are called by thy name, and upon Israel, whom thou didst make thy first-born.

Have compassion upon the holy city, even on Jerusalem, the city of thy rest.

Fill Zion with the sacred oracles, and thy temple with thy glory.

Give reward to them that wait upon thy word, and fulfill the prophecies that have been spoken in thy name,

that all upon the earth may know that thou art the Lord, the eternal God.

112 A CANTICLE OF THANKSGIVING

Praise the Lord! For it is good to sing praises to our God;

for he is gracious, and a song of praise is seemly.

The Lord builds up Jerusalem;

he gathers the outcasts of Israel.

He heals the brokenhearted,

and binds up their wounds.

He determines the number of the stars,

he gives to all of them their names.

Great is our Lord, and abundant in power;

his understanding is beyond measure.

The Lord lifts up the downtrodden,

he casts the wicked to the ground.

311

Sing to the Lord with thanksgiving;

make melody to our God upon the lyre!

He covers the heavens with clouds, he prepares rain for the earth,

he makes grass grow upon the hills.

He gives to the beasts their food,

and to the young ravens which cry.

Praise the Lord, O Jerusalem!

Praise your God, O Zion!

For he strengthens the bars of your gates;

he blesses your sons within you.

He makes peace in your borders;

he fills you with the finest of the wheat.   *Psalm 147:1-9, 12-14*

113 A THANKSGIVING OF ST. FRANCIS FOR ALL CREATED THINGS

O most high, omnipotent, good Lord God, to thee belong praise, glory, honor, and all blessing.

For our brother the sun, who is our day and who brings us the light, who is fair, and radiant with a very great splendor;

praised be our Lord.

For our sister the moon, and for the stars, which thou hast set clear and lovely in heaven;

praised be our Lord.

For our brother the wind, and for air and cloud, calms and all weather;

praised be our Lord.

For our sister water, who is very serviceable unto us and humble and precious and chaste;

praised be our Lord.

For our brother fire, by whom thou lightest up the night, and who is fair and merry, and very mighty and strong;

praised be our Lord.

For our mother the earth, which doth sustain us and keep us, and bringeth forth divers fruits, and flowers of many colors, and grass;

praised be our Lord.

For all those who pardon one another for thy love's sake, and who bear weakness and tribulation;

praised be our Lord.

Blessed are they who peaceably shall endure, walking by thy most holy will; for thou, O Most Highest, shalt give them a crown.

Praise ye and bless ye the Lord, and give thanks unto him, and serve him with great humility. Amen.

114 SANCTUS WITH BENEDICTUS

Holy, holy, holy:

Heaven and earth are full of thy glory!

Glory be to thee, O Lord most high!

Hosanna in the highest!

312

Blessed is he that comes in the name of the Lord.

Glory be to thee, O Lord most high!

115 LITANY OF PRAISE

Let us praise God:

For the day, for the glory and warmth of the sun, for the stir of life, and for honest toil that wins food and rest;

God be praised for the day.

For the earth, the sustainer of life; for the hills, the plains, and the valleys; for the beauty of meadows and fields, of flowers and of trees;

God be praised for the earth.

For the sky, for the shifting clouds, and for the glory of sunrise and sunset;

God be praised for the sky.

For the sea, that yields and receives again the water without which life would die, and is wonderful in its stillness and more wonderful in its storm;

God be praised for the sea.

For our food, and the pleasures he has given us in it, lest we should neglect the needs of life; may he help us to shun all waste and to rejoice in sharing with others;

God be praised for our food.

For the shelter from wind and weather, which hallowed by love becomes our home; may he strengthen our will that no one shall go hungry or ill-housed or ill-clad;

God be praised for our home.

Let us praise God in whom we live and move and have our being.

All praise be to God. Amen.

116 LITANY OF PRAISE

Let us praise God:

For our fathers and mothers, by whom he orders lives and comforts hearts, bringing strength to a house and sweetness to labor; may he hallow their work and direct their ways;

God be praised for good fathers and mothers.

For the gift of children; may he help us to train them to be reverent and truthful, that they may gladden our hearts and bring joy to the world;

God be praised for children.

For good friends to rejoice with us in our joys, to cheer us in trouble and to lighten our tasks; may he help us to repay them in fellowship and service;

God be praised for our friends.

For joy that heightens all our life and doubles our powers; may he help us to kindle it in the hearts of others by the gladness of our face;

God be praised for joy.

For mirth, that unites us with others and refreshes us for our work; may he help us to keep it kind and true;

God be praised for mirth.

For health, bringing wholesomeness of body and mind; may he help us to give our strength to his service;

God be praised for health.

Let us praise God for life.

All praise be to God. Amen.

For the trees in spring and the fruit blossoms, for the smell of the country after rain, for the green grass and the flowers, for cloud and sun and hills and mountain streams;

glory be to thee, O Lord, for ever and ever. Amen.

117 LITANY OF PRAISE

Let us praise God in gladness and humility:

For all great and simple joys, and for the weak things of the earth which have confounded the strong;

glory be to thee, O Lord.

For the gift of wonder and the joy of discovery, for the everlasting freshness of experience, for the newness of life each day as we grow older;

glory be to thee, O Lord.

For the fireside and the intimate talks of friendship, for the little traditions and customs of the home, for meals eaten together in fellowship, and for all the sanctities of family life;

glory be to thee, O Lord.

For games and holidays in the open air, for books and pictures and all our small possessions;

glory be to thee, O Lord.

For birds, for children and the joy of innocency, for the joy of work attempted and achieved, for the joy of harvest and the wedding feast;

glory be to thee, O Lord.

118 LITANY OF PRAISE

Let us praise God:

For the joy which is born of sympathy and sorrow, for the joy of the lost soul finding love again, and for the joy of the angels of God over one sinner that repenteth;

glory be to thee, O Lord.

For all pure comedy and laughter, and for the gift of humor and gaiety of heart;

glory be to thee, O Lord.

For all who have consecrated mirth with the love of Christ;

glory be to thee, O Lord.

For all singers and musicians, for all who work in form and color to increase the joy of life;

glory be to thee, O Lord.

For poets and craftsmen, for all who rejoice in their work and make things well;

glory be to thee, O Lord.

For all who have loved the common people and borne their sorrows in their hearts;

glory be to thee, O Lord.

For prophets and reformers who cry shame on all social wrong and point the way to fairer life for all the people;

glory be to thee, O Lord most high. Amen.

119 LITANY OF PRAISE

Let us praise God:
For all obscure and humble saints, who have made life sweeter and gentler;

glory be to thee, O Lord.

For all ignorant disciples, who have misunderstood the Christian doctrines, and yet lived in the companionship of Christ;

glory be to thee, O Lord.

For the image of Christ in ordinary people, their forbearance and their generosity, their good temper in crowds and railway trains, their courage and their kindness;

glory be to thee, O Lord.

For the glory of God shining in commonplace lives, for husband and wife scheming to please one another, for the sacrifices of both for their children;

glory be to thee, O Lord.

For all holy and humble men of heart, in whom the loveliness of our Savior Christ has been made manifest to the world;

glory be to thee, O Lord, now and evermore. Amen.

120 LITANY OF THANKSGIVING

O Father of all, who art wisdom and beauty and goodness, whose Spirit ever strives in the souls of men, we thank thee that thou hast made us heirs of all the ages of thy creative effort, and called us to share some part of thy burden of redemption;

glory be to thee, O Lord.

For the vision of thyself in our Lord and Savior Jesus Christ; for thy divine compassion which cares for us despite our weaknesses, cowardice, and self-love; and for thy leadership until this hour;

glory be to thee, O Lord.

For the radiance, mystery, and surprise of this dear world, for thy wisdom and beauty revealed in it, and for the love of friends which sweetens and enriches it;

glory be to thee, O Lord.

For the leaven of thy ideals of liberty and justice and brotherhood which have worked so terribly and still work so hopefully among the peoples of the earth;

glory be to thee, O Lord.

Because through suffering and weakness thou hast taught us patience, and given us the sense of dependence upon thee, because in health and strength thou hast given us to share thy joy in being active, and because in sorrow thou hast revealed to us the glory of others' kindness;

glory be to thee, O Lord.

For the disciplines of life, for the endurance which is learned through drudgery, for the work which is its own reward, for the difficulties which are the material of victory, thy victory in us;

glory be to thee, O Lord.

Because through the turmoil of life, we find thy peace, because for the adventure of life we need thy strength, and because in the supreme adventure of death, we have thy blessed hope;

glory be to thee, O Lord.

For the laughter of children, for mirth and wit, for the jest of gallant souls that makes us ashamed to be afraid, and for the cheerfulness of suffering folk, which shames us out of self-concern;

glory be to thee, O Lord.

For thy Church on earth, for the comfort and encouragement of the blessed company of faithful people, and above all for the sense of thy companionship with us, in loneliness and fellowship, in Sacrament and prayer;

glory be to thee, O Lord. Amen.

121 LITANY OF THANKSGIVING

Almighty God, fountain of all goodness, God of all grace, we bless thee for the earliest beginnings of thy work in us and in our children, for the awakening of faith, for gracious memories and holy desires, and for the ceaseless strivings of thy Spirit within us;

we praise thee, O God.

That thou hast succored us in times of temptation, remembered us when we have forgotten thee, pursued us when we have fled from thee, tarried for us with unwearied patience, and met us with forgiveness when we have turned back to thee;

we praise thee, O God.

For light and inspiration from thy holy Word, for moments of wonder and worship in thy house, for the fellowship of thy Church, for the reality of things unseen and eternal, and for every remembrance of friends who dwell with thee within the veil;

we praise thee, O God, Father, Son, and Holy Spirit. Amen.

122 ADORATION OF THE RISEN LORD

On the first day of the week, at early dawn, the women went to the tomb, taking the spices which they had prepared. And they found the stone rolled away from the tomb.

Hallelujah!

And the women departed quickly from the tomb with fear and great joy. And behold, Jesus met them and said, "Hail!"

Hallelujah!

And Mary stood weeping outside the tomb. And she said, "They have taken away my Lord, and I do not know where they have laid him." Saying this, she turned around and saw Jesus standing, but she did not know that it was Jesus. And Jesus said to her, "Mary." She turned and said to him, "Master."

Hallelujah!

That very day, two of the disciples were going to a village named Emmaus. While they were talking and discussing together, Jesus himself drew near, and went with them.

Hallelujah!

On the evening of that day, the doors being shut where the disciples were, Jesus came and stood among them, and said to them, "Peace be with you." When he had said this, he showed them his hands and his side.

Hallelujah!

Simon Peter said unto the disciples, "I am going fishing." They said to him, "We will go with you." And that night they caught nothing. But just as the day was breaking, Jesus stood upon the beach. And that disciple whom Jesus loved said to Peter, "It is the Lord."

Hallelujah!

Now may the God of peace, who brought again from the dead our Lord Jesus, that great shepherd of the sheep, by the blood of the eternal covenant, equip you with everything good that you may do his will, working in you that which is pleasing in his sight, through Jesus Christ: to whom be glory for ever and ever.

Hallelujah, hallelujah, hallelujah!

123 OUR LORD'S SUMMARY OF THE LAW

Our Lord Jesus Christ said: You shall love the Lord your God with all your heart, and with all your soul, and with all your mind. This is the great and first commandment.

Lord, have mercy upon us, and incline our hearts to keep this law.

And a second is like it, You shall love your neighbor as yourself.

Lord, have mercy upon us, and incline our hearts to keep this law.

A new commandment I give to you, that you love one another, even as I have loved you.

Lord, have mercy upon us, and write all these thy laws in our hearts, we beseech thee. Amen.

Matthew 22:37-39; John 13:34

IV.

Occasional Offices
of the Church

An Office for Licensing Persons to Preach

† *At the time appointed those who are to be licensed to preach, having satisfied the requirements of the Discipline, shall be presented by their respective pastors to the district superintendent and the District Conference. In the event there is no District Conference, this office may be used elsewhere at the discretion of the district superintendent. The secretary or other elder of the District Committee on Ministerial Qualifications shall say,*

Brethren, we present unto you *these persons* to be licensed to preach the Gospel of the Lord Jesus Christ:

† *Here let the names be read.*

† *The district superintendent shall then say,*

Brethren, you have heard the names of these persons who have completed the studies required for the license to preach and are recommended by the District Committee on Ministerial Qualifications. Their churches have inquired diligently concerning them and have found them to be fitted in character and skill for this sacred vocation. If there be any of you who know any reason why any one of them should not be licensed to preach the Gospel, let him arise now and declare the same.

† *If no impediment be alleged, the district superintendent shall then question those being licensed as follows:*

Do you believe you are moved by the Holy Spirit to preach the Word of God?

I do.

Will you strive to live a life in keeping with what you preach?

I will.

† *The district superintendent, addressing the conference, shall then say,*

Brethren, you have heard no objection to *any* candidate, and you have received *their* testimony in regard to *their* call and dedication. Will, then, you, the members of this District Conference, grant a license to preach to *these candidates* for the Christian ministry?

† *The vote shall be taken as the chairman may direct.*

† *The district superintendent, addressing the candidates who have received affirmative vote, shall say,*

321

You are hereby authorized to preach the Gospel in the congregation and to perform such other acts of service in the Church as you may be appointed to do. Take heed that you perform these duties faithfully as much as in you lies, the Lord being your helper.

† *The candidates shall kneel and the district superintendent shall pray, saying,*

Almighty God, whose Word is truth, in the keeping of which is eternal life: We thank thee for these persons whom this day we set aside in thy name as preachers of thy Gospel. Prepare them in body, mind, and spirit for their task, and continue them in thy grace, that they may increase and bless thy Church through their labors; through Jesus Christ our Lord. **Amen.**

† *Then the district superintendent shall say,*

Hear this commission from the Scriptures:

"Every one who calls upon the name of the Lord will be saved." But how are men to call upon him in whom they have not believed? And how are they to believe in him of whom they have never heard? And how are they to hear without a preacher? And how can men preach unless they are sent? As it is written, "How beautiful are the feet of those who preach good news!" But they have not all heeded the Gospel; for Isaiah says, "Lord, who has believed what he has heard from us?" So faith comes from what is heard, and what is heard comes by the preaching of Christ.

Romans 10:13-17

† *Then may the district superintendent say,*

The peace of God, which passeth all understanding, keep your hearts and minds in the knowledge and love of God, and of his Son Jesus Christ our Lord; and the blessing of God Almighty, the Father, the Son, and the Holy Spirit, be among you, and remain with you always. **Amen.**

An Office for Admission of Ministerial Candidates to Membership in an Annual Conference

† *An order of worship may precede this office. It may be used when the classes are voted into the Annual Conference, or at any other time the bishop may designate.*

† *Following a hymn of praise, the bishop shall cause the registrar, or other member of the conference, to read the names of those to be admitted on trial.*

† *The names having been read aloud, the candidates shall stand before the conference. Then the bishop shall address them, saying,*

Dearly beloved, this is a solemn hour in your life and a high moment in the proceedings of this conference. You are entering into a glorious fellowship. You are following in the footsteps of those who have sought to spread scriptural holiness through the lands of the earth. There is no calling more sacred than that which you now enter, and there is no privilege more meaningful than that which comes to you through this holy ministry. In the presence of this Annual Conference I ask you:

1. Are you convinced that you should enter the ministry of the Church?

2. Are you willing to face any sacrifices that may be involved?

3. Are you in debt so as to interfere with your work, or have you obligations to others which will make it difficult for you to live on the salary you are to receive?

4. If you are married, is your wife or husband in sympathy with your ministerial calling and willing to share in the sacrifices of your vocation?

5. For the sake of a disciplined example, and without implying moral superiority, are you willing to make a complete dedication of yourself to the highest ideals of the Christian ministry with respect to purity of life in body, in mind, and in spirit, and to bear witness thereto by abstinence from all indulgences, including alcoholic beverages and tobacco, which may injure your influence?

6. Are you willing to relate yourself in ministry to all persons without regard to race, color, or national origin, including receiving them into the membership and fellowship of the Church?

7. Will you keep before you as the one great objective of your life the advancement of God's kingdom?

323

† *The candidates having made appropriate response, the bishop shall pray as he is moved, or he may say,*

Let us pray.

Almighty God, our Father, accept our thanksgiving for *these* thy *servants* who *have* heeded Christ's call to the ministry of his Church; fill *them* with the gifts and graces needed in this sacred calling; prepare *them* to be true *shepherds* of the flock; stir up in *them* prophetic insight and priestly saintliness, that *they* may become true and faithful *ministers* of Christ's holy Church. In the name of the same Jesus Christ our Lord. **Amen.**

† *Here those received shall be seated.*

† *Here a hymn may be sung.*

† *Then the bishop shall cause the chairman of the Board of Ministerial Training, or some other elder of the conference, to present those to be admitted into full connection. Their names having been read aloud, the candidates shall stand before the conference, and the chairman, or other elder, addressing the bishop, shall say,*

I present to you *these* persons to be admitted into membership in full connection of the *N.* Annual Conference of The Methodist Church. *They have* fulfilled the requirements of the Discipline of our church, *they have* met the special rules of this conference, *they have* been examined as to character and competence for the ministry in the Church of Christ, and *they have* been elected to the membership of this conference. *They are* now presented to answer the questions required of all traveling preachers in The Methodist Church.

† *Then the bishop shall say,*

According to the usage and Discipline of The Methodist Church, you have indicated that you are convinced that you should enter the ministry of Christ's holy Church. You have declared that you are willing to face any sacrifice that may be involved in the consecration of life. You have indicated that you are so situated in life that you can accept the obligations of the itinerant minister. You have affirmed that you will abstain from those acts which may injure your work and influence as a minister of Christ, and that you will keep before you as the one great objective of your life the advancement of the kingdom of God. Give heed to the words of the Gospel of Christ when he said: "If any man will come after me, let him deny himself, and take up his cross, and follow me."

In accordance with the *Discipline* of The Methodist Church and the historic usages of our communion, you will in the presence of this conference give answer to the following questions:

1. Have you faith in Christ?
2. Are you going on to perfection?
3. Do you expect to be made perfect in love in this life?
4. Are you earnestly striving after it?
5. Are you resolved to devote yourself wholly to God and his work?
6. Do you know the General Rules of our church?
7. Will you keep them?
8. Have you studied the doctrines of The Methodist Church?
9. After full examination do you believe that our doctrines are in harmony with the Holy Scriptures?
10. Will you preach and maintain them?
11. Have you studied our form of church discipline and polity?
12. Do you approve our church government and polity?
13. Will you support and maintain them?
14. Will you diligently instruct the children in every place?
15. Will you visit from house to house?
16. Will you recommend fasting or abstinence, by both precept and example?
17. Are you determined to employ all your time in the work of God?
18. Are you in debt so as to embarrass you in your work?
19. Will you observe the following directions? (*a*) Be diligent. Never be unemployed. Never be triflingly employed. Never trifle away time; neither spend any more time at any one place than is strictly necessary. (*b*) Be punctual. Do everything exactly at the time. And do not mend our rules; but keep them; not for wrath, but for conscience' sake.

† *The candidates having made appropriate response, the bishop shall offer the following or some other prayer of consecration:*

O God, our heavenly Father, who didst manifest thy love in sending thine only begotten Son into the world that all might have life through him: Pour out thy Spirit upon thy Church, that it may fulfill thy command to preach the Gospel to every creature. Send forth, we beseech thee, laborers into thy harvest; fill them with the Holy Spirit and with faith; defend them in all dangers and temptations; and hasten the time when the fulness of the nations shall be gathered into thy kingdom; through the grace of Jesus Christ our Lord. **Amen.**

† Then the bishop shall give this or another blessing:

The peace of God, which passeth all understanding, keep your hearts and minds in the knowledge and love of God, and of his Son Jesus Christ our Lord; and the blessing of God Almighty, the Father, the Son, and the Holy Spirit, be among you, and remain with you always. **Amen.**

An Office for the Consecration of Deaconesses

† *At the time appointed, those to be consecrated deaconesses shall be presented to the bishop, or to an elder representing him, by one authorized for this purpose, who shall say,*

I present unto you *these persons* to be consecrated *deaconesses.*

† *Then the bishop, or other elder, shall say,*

Dearly beloved, *these are they* whom we purpose this day to consecrate *deaconesses* in the Church of God. After proper inquiry and due examination we have found *them* to be not unworthy and count *them* to be proper *persons* for this work and office.

† *This lesson shall then be read,*

When the Son of man comes in his glory, and all the angels with him, then he will sit on his glorious throne. Before him will be gathered all the nations, and he will separate them one from another as a shepherd separates the sheep from the goats, and he will place the sheep at his right hand, but the goats at the left.

Then the King will say to those at his right hand, "Come, O blessed of my Father, inherit the kingdom prepared for you from the foundation of the world; for I was hungry and you gave me food, I was thirsty and you gave me drink, I was a stranger and you welcomed me, I was naked and you clothed me, I was sick and you visited me, I was in prison and you came to me."

Then the righteous will answer him, "Lord, when did we see thee hungry and feed thee, or thirsty and give thee drink? And when did we see thee a stranger and welcome thee, or naked and clothe thee? And when did we see thee sick or in prison and visit thee?"

And the King will answer them, "Truly, I say to you, as you did it to one of the least of these my brethren, you did it to me."

Matthew 25:31-40

† *Then the bishop, or other elder, shall say to those to be deaconesses,*

Dearly beloved, we rejoice that in the providence of God a door of usefulness has been opened to you in the Church of Christ. You are to give *yourselves* to the service of the Lord, going about doing good. You are to minister to the poor, visit the sick, pray for the dying, care for the orphaned, seek the wandering, comfort the sorrowing, and lead the sinning to their Savior. Such service lays upon you solemn responsibility.

Do you believe that you are led of God to engage in this work and to assume the duties of this office?

I do.

Do you in the presence of God and of this congregation promise faithfully to perform the duties of a deaconess in the Church of God?

I do.

Will you be diligent in prayer, in the study of the Holy Scriptures, and in such other devotions as will help you to grow in the knowledge and love of God?

I will.

Will you be guided by the will and direction of those whom the Church may place over you in the doing of your work?

I will.

† *Then those to be consecrated shall kneel for silent prayer after which shall be said,*

O eternal God, the Father of our Lord Jesus Christ, who didst call Phoebe and Dorcas into the service of thy Church: Look upon *these* thy *servants* who *are* now to be set apart to the office of deaconess. Give to *them,* we pray thee, such understanding of thy holy Gospel, such firmness of Christian purpose, such diligence in service, and such beauty of life in Christ, that *they* may be to all whom *they* teach or serve a worthy revelation of the meaning and power of the Christian life. May *they* so order their time and nourish *their minds* and *hearts* that *they* may constantly grow in grace and in the knowledge of our Lord Jesus Christ, and may steadily increase in power to lead others unto him.

Grant that *they* may have strength of body, mind, and soul for the fulfillment of thy will in the holy task to which thou hast called *them;* and grant *them* thy Holy Spirit, that *they* may worthily discharge the work committed to *them,* to the blessing of mankind and to the praise of Christ our Savior. **Amen.**

† *Then the bishop, or other elder, laying his hands upon the head of each severally, shall say,*

I admit thee to the office of deaconess in the Church of God, in the name of the Father, and of the Son, and of the Holy Spirit. **Amen.**

† *A hymn may then be sung, all standing, after which the minister shall let the people depart with this blessing:*

May Christ dwell in your hearts through faith; that you, being rooted and grounded in love, may have power to comprehend with all the saints what is the breadth and length and height and depth, and to know the love of Christ which surpasses knowledge, that you may be filled with all the fulness of God.

Now to him who by the power at work within us is able to do far more abundantly than all that we ask or think, to him be glory in the Church and in Christ Jesus to all generations, for ever and ever. **Amen.**

An Office for the Commissioning of Missionaries and Deaconesses

† *This office may be included in an order of worship, following the sermon.*

† *Those to be commissioned as missionaries and deaconesses stand before the bishop, who shall address them, saying,*

Hear the words of our Lord Jesus Christ:

As the Father has loved me, so have I loved you.   *John 15:9a*

You did not choose me, but I chose you and appointed you that you should go and bear fruit and that your fruit should abide; so that whatever you ask the Father in my name, he may give it to you.   *John 15:16*

Go therefore and make disciples of all nations, baptizing them in the name of the Father and of the Son and of the Holy Spirit, teaching them to observe all that I have commanded you; and lo, I am with you always, to the close of the age.   *Matthew 28:19-20*

The Methodist Church, in its endeavor to carry out this great commission, has declared, "The supreme aim of missions is to make the Lord Jesus Christ known to all people in all lands as their divine Savior, to persuade them to become his disciples, and to gather these disciples into Christian churches; to enlist them in the building of the kingdom of God; to cooperate with these churches; to promote world Christian fellowship; and to bring to bear on all human life the spirit and principles of Christ."

Dearly beloved, we rejoice that you have purposed in your *hearts* to devote your *lives* to this task. Your labors may take you to the mountains and the plains, to isolated villages and teeming cities of this country, or to lands across the sea. You are to be among men as *those* who *serve* in teaching, preaching, and healing. In the varied activities of our common life you will ever testify to the infinite love of God shed abroad in Christ Jesus. Such a vocation confers a great privilege; it also lays upon you a solemn responsibility. What you have done alone with God in consecrating your *lives* to this service, we now ask you to do publicly in the presence of this congregation.

Do you sincerely believe that you have been led by the Spirit of God to engage in this work and to assume its responsibilities?

I do so believe.

In humble reliance upon divine grace, do you make it the supreme purpose of your life to give yourself unreservedly to the work of Christ in your appointed field?

I do, the Lord being my helper.

Will you be diligent in prayer, in the reading of the Holy Scriptures, and in such studies as help to the knowledge of God and his kingdom?

I will endeavor so to do.

Will you earnestly seek to carry forward your ministry in sincerity and in love, cooperating humbly with your fellow workers, under the direction of the Church?

I will, the Lord being my helper.

† *Then all shall bow for silent prayer, after which the bishop shall say,*

Almighty God, Father of all mercies: Graciously behold *these* thy servants now to be commissioned as *missionaries and deaconesses* of thy Church. Endue *them* with thy Holy Spirit, enrich *them* with thy heavenly grace, and strengthen *them* for the tasks which lie ahead; that in all *their* works, begun, continued, and ended in thee, *they* may glorify thy holy name, and advance thy blessed kingdom; through Jesus Christ our Lord. **Amen.**

† *Then the bishop, taking the hand of each severally, and giving the name, shall say,*

N., I commission you to take the Gospel of our Lord Jesus Christ into all the world, in the name of the Father, and of the Son, and of the Holy Spirit. **Amen.**

† *Then those who have been commissioned shall kneel, and the bishop shall offer prayer on their behalf.*

† *Following the prayer, those commissioned shall stand and face the people.*

† *When missionaries and deaconesses are present in the congregation, the bishop shall cause them to stand and, addressing them, shall say,*

Beloved in the Lord, you once stood where *these* now *stand,* answering the call of God in your hearts. Obedient to this divine imperative, you have labored at home and abroad, ministering to the needs of men and bringing to them words of life. We are justly proud of your work and are continually thankful for the fulness of your devotion.

These younger *workers* will look to you for help and guidance as *they go* forth to serve with you. I commend *them* to your love and care.

† *The missionaries and deaconesses present shall then say,*

We welcome you into our fellowship and into the joyous service of Christ and his kingdom. Your peace, joy, and welfare are now our own, and we pledge to you through the days ahead our unfailing support.

With you we renew our dedication to God and to the Church we delight to serve.

Now the God of peace make you perfect in every good work to do his will, working in you that which is well pleasing in his sight, through Jesus Christ; to whom be glory for ever and ever. Amen.

† *Then the bishop shall cause all the people to stand, and with them shall make this covenant, the bishop first saying, and the people responding:*

Dearly beloved, I commend to you *these persons* whom we this day have commissioned to carry into all the world the sacred and imperishable message of eternal salvation.

We rejoice to recognize you as *missionaries and deaconesses* of our church, and we thank God that you have dedicated your *lives* to his service.

In this holy moment we too are called to a renewed consecration of our lives to Christ and his kingdom. As *these* our fellow *workers go* forth upon *their* mission, let us assure *them* that we are with *them* in spirit and are supporting *them* by word and gift and deed.

We will follow you with our prayers; we will support your work with our gifts; and together we will strive to minister to the needs of our fellow men, and to bring them to the saving knowledge of our Lord Jesus Christ.

† *Then all shall say,*

We, being many, are one body in Christ, and every one members one of another.

United we pray: Thy kingdom come, thy will be done on earth as it is in heaven. And to this end we dedicate ourselves; in the name of the Father, and of the Son, and of the Holy Spirit. Amen.

† *Here let the people be seated and with heads bowed offer their personal intercessions for those who have just been commissioned and for the mission of the Church in the world.*

† *Here a hymn of dedication may be sung, after which the bishop shall let the people depart with this blessing:*

For this reason I bow my knees before the Father, from whom every family in heaven and on earth is named, that according to the riches of his glory he may grant you to be strengthened with might through his Spirit in the inner man, and that Christ may dwell in your hearts through faith; that you, being rooted and grounded in love, may have power to comprehend with all the saints what is the breadth and length and height and depth, and to know the love of Christ which surpasses knowledge, that you may be filled with all the fulness of God.

Now to him who by the power at work within us is able to do far more abundantly than all that we ask or think, to him be glory in the Church and in Christ Jesus to all generations, for ever and ever. **Amen.**

An Office for the Consecration of Directors of Christian Education and Directors of Music

† *This office may be used at the Annual Conference at the time of the report of the Conference Board of Education, or at some other time or place agreed upon.*

† *At the time appointed the executive secretary or president of the board, or someone designated by them, shall present to the bishop, or to some elder representing him, those who are to be consecrated, and having read aloud their names and respective offices, shall say,*

I present to you *these persons* who *have* been found to meet the standards set for *these offices,* and *are* qualified to be consecrated for the same.

† *Then the bishop shall question those to be consecrated as follows:*

Do you believe in your heart that you have been led by the Spirit of God to assume the responsibilities of the office in which you are to be consecrated?

I do so believe.

Will you be diligent in prayer, in the reading of the Holy Scriptures, and in other studies necessary to fulfill this office?

I will, the Lord being my helper.

Will you strive so to live that the power of God may be manifest in your life, and in this office and ministry, thus enabling you to bring others to an awareness of the presence of God and to become disciples of our Lord Jesus Christ?

I will, by God's grace.

Will you accept the duties which have been committed to your care, and will you endeavor to discharge them faithfully, to the glory of God and the service of his holy Church?

I will do so, the Lord being my helper.

Will you be loyal to the Church and accept the authority of those to whom the Church has committed the direction of your work?

I will, the Lord being my helper.

† *Then the bishop, taking the right hand of each person to be consecrated, and giving the name, shall say,*

334

N., I admit you to the office of director of Christian education in The Methodist Church, and may God's grace enable you to fulfill the same to his glory.

† *or,*

N., I admit you to the office of director of music in The Methodist Church, and may God's grace enable you to fulfill the same to his glory.

† *Then shall be read this lesson,*

I appeal to you therefore, brethren, by the mercies of God, to present your bodies as a living sacrifice, holy and acceptable to God, which is your spiritual worship. Do not be conformed to this world but be transformed by the renewal of your mind, that you may prove what is the will of God, what is good and acceptable and perfect.

For by the grace given to me I bid every one among you not to think of himself more highly than he ought to think, but to think with sober judgment, each according to the measure of faith which God has assigned him. For as in one body we have many members, and all the members do not have the same function, so we, though many, are one body in Christ, and individually members one of another. Having gifts that differ according to the grace given to us, let us use them: if prophecy, in proportion to our faith; if service, in our serving; he who teaches, in his teaching; he who exhorts, in his exhortation; he who contributes, in liberality; he who gives aid, with zeal; he who does acts of mercy, with cheerfulness.

Let love be genuine; hate what is evil, hold fast to what is good; love one another with brotherly affection; outdo one another in showing honor. Never flag in zeal, be aglow with the Spirit, serve the Lord.

Romans 12:1-11

† *Then the persons to be consecrated shall kneel, and the bishop shall offer this prayer of consecration,*

O eternal God, the Father of our Lord Jesus Christ, look upon *these* thy *servants* whom we consecrate this day. Grant that *they* may have strength of body, mind, and soul for the fulfillment of thy will, that *they* may worthily discharge the work committed to *them* to the blessing of mankind and the glory of Christ our Savior. **Amen.**

† *Then the bishop shall say,*

Now to him who by the power at work within us is able to do far more abundantly than all that we ask or think, to him be glory in the Church and in Christ Jesus to all generations, for ever and ever. **Amen.**

An Office for the Recognition of Officials in the Church

† *This office may be included in an order of worship when it is desired to recognize those who have been properly designated as office-bearers in the parish. The minister shall cause such to stand before him and, addressing them, shall say,*

Dearly beloved, you have been called of God, and chosen by this congregation, to assume special responsibilities in the administration of this church. Your duties include many tasks needful for its welfare and for the advancement of the kingdom of God. In addition, all of you share in the duty of counseling with your minister and of assisting him in the leadership of the spiritual and temporal life of the church. Above all it is your duty, as much as in you lies, to live before all men as becomes the Gospel.

Having well considered the nature and purpose of the office to which you have been called, will each of you accept this responsibility, and will you seek to accomplish the work and service it sets before you, to the honor and glory of our Lord Jesus Christ?

I will, the Lord being my helper.

† *Then the minister shall say,*

Let us pray.

O Lord our God, who art the only founder and keeper of thy Church: We thank thee that thou hast called thy servants to share in the work of thy kingdom. Grant them grace to give themselves wholly to this their task and service. Grant them sincerity and singleness of mind. Hold ever before them the example of their Lord, who pleased not himself, but gave himself up for us all, that, sharing his ministry and consecration, they may enter into his joy. Guide them in their work for thy Church. Prosper their counsels and their labors. Reward their fidelity with the knowledge that thou art using them for the accomplishment of thy purpose in Jesus Christ our Lord. **Amen.**

† *Then the minister, addressing the people, shall say,*

Dearly beloved, we rejoice to recognize these persons as office-bearers in this church. Do all you can to assist and encourage them in these offices into which they now have been inducted, giving them at all times your cooperation, your counsel, and your prayers.

† *Then the minister may add a blessing.*

An Office for the Recognition of Church School Officers and Teachers

† *This office may be included in an order of worship when the work of Christian education is the theme of the day, or at any other appropriate time.*

† *The minister shall cause the officers and teachers of the church school to stand before him and, addressing the congregation, shall say,*

Dearly beloved, we have gathered here in the presence of God to recognize those who have responded to his call to the work of teaching and administration in our church school. As they now present themselves to God for consecration to their various tasks, it is fitting that we, the members of this congregation, should with them consecrate our lives to the work with which they have been entrusted, and that we should publicly assume our obligation to support them by our loyalty and prayers, seeking with them and for them such measure of God's grace as may enable them to discharge their duties with faithfulness and godly fear.

† *Then the chairman of the Commission on Education or the minister may read the names of the officers and teachers of the church school. Following this, the minister and the officers and teachers shall read responsively, the minister beginning,*

There is one body and one Spirit, just as you were called to the one hope that belongs to your call, one Lord, one faith, one Baptism, one God and Father of us all, who is above all and through all and in all.

Now there are varieties of gifts, but the same Spirit; and there are varieties of service, but the same Lord.

For by grace you have been saved through faith; and this is not your own doing, it is the gift of God.

We have one Master, the Christ.

For we are fellow workmen for God; you are God's field, God's building.

For no other foundation can anyone lay than that which is laid, which is Jesus Christ.

I appeal to you therefore, brethren, by the mercies of God, to present your bodies as a living sacrifice, holy and acceptable to God, which is your spiritual worship.

The love of Christ controls us.

Do your best to present yourself to God as one approved, a workman who has no need to be ashamed, rightly handling the word of truth.

Who is sufficient for these things? Apart from him we can do nothing.

Now to him who by the power at work within us is able to do far more abundantly than all that we ask or think,

To him be glory in the Church and in Christ Jesus to all generations, for ever and ever. Amen.

† *Or Romans 12:1-8 may be read responsively or in unison.*

† *Here let the officers and teachers kneel, and the people be bowed. Then the minister shall say,*

Let us pray.

O God, who hast sent thy beloved Son to be unto us the way, the truth, and the life: Give thy blessing and the guidance of thy Holy Spirit to these thy servants, and to us all, that we, looking unto him, may set forward the teaching power of thy Church, to the nurture of thy children, the increase of thy kingdom, and the glory of thy Son Jesus Christ our Lord. **Amen.**

† *After which a hymn may be sung, and a blessing given.*

An Office for the Recognition of Choristers

† *This office may be included in an order of worship.*

† *The minister shall cause the choir director, with his choristers, to stand before him. The choir director shall say,*

I present these persons to be recognized as choristers in this church.

† *Then the minister, addressing the persons who are seeking admission as choristers, shall question them as follows:*

Do you desire to become a chorister in this church?

I do.

Will you endeavor always to be reverent in the house of God, and seek at all times to live a life in accordance with the Gospel?

I will, the Lord being my helper.

Do you promise obedience to those to whom the Church has committed authority over you?

I do.

† *The minister shall then say to the congregation,*

I commend to you these persons whom we now consecrate to the ministry of music in Christ's Church. Will you sustain them with your prayers and your spiritual support as you seek together to offer praise to God?

We will do so, with God's help.

† *Here shall be read this lesson,*

Let the word of Christ dwell in you richly, as you teach and admonish one another in all wisdom, and as you sing psalms and hymns and spiritual songs with thankfulness in your hearts to God. And whatever you do, in word or deed, do everything in the name of the Lord Jesus, giving thanks to God the Father through him.   *Colossians 3:16-17*

† *Then the minister may give the name of each chorister, and shall say,*

N., I admit you into the choir of this church. What you sing with your mouth, believe in your heart; what you believe in your heart, practice in your life. And may our heavenly Father give you grace to sing his praise and live to his glory, both in this world and in the world to come; through Jesus Christ our Lord. **Amen.**

† *Then the choir director and choristers shall kneel, and the minister shall say,*

Let us pray.

O Lord our God, who art worthy to be praised and to be held in reverence by all men: Give thy grace to the choristers of thy Church, that, singing together psalms and hymns and spiritual songs, they may make melody in their hearts to thee; through Jesus Christ our Lord. **Amen.**

† *Then all may say,*

Our Father, who art in heaven, hallowed be thy name. Thy kingdom come, thy will be done on earth as it is in heaven. Give us this day our daily bread. And forgive us our trespasses, as we forgive those who trespass against us. And lead us not into temptation, but deliver us from evil. For thine is the kingdom, and the power, and the glory, forever. Amen.

† *Then the minister may say,*

The Lord bless you and keep you: the Lord make his face to shine upon you, and be gracious to you: the Lord lift up his countenance upon you, and give you peace. **Amen.**

An Office for the Organizing of a Church

† *The district superintendent or other elder authorized by him, shall begin the service by making this declaration of purpose:*

Dearly beloved, we are met at this time to establish a new congregation of The Methodist Church, which is a part of the body of Christ; and to that end we dedicate ourselves and this hour.

The Church is of God, and will be preserved to the end of time, for the conduct of worship and the due administration of his Word and Sacraments, the maintenance of Christian fellowship and discipline, the edification of believers, and the conversion of the world. All, of every age and station, stand in need of the means of grace which it alone supplies.

† *Here a hymn may be sung.*

† *Then shall be read this lesson from the Old Testament:*

Behold, I will gather them from all the countries to which I drove them in my anger and my wrath and in great indignation; I will bring them back to this place, and I will make them dwell in safety. And they shall be my people, and I will be their God. I will give them one heart and one way, that they may fear me forever, for their own good and the good of their children after them. I will make with them an everlasting covenant, that I will not turn away from doing good to them; and I will put the fear of me in their hearts, that they may not turn from me. I will rejoice in doing them good, and I will plant them in this land in faithfulness, with all my heart and all my soul.   *Jeremiah 32:37-41*

† *Then shall follow this litany, the minister beginning, the people standing and responding:*

For the revelation of thyself which thou hast given to us through patriarchs, prophets, and sages,

we praise thy name, O Lord.

For salvation from sin through thy redeeming love, and for the ministry of the Gospel in all the world,

we praise thy name, O Lord.

For the call to discipleship, and for the joy of serving in the Church of Jesus Christ our Lord,

we praise thy name, O Lord.

For the desire of this people to be made a congregation in Christ's holy Church, in the hope that through them thy grace may be manifested, and thy people redeemed,

we praise thy name, O Lord, and pledge ourselves to thee this day. Amen.

† *Here let the people be seated.*

† *The district superintendent shall give opportunity for any to present themselves for membership by certificate of transfer or on profession of faith. When he is satisfied as to the genuineness of their faith and purpose, he shall receive them according to the offices of the church. After this he shall complete the organization of the church as prescribed in the* Discipline.

† *Whereupon the district superintendent shall say,*

By what name shall this church henceforth be known?

† *To which the pastor, chairman of the Official Board, or other official shall answer,*

It shall be called the *N.* Methodist Church.

† *Then shall the district superintendent say,*

In accordance with the laws and the *Discipline* of The Methodist Church, I hereby declare that the *N.* Methodist Church is duly constituted and organized for the glory of God, the proclamation of the Gospel, and the service of humanity.

† *Then shall be read this lesson from the New Testament:*

His divine power has granted to us all things that pertain to life and godliness, through the knowledge of him who called us to his own glory and excellence, by which he has granted to us his precious and very great promises, that through these you may escape from the corruption that is in the world because of passion, and become partakers of the divine nature. For this very reason make every effort to supplement your faith with virtue, and virtue with knowledge, and knowledge with self-control, and self-control with steadfastness, and steadfastness with godliness, and godliness with brotherly affection, and brotherly affection with love. For if these things are yours and abound, they keep you from being ineffective or unfruitful in the knowledge of our Lord Jesus Christ. For whoever lacks these things is blind and shortsighted and has forgotten that he was cleansed from his old sins. Therefore, brethren, be the more zealous to confirm your call and election, for if you do this you will never fall.

II Peter 1:3-10

† *A hymn may be sung.*

† *Then shall follow the sermon.*

† *After which the minister shall say,*

Let us pray.

† *Then the minister may offer prayer as he is moved, or he may say,*

O almighty God, whose Son Jesus Christ is the one foundation and the chief cornerstone of thy Church: Bless what we do now in organizing this church in thy name. Be thou, we beseech thee, the beginning, the increase, and the consummation of this our work, which is undertaken to thy glory; who with the Son and the Holy Spirit livest and reignest, one God, world without end. **Amen.**

† *Then a hymn may be sung and a blessing given.*

An Office for the Breaking of Ground for a Church Building

† *This office may be used within an order of worship, or separately.*

† *When the office is used separately, appropriate prayers, Scripture, and acts of praise may be used following the Scripture sentences.*

† *If the office is used within an order of worship, at the time appointed all shall proceed to the site set apart for the new church building, and the officiating minister shall say,*

Great is the Lord, and greatly to be praised in the city of our God.
Psalm 48:1

How lovely is thy dwelling place, O Lord of hosts! My soul longs, yea, faints for the courts of the Lord; my heart and flesh sing for joy to the living God. *Psalm 84:1-2*

Dearly beloved in the Lord: Forasmuch as devout and holy men have erected houses for the public worship and work of God, and separated them from all unhallowed, worldly, and common uses, in order to fill men's minds with greater reverence for his glorious majesty, and affect their hearts with greater devotion and humility in his service; which pious works have been approved of and graciously accepted by our heavenly Father; let us trust that he will also favorably approve our godly purpose of setting apart this place in solemn manner, that upon it there may be erected a building for the worship and work of God. Let us then faithfully and devoutly ask his blessing on this our undertaking.

Let us pray.

Almighty and everliving God, who art ever exalted yet always nigh: Grant to be present with us, who are here gathered together, to set apart this ground upon which we stand to the honor and glory of thy great name. Let thy Spirit descend upon thy church to be established here; and within its sanctuary let thy glory dwell. May thy love fill all who shall here seek thy face; and may thy presence be with them as they go forth from this place in the peace and power of thy Holy Spirit; through Jesus Christ our Lord. **Amen.**

† *Then all shall say,*

Our Father, who art in heaven, hallowed be thy name. Thy kingdom come, thy will be done on earth as it is in heaven. Give us this day

our daily bread. And forgive us our trespasses, as we forgive those who trespass against us. And lead us not into temptation, but deliver us from evil. For thine is the kingdom, and the power, and the glory, forever. Amen.

† *Here shall be read this lesson,*

I therefore, a prisoner for the Lord, beg you to lead a life worthy of the calling to which you have been called, with all lowliness and meekness, with patience, forbearing one another in love, eager to maintain the unity of the Spirit in the bond of peace. There is one body and one Spirit, just as you were called to the one hope that belongs to your call, one Lord, one faith, one baptism, one God and Father of us all, who is above all and through all and in all. But grace was given to each of us according to the measure of Christ's gift.

And his gifts were that some should be apostles, some prophets, some evangelists, some pastors and teachers, for the equipment of the saints, for the work of the ministry, for building up the body of Christ, until we all attain to the unity of the faith and of the knowledge of the Son of God, to mature manhood, to the measure of the stature of the fulness of Christ. We are to grow up in every way into him who is the head, into Christ, from whom the whole body, joined and knit together by every joint with which it is supplied, when each part is working properly, makes bodily growth and upbuilds itself in love.

Ephesians 4:1-7, 11-13, 15b-16

† *Then the minister may offer prayer as he is moved, following which he shall make this declaration:*

To the glory of God, in the presence of this congregation, I now direct that ground be broken for the N. Methodist Church. Upon you as members of this congregation rests the responsibility and privilege to cause a church to rise here which shall be devoted to the honor and worship of almighty God our Father, and to the glory of his blessed Son our Savior Jesus Christ.

† *Then as each of those selected turns a spadeful of earth, the minister shall say one of the following sentences, to which the people shall respond:*

That a church may rise here where little children shall learn to love God and grow in grace and goodness, and in favor with God and man,

we break this ground today.

That a church may rise here where through the years youth shall come to worship, pause to pray, and rise to serve,

we break this ground today.

That a church may rise here where the weary and heavy-laden shall find that inner peace which the world can neither give nor take away,

we break this ground today.

That a church may rise here where the Word of God shall be so read and preached that it shall become the Living Word, and the Sacraments so administered that all life shall become a sacrament,

we break this ground today.

That a church may rise here where multitudes shall be refreshed in spirit, relieved from pain, released from bondage, and redeemed from sin,

we break this ground today.

That a church may rise here where the grace of God may be manifest, making our human loves constant, our homes Christlike, and our families creative centers of Christian witness,

we break this ground today.

That a church may rise here where all who bow in sorrow shall rise in faith in him in whom to believe is life eternal,

we break this ground today.

† *Then the minister shall say, the people responding,*

The Lord be with you.

And with thy spirit.

Let us pray.

Almighty and everlasting God, in communion with the saints in all the ages, and remembering the heritage that has been given us, we offer thee our praise and thanksgiving.

O Lord, hear our prayer.

Help us to accept the privilege and responsibility of this thy fellowship of faith; here may we keep the unity of the Spirit in the bond of peace.

So may we fulfill the law of love.

Enable us, by thy grace, to dedicate ourselves this day to the solemn task which thou dost lay upon our hearts and consciences.

In all that we do, be thou, O Lord, our strength and help.

Reveal to us the beauty of thy perfect law and the joy of our living Lord, that with glad hearts we may show forth our thankfulness, and serve thee all our days to the glory of thy blessed name.

Be thou, O Lord, our guide and help for evermore. Amen.

† *Then the minister shall let the people depart with a blessing.*

An Office for the Laying of the Cornerstone of a Church Building

† *This office may be used within an order of worship, or separately.*

† *When the office is used separately, a hymn may be sung before or after the Scripture sentences.*

† *If the office is used within an order of worship, at the time appointed all shall proceed to the site of the new building, and the officiating minister, standing by the cornerstone, shall say,*

Our help is in the name of the Lord, who made heaven and earth.

Psalm 124:8

Unless the Lord builds the house, those who build it labor in vain.

Psalm 127:1a

Dearly beloved, we are assembled to lay the cornerstone of a new house for the worship of almighty God. Therefore let us faithfully and devoutly seek his blessing on this our undertaking.

Let us pray.

Almighty and everlasting God, who art ever exalted and yet always near: Grant that we may worthily offer unto thee, the Father, the Son, and the Holy Spirit, this foundation which is laid for the building of a temple and a sanctuary where thy glory shall be manifest among us, and where all people shall come to call upon thy name; through Jesus Christ our Lord. **Amen.**

† *Then all shall say,*

Our Father, who art in heaven, hallowed be thy name. Thy kingdom come, thy will be done on earth as it is in heaven. Give us this day our daily bread. And forgive us our trespasses, as we forgive those who trespass against us. And lead us not into temptation, but deliver us from evil. For thine is the kingdom, and the power, and the glory, forever. Amen.

† *Then this psalm shall be read responsively, the minister beginning,*

The earth is the Lord's and the fulness thereof,
the world and those who dwell therein;
for he has founded it upon the seas,
and established it upon the rivers.

Who shall ascend the hill of the Lord?
And who shall stand in his holy place?
He who has clean hands and a pure heart,
who does not lift up his soul to what is false,
and does not swear deceitfully.
He will receive blessing from the Lord,
and vindication from the God of his salvation.
Such is the generation of those who seek him,
who seek the face of the God of Jacob.
Lift up your heads, O gates!
and be lifted up, O ancient doors!
that the King of glory may come in.
Who is this King of glory?
The Lord of hosts,
he is the King of glory! *Psalm 24:1-7, 10*

† *Then shall be said or sung the* Gloria Patri.

† *Then shall be read this lesson:*

So then you are no longer strangers and sojourners, but you are fellow citizens with the saints and members of the household of God, built upon the foundation of the apostles and prophets, Christ Jesus himself being the chief cornerstone, in whom the whole structure is joined together and grows into a holy temple in the Lord; in whom you also are built into it for a dwelling place of God in the Spirit. *Ephesians 2:19-22*

† *Here may follow a prayer, offering, anthem, and hymn as desired.*

† *Then the minister, standing by the cornerstone, shall exhibit to the people a box to be placed in the stone, containing such articles as a Bible,* The Methodist Hymnal, *the latest* Discipline, *church periodicals, names of the pastor, Official Board, the building committee of the church, with such other documents as may be desired.*

† *Then, standing at the side of the cornerstone, the minister shall read the following Scripture sentences:*

Behold, I am laying in Zion for a foundation a stone, a tested stone, a precious cornerstone, of a sure foundation. *Isaiah 28:16*

Take heed now, for the Lord has chosen you to build a house for the sanctuary; be strong, and do it. *I Chronicles 28:10*

Fear not, be not dismayed; for the Lord God, even my God, is with you. He will not fail you or forsake you, until all the work for the service of the house of the Lord is finished. *I Chronicles 28:20*

According to the commission of God given to me, like a skilled master builder I laid a foundation. *I Corinthians 3:10a*

For no other foundation can any one lay than that which is laid, which is Jesus Christ. *I Corinthians 3:11*

† *Then, with the aid of the builder, the minister shall lay the stone in its place; after which he shall say, the people responding,*

Praise the Lord, because the foundation of the house of the Lord is laid!

Praise the Lord. Hallelujah!

† *Then the minister shall place his hand upon the stone and say,*

Let us pray.

Almighty God, on whom we build all our hopes for this life and that which is to come: Visit, we beseech thee, with thy lovingkindness this place whereon we lay the foundation of a house to the praise and honor of thy holy name. Accept the act by which we lay this cornerstone. Bless those whose offerings enable us to build this house of worship. Graciously guard and direct those who labor in erecting it, shielding them from accident and peril. May the walls of this building rise in security and in beauty; and may the hearts of these thy people be fitly joined together into a living temple, builded upon the foundation of the apostles and prophets, Jesus Christ being the chief cornerstone. **Amen.**

† *Then may be added this prayer by the minister or by the minister and people together,*

O Lord God, when thou givest to thy servants to endeavor any great matter, grant us also to know that it is not the beginning, but the continuing of the same unto the end, until it is thoroughly finished, which yieldeth the true glory; through him who for the finishing of thy work laid down his life, our Redeemer Jesus Christ. **Amen.**

† *Then a hymn or a doxology may be sung, and the minister shall let the people depart with a blessing.*

An Office for the Opening or Consecrating of a Church Building

† *This office may be used for opening or consecrating a sanctuary, a church school building, or a parish house.*

† *The service may begin with a prelude.*

† *A hymn may be sung, the people standing.*

† *Then the officiating minister shall say, the people responding,*

Serve the Lord with gladness.

Enter into his gates with thanksgiving, and into his courts with praise.

O come, let us worship and bow down, let us kneel before the Lord our maker.

For he is our God, and we are the people of his pasture, and the sheep of his hand.

† *Here let the people be seated.*

† *Then the minister shall say,*

Let us pray.

O God, eternal and ever blessed, who delightest in the assembling of thy people in the sanctuary: Hear our prayer for this house, which we would devote henceforth to the honor of thy name. Grant, we beseech thee, that peace and prosperity may be found within these walls, that thy glory may be the light thereof, and that we, and all who come within it, may be satisfied with the goodness of thy house; through Jesus Christ our Lord. **Amen.**

† *Then all shall say,*

Blessed be thy name, O Lord, that thou hast given to thy servants a holy will and sacred desire, to erect and sanctify to thine own worship this building, which we now open for thine honor and glory. Grant that we, and all who come within these portals, shall ever make right use of it, and that the splendor of thy presence shall be manifest therein, and the hearts of thy people be ever blessed; through Jesus Christ our Lord. Amen.

† *An anthem may be sung.*

† *Here let the people stand. Then this canticle shall be said responsively; all shall remain standing until after the affirmation of faith.*

Arise, shine; for your light has come,
  and the glory of the Lord has risen upon you.
For behold, darkness shall cover the earth,
  and thick darkness the peoples;
but the Lord will arise upon you,
  and his glory will be seen upon you.
And nations shall come to your light,
  and kings to the brightness of your rising.
The abundance of the sea shall be turned to you,
  the wealth of the nations shall come to you.
Your gates shall be open continually,
  day and night they shall not be shut.
Violence shall no more be heard in your land,
  devastation or destruction within your borders;
you shall call your walls Salvation,
  and your gates Praise.
The sun shall be no more
your light by day,
  nor for brightness shall the moon
  give light to you by night;
but the Lord will be your everlasting light,
  and your God will be your glory.
Your sun shall no more go down,
  nor your moon withdraw itself;
for the Lord will be your everlasting light,
  and your days of mourning shall be ended.

Isaiah 60:1-3, 5b, 11a, 18-20

† *Here shall be sung the* Gloria Patri.

† *Then the minister shall say,*

Let us unite in this historic confession of the Christian faith:

I believe in God the Father Almighty, maker of heaven and earth;
  And in Jesus Christ his only Son our Lord: who was conceived by
the Holy Spirit, born of the Virgin Mary, suffered under Pontius
Pilate, was crucified, dead, and buried; the third day he rose from
the dead; he ascended into heaven, and sitteth at the right hand of
God the Father Almighty; from thence he shall come to judge the
quick and the dead.

I believe in the Holy Spirit, the holy catholic Church, the communion of saints, the forgiveness of sins, the resurrection of the body, and the life everlasting. Amen.

† *Then shall follow one or more of these lessons: I Kings 8:22-30; I Corinthians 3:9-23; Hebrews 10:19-25. For a church school building: Deuteronomy 6:4-9; Ephesians 4:11-13; Matthew 28:19-20. For a parish house: I John 1:1-7.*

† *Here prayer shall be offered.*

† *Parish notices may be given.*

† *An offering may be received, after which a prayer of dedication shall be said or sung.*

† *At the discretion of the minister the offering and prayers may follow the sermon.*

† *Here a hymn may be sung.*

† *Then shall follow the sermon.*

† *Following the sermon or the offering, a hymn may be sung, and an invitation to Christian discipleship given, after which the officiating minister shall make this declaration:*

In holy reverence, and in confidence that God our Father will accept that which we do in his name, I now declare this house to be open for the worship of almighty God.

† *When the building being consecrated is the church sanctuary, the minister shall then say,*

For the preaching of God's Word; for the due administration of the holy Sacraments; for the conversion of sinners, the edification of believers, and the salvation of the world, we reverently set apart and consecrate this building, in the name of the Father, the Son, and the Holy Spirit. **Amen.**

† *When it is a church school building or parish house, the minister shall say,*

For nurture in the truth of the Holy Scriptures; for Christian teaching, fellowship, and service, we reverently set apart and consecrate this building, in the name of the Father, the Son, and the Holy Spirit. **Amen.**

† *Then the minister shall offer one or more of the following prayers:*

Now therefore, O Lord, let thine eyes be open toward this house day and night; and let thine ears be ready toward the prayers of thy children, which they shall make unto thee in this place. And whensoever thy servants shall make to thee their petitions, do thou hear them, and when thou hearest, forgive. **Amen.**

Grant, O Lord, we beseech thee, that thy ministers may be clothed in righteousness, and thy saints rejoice in thy salvation. And may we all, with thy people everywhere, grow up into a holy temple in thee, O Lord, and be at last received into the glorious temple above, the house not made with hands, eternal in the heavens. To the Father, the Son, and the Holy Spirit, be glory and praise, world without end. **Amen.**

O God, who hast built thy Church upon the foundation of the apostles and prophets, Jesus Christ himself being the chief cornerstone: Save the community of thy people from cowardly surrender to the world, from rendering unto Caesar what belongs to thee, and from forgetting the eternal Gospel amid the temporal pressures of our troubled days.

For the unity of the Church we pray, and for her fellowship across the embittered lines of race and nation; and to her growth in grace, her building in love, her enlargement in service, her increase in wisdom, faith, charity, and power we dedicate our lives; through Jesus Christ our Lord. **Amen.**

Blessed Lord, who hast caused all holy Scriptures to be written for our learning: Grant that we may in such wise hear them, read, mark, learn, and inwardly digest them, that by patience, and comfort of thy holy Word, we may embrace, and ever hold fast, the blessed hope of everlasting life, which thou hast given in our Savior Jesus Christ. **Amen.**

O God, who hast sent thy beloved Son to be unto us the way, the truth, and the life: May thy blessing attend this enlargement of our opportunities; grant us, we beseech thee, the guidance of thy Holy Spirit, that we, looking ever unto him, may set forward the teaching power of thy Church, to the nurture of thy children, the increase of thy kingdom, and the glory of thy Son Jesus Christ our Lord. **Amen.**

† *Here a hymn may be sung, after which the minister shall let the people depart with a blessing.*

An Office for the Dedication of a Church Building

† *This office may be used for the dedication of a sanctuary, a church school building, or a parish house.*

† *The service may begin with a prelude.*

† *A hymn may be sung, the people standing.*

† *Then the officiating minister shall say, the people responding,*

This is the day which the Lord has made; let us rejoice and be glad in it.

I was glad when they said to me, "Let us go to the house of the Lord!"

This is none other than the house of God, and this is the gate of heaven.

Blessed be the Lord; may his glory fill the whole earth!

† *Here let the people be seated.*

† *Then the minister shall say,*

Let us pray.

Almighty and everlasting God, whom the heaven of heavens cannot contain, yet who art willing to have a house fashioned by man, wherein thine honor dwelleth and where men may worship thee: Of thy love and mercy, we beseech thee, vouchsafe thy presence here, that this building which we have reared to the glory of thy name, and do now wholly devote and dedicate to thee, may by thee be accepted and hallowed, to the end that souls may here be gathered, nourished in thy love, and made fruitful in thy service; through Jesus Christ our Lord. **Amen.**

† *Then all shall say,*

O God, by whose providence we celebrate the dedication of this church: Send down upon us, we beseech thee, thy heavenly blessing; and, because holiness becometh thine house for ever, make us living temples, holy and acceptable unto thee; through Jesus Christ our Lord. Amen.

† *An anthem may be sung.*

† *Here let the people stand. Then this psalm shall be said responsively; all shall remain standing until after the affirmation of faith.*

The earth is the Lord's and the fulness thereof,
the world and those who dwell therein;

for he has founded it upon the seas,
  and established it upon the rivers.
Who shall ascend the hill of the Lord?
  And who shall stand in his holy place?
He who has clean hands and a pure heart,
  **who does not lift up his soul to what is false,
  and does not swear deceitfully.**
He will receive blessing from the Lord,
  and vindication from the God of his salvation.
Such is the generation of those who seek him,
  who seek the face of the God of Jacob.
Lift up your heads, O gates!
and be lifted up, O ancient doors!
  that the King of glory may come in.
Who is the King of glory?
  **The Lord, strong and mighty,
  the Lord, mighty in battle!**
Lift up your heads, O gates!
and be lifted up, O ancient doors!
  that the King of glory may come in!
Who is this King of glory?
  **The Lord of hosts,
  he is the King of glory!**   *Psalm 24*

† *Here shall be sung the* Gloria Patri.
† *Then the minister shall say,*
Let us unite in this historic confession of the Christian faith:
  **I believe in God the Father Almighty, maker of heaven and earth;
  And in Jesus Christ his only Son our Lord: who was conceived by
  the Holy Spirit, born of the Virgin Mary, suffered under Pontius
  Pilate, was crucified, dead, and buried; the third day he rose from
  the dead; he ascended into heaven, and sitteth at the right hand of
  God the Father Almighty; from thence he shall come to judge the
  quick and the dead.**
  I believe in the Holy Spirit, the holy catholic Church, the com-

356

munion of saints, the forgiveness of sins, the resurrection of the body, and the life everlasting. Amen.

† *Then shall be read one or more of the following or other lessons: I Kings 8:22-30; Isaiah 55:6-13; Matthew 16:13-18; Ephesians 2:13-22. For a church school building: Jeremiah 31:31-34; Luke 2:40-52. For a parish house: Matthew 7:24-27.*

† *Parish notices may be given.*

† *An offering may be received, after which a prayer of dedication shall be said or sung.*

† *At the discretion of the minister the offering may follow the sermon.*

† *Here a hymn may be sung.*

† *Then shall follow the sermon.*

† *Following the sermon or the offering, the officiating minister shall cause to stand before him the persons designated to present the building for dedication, who shall say,*

We present this building to be dedicated to the glory of God and the service of men.

† *When the building being dedicated is the church sanctuary, or is to bear any specific name, the minister shall say,*

By what name shall this *church* henceforth be known?

† *To which shall be answered,*

It shall be called the *N. Methodist Church.*

† *Then the minister shall say,*

Beloved in the Lord, we rejoice that God has put it into the hearts of his people to build this house to the glory of his name. I now accept this building *to be known as the N. Methodist Church,* that we may dedicate it, and so set it apart for the worship of almighty God and the service of men. Let us therefore, as we are assembled, solemnly dedicate this place to its proper and sacred uses.

† *Then, all standing, the minister shall say, the people responding,*

To the glory of God the Father, who has called us by his grace;
To the honor of his Son, who loved us and gave himself for us;
To the praise of the Holy Spirit, who illumines and sanctifies us;
 we dedicate this house.

For the worship of God in prayer and praise;
For the preaching of the everlasting Gospel;
For the celebration of the holy Sacraments;

we dedicate this house.

For the comfort of all who mourn;
For strength to those who are tempted;
For light to those who seek the way;

we dedicate this house.

For the hallowing of family life;
For teaching and guiding the young;
For the perfecting of the saints;

we dedicate this house.

For the conversion of sinners;
For the promotion of righteousness;
For the extension of the kingdom of God;

we dedicate this house.

In the unity of the faith;
In the bond of Christian brotherhood;
In charity and good will to all;

we dedicate this house.

In gratitude for the labors of all who love and serve this church;
In loving remembrance of those who have finished their course;
In the hope of a blessed immortality through Jesus Christ our Lord;

we dedicate this house.

† *Then all shall say,*

We now, the people of this church and congregation, compassed about with a great cloud of witnesses, grateful for our heritage, sensible of the sacrifice of our fathers in the faith, confessing that apart from us their work cannot be made perfect, do dedicate ourselves anew to the worship and service of almighty God; through Jesus Christ our Lord. Amen.

† *Then the officiating minister, standing by the Lord's Table, shall say,*

Let us now offer unto God our petitions and intercessions for his blessing and grace.

† *Then the minister, with other ministers whom he may invite to assist him, shall kneel before the Lord's Table, and shall severally offer one or more of the following prayers:*

O eternal God, mighty in power and of majesty supreme, whom the heavens cannot contain, much less the walls of temples made with hands: Graciously accept, we pray thee, the dedication of this house to thine honor and glory. **Amen.**

Grant, O Lord, that by thy holy Word, which shall be read and preached in this place, and by thy Holy Spirit grafting it inwardly in all hearts, the hearers thereof may both perceive and know what things they ought to do, and may have power and strength to fulfill the same. **Amen.**

Grant, O Lord, that all who here share in the Sacraments, the ministry of the Word, and the fellowship of praise and prayer may know that thou art in this place, may hear thy voice within their hearts, and may go forth to extend to the uttermost bounds of life our Lord Christ's kingdom. **Amen.**

Regard, O Lord, the supplications of thy servants, and grant that whosoever in this house shall be received by Baptism into the congregation of Christ's flock may be so empowered by the Holy Spirit as to continue Christ's faithful soldier and servant until his life's end. **Amen.**

Grant, O Lord, that they who in this church shall in their own persons renew the promises and vows taken at their Baptism, may come into the full membership of thy Church, and receive such grace through thy Holy Spirit, that they may ever continue faithful until their life's end. **Amen.**

Grant, O Lord, that whosoever shall receive in this place the Sacrament of our Lord's holy Supper, may come to that holy ordinance with faith and true repentance; and, being filled with thy grace and heavenly benediction, may to their great and endless comfort obtain remission of their sins, and continue living ever as unto thee. **Amen.**

Grant, O Lord, that whosoever shall be joined together in this place in holy matrimony may faithfully perform and keep the vow and covenant between them made, and remain in perfect love together until their life's end. **Amen.**

Grant, O Lord, that, as thy people meet in this place, to consider reverently and faithfully the affairs of the church and congregation, it may so be that all may be one in that spiritual discipline which thou dost enjoin upon thy disciples, so that they may act wisely and well as faithful stewards in the ministration of the temporal and spiritual affairs of thine earthly kingdom. **Amen.**

Almighty, everlasting God, bless, we beseech thee, and take under thy protection thy children. Pour into their hearts thy grace, that they may be here enlightened and instructed to learn what is pleasing to thee, and may grow in wisdom and stature, and in favor with thee and with their fellow men; through Jesus Christ our Lord. **Amen.**

Almighty God, who through thy Son our Lord hast called us into light, wherein we may have fellowship with thee and with one another: Grant that here thy people may meet in devotion to thee; here may thy way be taught, thy name hallowed, and thy glory praised. Here may life be nourished and guided, and the bonds of fellowship in Christ be nurtured in mutual love and selfless purpose; through Jesus Christ our Lord. **Amen.**

† *Then shall be said,*

Now, therefore, O Lord, let thine eyes be open toward this house day and night; and let thine ears be ready toward the prayers of thy children, which they shall make unto thee in this place. An whensoever thy servants shall make to thee their petitions, do thou hear them, and when thou hearest, forgive. **Amen.**

Grant, O Lord, we beseech thee, that thy ministers may be clothed with righteousness, and thy saints rejoice in thy salvation. And may we all, with thy people everywhere, grow up into a holy temple in thee, O Lord, and be at last received into the glorious temple above, the house not made with hands, eternal in the heavens. To the Father, and the Son, and the Holy Spirit, be glory and praise, world without end. **Amen.**

† *Here a hymn may be sung, after which the minister shall let the people depart with a blessing.*

An Office for the
Dedication of a School, College, or University Building

† *The service may begin with a prelude.*

† *The officiating minister shall say, the people standing and responding,*
O worship the Lord in the beauty of holiness: fear before him, all the earth.

They that worship him must worship him in spirit and in truth.

† *Then the minister shall make this declaration,*
Dearly beloved, this building, which by the favor of God and the labor of man has been so far completed, embodies the obligation of each generation to impart its treasures of wisdom and knowledge to the generation following. For the fulfillment of this task we need, not only the best that men can do, but above all the blessing of almighty God. Let us therefore bring to him our praises for his aid in this undertaking, and our prayers on behalf of those who by their gifts or their service shall unite in fulfilling the purpose for which this building is prepared.

† *Here a hymn may be sung.*

† *Here let the people be seated.*

† *Then shall be read these lessons,*

> Happy is the man who finds wisdom,
>> and the man who gets understanding,
> for the gain from it is better than gain from silver
>> and its profit better than gold.
> She is more precious than jewels,
>> and nothing you desire can compare with her.
> Long life is in her right hand;
>> in her left hand are riches and honor.
> Her ways are ways of pleasantness,
>> and all her paths are peace.
> She is a tree of life to those who lay hold of her;
>> those who hold her fast are called happy.
> The Lord by wisdom founded the earth;
>> by understanding he established the heavens;
> by his knowledge the deeps broke forth,
>> and the clouds drop down the dew.

361

My son, keep sound wisdom and discretion;
    let them not escape from your sight,
    and they will be life for your soul
        and adornment for your neck.   *Proverbs 3:13-22*

Enter by the narrow gate; for the gate is wide and the way is easy, that leads to destruction, and those who enter by it are many. For the gate is narrow and the way is hard, that leads to life, and those who find it are few.

Every one then who hears these words of mine and does them will be like a wise man who built his house upon the rock; and the rain fell, and the floods came, and the winds blew and beat upon that house, but it did not fall, because it had been founded on the rock. And every one who hears these words of mine and does not do them will be like a foolish man who built his house upon the sand; and the rain fell, and the floods came, and the winds blew and beat against that house, and it fell; and great was the fall of it.   *Matthew 7:13-14, 24-27*

† *Here a hymn may be sung.*

† *Then shall follow the address.*

† *Here an offering may be received, after which a prayer of dedication may be said or sung.*

† *Then the minister shall say, the people standing and responding,*

    Wisdom has built her house,
    she has set up her seven pillars.
      Does not wisdom call,
      does not understanding raise her voice?
    On the heights beside the way,
    in the paths she takes her stand;
      beside the gates in front of the town,
      at the entrance of the portals she cries aloud:
    "To you, O men, I call,
    and my cry is to the sons of men.
      O simple ones, learn prudence;
      O foolish men, pay attention.
    Hear, for I will speak noble things,
    and from my lips will come what is right;
      for my mouth will utter truth;
      wickedness is an abomination to my lips.

Take my instruction instead of silver,
and knowledge rather than choice gold;
for wisdom is better than jewels,
and all that you may desire cannot compare with
her."
But where shall wisdom be found?
And where is the place of understanding?
Behold, the fear of the Lord, that is wisdom;
and to depart from evil is understanding.

Proverbs 9:1; 8:1-7, 10-11; Job 28:12, 28

† *Here shall be said or sung the* Gloria Patri.

† *Here let the Board of Trustees or the proper committee stand up*
before the people, and let one of them say to the minister,

We present this building to be dedicated to the glory of almighty God,
and for his service in the enlightenment of his children.

† *If the building is to be a memorial, there shall be added,*

. . . in loving memory of *N*.

† *Then the minister shall say, the people standing and responding,*

Dearly beloved, it is right and proper that buildings erected for such
service in the name of our Lord and Savior Jesus Christ should be
formally and devoutly set apart for their special uses. For such a dedication we are now assembled. And, as the dedication of this building is vain
without the solemn consecration of those whose gifts and labors it represents, let us now give ourselves anew to the service of God: our souls,
that they may be renewed after the image of Christ; our bodies, that they
may be fit temples for the indwelling of the Holy Spirit; and our labors
and business, that they may be according to God's holy will, and that
their fruit may tend to the glory of his name and the advancement of
his kingdom.

In the name of the Father, and of the Son, and of the Holy Spirit,
we dedicate this building.

To the holy ministry of education,
we dedicate this building.

To the spiritual enrichment of all who shall come here in pursuit of
knowledge,
we dedicate this building.

To the loyal service of those whose training and devotion have prepared them to lead students toward the truth,

we dedicate this building.

To that ministry of administration upon whose ability and fruitfulness depends the wise conduct of its affairs,

we dedicate this building, and we dedicate ourselves anew to that service of our fellow men wherein can best be performed our true service of God, in obedience to the spirit of the Master when he said: "You shall love the Lord your God with all your heart, and your neighbor as yourself."

† *Then the minister shall say,*

Let us pray.

Almighty God, our heavenly Father, whose eyes are ever toward the righteous, and whose ears are ever open unto their cry: Graciously accept, we pray thee, this building which we now dedicate to thee, to thy service, and to thy glory, that in it love and wisdom may unite to make plain the path of knowledge to those who gather here; and we beseech thee, receive us thy servants who here dedicate ourselves anew to thee and to those offices of fellowship and good will in which thou art well pleased. Grant that those who come here, whether as administrators, teachers, or students, may come with pure minds, upright purpose, and steadfast endeavor to learn and to do thy holy will; through Jesus Christ our Lord. **Amen.**

God of our fathers, we offer thee our heartfelt thanks for all thy servants, the parents and teachers, the benefactors and friends, by whose love and devotion we have come into our great inheritance of health, truth, and piety. Help us to guard faithfully this great boon, to profit by it, to augment it, and loyally to pass it on to the coming generation, that they through us may rise up to serve thee; in the name of Jesus Christ our Lord. **Amen.**

† *Then the minister shall let the people depart with a blessing.*

An Office for the Dedication of a Hospital

† *The service may begin with a prelude.*

† *The officiating minister shall say, the people standing and responding,*

Our help is in the name of the Lord,

who made heaven and earth.

O give thanks to the Lord, for he is good,

for his steadfast love endures for ever.

† *Then the minister shall make this declaration,*

Dearly beloved, this building, which by the favor of God and the labor of man has been so far completed, is a symbol of that care for the sick and the suffering which was supremely exemplified in the Lord Jesus, and which has always inspired those who follow him. We believe that the heavenly Father not only desires, but gladly accepts, the service of comfort and healing for which this building is to provide, and that he looks with favor upon the dedication of the building to himself and to the welfare of his children.

Let us therefore bring to him our praises for his guidance and aid in this undertaking, and our prayers on behalf of those who by their gifts or their services shall unite in fulfilling those purposes of love and skill for which this building is prepared.

† *A hymn may be sung.*

† *Here let the people be seated.*

† *Then shall be read these lessons:*

The Spirit of the Lord God is upon me,
   because the Lord has anointed me
to bring good tidings to the afflicted;
   he has sent me to bind up the brokenhearted,
to proclaim liberty to the captives,
   and the opening of the prison to those who are
      bound;
to proclaim the year of the Lord's favor,
   and the day of vengeance of our God;
   to comfort all who mourn;

to grant to those who mourn in Zion—
> to give them a garland instead of ashes,
the oil of gladness instead of mourning,
> the mantle of praise instead of a faint spirit.
Strengthen the weak hands,
> and make firm the feeble knees.
Say to those who are of a fearful heart,
> "Be strong, fear not!
Behold, your God
> will come with vengeance,
with the recompense of God.
> He will come and save you."
Then the eyes of the blind shall be opened,
> and the ears of the deaf unstopped;
then shall the lame man leap like a hart,
> and the tongue of the dumb sing for joy.

Isaiah 61:1-3ab; 35:3-6a

The disciples of John told him of all these things. And John, calling to him two of his disciples, sent them to the Lord, saying, "Are you he who is to come, or shall we look for another?"

In that hour he cured many of diseases and plagues and evil spirits, and on many that were blind he bestowed sight. And he answered them, "Go and tell John what you have seen and heard: the blind receive their sight, the lame walk, lepers are cleansed, and the deaf hear, the dead are raised up, the poor have good news preached to them. And blessed is he who takes no offense at me."

Luke 7:18-19, 21-23

† *Here a hymn may be sung.*

† *Then may follow an address.*

† *Here an offering may be received, after which a prayer of dedication may be said or sung.*

† *Then the minister shall say, the people standing and responding,*

> Bless the Lord, O my soul;
> and all that is within me, bless his holy name!
>
> **Bless the Lord, O my soul,**
> **and forget not all his benefits,**
>
> who forgives all your iniquity,
> who heals all your diseases,

who redeems your life from the Pit,
who crowns you with steadfast love and mercy.

As a father pities his children,
so the Lord pities those who fear him.

For he knows our frame;
he remembers that we are dust.

As for man, his days are like grass;
he flourishes like a flower of the field;

for the wind passes over it, and it is gone,
and its place knows it no more.

But the steadfast love of the Lord is from everlasting
to everlasting
upon those who fear him,
and his righteousness to children's children,

to those who keep his covenant
and remember to do his commandments.

Bless the Lord, O you his angels,
you mighty ones who do his word,
hearkening to the voice of his word!

Bless the Lord, all his hosts,
his ministers that do his will!

Bless the Lord, all his works,
in all places of his dominion.

Bless the Lord, O my soul!

Psalm 103:1-4, 13-18, 20-22

† *Then shall be said or sung the* Gloria Patri.

† *Here let the Board of Trustees or the proper committee stand before the people, and let one of them say to the minister,*

We present this building to be dedicated to the glory of almighty God, and for his service in the relief of the sick and the suffering.

† *If the building is to be a memorial, there shall be added,*

. . . in loving memory of *N.*

† *Then the minister shall say, the people standing and responding,*

Dearly beloved, it is right and proper that buildings erected for such service in the name of our Lord and Savior Jesus Christ should be

367

formally and devoutly set apart for their special uses. For such a dedication we are now assembled. And, as the dedication of this building is vain without the solemn consecration of those whose gifts and labors it represents, let us now give ourselves anew to the service of God: our souls, that they may be renewed after the image of Christ; our bodies, that they may be fit temples for the indwelling of the Holy Spirit; and our labors and business, that they may be according to God's holy will, and that their fruit may tend to the glory of his name and the advancement of his kingdom.

In the name of the Father, and of the Son, and of the Holy Spirit,

we dedicate this building.

To the holy ministry of healing, and the sustaining power of the Holy Spirit in time of pain and suffering,

we dedicate this building.

To the skill and wisdom that bring relief and cure, and to the patient research that uncovers fresh resources with which to serve the public health,

we dedicate this hospital, and we dedicate ourselves anew to that service of our fellow men wherein can best be performed our true service of God, in obedience to the spirit of the Master when he said: "You shall love the Lord your God with all your heart, and your neighbor as yourself."

† *Then shall be offered one or more of the following prayers, the minister first saying,*

Let us pray.

Almighty God, our heavenly Father, whose eyes are ever toward the righteous, and whose ears are ever open unto their cry: Graciously accept, we pray thee, this building which we now dedicate to thee, to thy service, and to thy glory, that in it skill and tenderness may unite to bring health and cure to those who come for aid; and we beseech thee, receive us thy servants who here dedicate ourselves anew to thee and to those offices of love and good will in which thou art well pleased. Grant that those who come here in weakness may be made strong, that those who come in pain may find relief, and that those who come in sorrow may find joy and gladness; and the praise shall be thine forever; through Jesus Christ our Lord. **Amen.**

O blessed Lord, our heavenly Father, who hast power over life and death, over health and sickness: Give strength, wisdom, and gentleness to all thy ministering servants, all physicians and surgeons, nurses and watchers by the sick, that, always bearing thy presence with them, they may not only heal but bless, and shine as lamps of hope in the darkest hours of distress and fear; through Jesus Christ our Lord. **Amen.**

O most merciful Father, we look to thee for thy grace on behalf of those who, coming here in grievous illness, may not return to earthly joys and sorrows, but pass from here into that life immortal where thou dost receive all who put their trust in thee. Thou hast said that as the heavens are higher than the earth, so are thy ways higher than our ways; yet, knowing that all thy children are safe in thy tender and unfailing love, we pray that the blessed ministry of thy Holy Spirit may sustain them, and that light eternal may shine upon them. **Amen.**

And now, O loving Father, we bow before thee, of whom the whole family in heaven and earth is named, praying that thou wilt grant us, according to the riches of thy glory, to be strengthened with might by thy Spirit in the inner man; that Christ may dwell in our hearts by faith; that we, being rooted and grounded in love, may be able to comprehend with all the saints what is the breadth and length and height and depth, and to know the love of Christ which surpasses knowledge, that we may be filled with all the fulness of God. **Amen.**

† *Then the minister shall let the people depart with a blessing.*

An Office for the
Dedication of a Church Organ or Other Instruments
for Sacred Music

† *This office is intended for use within an order of worship. When used separately, appropriate Scripture sentences, lessons, acts of praise, and prayers may be added.*

† *The minister shall cause to stand before him the donor or one designated for this purpose, who, naming the instrument, shall say,*

We present this *organ* to be dedicated to the glory of almighty God, and for service in this church.

† *If the instrument is to be a memorial, there shall be added,*

. . . in loving memory of *N.*

† *Then the minister shall say, the people standing and responding,*

It is good to give thanks to the Lord,

to sing praises to thy name, O Most High;

to declare thy steadfast love in the morning,

and thy faithfulness by night,

to the music of the lute and the harp,

to the melody of the lyre.

For thou, O Lord, hast made me glad by thy work;

at the works of thy hands I sing for joy. *Psalm 92:1-4*

† *Then shall be said or sung by all the* Gloria Patri.

† *Here dedicatory music shall be played on the instrument or instruments to be dedicated, the people seated.*

† *After which the minister shall say,*

Our Father, whom the generations have worshiped with concord of sweet sound: Be pleased to accept this instrument as a means of praising thee. Grant that its music may be a blessed benediction upon all who worship here. Vouchsafe, we beseech thee, to all musicians who shall sound its notes, and to all worshipers who shall be lifted godward by its voice, that there may come at times the sweep of hallelujahs, from the heavenly hosts, and the whispers of thy voice from thine eternal grace. **Amen.**

Therefore with angels and archangels, and with all the company of heaven, we laud and magnify thy glorious name, evermore praising thee and saying:

† *Then all shall sing or say,*

Holy, holy, holy, Lord God of hosts: Heaven and earth are full of thy glory! Glory be to thee, O Lord most high! Amen.

† *If this be the conclusion of the service, the minister shall let the people depart with a blessing.*

An Office for the Dedication of a Memorial

† *This office is intended for use within an order of worship. When used separately, appropriate Scripture, hymns, and prayers may be added.*

† *The minister shall cause to stand before him the donor or one designated to present the memorial, who, naming the memorial, shall say,*

We present this *memorial* to be dedicated to the glory of almighty God, and for service in this church, in loving memory of N.

† *To which one designated to accept the memorial may say,*

We accept this gift as a sacred trust, and shall guard it reverently, in honor of the faithful and devoted life in whose memory it is given.

† *Then the minister shall say,*

In the name of the Father, and of the Son, and of the Holy Spirit, we dedicate this *memorial* to the glory of God, and in memory of his *servant* N. The memory of the righteous is ever blessed.

Give unto the Lord the glory due unto his name; worship the Lord in the beauty of holiness.

Let us pray.

Almighty God our heavenly Father, without whom no words or works of ours have meaning, but who dost accept the gifts of our hands as the tokens of our devotion: Grant thy blessing upon us as we dedicate this gift to thy glory. May this memorial which we now dedicate be an enduring witness before all thy people of the faithful service of thy servant. May our lives, being consecrated unto thy service, be joined with thy faithful ones into that building which groweth unto a holy temple in the Lord. **Amen.**

† *If this be the conclusion of the service, the minister shall let the people depart with a blessing.*

An Office for the Blessing of a Dwelling

† *The minister shall read one or more of the following Scripture sentences:*

Grace to you and peace from God our Father and the Lord Jesus Christ.
Romans 1:7b

Beloved, let us love one another; for love is of God, and he who loves is born of God, and knows God.
I John 4:7

If we love one another, God abides in us and his love is perfected in us.
I John 4:12b

† *Then the minister shall say,*

Dearly beloved, we have gathered here to seek God's blessing upon this home, which, by the favor of God and the labor of man, has been so far completed, and which is a symbol of that loving care which was bestowed upon the world by our heavenly Father, and exemplified in the life of our Lord Jesus Christ.

Let us therefore bring to him our praise and thanksgiving for his goodness and mercy, and give ourselves anew to his service: our souls, that they may be renewed after the image of Christ; our bodies, that they may be fit temples for the indwelling of the Holy Spirit; our labors and love, that they may be according to God's holy will.

Let us pray.

O God, who dost govern all things in heaven and earth, and dost make all things new through thine almighty Word: Every day we give thanks unto thee, and praise thy name for ever and ever. Shed forth upon us, we beseech thee, thine everlasting light that we, beholding thy glory, may be ever devoted to thee, by whose wisdom we were created, by whose providence we are governed, and by whose love we are redeemed; through Jesus Christ our Lord. **Amen.**

† *Then all shall say,*

Our Father, who art in heaven, hallowed be thy name. Thy kingdom come, thy will be done on earth as it is in heaven. Give us this day our daily bread. And forgive us our trespasses, as we forgive those who trespass against us. And lead us not into temptation, but deliver us from evil. For thine is the kingdom, and the power, and the glory, forever. Amen.

† *Then may be read this lesson.*

For this reason I bow my knees before the Father, from whom every family in heaven and on earth is named, that according to the riches of his glory he may grant you to be strengthened with might through his Spirit in the inner man, and that Christ may dwell in your hearts through faith; that you, being rooted and grounded in love, may have power to comprehend with all the saints what is the breadth and length and height and depth, and to know the love of Christ which surpasses knowledge, that you may be filled with all the fulness of God.

Now to him who by the power at work within us is able to do far more abundantly than all that we ask or think, to him be glory in the church and in Christ Jesus to all generations, for ever and ever. Amen.

Ephesians 3:14-21

† *Then the minister shall say, the people responding,*

In the name of the Father, and of the Son, and of the Holy Spirit, we bless this home, committing to God's love and care this house and all who dwell therein.

Glory be to God most high!

† *Then the minister shall say,*

Unless the Lord builds the house, those who build it labor in vain.

Psalm 127:1

By wisdom a house is built, and by understanding it is established; by knowledge the rooms are filled with all precious and pleasant riches.

Proverbs 24:3-4

Let us pray.

O almighty God, whose Son our Lord did by his presence bless the home in Bethany: Bless, we beseech thee, this home, that thy love may rest upon it, and that thy promised presence may be manifest in it. May all the members of this household grow in grace and in the knowledge of thee, and of our Lord and Savior Jesus Christ. Teach them to love one another as thou didst give us commandment; and help us all to choose that better part which shall not be taken away from us; through the same Jesus Christ our Lord. **Amen.**

The Lord bless you and keep you; the Lord make his face to shine upon you, and be gracious to you; the Lord lift up his countenance upon **you,** and give you peace, now and for evermore. **Amen.**

V

Services in the
Methodist Tradition

The Order for Morning Prayer

In 1784 John Wesley sent to the Methodist societies in America, then in the process of becoming the Methodist Episcopal Church, *The Sunday Service of the Methodists in North America, with other occasional services.*

This consisted of Mr. Wesley's adaptation of such basic services from the Book of Common Prayer of the Church of England as Morning and Evening Prayer, the orders for the administration of the Sacraments, the litany, and other offices. While edited versions of *The Order for Morning Prayer* from this collection have been variously printed elsewhere, it is here reproduced in the original form as prepared by Mr. Wesley.

Every Lord's Day

At the Beginning of Morning Prayer, the Minister shall read with a loud Voice some one or more of these Sentences of the Scriptures that follow: And then he shall say that which is written after the said Sentences.

When the wicked man turneth away from his wickedness that he hath committed, and doeth that which is lawful and right, he shall save his soul alive. *Ezek.* xviii. 27.

The sacrifices of God are a broken spirit: a broken and a contrite heart, O God, thou wilt not despise. *Psal.* li. 17.

To the Lord our God belong mercies and forgiveness, though we have rebelled against him: neither have we obeyed the voice of the Lord our God, to walk in his laws which he set before us. *Dan.* ix. 9, 10.

I will arise, and go to my father, and will say unto him, Father, I have sinned against Heaven and before thee, and am no more worthy to be called thy son. *Luke* xv. 18, 19.

Enter not into judgment with thy servant, O Lord; for in thy sight shall no man living be justified. *Psal.* cxliii. 2.

Dearly beloved brethren, the Scripture moveth us, in sundry places, to acknowledge and confess our manifold sins and wickedness, and that we should not dissemble or cloke them before the face of Almighty God, our heavenly Father; but confess them with an humble, lowly, penitent, and obedient heart; to the end that we may obtain forgiveness of the same, by his infinite goodness and mercy. Wherefore I pray and beseech you, as many as are here present, to accompany me with a pure heart and humble voice, unto the throne of the heavenly grace, saying after me.

A general Confession, to be said by the whole Congregation, after the Minister, all kneeling.

Almighty and most merciful Father, We have erred and strayed from thy ways like lost sheep. We have followed too much the devices and desires of our own hearts. We have offended against thy holy laws. We have left undone those things which we ought to have done; And we have done those things which we ought not to have done; And there is no health in us. But thou, O Lord, have mercy upon us, miserable offenders. Spare thou them, O God, which confess their faults. Restore thou them that are penitent; According to thy promises declared unto mankind in Christ Jesus our Lord. And grant, O most merciful Father, for his sake, That we may hereafter live a godly, righteous, and sober life; To the glory of thy holy Name. Amen.

Then the Minister shall say,

O Lord, we beseech thee, absolve thy people from their offences; that, through thy bountiful goodness, we may be delivered from the bands of those sins, which by our frailty we have committed. Grant this, O Heavenly Father, for Jesus Christ's sake, our blessed Lord and Saviour.

The People shall answer here, and at the End of all other Prayers. Amen.

Then the Minister shall say the Lord's Prayer; the People also repeating it with him, both here, and wheresoever else it is used in Divine Service.

Our Father who art in Heaven, Hallowed be thy Name; Thy kingdom come; Thy Will be done on Earth, As it is in Heaven: Give us this day our daily bread; And forgive us our trespasses, As we forgive them that trespass against us; And lead us not into temptation; But deliver us from evil: For thine is the Kingdom, and the Power, and the Glory, For ever and ever. Amen.

Then likewise he shall say,

O Lord, open thou our lips.

Answ. And our mouth shall shew forth thy praise.

Minist. O God, make speed to save us;

Answ. O Lord, make haste to help us.

Here all standing up, the Minister shall say,

Glory be to the Father, and to the Son, and to the Holy Ghost;

Answ. As it was in the beginning, is now, and ever shall be, world without end. Amen.

Minist. Praise ye the Lord.

Answ. The Lord's Name be praised.

Then shall follow the Psalms, in order as they are appointed. And at the End of every Psalm, shall be repeated,

Glory be to the Father, and to the Son, and to the Holy Ghost;

As it was in the beginning, is now, and ever shall be, world without end. Amen.

Then shall be read distinctly, the First Lesson taken out of the Old Testament, as is appointed in the Table of proper Lessons: He that readeth, so standing, and turning himself as he may be best heard of all. And after that, shall be said the following Hymn:

We praise thee, O God: we acknowledge thee to be the Lord.

All the earth doth worship thee, the Father everlasting.

To thee all Angels cry aloud: the Heavens, and all the powers therein.

To thee Cherubim and Seraphim continually do cry,

Holy, holy, holy, Lord God of Sabaoth;

Heaven and Earth are full of the Majesty of thy Glory.

The glorious company of the Apostles praise thee.

The goodly fellowship of the Prophets praise thee.

The noble army of Martyrs praise thee.

The Holy Church throughout all the world doth acknowledge thee;

The Father of an infinite Majesty;

Thine honourable, true, and only Son;

Also the Holy Ghost, the Comforter.

Thou art the King of glory, O Christ;

Thou art the everlasting Son of the Father.

When thou tookest upon thee to deliver man, thou didst not abhor the Virgin's womb.

When thou hadst overcome the sharpness of death, thou didst open the kingdom of Heaven to all believers.

Thou sittest at the right hand of God, in the glory of the Father.

We believe that thou shalt come to be our Judge.

We therefore pray thee, help thy servants, whom thou hast redeemed with thy precious blood.

Make them to be numbered with thy Saints in glory everlasting.

O Lord, save thy people, and bless thine heritage.

Govern them, and lift them up for ever.

Day by day we magnify thee;

And we worship thy name ever, world without end.

Vouchsafe, O Lord, to keep us this day without sin.

O Lord, have mercy upon us: have mercy upon us.

O Lord, let thy mercy lighten upon us, as our trust is in thee.

O Lord, in thee have I trusted: let me never be confounded.

Then shall be read in like manner the Second Lesson, taken out of the New Testament: and after that, the following Psalm:

O Be joyful in the Lord, all ye lands: serve the Lord with gladness, and come before his presence with a song.

Be ye sure that the Lord he is God; it is he that hath made us, and not we ourselves: we are his people, and the sheep of his pasture.

O go your way into his gates with thanksgiving, and into his courts with praise: be thankful unto him, and speak good of his Name.

For the Lord is gracious, his mercy is everlasting: and his truth endureth from generation to generation.

Glory be to the Father, and to the Son, and to the Holy Ghost;

As it was in the beginning, is now, and ever shall be, world without end. Amen.

Then shall be said the Apostles' Creed by the Minister and the People, standing.

I Believe in God the Father Almighty, Maker of Heaven and Earth:

And in Jesus Christ his only Son our Lord; Who was conceived by the Holy Ghost; Born of the Virgin Mary; Suffered under Pontius Pilate; Was crucified, dead, and buried, He descended into hell: The third day he rose again from the dead: He ascended into Heaven, And sitteth on the right hand of God, the Father Almighty; From thence he shall come to judge the quick and the dead.

I believe in the Holy Ghost; The Holy Catholick Church; The Communion of Saints; The Forgiveness of Sins; The Resurrection of the Body, And the Life everlasting. Amen.

And after that, the Minister shall pronounce with a loud Voice,

The Lord be with you;

Answ. And with thy spirit.

Minister. Let us pray.

Lord, have mercy upon us.

Answ. Christ have mercy upon us.

Minist. Lord, have mercy upon us.

Then shall follow three Collects; the first of the Day, which shall be the same that is appointed at the Communion; the second for Peace; the third for Grace to live well; all devoutly kneeling.

The second Collect, for Peace.

O God, who art the author of peace, and lover of concord, in knowledge of whom standeth our eternal life, whose service is perfect freedom; Defend us thy humble servants in all assaults of our enemies; that we, surely trusting in thy defence, may not fear the power of any adversaries, through the might of Jesus Christ our Lord. Amen.

The Third Collect, for Grace.

O Lord our heavenly Father, Almighty and everlasting God, who hast safely brought us to the beginning of this day; defend us in the same with thy mighty power; and grant that this day we fall into no sin; neither run into any kind of danger: but that all our doings may be ordered by thy governance, to do always that is righteous in thy sight, through Jesus Christ our Lord. Amen.

Then these Prayers following are to be read.
A Prayer for the Supreme Rulers.

O Lord, our heavenly Father, high and mighty, King of kings, Lord of lords, the only Ruler of princes, who dost from thy throne behold all the dwellers upon earth; Most heartily we beseech thee, with thy favour to behold the Supreme Rulers of these United States, and so replenish them with the grace of thy Holy Spirit, that they may alway incline to thy will, and walk in thy way; through Jesus Christ our Lord. Amen.

Almighty God, who hast given us grace at this time with one accord, to make our common supplications unto thee, and dost promise that when two or three are gathered together in thy Name, thou wilt grant their requests; Fulfil now, O Lord, the desires and petitions of thy servants, as may be most expedient for them: granting us in this world knowledge of thy truth, and in the world to come life everlasting. Amen.

2 Cor. xiii 14.

The grace of our Lord Jesus Christ, and the love of God, and the fellowship of the Holy Ghost, be with you all evermore. Amen.

Here endeth the Order of Morning Prayer

An Order of Worship
for Such as Would Enter into
or Renew Their Covenant with God

For Use in a Watch Night Service,
on the First Sunday of the Year, or Other Occasion

"On December 25, 1747, John Wesley strongly urged the Methodists to renew their Covenant with God. His first Covenant Service was held in the French Church at Spitalfields on August 11, 1755, when he recited the words of 'that blessed man Richard Alleine,' which he published that year in the 'Christian Library.' Wesley issued this as a pamphlet in 1780, and the form was used without alteration for nearly a century. Various modifications were then made, till a form was prepared which gave the people a larger share in the devotions. That form has now been revised with a deep sense of the importance of a service which has been a fruitful source of blessing to Methodism ever since 1755."

The Book of Offices, The Methodist Church
of Great Britain and Ireland

The covenant hymn, "Come, let us use the grace divine," was written for this service by Charles Wesley.

† *Let the service of worship begin at the time appointed. Let the people kneel or bow in silent prayer upon entering the sanctuary.*

† *The following or some other suitable hymn shall be sung:*

> Come, let us use the grace divine,
>   And all, with one accord,
> In a perpetual covenant join
>   Ourselves to Christ the Lord:
>
> Give up ourselves, through Jesus' power,
>   His name to glorify;
> And promise, in this sacred hour,
>   For God to live and die.
>
> The covenant we this moment make
>   Be ever kept in mind:
> We will no more our God forsake,
>   Or cast his words behind.

We never will throw off his fear
  Who hears our solemn vow;
And if thou art well pleased to hear,
  Come down, and meet us now.

To each the covenant blood apply,
  Which takes our sins away;
And registers our names on high,
  And keep us to that day. Amen.

† *After this the minister shall say,*

Let us pray.

Almighty God, unto whom all hearts are open, all desires known, and from whom no secrets are hid: Cleanse the thoughts of our hearts by the inspiration of thy Holy Spirit, that we may perfectly love thee, and worthily magnify thy holy name; through Christ our Lord. **Amen.**

† *Then all shall say,*

Our Father, who art in heaven, hallowed be thy name. Thy kingdom come, thy will be done on earth as it is in heaven. Give us this day our daily bread. And forgive us our trespasses, as we forgive those who trespass against us. And lead us not into temptation, but deliver us from evil. For thine is the kingdom, and the power, and the glory, forever. Amen.

† *Then shall be read John 15:1-8, the people being seated.*

† *Then the minister shall say,*

Dearly beloved, the Christian life, to which we are called, is a life in Christ, redeemed from sin by him, and through him consecrated to God. Upon this life we have entered, having been admitted into that new covenant of which our Lord Jesus Christ is mediator, and which he sealed with his own blood, that it might stand forever.

On one side the covenant is God's promise that he will fulfill in and through us all that he declared in Jesus Christ, who is the author and perfecter of our faith. That his promise still stands we are sure, for we have known his goodness and proved his grace in our lives day by day.

On the other side we stand pledged to live no more unto ourselves, but to him who loved us and gave himself for us and called us to serve him that the purposes of his coming be fulfilled.

From time to time we renew our vows of consecration, especially when we gather at the table of the Lord; but on this day we meet expressly, as generations of our fathers have met, that we may joyfully and solemnly renew the covenant which bound them and binds us to God.

Let us then, remembering the mercies of God and the hope of his calling, examine ourselves by the light of his Spirit, that we may see wherein we have failed or fallen short in faith and practice and, considering all that this covenant means, may give ourselves anew to God.

ADORATION

† *Then the minister shall say, the people responding,*

Let us adore the Father, the God of love who created us;
who every moment preserves and sustains us;
who has loved us with an everlasting love, and given us the light of the knowledge of his glory in the face of Jesus Christ.

We praise thee, O God; we acknowledge thee to be the Lord.

Let us glory in the grace of our Lord Jesus Christ;
who, though he was rich, yet for our sakes became poor;
who went about doing good and preaching the Gospel of the kingdom;
who was tempted in all points like as we are, yet without sin;
who became obedient unto death, even the death of the cross;
who was dead, and liveth for evermore;
who opened the kingdom of heaven to all believers;
who sitteth at the right hand of God in the glory of the Father.

Thou art the King of glory, O Christ.

Let us rejoice in the fellowship of the Holy Spirit, the Lord and giver of life, by whom we are born into the family of God, and made members of the body of Christ;
whose witness confirms us;
whose wisdom teaches us;
whose power enables us;
who waits to do for us exceeding abundantly above all that we ask or think.

All praise to thee, O Holy Spirit. Amen.

† *Here shall follow a period of silent prayer.*

THANKSGIVING

† *Then the minister shall say, the people responding,*

Let us rise and give thanks to God for his manifold mercies.

† *Here let the people stand.*

O God our Father, the fountain of all goodness, who hast been gracious to us through all the years of our life: We give thee thanks for thy loving-kindness which hath filled our days and brought us to this time and place.

We praise thy holy name, O Lord.

Thou hast given us life and reason, and set us in a world which is full of thy glory. Thou hast comforted us with kindred and friends, and ministered to us through the hands and minds of our fellows.

We praise thy holy name, O Lord.

Thou hast set in our hearts a hunger for thee, and given us thy peace. Thou hast redeemed us and called us to a high calling in Christ Jesus. Thou hast given us a place in the fellowship of thy Spirit and the witness of thy Church.

We praise thy holy name, O Lord.

In darkness thou hast been our light, in adversity and temptation a rock of strength, in our joys the very spirit of joy, in our labors the all-sufficient reward.

We praise thy holy name, O Lord.

Thou hast remembered us when we have forgotten thee, followed us even when we fled from thee, met us with forgiveness when we turned back to thee. For all thy long-suffering and the abundance of thy grace,

We praise thy holy name, O Lord. Amen.

† *Here shall follow a period of silent prayer, the people seated.*

CONFESSION

† *Then the minister shall say, the people responding,*

Let us now examine ourselves before God, humbly confessing our sins and watching our hearts, lest by self-deceit we shut ourselves out from his presence.

Let us pray.

O God our Father, who hast set forth the way of life for us in thy beloved Son: We confess with shame our slowness to learn of him, our reluctance to follow him. Thou hast spoken and called, and we have not given heed; thy beauty hath shone forth, and we have been blind; thou hast stretched out thy hands to us through our fellows, and we have passed by. We have taken great benefits with little thanks; we have been unworthy of thy changeless love.

Have mercy upon us and forgive us, O Lord.

Forgive us, we beseech thee, the poverty of our worship, the formality and selfishness of our prayers, our inconstancy and unbelief, our neglect of fellowship and of the means of grace, our hesitating witness for Christ, our false pretenses, and our willful ignorance of thy ways.

Have mercy upon us and forgive us, O Lord.

Forgive us wherein we have wasted our time or misused our gifts. Forgive us wherein we have excused our own wrongdoing or evaded our responsibilities. Forgive us that we have been unwilling to overcome evil with good, that we have drawn back from the cross.

Have mercy upon us and forgive us, O Lord.

Forgive us that so little of thy love hath reached others through us, and that we have borne so lightly wrongs and sufferings that were not our own. Forgive us wherein we have cherished the things that divide us from others, and wherein we have made it hard for them to live with us, and wherein we have been thoughtless in our judgments, hasty in condemnation, grudging in forgiveness.

Have mercy upon us and forgive us, O Lord.

If we have made no ventures in fellowship, if we have kept in our heart a grievance against another, if we have not sought reconciliation, if we have been eager for the punishment of wrongdoers and slow to seek their redemption,

Have mercy upon us and forgive us, O Lord.

† *Then, the people still kneeling or bowed, the minister shall rise and say,*

Let each of us in silence make confession to God.

† *After a period of silent prayer the minister and people shall say,*

Have mercy upon me, O God, according to thy lovingkindness; according to the multitude of thy tender mercies blot out my transgressions. Wash me thoroughly from mine iniquity, and cleanse me from my sin. Create in me a clean heart, O God; and renew a right spirit within me. Amen.

† *Then the minister shall say,*

This is the message we have heard from him, and proclaim to you, that God is light, and in him is no darkness at all. If we walk in the light, as he is in the light, we have fellowship one with another, and the blood of

Jesus Christ his Son cleanses us from all sin. If we say we have no sin, we deceive ourselves, and the truth is not in us. If we confess our sins, he is faithful and just, and will forgive our sins, and cleanse us from all unrighteousness.

† *Here shall be sung a hymn.*

THE COVENANT

† *Then, the people standing, the minister shall say,*
And now, beloved, let us bind ourselves with willing bonds to our covenant God, and take the yoke of Christ upon us.

This taking of his yoke upon us means that we are heartily content that he appoint us our place and work, and that he alone be our reward.

Christ has many services to be done; some are easy, others are difficult; some bring honor, others bring reproach; some are suitable to our natural inclinations, and temporal interests, others are contrary to both. In some we may please Christ and please ourselves; in others we cannot please Christ except by denying ourselves. Yet the power to do all these things is assuredly given us in Christ, who strengthens us.

Therefore let us make the covenant of God our own. Let us engage our heart to the Lord, and resolve in his strength never to go back.

Being thus prepared, let us now, in sincere dependence on his grace and trusting in his promises, yield ourselves anew to him.

† *Here let the people kneel or bow, and the minister say in the name of all,*
O Lord God, holy Father, who hast called us through Christ to be partakers in this gracious covenant: We take upon ourselves with joy the yoke of obedience, and engage ourselves, for love of thee, to seek and do thy perfect will. We are no longer our own, but thine.

† *Then all shall say,*
I am no longer my own, but thine. Put me to what thou wilt, rank me with whom thou wilt; put me to doing, put me to suffering; let me be employed for thee or laid aside for thee, exalted for thee or brought low for thee; let me be full, let me be empty; let me have all things, let me have nothing; I freely and heartily yield all things to thy pleasure and disposal.

And now, O glorious and blessed God, Father, Son, and Holy Spirit, thou art mine, and I am thine. So be it. And the covenant which I have made on earth, let it be ratified in heaven. Amen.

† *Here all shall stand and say or sing responsively,*
Lift up your hearts.

We lift them up unto the Lord.

Let us give thanks unto the Lord.

It is meet and right so to do.

It is very meet, right, and our bounden duty that we should at all times and in all places give thanks unto thee, O Lord, holy Father, almighty, everlasting God.

Therefore with angels and archangels, and with all the company of heaven, we laud and magnify thy glorious name, evermore praising thee, and saying:

Holy, holy, holy, Lord God of hosts: Heaven and earth are full of thy glory! Glory be to thee, O Lord most high! Amen.

† *Then may follow the Holy Communion, beginning with the prayer of consecration; or else immediately a hymn may be sung and a blessing given.*

A Form for Use in Observance of the Love Feast

† *Traditionally, worshipers were seated in a circle or around a table. Bread was broken into small portions, or a common loaf was passed from hand to hand. A loving cup with two handles was provided for water, but later individual glasses were used.*

A HYMN OF PRAISE

THE SCRIPTURE

VOLUNTARY PRAYERS AND THE LORD'S PRAYER

AN ADDRESS

A HYMN OF CHRISTIAN FELLOWSHIP

THE PASSING OF THE BREAD   † *Here this blessing shall be said:*
Blessed art thou, O Lord, God of the universe, who dost bring forth bread from the earth. **Amen.**

OFFERING FOR THE POOR

THE PASSING OF THE CUP   † *Here this promise shall be said:*
Jesus Christ said, Whosoever drinketh of the water that I shall give him shall never thirst. **Amen.**

A THANKSGIVING IN UNISON   † *To be said by all:*

Blessed art thou, O God, the author of all sustenance, who hast nourished us from our youth up. Fill, we beseech thee, our hearts with joyfulness, that in thy bountiful providence we may serve thee with every good work; through Jesus Christ our Lord, to whom with thee and the Holy Ghost be all glory and power, honor and worship, both now and for evermore. Amen.

TESTIMONIES

A HYMN OF THANKSGIVING

A BLESSING

Resources for Use in the Observance of Aldersgate Sunday

FROM JOHN WESLEY'S *Journal,* May, 1738

After describing his renunciation of all dependence on his own good works as the ground of hope for salvation, and his earnest though as yet unavailing search for a "justifying, saving faith," and a "trust" in Christ for his sole "justification, sanctification, and redemption," Mr. Wesley went on to write:

"I continued thus to seek it (though with strange indifference, dullness, and coldness, and unusually frequent relapses into sin) till *Wednesday,* May 24. I think it was about five this morning, that I opened my Testament on those words, 'There are given unto us exceeding great and precious promises, even that ye should be partakers of the divine nature' (2 Pet. i. 4). Just as I went out, I opened it again on those words, 'Thou art not far from the kingdom of God.' In the afternoon I was asked to go to St. Paul's. The anthem was, 'Out of the deep have I called unto Thee, O Lord: Lord, hear my voice. . . . O Israel, trust in the Lord: for with the Lord there is mercy, and with Him is plenteous redemption.'

"In the evening I went very unwillingly to a society in Aldersgate Street, where one was reading Luther's *Preface to the Epistle to the Romans.* About a quarter before nine, while he was describing the change which God works in the heart through faith in Christ, I felt my heart strangely warmed. I felt I did trust in Christ, Christ alone for salvation; and an assurance was given me that He had taken away *my* sins, even *mine,* and saved *me* from the law of sin and death.

"I began to pray with all my might for those who had in a more especial manner despitefully used me and persecuted me. I then testified openly to all there what I now first felt in my heart. But it was not long before the enemy suggested, 'This cannot be faith; for where is thy joy?' Then was I taught that peace and victory over sin are essential to faith in the Captain of our salvation; but that, as to the transports of joy that usually attend the beginning of it, especially in those who have mourned deeply, God sometimes giveth, sometimes withholdeth them, according to the counsels of His own will."

From Luther's Preface to the Epistle to the Romans

To fulfill the law is to do with willingness and love the works which the law requires.

Such willingness is bestowed upon us by the Holy Spirit through faith in Jesus Christ.

But the Spirit is not given except through the word of God which preaches Christ.

As Paul said: "If thou shalt confess with thy mouth the Lord Jesus, and shalt believe in thine heart that God hath raised him from the dead, thou shalt be saved."

So faith makes righteous for it brings the Spirit through the merits of Christ.

And the Spirit makes the heart free and willing as the law requires; and then good works proceed of themselves from faith.

Now sin is not only outward bodily action but inner impulse as well.

No outward deed can be committed unless the whole man exerts himself in the doing of it.

Unbelief arouses sin and the inclination to do evil.

Faith brings the Spirit with its inclination to do good works.

Grace is the good will or favor of God toward us which moved him to share Christ and the Holy Spirit with us.

Therefore, when we believe in Christ, we have the beginning of the Spirit in us.

Faith is a divine work in us, which transforms us, begets us anew from God, bringing with it the Holy Spirit.

O this faith is a living, busy, active, powerful thing!

Such confidence and personal knowledge of divine grace makes its possessor joyful, bold, and full of warm affection toward God and all created things—

All of which the Holy Spirit works in us through faith. Pray God that he may work this faith in you.

An Aldersgate Prayer

O almighty God, who in a time of great need didst raise up thy servants John and Charles Wesley, and by thy Spirit didst inspire them to kindle a flame of sacred love which leaped and ran, an inextinguishable blaze: Grant, we beseech thee, that all those whose hearts have been warmed at these altar fires, being continually refreshed by thy grace, may be so devoted to the increase of Scriptural holiness throughout the land, that in this our time of great need, thy will may fully and effectively be done on earth as it is in heaven; through Jesus Christ our Lord. **Amen.**

Acknowledgment of Sources

Acknowledgment is due authors and publishers who have granted permission for use of copyright materials in this book. They are listed below, and specific items in the Index of First lines are identified by the initials preceding these sources.

ACF   A. Campbell Fraser, *A Book of Prayers*. Oxford: Basil Blackwell & Mott, 1932.

AD   *Acts of Devotion,* compiled by F. W. Dwelly. London: SPCK, 1927.

AFT   A. F. Thornhill, *Family Prayers*. London: Longmans, Green & Co., 1908.

BCS   *A Book of Church Services*. Boston: Pilgrim Press, 1922.

BO   *The Book of Offices*. 3rd ed. New York: The Church Pension Fund, 1960.

BP   John Heuss, *A Book of Prayers*. New York: Morehouse-Barlow, 1957.

BPS   *A Book of Prayers for Schools,* edited by Hugh Martin. London: SCM Press, 1936.

BPSt   *A Book of Prayers for Students*. 4th ed. London: SCM Press, 1923.

BWFC   *A Book of Worship for Free Churches*. New York: Oxford University Press, 1948.

CBB   Eric Milner-White, *The Cambridge Bede Book*. London: Longmans, Green & Co.

CFM   C. F. Miller, *Prayers for Parish Worship*. London: Oxford University Press, 1948.

CHB   Charles H. Brent, *With God in Prayer*. Philadelphia: Macrae-Smith, 1907.

CMJ   Charles Michael Jacobs, *Helps on the Road*. Philadelphia: United Lutheran Publishing House, 1933.

COC   *The Book of Common Order of the United Church of Canada*. Toronto: United Church Publishing House, 1932.

COS   *The Book of Common Order of the Church of Scotland*. By Authority of the General Assembly. London: Oxford University Press, 1952.

CSB   *Common Service Book of the Lutheran Church*. Philadelphia: The United Lutheran Church in America, 1919.

CSI   *The Book of Common Worship of the Church of South India*. London: Oxford University Press, 1962.

CSM   Charles S. Martin, in Rodemayer, *The Pastor's Prayerbook*.

CWC   *The Book of Common Worship,* edited by W. P. Thirkield and Oliver Huckel. New York: E. P. Dutton & Co., 1932.

CWM   Charles W. Merriam, *Church Worship Book.* Boston: Pilgrim Press, 1931.

DHC   Bishop Douglas H. Crick.

DRJ   Donald R. Jessup.

DW   *Divine Worship.* Approved by the Conference for Optional Use in Methodist Churches. London: Epworth Press, 1935.

EBW   Edwin B. Womack.

EFT   Ernest Fremont Tittle, *A Book of Pastoral Prayers.* Nashville: Abingdon Press, 1951.

EL   Elvet Lewis, *The Book of Jeremiah.* London: Lutterworth Press.

EXL   G. F. Cope, J. G. Davies, and D. A. Tytler, *An Experimental Liturgy.* Richmond: John Knox Press, 1958.

FBM   F. B. Macnutt, *The Prayer Manual.* London: A. R. Mowbray, 1951.

FCBP   *A Free Church Book of Common Prayer.* New York: E. P. Dutton & Co., 1929.

FDG   Fred D. Gealy.

FRB   Bishop F. R. Barry

GV   Gregory Vlastos.

HA   Harold Anson.

HEF   Harry Emerson Fosdick, *A Book of Public Prayers.* New York: Harper & Row, 1959.

HVD 32   Henry van Dyke, in *The Book of Common Worship.* Rev. ed. Philadelphia: Board of Christian Education of the Presbyterian Church, U.S.A., 1932.

HVD 46   Henry van Dyke, in *The Book of Common Worship.* Philadelphia: Board of Christian Education of the Presbyterian Church, U.S.A., 1946.

ICF   Industrial Christian Fellowship, prayer in Macnutt, *The Prayer Manual.*

JB   John Baillie, *A Diary of Private Prayer.* New York: Charles Scribner's Sons, 1936.

JCB   Bishop James C. Baker.

JFN   Joseph Fort Newton, *Altar Stairs.* New York: The Macmillan Company, 1928.

JH   John Hunter, *Devotional Services.* London: J. M. Dent & Sons, 1936.

JMT   J. M. Todd, *Prayers and Services for Christian Festivals.* London: The Independent Press, 1951.

JUS   John Underwood Stephens, *Prayers of the Christian Life.* New York: Oxford University Press, 1952.

KPG   *The Kingdom, the Power, and the Glory.* An American Edition of the Grey Book. New York: Oxford University Press, 1933.

LBB   Fred D. Gealy, *Let Us Break Bread Together.* Nashville: Abingdon Press, 1960.

NBH   Bishop Nolan B. Harmon.

ACKNOWLEDGMENT OF SOURCES

OJH   Bishop Oliver J. Hart.

OS   *Occasional Services for the Use of the Lutheran Churches Cooperating in the Commission on the Liturgy and Hymnal.* Minneapolis: Augsburg Publishing House, 1962.

PB   Paul Burt.

PCL   *Prayers for the Church Service League.* Boston: Protestant Episcopal Diocese of Massachusetts, 1937.

PCY   *Prayers for the Christian Year.* By Authority of the General Assembly of the Church of Scotland. London: Oxford University Press, 1935.

PD   Percy Dearmer, *The Sanctuary.* London: Rivingtons, 1905.

PNW   John W. Suter, *Prayers for a New World.* New York: Charles Scribner's Sons, 1964.

POS   John W. Suter, *Prayers of the Spirit.* New York: Harper & Row, 1943.

RN   Reinhold Niebuhr.

RNR   Robert N. Rodemayer, *The Pastor's Prayerbook.* New York: Oxford University Press, 1960.

RT   Richard Tatlock, *A Book of Prayers.* London: Cassell and Company.

SBO   *Service Book and Ordinal of the Presbyterian Church of South Africa.* 2nd ed. Glasgow: Jackson, Son & Company, 1929.

SEJ   Sherman E. Johnson.

UMN   Ursula M. Niebuhr.

UP   *The Union Prayerbook for Jewish Worship.* Rev. ed. Cincinnati: Central Conference of American Rabbis, 1953.

WAK   W. A. Knowles, *Euchologian.* London: William Blackwood & Sons.

WEO   W. E. Orchard, *The Order of Divine Service for Public Worship.* 2nd ed. London: Oxford University Press, 1926.

WLS   Willard L. Sperry, *Prayers for Private Devotions in War-Time.* New York: Harper & Bros., 1943.

WR   Walter Rauschenbusch, *Prayers of the Social Awakening.* Boston: Pilgrim Press, 1909.

WRB   Walter Russell Bowie, *Lift Up Your Hearts.* Enlarged ed. Nashville: Abingdon Press, 1956.

Index of First Lines

INDEX OF FIRST LINES

408

411

INDEX OF FIRST LINES

Index of Scripture References

NEW TESTAMENT

INDEX OF SCRIPTURE REFERENCES

APOCRYPHA

Index of Subjects

Salutations, 201

Sanctus, prefaces to, 23

Scripture lessons. *See* Lessons

Scripture sentences or calls to worship, 168, 349-50; Advent, 66-67; All Saints' Day, 160; Ash Wednesday, 90; Christmas, 71, 73-74; Eastertide, 113-14, 115-17; Epiphany, 81-84; Good Friday, 103, 109; Kingdomtide, 148-51; Lenten Season, 92-94, 98-99, 100-101; Pentecost, 126-27, 130, 132-36, 145, 146-47; Thanksgiving Day, 162

Self-surrender, prayer for, 245

Sick, prayers for, 233-35; prayers for those who care for, 235

Singleness of heart, prayer for, 187

Small group worship, form for, 249

Space age, prayer for, 192

Steadfastness, prayers for, 247

Student Day, 145-46

Suffering, prayers for the, 236-37

Sunday Service of John Wesley, 377-81

Sundays after Easter: collects, 119-20, 122, 123, 124; invocations, 117-19, 123; litany, 120-21; prayers, 122, 123-25; Scripture sentences or calls to worship, 115-17

Sundays after Pentecost, 9, 61; collects, 138-41, 146, 147; invocations, 136-38, 145-46, 147; litany, 144-45; prayers, 141, 143-44, 146, 147; Scripture sentences or calls to worship, 132-36, 145, 146-47

Supplication, 213

Table graces, 229-32

Teachers: church school, recognition of, 337-38; prayer for, 242

Te Deum, 160-61, 283-84

Thanksgiving: canticle, 311-12; litanies, 315-16; in love feast, 389; prayers of,

Thanksgiving—*cont'd*
163, 181-84, 389; for restored health, 236; in service renewing covenant with God, 384-85

Thanksgiving Day, 64, 162-65

Thomas Aquinas, prayer of, 244

Travelers, prayers for, 238-39

Trinity Sunday, 64, 130-32

Truth, prayer for loyalty to, 247-48; prayer to speak, 248

Understanding, prayers for, 248

Union, church, prayer for, 185

Unity of God's people, prayer for, 185

Universal Bible Sunday, 64

University building dedication, 361-64

Versicles, 200-201

Veteran's Day, 161-62

War, prayer for protection from, 191-92; prayer for those suffering under, 240

Watch Night, 64, 77-78, 382-88

Wedding, wedding anniversary, prayers for, 226-27; *see also* Marriage

Wesley, Charles, 382

Wesley, John, 382; graces of, 229-30; quotation from *Journal* of, 390; Sunday Service of, 377-81

Whitsunday, 63, 65; collects, 127-28; invocations, 127; prayers, 128-29; Scripture sentences or calls to worship, 126-27; *see also* Pentecost season

Words of Christ on the cross, 104-8

World Order Sunday, 64

Worship: calls to, *see* Scripture sentences or calls to worship; orders of, *see* Orders of worship

Youth, baptism of, 9-11